Palgrave Socio-Legal Studies

Series Editor
Dave Cowan
School of Law
University of Bristol
Bristol, UK

'*Children, Young People and the Press* is exemplary critical criminology: an original interdisciplinary study of young people and the print media in Northern Ireland under transition. This multifaceted empirical investigation shows how the press has targeted and demonised 'deviant' youth, and to what effect. Gordon's work is thoughtfully structured, clear and lively in expression, and forceful in argument: a rich asset for students of youth, media, law and society.'

—Scott Poynting, *Western Sydney University and Queensland University of Technology, Australia*

'Every generation seems to succumb to fears about the generations that follow. Such moral panics about "the kids today" appear particularly misplaced in the context of a society in transition from a troubled past like Northern Ireland. In this insightful and rigorously evidenced analysis, Gordon argues instead in favour of listening to the voices of young people themselves as they represent our best hope for a brighter future.'

—Shadd Maruna, *University of Manchester, UK*

'Conflict takes away childhoods and its legacy into the peace can destroy children's future. This expertly argued book draws on detailed research to address how children are represented in the print media in transitional societies and how these representations contribute to the problems youth are seen as presenting. It is cogently argued, very well written and erudite in its coverage. It is a wonderful addition to youth studies and transitional justice.'

—John D. Brewer, *Queen's University Belfast, Northern Ireland*

'This book offers a valuable contribution to criminological literature, in particular the growing body of empirically-informed critical youth justice scholarship. Gordon examines an issue of international significance in an incisive, cogent and articulate manner. A must-read for students and professionals with an interest in media influence upon constructing understandings of youth offending.'

—Stephen Case, *Loughborough University, UK*

The Palgrave Socio-Legal Studies series is a developing series of monographs and textbooks featuring cutting edge work which, in the best tradition of socio-legal studies, reach out to a wide international audience.

More information about this series at
http://www.palgrave.com/gp/series/14679

Faith Gordon

Children, Young People and the Press in a Transitioning Society

Representations, Reactions and Criminalisation

Faith Gordon
University of Westminster
History, Sociology and Criminology
London, UK

Palgrave Socio-Legal Studies
ISBN 978-1-137-60681-5   ISBN 978-1-137-60682-2   (eBook)
https://doi.org/10.1057/978-1-137-60682-2

Library of Congress Control Number: 2018933518

Cover illustration: northlightimages

Printed on acid-free paper

This Palgrave Macmillan imprint is published by Springer Nature
The registered company is Macmillan Publishers Ltd.
The registered company address is: The Campus, 4 Crinan Street, London, N1 9XW, United Kingdom

For my God-daughter, Iona

Acknowledgements

The subject of children, young people and media representations has been with me now for over a decade and throughout my journey, there were many people who provided encouragement.

The writing of this book commenced during my time working in the School of Law, Queen's University Belfast. Thank you to my PhD supervisors, Professor Phil Scraton and Professor Anne-Marie McAlinden, for their comments and suggestions on my PhD study, which became the foundation for this monograph. I would like to acknowledge The Department of Education and Learning in Northern Ireland who provided me with a PhD scholarship, which made the extended empirical research possible.

At Queen's University, Professor Sally Wheeler, Head of School, Professor Anne-Marie McAlinden, Director of Research and Professor Scott Poynting, External Examiner (University of Auckland), were supportive in encouraging me to submit a book proposal. Many thanks to Professor Dave Cowan, Series Editor and Aléta Bezuidenhout, Palgrave for their support, guidance and patience throughout the writing process. Most recently thank you to Steph Carey and Josie Taylor for their support at the final stages of the submission process.

Sincere thanks to the 28 interviewees who took time out of their busy schedules to participate in the primary research. I am extremely grateful to the 33 children and young people who so generously gave up their leisure time to participate and share their insights and experiences with me and to the subsequent 171 children and young people I met and engaged with during my post-doctoral research project.

At home in Northern Ireland, I have a number of former colleagues and friends who have maintained ongoing interest in my research and career development and have provided guidance and friendship along the way: Professor Norma Dawson; Professor Shadd Maruna; Professor Laura Lundy; Professor John Brewer; Professor Joanne Hughes; Dr. Ciara Hackett; Dr. Cheryl Lawther; Dr. John Stannard; Dr. Heather Conway; Dr. Bronagh Byrne; Dr. Sharon Thompson; Koulla Yiasouma; Tara Mills, Ronan Lavery QC; Sharon Whittaker; Natalie Whelehan; Edel Quinn; Niall Enright; Sara Boyce.

The monograph has travelled with me to my new home in London and I am grateful to the new friendships and working relationships formed at the University of Westminster, the Institute of Advanced Legal Studies and further afield.

At the University of Westminster, I would like to thank my colleagues in the Department of History, Sociology and Criminology for assisting me to settle into a new city and the Department. In particular, I have benefitted from the excellent mentoring of Professor Lisa Webley and Mr. Tony Burke. Professor Webley has offered a tremendous amount of insight, support and friendship – she remains an inspiration in terms of her teaching and research achievements and she is one of the most collegial and supportive people I have met in academia to date.

At the University of Westminster, encouragement has also been provided by Neena Samota; Professor Sarah Niblock; Elaine Fisher; Dr. Margherita Sprio; Juliet Allen, Dr. Petros Karatsareas; Dr. Russell Orr; Dr. Victoria Brooks; Dr. Simon Flacks; Dr. Ed Bracho; Dr. Andy Aresti and Dr. Sacha Darke and many others working in the Faculty of Social Sciences and Humanities. Further to this, thanks are due to Professor Andrew Linn, Pro Vice-Chancellor and Dean of the Faculty of Social Sciences and Humanities, Dr. Martin Doherty, Professor Terry Lamb, Dr. Thomas Moore and Professor Malcolm Kirkup for their support regarding the establishment of the *Youth Justice Network*, which I am Director of at the University of Westminster.

My greatest thanks is to David Manlow, Course Leader in Criminology, for his ongoing encouragement, positive energy and belief in me (especially when my own self-belief waivered!) that I could make it across the finish line with this project. His dedication to our students is truly inspirational and I am learning a lot from him. It was the coffees and chats with David about the monograph (plus his music suggestions) that has gotten me over the finish line!

More recently, I am grateful for the collegial support of the Information Law and Policy Centre at the Institute of Advanced Legal Studies. The Director of the Centre, Dr. Nora NiLoideain has been extremely supportive of my research interests and the development of my latest work in the area of children's rights in the digital age. I am very excited about undertaking my role as a Research Associate of the Centre.

Encouragement was kindly provided by a number of family, friends and neighbours in Annaclone, Belfast, London and further afield, in particular: Dr. Therese O'Reilly; Adrian Marshall; Phil Luney; Ronan Doran; Nuala Cosgrave; Annette MacArtain-Kerr; Kat Mervyn; Una Murphy and Brian Pelan; Margaret Dodds; Madeleine Hillis; Patrick McAnearney; Frankie McKinley; Betty, Raymond and Fiona McCullough; Betty Johnston, Elizabeth Heath and family; Katie Barron and Rob Thompson; Jack Nouril; Clover Southwell; Rev. Diane Clutterbuck; Bob Matthews; Ellie-May, Clare and Paul Horrell; Dr. Humera Iqbal and husband, Hak; Dr. Keir Irwin-Rodgers; Holly Powell-Jones; Emma Nottingham; Monika Baylis; Dr. Victoria Knight; Lucy Baldwin; Dr. Paul Reilly; Dr. Stuart Miller; Professor Steve Case; Professor Bernard Schissel; Dr. Helena Gosling and colleagues at Liverpool John Moores University; James Lee; Paul Jordan; Assan Ali; Dr. Emily Falconer, partner David and Iona; Dr. Ludivine Broch and Elliott; Mary and John Hicks; Miriam, Adam and Ezra Kennedy and my Flatmates in London (Karin, Ash, Matt and Will).

The staff working in the following organisations: Headliners, IARS, Include Youth, Save the Children NI, Terry Enright Foundation and London Youth, continue to inspire me. I am honoured to be a trustee of Headliners and to see first-hand the difference staff make to the lives of children and young people who are experiencing marginalisation and exclusion.

On a personal level, the greatest thanks of all is due to my parents, Kenny and Isobel, my sister, Serena and her husband, Jonathan. Over the years, they have been so supportive and encouraging of my work. Their belief in me completing the monograph never waivered and that is what truly kept me going.

Contents

Abbreviations

ABC	Audit Bureau of Circulation
ACPO	Association of Chief Police Officers
AEPs	Attenuating Energy Projectiles
ASBO/ASBOs	Anti-social Behaviour Order/s
BBC	British Broadcasting Corporation
BECTU	Broadcasting, Entertainment, Cinematograph and Theatre Union
CCTV	Closed Circuit Television
CD	Compact Disk
CDA	Crime and Disorder Act 1998
CJI	Criminal Justice Inspectorate Northern Ireland
CJR	Criminal Justice Review
COPs	Colloquial Term for Police Officers
CPS	Crown Prosecution Service
CRC	United Nations Committee on the Rights of the Child
CS GAS	2-chlorobenzalmalononitrile/Tear Gas
CSJ	Centre for Social Justice
DHSSPNI	Department of Health, Social Services and Public Safety Northern Ireland
DOJ NI	Department of Justice Northern Ireland
DPP	District Policing Partnership
DUP	Democratic Unionist Party
ECHR	European Convention on Human Rights
EU	European Union
FOI	Freedom of Information
GCSE	General Certificate of Secondary Education
HRA	Human Rights Act 1998
IRA	Irish Republican Army
MLA	Member of the Legislative Assembly

MP	Member of Parliament
NGO	Non-Governmental Organisation
NI	Northern Ireland
NIACRO	Northern Ireland Association for the Care and Resettlement of Offenders
NICCY	Northern Ireland Children's Commissioner
NIHRC	Northern Ireland Human Rights Commission
NIO	Northern Ireland Office
NUJ	National Union of Journalists
OAP	'Old Age Pensioner'
OFCOM	Office of Communications
PACE	Police and Criminal Evidence (NI) Order 1989
PCC	Press Complaints Commission
PHA	Public Health Agency
POCVA	Protection of Children and Vulnerable Adults (NI) Order 2003
PPS	Public Prosecution Service Northern Ireland
PR	Public Relations
PSNI	Police Service of Northern Ireland
RA	Irish Republican Army (colloquial abbreviation)
ROI	Republic of Ireland
RUC	Royal Ulster Constabulary
SAS	Special Air Service
SBN	*South Belfast News*
SDLP	Social and Democratic Labour Party
SF	Sinn Féin
TV	Television
UDA	Ulster Defence Association
UK	United Kingdom
UN	United Nations
UNCRC	United Nations Convention on the Rights of the Child
UNICEF	United Nations Children's Fund
US/USA	United States/United States of America
UTV	Ulster Television
UUP	Ulster Unionist Party

List of Tables

Part I

The Theoretical Context

1

Researching the Media Representations of Children and Young People

Young people are continuously the focus of what are often misplaced anxieties and 'moral panics' and as Austin and Willard (1998: 1) assert, this is often heighted during times of 'perceived … change':

> 'Youth' becomes a metaphor for perceived social change and its projected consequences, and … is an enduring locus for displaced social anxieties. Pronouncements such as 'the problems of youth today', [are] used as a scapegoat for larger social concerns.

Northern Ireland is a society emerging from 30 years of conflict. In negotiating the impact of change and transition, children and young people living in marginalised and segregated communities in Northern Ireland, continue to experience the legacy of the Conflict and 'persistent economic disadvantage' (see McAlister et al. 2009: 147). This monograph focuses on the role of the print media[1] in creating negative representations and maintaining negative ideological constructions of children and young people, in particular those who are the most marginalised, those considered anti-social within their communities and those in conflict with the law.[2] Contextually, the devolution of criminal justice decision-making powers in April 2010, following a period of 38 years of direct rule, the appointment of a local Minister for Justice, as well as the commencement of a Youth Justice Review,[3] provided a unique setting for the empirical study upon which this book is based. Thus, the empirical research covers a unique period in exploring justice and punishment in the context of real change and transition.

© The Author(s) 2018
F. Gordon, *Children, Young People and the Press in a Transitioning Society*,
Palgrave Socio-Legal Studies, https://doi.org/10.1057/978-1-137-60682-2_1

While Northern Ireland has experienced the impact of a Peace Process heralding the beginnings of transition from several generations of conflict, a wider body of literature focuses on the assumed deviant behaviour of children and young people. Historical analyses demonstrate that this process of packaging and repackaging the concept of problem youth is not new (Pearson 1983; Brown 1998; Jewkes 2009). For example, in the 1960s following a period of economic austerity, Mods and Rockers were viewed as having been corrupted by a new teenage prosperity (Cohen 1972), while a decade prior teddy boys were represented as the product of wartime childhoods, adversely affected by absent fathers (Wilkins 1960). The same repeated 'rigidly immovable vocabulary' and 'complaints' about youth in media and political discourses are part of 'this ages-old tapestry' and notably, such 'problems' are often 'held up as something entirely new and unprecedented' (Bessant and Watts 1998: 7).

Bessant and Hil (1997: 4) argue that contemporary distress about young people is linked to a popular uncertainty about the future. Thus, representations based on current pessimistic portrayals of young people as 'bad, troubling and troublesome' often 'reveal more about the apprehensions, fantasies and anxieties' of adults or in the case of the media, 'those doing the reporting', than they do about the young people they are portraying (Bessant and Hil 1997: 4).[4] Derived in Becker's (1963) work, several criminological studies demonstrate how the identification and treatment of individuals or social groups as outsiders, typically the targets of stereotypical media portrayals, are relegated to the margins of society and blamed for a range of social ills. Curran (2002: 109) asserts that this 'deflect[s] wider social conflict and reinforce[s] dominant social and political norms'.

Reflecting critically on popular discourse and political debate, this monograph critically addresses the prominence of negative media representations, the maintenance of negative ideological constructions and government responses directed towards children and young people. Significantly, the empirical research was timely, beginning in October 2008, at the time of the publication of the United Kingdom's (UK) Concluding Observations of the United Nations Committee on the Rights of the Child (CRC). In its Concluding Observations, the CRC strongly emphasised the existence of:

[A] general climate of intolerance and negative public attitudes towards children, especially adolescents, which appears to exist in the State party, including in the media, may be often the underlying cause of further infringements of their rights. (CRC, October 2008: para 24)

The Committee also criticised the Government for not taking 'sufficient measures to protect children, notably, from negative media representation and public "naming and shaming"' (CRC, October 2008: para 36). Thus, internationally concerns exist surrounding both media representations of children and young people and the lack of appropriate responses from the state and state agencies.

While such concerns have been raised locally, nationally and internationally, there has been no academic research analysing media content, to unpack how the media in Northern Ireland represent children and young people and to assess the impact of negative media content on public perceptions and political responses. In addressing the gap in the academic literature, the empirical chapters present a critical analysis of newspaper content over an extended period and establish how children and young people in Northern Ireland are represented in media discourse.

In societies that have experienced conflict and violence followed by transition to peace, the legacy of conflict presents particular challenges (see O'Rawe 2011). While transition from the Conflict and the ensuing peace process in Northern Ireland are marked particularly by the power-sharing arrangement within the Assembly, in communities the unaddressed issues of the Conflict's legacy continue to impact on the lives and experiences of children, young people and their families (see McAlister et al. 2009). The timing of the study upon which this monograph is based, provides the first opportunity to consider whether the UK Government's legacy regarding criminal justice and youth justice legislation, policy and practice, has been inherited or contested by the devolved administration in Northern Ireland. Thus, the research timing is opportune for structural changes to be considered and implemented in the field of youth justice and within the criminal justice system in Northern Ireland.

There is an extensive body of academic research exploring the complex relationships between crime, deviance, criminal justice, the media and popular culture (see for example: Young 1971; Cohen 1972; Chibnall 1973, 1977; Hall et al. 1978; Cohen and Young 1981; Schlesinger and Tumber 1994; Durham et al. 1995; Aggleton 1987; Surette 1998; Wykes 2001; Reiner 2002). Within Northern Ireland the existing literature on the media has focused mainly on the representation of the Conflict and violence, as the Conflict or Troubles[5] have dominated much of Northern Ireland's past (see Schlesinger et al. 1983; Rolston 1991; Miller 1993; Rolston and Miller 1996). An exception is Greer's (2003) research into the media's representation of sex offending in Northern Ireland and contemporary comparative studies, such as Wolfsfeld's (2004) research that has focused on the media's role in peace-keeping. While valuable, the literature has neglected the media's representation of social groups, particularly individuals and groups experiencing marginalisation and social exclusion.

As a social group, children and young people have been the focus of numerous studies on media representation produced by national and international scholars (see for example: Franklin and Petley 1996; Bessant and Hil 1997; Crane 1997; Davies 1997; McMahon 1997; Schissel 1997; Simpson 1997; Tait et al. 1997; Wearing 1997; Collins et al. 2000; Holland 2004; Poynting et al. 2004; Andersson and Lundstrom 2007; Green 2008a, 2008b; Lumsden 2009). There are existing analyses of media representations of children and young people during the Conflict in Northern Ireland. For example, Cairns (1987) describes how British media images and accounts of the civil rights 'riots' in Belfast and Derry/Londonderry[6] in 1969, 'vividly portrayed … youths and children fighting'. Similarly Brocklehurst (2006: 100; see also Holland 2004) states that, 'child stone-throwers and petrol bombers in the front line attracted a great deal of front-page coverage and shocked comment'. Such research however was not based on print media content analysis over an extended period. Further, research has not considered the media's representation of children and young people in Northern Ireland and the impact of negative ideological constructions.

Against the backdrop of McLaughlin's (2006: 60) prediction that the 'transition from conflict to peace' will present 'profound … challenges' for the media in Northern Ireland, this study explores the role of the media at a time of change and transition. In exploring the role of the media and the impact of negative media representations on social reaction, this study also includes the voices of editors and journalists, who produce media content (see Lashmar 2010). It also addresses the call by McRobbie and Thornton (1995) to explore whether 'folk devils' play a role in the creation of moral panics. This is achieved by including the voices of children, young people and their advocates, often absent from previous academic research on media representation. Further, content analysis of print media content and a case study of what is framed as youth involvement in 'sectarian' rioting in July 2010, explores how the media represent children and young people at a time of change and transition in Northern Ireland.

Theoretical Framework and Research Context

The theoretical framework adopted is derived in critical analysis within criminology. It draws on literature and key debates within the fields of media and communication studies, sociology, social policy and youth studies. Specifically, reflecting on the legacy of critical criminological research (Becker 1963; Young 1971; Cohen 1972; Chibnall 1977; Hall et al. 1978), the research is concerned with unravelling 'the ways in which taken-for-granted talk' (Walklate 1998: 34) about children and young people's perceived involvement in anti-social behaviour and crime, is maintained, amplified and responded to in media, popular and political discourses.

Critical analysis 'focuses on the ideologies that sustain domination' (David and Sutton 2011: 77). In exposing 'malpractices, injustices, and exploitation', it takes into account how 'underlying social structures … oppress' (Henn et al. 2009: 17), 'marginalise and consequently criminalise some groups', such as children and young people (Walklate 1998: 35). This perspective explores the 'complex interplay between structure and agency', which considers how individuals 'are not seen either as the sole determiners of what they can and cannot do or how they are seen or not seen' (Walklate 1998: 35). In challenging hierarchies of credibility, dominant discourses and constructions of knowledge (Jupp 2006a; Stubbs 2008), as well as the interests they represent (Anthony and Cunneen 2008), this approach sets an oppositional agenda (Scraton 2007: 10). It does so by seeking out, recording, championing and valuing the view from below (Scraton 2007: 10). The experiences of those most marginalised, as well as a consideration of how power operates in society, helps to 'explain generalised oppression in order to precipitate social change' (Henn et al. 2009: 17).

This book also draws on concepts developed within the labelling perspective - deviancy amplification, folk devils and moral panics and the construction of crime news. Becker (1963) and Lemert (1972) proposed that actions and behaviours come to be identified as deviant through the process of labelling. As Aggleton (1987: 8) has pointed out, it is a process rarely uncontested, often involving people struggling to reject the labels others place on them. The process involves the application of power, with some groups more powerful in establishing their interpretation of a situation as the right and reasonable version (Aggleton 1987: 9). Thus, the labelling perspective is significant in directing attention to, and exploring the 'processes' by which, particular actions come to be defined as 'deviant'.

Similarly, deviancy amplification not only assures that the media frequently exaggerate what happens, but also it refers to a type of effect. According to Barrat (1994: 36), the effect is a process by which fictional and non-fictional representations of deviance feed back and impact on the perceptions and behaviour of individuals. The outcome is often an apparent increase in the amount of deviance (Barrat 1994: 36) or a perception that there is an increase, reflecting and confirming the stereotypes.

Young (1971), Cohen (1972), Chibnall (1977) and Hall et al. (1978) produced the pivotal studies on deviance amplification, folk devils, moral panics and constructions of crime news. They argued that the media amplification of deviance contributed to the creation of moral panics and folk devils, with individuals and groups demonised, labelled and ascribed outsider status. Young (2008: 176) states that the findings from this research 'seem to represent major structural and value changes in industrial society as refracted through the prism of youth'. In particular, Cohen's work in the early 1970s was seminal in highlighting the role the media has played in influencing society's negative perception of children and young people in conflict with the law. This book will consider the role of the media in constructing negative images of children and young people, in particular those in conflict with the law. Drawing on Cohen's (1972) conceptualisation of folk devils and moral panics, this study will explore the impact of labelling and demonisation on children and young people who are framed as contemporary 'folk devils' in Northern Ireland.

Northern Ireland: A Society in Transition

Critical analysis sets out to locate 'crime', 'deviance' and 'social conflict', 'within their *determining contexts*' of 'age', 'social class', 'gender', 'sexuality' and 'race' (Chadwick and Scraton 2006: 97, original emphasis). This approach influences the questions posed by critical social research (David and Sutton 2011: 77). Against this theoretical backdrop, this book considers the content, focus and impact of media representations of children and young people in Northern Ireland. Following a period of over 30 years of conflict, Northern Ireland is a society in transition and the legacy of the Conflict remains a significant and largely unaddressed contemporary issue. Thus, in addition to the determining contexts of age, class and gender, the legacy of the Conflict and the dynamics of transition are central contextual considerations.

There is a body of literature documenting the origins and impact of the Conflict (see Gillespie 2009). Ruane and Todd (1996: 1) argue that during the Conflict, violence 'damaged the whole fabric of the liberal democratic state and civic culture'. They note that: 'normal' judicial processes were suspended; there were repeated breaches of human rights; collusion between members of the security forces and paramilitaries; paramilitaries took over the functions of the police in many areas and there existed 'the demonisation of the "enemy"' (Ruane and Todd 1996: 1). Space was divided with the erection of social and physical barriers in Northern Ireland, resulting in open communities being turned into closed ones (Ruane and Todd 1996: 1). Jarman (1997: 2) observes that, 'it is impossible to ignore the prominent role that historical events ... continue to play in the political and social life of Northern Ireland'.

Significantly, Northern Ireland has the youngest population of any jurisdiction in the UK (Save the Children and ARK 2008). It is one of the poorest regions in the European Union (EU), with more than one third of children and young people living in poverty (Save the Children and ARK 2008). When conducting research in Northern Ireland, the effects and legacy of the Conflict are paramount, as children, young people and their parents continue to suffer from conflict-related trauma, with a high proportion of working class communities experiencing social exclusion and extreme economic marginalisation (Scraton 2007: 150). As Scraton (2007: 148) argues, 'several generations have endured pervasive sectarianism, hard-line policing, military operations and paramilitary punishments'. For many children 'the notions of post-conflict or transition are distant possibilities as sectarianism entrenches hatred for the "other"' (Kilkelly et al. 2004: 245). As Barber (2009: 126) observes, 'children and young people in Northern Ireland have obviously paid a price for the political violence that has tainted the region'.

Paramilitaries' violence against children and young people has been endemic within Loyalist/Unionist/Protestant and Nationalist/Republican/Catholic communities.[7] Children and young people have been refugees, exiles for anti-social behaviour[8] or the victims of punishment beatings (Hillyard et al. 2005: 190). A community worker summarised the emotional effects of the conflict as having a major impact on 'children's education, their mental health and their ability to participate in society' (quoted in Scraton 2007: 149). Similar concerns were raised by Smyth et al. (2004: 43), who noted that those children deeply affected by the Conflict had 'difficulties in concentration and the aggressive behaviour that followed their traumatisation was misinterpreted by others, being seen as deliberately disruptive behaviour'.

In Northern Ireland official discourse notes that 'young people are often regarded with fear, suspicion and mistrust' (Northern Ireland Office (NIO) Statistics and Research Branch 2003, cited in Hamilton et al. 2003: 13), thus viewed as threatening and intimidating, as perpetrators of 'anti-social behaviour', of social disruption and as initiators of sectarian tensions and disorder (see Jarman and O'Halloran 2001; Jarman et al. 2002). Such feelings and suspicions may arise from little more than having groups of young people hanging around on street corners (see Hamilton et al. 2003: 13). This book considers the significance of negative media representations on targeting youth, and their manifestation in punishment attacks, beatings and exiling.

Further, it considers the added dimension and consequences of naming and shaming and social reaction in a post-conflict society.

The paramilitary ceasefires in the early 1990s, followed by the Belfast/Good Friday Agreement in 1998 brought change, with the formation of the locally elected Northern Ireland Assembly and the establishment of the Police Service of Northern Ireland (PSNI) in 2001, following the Patten Commission recommendations (NIO 1999). From 1998, however, it took a further nine years for the Northern Ireland Executive to be established and to form political relations considered stable (Gillespie 2009). Significantly, under the Northern Ireland Act 1998, decision-making powers in criminal justice and policing remained the responsibility of the UK Secretary of State for Northern Ireland. Following the St Andrews Agreement 2006, Republican Sinn Féin, previously opposing the operational role and function of the police in Northern Ireland, in 2007 accepted the PSNI.

Following the Hillsborough Agreement 2010, criminal justice decision-making powers were devolved from the UK Government to the Northern Ireland Assembly in April 2010. In political and media discourse it was represented as, 'the final piece in the devolution puzzle',[9] with Northern Ireland's First Minister asserting: 'Throughout history there are times of challenge and defining moments. This is such a time. This is such a moment' (quoted by BBC News, 9 March 2010a).[10] International figures such as Hillary Clinton, United States (US) Secretary of State, commended Northern Ireland's political leadership and described devolution as 'an important step in ensuring a peaceful and prosperous future … for generations to come' (quoted by *Guardian*, 9 March 2010).[11]

Moving from violence to political stability, societies in transition from periods of conflict face significant challenges (Aughey 2005). In Northern Ireland, they include ongoing dissident republican activity. As McEvoy (2008: 67) notes, republican dissidents oppose Sinn Féin's endorsement of the Belfast/Good Friday Agreement and the abandonment of the 'armed struggle'. Contemporary academic analyses note that Sinn Féin politicians are 'presented with similar challenges to their authority by growing support for the dissidents from sections of alienated nationalist youth' (Bean 2011: 166). This projects youth as a threat to the stability of the 'peace process' in Northern Ireland. Significantly, such analyses are not based on qualitative empirical research. In contrast, this book is grounded in qualitative research, identifying 'hidden' voices and ensuring their contribution. It challenges 'official' or dominant discourses. Contextually, the legacy of the Conflict, sectarianism, contested spaces and segregation, the persistence of paramilitarism, the policing deficit, the context of punishment beatings, shootings, exiling, the current transition and devolution of policing and justice, are considered.

Identifying the Research Focus and Establishing the Methodology

This book examines the proposition that negative images and ideological constructions of children and young people published in the media, have a significant impact on public perceptions, and on policy responses directed particularly towards those in conflict with the law or considered anti-social within their communities. The issue of addressing children and young people as a special case with regard to media reporting, as noted by the United Nations Convention on the Rights of the Child (UNCRC), is considered.

Further, the book explores the perceived impact of negative representations on children's and young people's advocates and its significance for the effectiveness of service provision. Thus, in analysing the Northern Ireland media representations of children and young people, it considers the impact of, and reactions to those representations. The empirical research employs the following research methods: documentary analysis; discourse analysis; content analysis; semi-structured qualitative interviews with a range of professional people, from those working in the media, to those working in the children and youth sectors, politicians, the PSNI, the equality and human rights sector; and focus groups with children and young people.

The complex and combined strength of the approach and research methods employed enables this study to achieve a fully rounded examination of the relationship between media representation, children and young people's lives and the politics of a society in transition. David and Sutton (2011: 19) assert that research studies 'may adopt a combination of methods' to achieve specific ends and to strengthen the overall empirical findings. Further, Noaks and Wincup (2004: 8) observe that in social research, arguments have been advanced and show support for combining research methods, with the use of methods carefully and appropriately built into the research strategy adopted.

Content and Discourse Analysis of Media Coverage

Newspaper content was collected from eight newspapers over six months, with 627 newspapers collected for analysis, from 1 March 2010 to 31 August 2010 (inclusive). Details of each newspaper, its circulation and readership figures, and a justification of the selected time period, are outlined in Appendix 1. The method of collecting newspapers daily ensured that findings were based on an analysis of original newspapers, in the format encountered by readers. This method ensured that analysis was not 'de-saturated', nor was 'text … stripped away from the contextual images and juxtapositions that readers' consume when they encounter news items (Green 2008a: 201). Each page of every newspaper was searched to identify news items, followed by a comprehensive process of logging the media items into electronic table format (Microsoft Word) and also a process of re-checking for complete accuracy. The process of logging data in a tabular format facilitated the analysis of the data and information collected. The data, therefore, was manageable and similar to qualitative interview transcripts, it provided the researcher with a structure on which to base the analysis.

In total, 2,456 media items referred directly to children, young people and their advocates in Northern Ireland. When analysing the print media newspaper articles, main news stories, comment sections and any written commentary, the data analysis reflected on the form, style, intentions, substance of the media message, the characteristics of the content and the prominence of the story. Further, the analysis considered who was quoted or given 'expert status', whether the voices of children, young people and their advocates featured and whether there was a follow-up or sustained coverage.

Unlike previous media content analysis studies, this research is not limited to a text-only approach, as it includes also an analysis of visual images employed by the media. In this, the researcher acknowledges the importance of analysing both the language and image aspects of news items, as this is how the reader 'encounters' coverage. There has been criticism of text-only analyses and several scholars have asserted that researchers should explore the form and impact of visual images within media coverage (see Greer 2007; McLaughlin and Greer 2007, cited in Green 2008a: 201). In addressing such criticism, this book considers how particular messages and negative constructions of young people are communicated through visual images (see Davies 1997). Further, it analyses the impact of negative visual representations on children, young people and their advocates.

Qualitative Semi-structured Interviews and Focus Groups

A significant criticism of research on media representation (Lashmar 2010) is the insularity: that some content analysis studies fail to explore the meanings and interpretations that people attach to media coverage, while others neglect to consider the context in which the media operates. This study prioritises the inclusion of the voices of the primary definers and the 'hidden' voices of children and young people's advocates.

The study included 28 semi-structured interviews conducted with youth workers, community workers, those working in the equality and human rights sectors, research and policy officers and advocates working in the children and youth sector/non-governmental organisations (NGOs), the Northern Ireland Children's Commissioner, a spokesperson from the PSNI, journalists, editors, television news reporters, radio reporters, politicians (several sit on the Northern Ireland Policing Board and several are members of the Justice Committee at Stormont) and local councillors (see Appendix 2 for list and reference key).

In its inception a central aim of this research was to include the 'view from below'; a view often marginalised in media discourse and missing from previous research on children and young people's representation in the media. Six focus groups with 33 children and young people, aged 14–23 years, gained the direct views of a group marginalised and absent from media discourse. The focus groups spanned three counties in Northern Ireland, taking place in Belfast (County Antrim), Derry/Londonderry (County Derry/Londonderry) and Bangor (County Down).

Regarding gender, the focus groups involved 15 young women and 18 young men. Two focus groups involved children and young people engaged with their own forms of media to challenge stereotypes of children and young people printed in the 'mainstream' media. Significantly, the focus groups involved children and young people in care, those who have been in contact with the criminal justice system and young people who have been bereaved by suicide. The focus groups provided the children and young people who participated, the opportunity to present their views, experiences and first-hand accounts of the impact of media reporting, 'naming and shaming' and media intrusion.

Structure

The first section of the book explores the key national and international academic literature and previous studies on the role and functions of the media. This includes the key theoretical debates on deviancy amplification, folk devils and moral panics. It will assess the media's impact on criminal justice policies and on public opinion of, and support for authoritarian ideologies and policies. The section will conclude with an examination of the media's role in the process of social reaction and the tangible consequences for children and young people.

The book then focuses on the primary research including analysis of: the legacy of the Conflict, sectarianism; contested spaces and segregation; the persistence of paramilitarism; the policing deficit; the context of punishment beatings, shootings and exiling; the transition and devolution of policing and justice in Northern Ireland. The empirical findings explored in this book will confirm the proposition that children and young people are convenient scapegoats, as the negative reputation ascribed to them invariably diverts attention from the structural and institutional issues that are inevitable in a society accommodating a gradual transition from conflict.

The book provides, through a case study of the riots in Belfast and Derry/Londonderry, a new contemporary insight into how close the relationship between the state, state agencies such as the PSNI and the media, are in a transitioning society. Further it demonstrates the impact of the informal and formal policing of children and young people in their communities. While unravelling the ways in which taken-for-granted talk about children and young people's perceived involvement in 'anti-social behaviour' and 'crime' is maintained, amplified and responded to in media, popular and political discourses, this book will place the empirical work theoretically and politically within an international context and will consider the future 'way forward' in terms of ongoing debate in other countries.

It will also discuss issues central to the research process of carrying out critical social research and the challenges faced when interviewing 'primary definers' and providing an opportunity for the 'view from below' to be heard. It will conclude by proposing future considerations and challenges for academic research and policy intervention demonstrating the potential institutional impact of the research.

Notes

1. Throughout the monograph, the term 'media' refers to the traditional definition of the media, as consisting of newspapers (the print media), radio (broadcast media) and news bulletins and programs (televised media). However, the empirical research consists of analysis of the print media/newspapers. In the empirical chapters (Chaps. 4, 5, 6, 7 and 8), the term 'media' is typically employed to refer to the print media/newspapers.
2. The phrase 'in conflict with the law' is typically employed to refer to children and young people who come to the attention of the police. Children and young people 'in conflict with the law' may not have been formally arrested or prosecuted, however they have come into contact with the police or the criminal justice system.
3. The Hillsborough Agreement (NIO 2010: 7) outlined the need for a 'review of how children and young people are processed at all stages of the criminal justice system, including detention, to ensure compliance with international obligations and best practice'. The Hillsborough Agreement

can be accessed here: http://www.nio.gov.uk/agreement_at_hillsborough_ castle_5_february_2010.pdf (accessed on 12 February 2010). The Youth Justice Review Team consisted of Mr John Graham, current Director the Police Federation for England and Wales, Dr Stella Perrott, former Head of the Care and Justice Division in the Scottish Government and Kathleen Marshall, a solicitor. The report published in 2011 presents 31 recommendations for changes to the youth justice system in Northern Ireland. The report can be accessed from: http://www.dojni.gov.uk/index/publications/ publication-categories/pubs-criminal-justice/review-of-youth-justice--- large-print-version-of-report.pdf (accessed on 1 October 2011).

4. This is particularly evident in relation to the difference in the 'perception' and 'reality' of children and young people's involvement in 'crime' (see Schissel 1997; Poynting et al. 2004). In Northern Ireland, the Department of Justice's bulletin (February 2012a) outlines the stark difference between the perceptions of crime and 'high levels of worry', 'despite the lower prevalence of crime'. See: http://www.northernireland.gov.uk/index/media-centre/news- departments/news-doj/news-doj-29022012-perceptions-of-crime.htm (accessed on 30 August 2012).

5. The 'Troubles' is a reference to the Conflict in Northern Ireland. It is typically employed interchangeably to refer to the period of 30 years of conflict and violence in Northern Ireland.

6. There is contestation locally surrounding the name of this city. Thus, Derry/ Londonderry is referred to throughout the monograph, empirical interviews and focus groups, using both of the local names. This recognises the conflicting and differing beliefs and preferences of society in Northern Ireland and it ensures that the researcher does not express or impose any perceived political allegiance or personal opinion.

7. As McAlister et al. (2009: 25) note, approximately 95 percent of social housing in Northern Ireland is segregated by religious affiliation – namely Loyalist/ Unionist/Protestant and Nationalist/Republican/Catholic. Thus, division or 'segregation' in both 'public housing' and in 'schooling', 'remain defining features of social, political and cultural experiences and opportunities in Northern Ireland' (McAlister et al. 2009: 25).

8. Given the broad definition of what 'anti-social behaviour' is, it is vague and open to interpretation. It has resulted in ASBOs being given for a range of minor and what have been classed as 'silly ASBOs'. See: http://news.bbc.co. uk/1/hi/wales/south_east/4902092.stm (accessed on 3 March 2010).

9. See: http://news.bbc.co.uk/1/hi/northern_ireland/8457650.stm (accessed on 10 February 2010); http://news.bbc.co.uk/1/hi/8459824.stm (accessed on 27 April 2010).

10. See: http://news.bbc.co.uk/1/hi/northern_ireland/8558466.stm (accessed on 27 April 2010).

11. See: http://www.guardian.co.uk/politics/2010/mar/09/stormont-northern- ireland-policing-vote (accessed on 10 March 2010).

2

The Significance and Impact of the Media in Contemporary Society

Research within media and cultural studies labels contemporary society as being media saturated (Allan 1999; Potter 2010). As Albertazzi and Cobley (2010: 1) assert:

> Anyone who seeks to underestimate the centrality of the media in contemporary … life does so at their peril. Today, arguably more than at any time in the past, media are the key players in contributing to what defines reality.

The mass media is a significant, powerful and pervasive social institution embedded into contemporary society, which is experiencing 'unprecedented levels of media saturation and social change' (Devereux 2007: 2), particularly since the advent of the internet.[1] The centrality and impact of the mass media in society have long been topics of great intellectual concern. Theoretically and empirically by 'defamiliarising the familiar' (Wright Mills 1976) academics from the 1970s onward, firstly began to critically question the objectivity of media reporting. During this period, critical criminologists produced pivotal studies on 'folk devils', 'moral panics', deviancy amplification and construction of crime news (Young 1971; Cohen 1972; Chibnall 1977; Hall et al. 1978). This chapter explores the significance of the media and the impact it has on the meaning-making processes in society. In particular, it will focus on exploring how the media can influence popular culture and the impact of media portrayals of crime on societal perceptions, responses and reactions.

© The Author(s) 2018
F. Gordon, *Children, Young People and the Press in a Transitioning Society*,
Palgrave Socio-Legal Studies, https://doi.org/10.1057/978-1-137-60682-2_2

Role and Functions of the Media in Contemporary Society

The media and an audience or readership's engagement with media content is integral to the meaning-making processes in contemporary society. The role and practices of those working in the mass media are informed and influenced by particular interests, customs, norms and values (Craig 2004). The communicative contexts in which messages are produced and presented, illustrate the knowledge management functions and ideological control within the news making process (Craig 2004: 3, 10). The representational powers and communicative function of the media has 'blurred divisions between the public and private' and 'between factual and fictional forms of representation' (Craig 2004: 4).

The media have a number of further functions, which demonstrate the social, cultural, political and economic dimensions of their role (Silverstone 1999a). These functions include informing, educating, socialising and entertaining the audience or readership; transmitting culture and heritage from one generation to the next; pointing out threats and opportunities for individuals and societies and in editorialising and interpreting 'the news of the day' (Lasswell 1948; Wright 1960, cited in Perry 2002: 72). The media performs a gate-keeping function by 'allowing certain things through, while ignoring or filtering out others'; an agenda setting function, which establishes 'what is to be talked about' and also a reality-defining effect (Corner and Hawthorn 1993: 173). Those working in the media typically identify their functions as serving the public interest and acting as, 'the watchdog of the state' (McQuail 1991: 70).

For millions of people reading newspapers provides 'a regular form of ... training in knowing where ... [they] are and how best to do things' (Mercer 1992: 37). As O'Sullivan et al. (2003: 4) assert, acceptance of 'regular contact with the media for information, news opinion, entertainment' and '"ideas" about what is happening around the world to what is happening in their own community, is "natural"'. This process is 'deeply bound up with ... attempts to maintain a coherent sense of "who" and "where" a person thinks they are', reinforcing 'their ongoing "sense of identity"' (O'Sullivan et al. 2003: 4). How the audience or readership receive, engage with and interpret the meaning of media content is significant. Reflective of the traditional 'model' of the audience, Surette (1998: xi) concludes, most interact with the media as passive rather than as critical consumers. Accordingly, an audience or readership are therefore conditioned to receive media content 'without considering where the material comes from, what effect it has on their attitudes and perceptions, and how it affects society' (Surette 1998: xi).

In contrast, Knight (2016: 74–76) draws on the theorisations of Ang (1990b), Silverstone (1999b) and Gorton (2009), to demonstrate how the nature and composition of the audience remains complex. In particular in the digital age, audiences are difficult to define, observe and cannot be described as a 'fixed group', as they are in effect plural and diverse (Knight 2016; see also Moores 1993). In moving beyond the traditional models of referring to the audience as inherently passive receivers of messages (Surette 1998), Morley (1997: 87) asserts that it might be more appropriate to consider the audience as 'less of an undifferentiated mass of individuals than as a complicated pattern of overlapping sub-groups and subcultures, within which individuals are situated'. Other theoretical perspectives characterise the active nature of the individual audience member and explore the social aspects of media consumption, positioning engagement as central rather than assuming passivity on the part of the audience (Knight 2016; see also Radway 1984).

As Ericson et al. (1987: 10) argue, the news media, given its 'importance to other control agents … are one of the most important and powerful institutions in society'. In complete contrast to pluralists, who consider that the media are truly independent (Glover 1984: 53)[2] and operate in the public interest, Marxists analysis has argued that the dominant class is 'able to regulate the production and distribution of … ideas'. As Hall (1997: 6) asserts, capitalism is a determining process, both in the search of economic profit and in the ideological sense of promoting dominant values in media reporting. Inevitably, capitalism has an effect on the content of media, which typically reflects ruling-class interests.

It is evident that a very high percentage of what the audience or readership see, hear and read in the mainstream media sphere, derives from a small number of extremely large companies, which dominate the market (Glover 1984: 49; Hart 1991; Curran and Seaton 1992).[3] Media organisations possess a number of the same attributes as other large-scale industrial organisations (Curran et al. 1988). These include 'an internal division of labour and role differentiation', with those working to achieve 'clearly specified and accepted institutional goals', which have been 'translated into specific policies and … practices' (Curran et al. 1988: 17). The existence of a management structure (Cole 2005) with power 'located at the top of the hierarchy' (Curran et al. 1988: 18) raises concerns that individuals at the 'top' can use 'media outlets … to exercise… power and influence' (O'Sullivan et al. 2003: 143). The concentration of ownership also results in most of the media being subjected to similar influences as other capitalist enterprises (Murdock and Golding 1977).[4]

Alongside the media's connection to capitalism, it is connected to the political system (Whale 1980; Khabaz 2006). Gallagher (1982: 160) asserts that this connection is one of the most crucial of all the relationships that bind the media to wider society. High profile relationships between British Prime Ministers and media owners, such as Rupert Murdoch and Margaret Thatcher (Shawcross 1992; Thompson 1997) and Murdoch and Tony Blair (Greenslade 2003), emphasise the significance of power relations and how politicians and the media work together to promote and defend their own agendas.[5] Therefore, by exploring the process of 'who is communicating with whom, by what means, for what purposes, with what effects and in whose interests?', an insight can be gained into 'the kind of societies' that exist and the way in which power and control operate (Eldridge et al. 1997: 6).

Control in the media sphere is two-fold; institutional control, such as financial, bureaucratic, technological and direct control over content, by setting agendas, providing explanations and constructing their 'own versions of events … as natural and authentic' (Masterman 1990: 6). This emphasises the extent to which media output or the ideological content, is shaped by those in power (Gallagher 1982: 152; McQuail 2000: 82). The industrialised structure of the media places limits on who can access the means of communication. Power is implicit in the process, with a small minority in a privileged position to shape, establish and promote their agendas. This illustrates clearly what Marx (1945, cited in Barrat 1994: 61) describes as the promotion of 'the dominant ideas… of the dominant class', whereby the media maintain conformity of certain views and promote certain economic and political agendas, whilst excluding or marginalising opposing viewpoints.

Power relations, ownership and control impact on 'the precise structures of news reports' (van Dijk 1991: 41), which emerge carrying 'the marks of the technical and organizational structure' in which they are created (Golding and Elliott 1999: 119). Journalists inherit and work according to media rules and professional codes, to reproduce 'the standard choices of the powerful' (Herman 1990: 77). Curran et al. (1988: 18–19) argue that when exploring the relationship between the ideology implicit in media messages and 'the interests of those in control', researchers must explore the professional ideologies, work practices and constraints experienced by media professionals. Gieber's (1999: 218) research on newsroom practice concludes that the main priority of journalists was getting the copy into the newspaper, with 'the editor … preoccupied with … mechanical pressures … rather than the social meanings and impact of the news'.

News is a manufactured product (McQuail 1972) and subject to sifting, selection, evaluation, structuring and classification (Briggs and Cobley 1998: 12). Those who create the news construct their representations and accounts of reality. As Herman and Chomsky (1988: 2) state:

> The raw material of the news must pass through successive filters, leaving only the cleansed residue fit to print. They fix the premises of discourse and interpretation, and the definition of what is newsworthy in the first place ... The elite domination of the media and marginalization of dissent ... results from the operation of these filters.

News is 'produced by an industry, shaped by the bureaucratic and economic' structures and by the relations with other industries such as the government (Fowler 1994: 222). Very few news events are observed directly by journalists, most are gathered from secondary sources and are re-packaged (Barrat 1994: 93). This has certainly become much more the practice in the digital age, with increased 'desk-top' based journalism and the use of the internet by journalists to source news stories, imagery and 'facts'. News 'derives ... from the sources and contexts of its production' (Rock 1982, cited in Robson 2004: 34), is articulated from a particular ideological position' and in turn reflects and shapes the 'prevailing values of society' (Fowler 1994: 10, 222). The outcome is a selected and 'constructed representation constitutive of "reality"' (Barker 2000: 260), evident both in the language employed and in 'other signs like photographs' and images (Bignell 1997: 81).

Typically, journalists, editors and others working in the media, present a news account/item as an 'objective', 'impartial *translation* of reality' (Allan 1999: 4, original emphasis). Further, often they present themselves as unaware of news selection and filtering processes. Rather:

> News journalists often describe their thinking as so instinctive that it defies explanation. Split-second decision-making, gut instinct, curiosity and a 'nose' for news are highly prized attributes of any reporter or editor. (Machin and Niblock 2006: 1)

Decisions made by editors and journalists about which stories or events to cover and how, and which to exclude, reflects what is deemed as newsworthy (Newburn 2007: 85). Personal whims, the norms, rules and conventions of the office, time pressures, and the need to make profit, are factors which each influence the selection process (Barrat 1994: 92). As Curran and Seaton (1992: 265) assert, the media's need 'to secure instant attention creates a strong prejudice in favour of familiar stories and themes'. This highlights how convention operates in the newsroom and how editors and journalists set the terms of what is significant and what is not (Bignell 1997: 82).

The criteria of newsworthiness relate closely to news values, which govern what will be selected (Braham 1982: 275), how it will be constructed and presented and the degree of exposure or prominence the news item will receive. News values are professionalised, gained through training on the job (Branston and Stafford 2003: 136). As Barrat (1994: 94) observes, 'journalists are probably the worst people to ask about news values'. Insight has been gained from observing editors and journalists (Chibnall 1975, 1977; North 2009; Mawby 2010) or analysing the content of stories produced (Naylor 2001; Berrington and Honkatukia 2002; Shipman 2002; Gado 2008; Green 2008a, 2008b). As argued in Chap. 1, one major criticism of such research is the 'insular' approach some studies have taken (Lashmar 2010). The primary research upon which this monograph is based, is concerned with analysing media content, considering how and why the media operates the way it does, as well as exploring the meanings and interpretations that people attach to media coverage and representations.

Galtung and Ruge (1965, 1982) were the first to formulate a list of criteria for newsworthiness, mostly commonly referred to as news values (Wykes 2001). Their list includes: frequency, whether or not the event occurred suddenly and whether it fits well with the organisation's news schedule; negativity, as bad news is considered more newsworthy than good news; the importance of the event; cultural proximity; continuity, as a story which has already been in the news gathers a kind of inertia; how personal the story is, in terms of human interest (Galtung and Ruge 1982: 53). Dramatisation, exaggeration and hyperbole are further rhetorical tricks or values (van Dijk 1991, cited in Conboy 2006: 16). News values not only influence the prominence of the news item, but the way in which it is presented, with journalists making the most of topical, dramatic, titillating and personality aspects (Barrat 1994: 100; Fowler 1994: 12–17).

If a story is accompanied by a vivid photograph or dramatic piece of news film, these aesthetic components heighten the impact of the news item, which then make it more likely to be given a higher priority (Barrat 1994: 97). With this in mind, Chibnall (1977) and Wykes (2001) expanded the original list of news values to include: conformity/ non-conformity; cleanliness/ dirtiness; commitment/ non-commitment; safety/ danger; puritanism/ pleasure; natural/ cultural. These news values are significant in contributing to how news is selected and constructed. Their meaning further emphasises the 'us' and 'them' distinction, which divides the 'law-abiding' from those individuals or social groups that are labelled criminal or deviant. In revisiting the original analysis of news values, Wykes (2001: 23) argues that in the contemporary setting, sexuality and broader cultural relations around gender, ethnicity and age, need to be considered.

How news values operate in the newsroom to include and exclude stories from the news schedule has an impact on the information the readership is provided with. Galtung and Ruge (1982: 58–59, original emphasis) have long argued that *negative* news is preferred to positive news, as it enters the news channel more easily, satisfies the *frequency* criterion better and it is more *unexpected*, seen to be more rare and thus, less predictable. Crime, deviance and offenders regularly feature in media coverage and are framed as negative news. This influences the way in which the audience or readership view crime in contemporary society.

The selection of news also influences the portrayal of movements, causes or significant events. Barrat (1994: 95–97) uses the example of feminist protests to illustrate how the focus on 'scenes of emotion and … violence' were 'given primary position', whilst the protestors' arguments were secondary and generally not included. Ericson et al. (1987: 9) argue that, 'the very act of discovering and construing events … in journalistic terms blinds the journalist' and 'the result is not the whole truth but truth reduced to the genre capacities' of the news item. Therefore, journalistic custom and practice, restricts and shapes not only what is reported but how it is reported and whose voices are included.

How journalistic custom and practice operates is also evident in the choice of language and imagery employed by journalists. As van Dijk (1991: 50–51) asserts, 'headlines … have important textual and cognitive functions', they have ideological implications, 'may bias the understanding process', with a catchy title for readers appearing the main priority of many editors. Headlines function as tone setters and signposts (Archers and Jones 2003: 18). Similarly images and photographs are 'worked on, chosen, composed, constructed … according to professional, aesthetic or ideological norms' (Barthes 1977: 19). The relationship between language and imagery in news reports can often be significant, with photographs gaining 'some of their meaningfulness from the … context in which they appear', often functioning as 'proof' that the media message is 'true' (Bignell 1997: 98–99). In producing representations, through language and imagery, the news-making process impacts on meaning in the public domain and thus, inevitably directly impacts on popular culture.

Impact of Media Representation on Popular Culture

Popular culture is heavily influenced by media messages, which permeate people's everyday lives (Ang 1990b: 155). In forming part of the social fabric of contemporary society, specific media content plays 'an important role in … day-to-day … interactions' (Devereux 2003: 11) and 'a pivotal role in orga- nizing the images and discourse through which people make sense of the world' (Golding and Murdock 1991: 15). To an extent it has become an unchallenged aspect of everyday life (O'Sullivan et al. 2003: 140), with con- sumers' intimate familiarity often resulting in them taking the media and media messages for granted (Croteau and Hoynes 2003). Effectively, as an unchallenged social institution, the media are in a powerful position to create media messages, which not only shape the audience's understanding, but impact on popular culture and audience judgements.

In exploring the role of the media in contemporary society, 'the practices and ideology which lies behind the making of the news' (Schlesinger 1987: 11) is pivotal in assessing the impact of the media on popular culture. Ideology shapes people's view of the world, by presenting a system of beliefs, used to make judgements about society (Lacey 1998: 98). Meanings are read into signs and the ideological process of reading such signs (Schirato and Yell 2000: 18), underpins and endows what it is to belong to a particular nation, social class, age group, race, gender, sexuality, (dis)able(d) group, for example (Briggs and Cobley 1998: 279). Therefore, the central function of ideology is to ensure that the existing system appears natural and acceptable to everyone (Bignell 1997: 26).

Power is at the core of ideology, with meanings serving to support power relationships and dominant economic and political interests (Corner and Hawthorn 1993: 7). Most communication is shaped and takes place within settings of inequality, whereby 'particular prejudices, discriminations and evaluations' are reinforced by the representation of the system as neutral (Corner and Hawthorn 1993: 7) or naturalised (Schirato and Yell 2000: 73). Journalistic custom and practice are central in reproducing ideology, which reinforces the interests of the economically and politically powerful. Dominant ideologies reflect and maintain the unequal distribution of power and wealth in contemporary society, placing individuals and groups in the margins, with little or no means of challenging their position or how they are represented.

Media representations are 'the bearers of ideology' (Briggs and Cobley 1998: 279). In constructing and promoting meanings 'which privilege one culture, or one section of a culture … over another' (Schirato and Yell 2000: 73) and by trading in stereotypes (Briggs and Cobley 1998: 279), the 'codified conventions' of the media 'contribute to the *naturalization* of … social divisions and inequalities' in contemporary society and 'reaffirm … inequalities as being *appropriate, legitimate* or *inevitable* in ideological terms' (Allan 1999: 49, original emphasis). Narratives and explanations of events, practices and activities in the media, 'attempt to draw attention away from the material … conditions in which people live', with 'the political and economic realities that define and determine people's existences', perpetuating 'inequality' and 'oppression' (Schirato and Yell 2000: 77–78).

Significantly, as Bryant and Zillmann (2002: 21) assert, the media's 'capacity … to reach large audiences', carries with it 'the risk of misleading the public' if the information or representations they disseminate prove to be 'distorted, inaccurate or in error'. Not only does the ideological process of news making naturalise, reinforce and maintain inequalities, it also provides an accessible platform from which those in power can ensure their position is maintained and their agenda is promoted. However, this platform is not easily accessible to those who are marginalised. This continuous ideological process assumes that the discourse presented in media content is that of those dominant and powerful members of contemporary society.

From the 1970s onward, developed the concept of discourse to complement the theory of ideology (Cormack 2000). Discourse theory focuses on the workings of representation (Briggs and Cobley 1998: 279–280) to illustrate how meanings and values reproduce power relations (Schirato and Yell 2000: 59). Foucault (1970, 1972) argues that discourse concerns both language and practice, which 'constructs, defines and produces … objects of knowledge' and at the same time excludes 'other ways of reasoning as unintelligible' (Barker 1999: 26), which highlights the regulation of what can be said under determinate social and cultural conditions and who can speak, when and where (Barker 2000: 79). As Hall (1997: 47) observes, Foucault's later writing became concerned with how 'knowledge was put to work through discursive practices in specific institutional settings to regulate the conduct of others'.

The relationship and connection between how an individual or social group is represented in media discourse and how they are treated, is significant. As van Zoonen (1996: 38–39) asserts:

[T]he process of discourse … and the product … (meanings and narratives) … privilege certain meanings above others … the power of discourse lies … in its capacity to define what is a social problem … also in its prescriptions of how an issue should be understood, the legitimate views on it, the legitimacy and deviance of the actors involved, the appropriateness of certain acts etc.

The promotion of dominant discourses is 'part and parcel of everyday mainstream media content', as dominant groups in society, who hold 'the greatest economic or cultural capital', have greater opportunities 'to promote their ideologies to wider audiences', via the media (van Zoonen 1996: 81). This process refers to hegemony, a theory developed by the Italian Marxist, Antonio Gramsci and members of the Frankfurt School for Social Research and promoted by the Centre for Contemporary Cultural Studies at Birmingham University. Hegemony can be described as 'that which goes without saying', 'the givens' or 'common-sense realities', which maintain the dominance of the ruling class (Berger 1998: 56; Williams 1977). It exposes how 'through images and texts … consent to a dominant ideological position is won', which further emphasises the media as a powerful and active tool of social control (Lacey 1998: 113–114).

Drawing on the theory of cultural hegemony, research produced by Birmingham's Centre for Contemporary Cultural Studies asserted that 'the unconscious internalization of the assumptions of the dominant culture by journalists' and the 'reliance on powerful groups and institutions as sources' (Curran 2002: 110), resulted in a taken-for-grantedness (Hall 1986) of dominant representations and the downgrading of opposing or alternative meanings. Within the hegemonic model, ideology in news, was the 'outcome of routine attitudes … working practices … conventions and codes' operating within the media (Barker 2000: 262). The model does not assert that there is no space available for opposing or alternative viewpoints in media content, rather it argues that the current organisation of the media and the existence of struggles between competing ideologies within the social world, remain challenges.

In constructing representations, the media are in a powerful position to continuously represent someone, a group, certain acts and behaviours, in such a way that the audience's or readership's view of them becomes fixed or frozen (Glover 1984: 27). Stereotyping is a conventional process active in media representation, whereby a person or group is labelled, portrayed or represented, via a process of categorisation and evaluation, which results in the audience or readership easily grasping negative characteristics and presuming they belong to an entire social group (O'Sullivan et al. 2003: 78). This process has the potential to give rise to social prejudices and in ideological terms it is a means by which support is provided for one group's differential and discriminatory treatment of another, as it marks out acceptable boundaries and points out those who do not fully belong (Glover 1984: 27). Further to this, it illustrates how power relations operate and are utilised by those in power, to maintain and reinforce their position.

It has been established that the structure of the media places constraints or limits on those who have access to it (Becker 1967). Typically, it is a small number of powerful individuals who are granted the position to communicate on a society-wide basis. Gerbner (1972, cited in Barrat 1994: 14–15) acknowledges this when he argues that, in society, 'never have so many people … shared so much of a common system of messages and images [with] … assumptions about life, society and the world embedded in them – while having so little to do with their making'. While audiences do not play an active role in how media content is produced, they do play an active role in interpretation (Ang 1990a; Tolson 1996). Media audiences use and interpret media content and messages 'according to the logic of their own social, cultural and individual circumstances', with content 'framed by shared cultural meanings and practices' (van Zoonen 1996: 40; Barker 2000: 271).

Audiences are active creators of meaning (Barker 1999: 111), in that they decode media content from different social positions, having developed the skill according to particular social and cultural codes and conventions. Media content is structured in dominance which produces a preferred meaning (Hall 1986) that usually coincides with the perceptions of the dominant sections of society (Fiske and Hartley 1989).[6] Perceptions and ideas are therefore shaped in this way (Masterman 1990: 3), which can have an impact on the 'thoughts and behaviours' of the audience or readership (Caliendo 2011: 74), in terms of prejudice, or the way in which 'we think and feel about ourselves' or 'others' (Corner and Hawthorn 1993: 173).

The formation of print news, news values and how readers engage with media content, is a 'process in which stereotypes are the currency of negotiation' (Fowler 1994: 17). Within this process the audience plays a key role in accepting and internalising such ways of thinking. Stereotypes reflect 'a particular set of ideological values', 'become consensus views' and are most 'often used by individuals', such as the media, in reference to 'people, or peoples, they do not know' (Lacey 1998: 138–139). Class, race, sexuality, age and gender, all of which are social constructs, have stereotypes associated with them. Media consumption is often specialised and motivated by a person's specific enthusiasms and prejudices (Briggs and Cobley 2002: 1). Therefore, when 'audience recognition' and acceptance of stereotypes occur, 'the status of consensus' is applied (Lacey 1998: 139). Further, the hegemonic function of stereotypes is to serve and naturalise existing power relationships in society (Lacey 1998: 139), for example between adults and children and young people. The result is the justification of 'social disadvantages and injustices' (Glover 1984: 27).

Stereotypes 'reduce persons to a set of exaggerated, usually negative, character traits' (Barker 1999: 75). Not only does the process of stereotyping illustrate power relations and the 'connection between representation, difference and power' (Hall 1997: 259), it focuses on individuals or social groups who are '"abjected" or "thrown out" from the "normal" order of things', and it 'simultaneously establishes who is "us" and who is "them"' (Barker 1999: 75). Therefore, 'how that group is represented in the sense of spoken for and on behalf of', are factors which impact on 'how groups see themselves and others like themselves', 'their place in society' and 'their right to the rights a society claims to ensure its citizens' (Dyer 1993: 1). Media representation is central to how a group is seen and this determines how they are treated, thus, how others treat them is 'based on' how they 'see them' (Dyer 1993: 1).

Stereotyping relates closely to agenda setting, 'a process whereby the terms of reference for debate are fixed to suit the interests of the powerful' (Barrat 1994: 52). The traditional news making process provides the powerful that opportunity to represent their views as being consistent with a larger 'public consensus' (Allan 1999: 71), when in effect it is the presentation of 'the elite consensus' (Curran 1998: 85). Further, it refers to the 'causal relationship' between media content and 'subsequent public perception of what … important issues … are' (McNair 2009: 21–22), with 'omission' as well as 'inclusion' helping 'to structure public perception' (Goodwin 1990: 48). As Camargo Heck (1980: 124, original emphasis) succinctly concludes, 'it is not only what is *said* that has a significance but also the *way* it is said, and what is *not said but could be said*'.

The impact of material problems and conditions, as well as the structure of society, which reinforces inequality, continues to be ignored and unaddressed in media coverage. Related to this, are the difficulties that marginalised social groups experience in seeking to have their voices heard. It is evident that gaining access to the media to express opinion, to challenge media representations or to seek redress, is constrained by power relations in contemporary society. As this chapter establishes, journalistic custom and practice ensure that the most politically and economically powerful have the monopoly as 'credible' sources of information on events or issues.

'Institutional' and 'organizational ties' 'leave journalists in a state of dependency with respect to sources' (Ericson et al. 1999: 280). The result is the 'over-accessing' of those in 'powerful and privileged institutional positions' (Hall et al. 1978: 58). Such 'authoritative' voices are 'routinely available' (Masterman 1990: 122) and news organisations regularly in choosing a 'self-effacing formulae', delegate 'considerable editorial control to these sources' (Curran 1998: 85). Becker's (1967: 241) theory on the 'hierarchy of credibility', highlights how those 'at the top' have their views 'regarded as the most credible account available', as they have the most 'knowledge' of 'the truth' (see also Hall 1986; Allan 1999). This process defines the scope of debate, with 'primary definers' (Becker 1967) giving 'the initial definition or … interpretation of the news topic to be processed' (Allan 1999: 71) and in doing so, they set the agenda and 'the boundaries within which the debate should take place' (Barrat 1994: 52). Whilst this does not 'prohibit all debate or disagreement' (Barrat 1994: 52), it does reveal that news production is 'mainly a one-way traffic', with '"Them" telling "us" what they want us to know' (Masterman 1990: 121).

This 'structured relationship' between the media and the 'hierarchy of institutional definers' (Allan 1999: 71) steers 'too much towards authority figures and too little towards ordinary and marginalised voices' (Machin and Niblock 2006: 24). Politicians, judges, civil servants, business executives, 'personality' figures, religious figures and others in key powerful positions are provided with 'organized media access' (van Dijk 1991: 152–153). 'Others' struggle to gain access, as it is often 'socio-economically determined' (van Dijk 1991: 152–153). The media provide 'an illusion of "openness", presenting itself as a forum for competing points of view', but in reality '"discourse" or agenda … sets the limits to what shall and, more importantly, what shall *not*, be discussed by society' (Barrat 1994: 53, original emphasis). When alternative views are included, they 'rarely act to structure the overall framework of debate' and if 'information' provided 'contradicts the dominant view', it appears in the media 'as fragments' and is 'never explored by news personnel as a rational … explanation' (Goodwin 1990: 48). As Gross (1992: 131) contends, when marginalised groups 'attain visibility', their viewpoints appear 'only within a framework set out by' the mainstream media.

Crime, Punishment, Media and Public Opinion

As established above, the news is both an ideological and social construct, with editors and journalists playing a central role in selecting, shaping and framing the information that is released to the public. This is particularly significant when the public has little or no direct experience of an issue, gaining all or most of its information from the media. Crime, offenders and punishment are examples of this. The connection between media representation and societal treatment, not only restricts who has access to the media, but it results in the maintenance, reinforcement and naturalisation of inequalities. Such inequalities impact on the most marginalised individuals and social groups. This illustrates the hegemonic function of the media and how the promotion and maintenance of dominant ideologies and discourses play out in contemporary society.

Pivotal studies produced by sociologists and critical criminologists from the 1970s onward, have confirmed this link between representation and treatment (Young 1971; Cohen 1972; Hall et al. 1978; Pearson 1983). In questioning 'the media as purveyors of particular social constructions of reality' (Kidd-Hewitt 1995: 13), this influential body of research argues that the media's 'stereotypical' and 'misleading portrayals' of certain groups in society, helps 'to deflect wider social conflict and reinforce dominant social and political norms' (Curran 2002: 109). This is evident in the media's reporting and representation of crime, deviance and offenders, as journalists draw on 'a rich seam of source material' provided by 'official sources' (Bessant and Hil 1997: 1). As argued above, alternative voices and opposing viewpoints rarely feature in media coverage on crime and when they do, their comments are placed within the framework set out by the 'primary definers'.

Critical literature and research on how crime is represented in the contemporary media, argues that crime journalism embodies and reflects a particular way of seeing the social world. This is significant, as Wykes (2001: 3) points out:

> Crime news mobilises the extremes of value judgments ... good and bad, innocent and guilty, heroes and villains, victims and abusers. It is the site of our national conscience and moral codes.

Media reporting on crime produces 'a cultural effect' that is 'profoundly ideological' in disguising 'the social and political forces' that ultimately influence 'the shape of events' and representations (Curran et al. 1980: 306). This part of the chapter explores the implications of social reactions to crime and deviance and how public opinion impacts on those who are labelled and demonised. Through an analysis of pivotal studies on 'labelling', 'outsiders', 'secondary deviance', 'deviancy amplification', 'folk devils' and 'moral panics', it concentrates on research with children and young people. It argues that the media, in limiting, framing and shaping information on crime, presents a distorted and exaggerated picture of crime and offenders in contemporary society.[7] This is evidenced in national and international research, which concludes that the print media disproportionately represent children and young people as perpetrators.

Crime, as a staple of the contemporary media (Newburn 2007: 84), is more often than not the topic of the lead story or the front page headline 'grabber' (Surette 1998: x). Crime and the criminal justice system, 'given their centrality to public life … are crucial fields for everyday news-reporting' (Schlesinger and Tumber 1994: 271). Marsh and Melville (2009: 1) assert that within the general population there is a 'vast and seemingly insatiable interest … in crime and criminals'. As previously outlined, in responding to 'the pressure of supply and demand in producing news for mass consumption' (Schissel 2006: 42), journalism always produces 'a selective, partial account of reality' (McNair 1994: 34). It is asserted that the media, more than any other source have the greatest influence on the public's perception of crime (Muraskin and Domash 2007: 7).[8] Crime reporters therefore have the capacity, significant power and opportunity to shape public opinion and a more broadly held understanding and knowledge of crime, offenders and punishment.

Reiner (2007) refers to the process and formation of crime news as 'hegemony in action'. In highly competitive and market-driven environments, journalists and editors select events according to the criteria of 'newsworthiness', and make the most out of 'the shock value' of crime stories, with specific aspects often presented as more salient to the audience than others (Nichols 2010). As a result of this process, certain aspects appear more 'noticeable', 'meaningful' and 'memorable' to audiences (Entman 1993: 51). This has led to the media often presenting 'a seriously distorted picture of criminal activity … crime and criminals' (Durham et al. 1995: 143–144). This is particularly evident in the reporting of youth crime, which 'is deemed "newsworthy" because … it makes for dramatic appeal and "good copy"' (Bessant and Hil 1997: 1).

Fulfilling a number of the news values as outlined above, crime and in particular youth crime and violence are packaged as 'bad news', as they fit with the well-established 'tried and tested formulas' of 'news-production' (Bessant and Hil 1997: 1). Similarly, news values also influence how 'political violence' or 'disorder' is presented. As Reiner (2007: 324) asserts, they are always framed 'in terms of individual pathology rather than "ideological opposition"', and as 'discrete criminal events, not manifestations of structural conflict'. The media's representation of inner-city uprisings, such as the Brixton 'riots' and miners' strikes in England in the early 1980s are examples of the media's pathologising of individuals and social groups (Khabaz 2006). Stereotypes linked to age, race, gender and class, are evoked to frame 'criminal events' in terms of individual pathology and are used politically to validate and gain public support for harsh responses. By omitting discussion, debate or acknowledgement of social and structural context, the media provides the outlet through which dominant political and ideological assertions can be maintained, at the expense of 'others' who are portrayed as creating 'problems' for themselves.

As occurred in the examples of the media's framing of the inner-city uprising and strikes in the 1980s, crime journalists work according to their long-established formulas and news values to present events and individuals in a certain way and also to propose 'solutions'. Crime and deviance are presented according to particular journalistic customs and practices. In particular, as a result of news values, the media frame crime and offenders in an identifiable and dramatic way, ensuring that stories of incidents of crime, appeal to and reach as large an audience as possible. Glover (1984: 57) argues that news formulas tend 'to ignore the diversity of ... beliefs' or opposing viewpoints that may exist in contemporary society. They also ensure that certain explanations and proposed responses are validated by 'official' sources and 'authoritative' voices. The process, in fulfilling 'the economic necessity of reaching as big a circulation as possible' (Glover 1984: 57), spreads 'ideological views' which reflect dominant ideologies and the social order (Newburn 2007: 85).

The media exert 'exceptional political' and 'ideological power' (McNair 1994: 48) in defining what issues or individuals and social groups are viewed as 'problems' and in playing a significant role in outlining 'solutions' (Schlesinger and Tumber 1994: 149). In light of the media's reliance on 'official sources' for information, as well as the promotion of dominant ideologies, the media's reporting on policing, punishment and criminal justice policies and practices, reinforce and show support for 'official' responses to crime. This includes framing crime responses according to 'the "law and order" narrative' (Reiner 2007: 327). As a result other approaches or proposed approaches are not included, are marginalised or discredited.

In shaping and framing the information the public receive on crime, the media not only exaggerate the level of crime that occurs, but they portray disproportionately certain social groups, as offenders or perpetrators. This is particularly evident in the media's representation of young people. Young people, as a relatively powerless and marginalised social group, are regularly the focus of media reporting on crime and punishment. Bessant and Hil (1997: 2–3) argue that, 'the media reserves its most vociferous reporting for the apparent "crime waves" and "social problems" generated by certain sections of the youth population'. As Hall et al. (1978) observe, the media's selection of crime stories rarely focus on crimes of the powerful, rather they concentrate on powerless groups, such as young people, with media content regularly 'sympathetic to the justice system rather than to the offender' (Newburn 2007: 85).

Further to this, Glover (1984: 66) argues that crime reporters 'are constrained by their relations with their sources', with many quotations and opinions gathered from those holding powerful positions in contemporary society.

It is the information gained from influential 'definers' that regularly frames the direction and messages of stories on crime and deviance. Access to sources, responses from those in power and public reaction, each impact on how stories are framed and also on the period of time that certain stories on crime will remain in the public domain, via extended media coverage.

Specifically with regard to crime, there is a wealth of contemporary national and international research, which confirms that media coverage of youth slants towards 'distortion, exaggeration and misrepresentation' (see Glover 1984; Simpson 1997; Schissel 1997, 2006, 2008; White 2002; Osgerby 2004; France 2007; Springhall 2008). Tabloid press reporting is fraught with stereotypical representations of youth (Schissel 2006), which 'create categories of evil outsiders to contrast with the inner community of their own readers' (Wykes 2001, cited in Conboy 2006: 104). Journalists, in line with custom, practice and news values, employ 'a wide range of emotive terms to emphasize both the nature of the outsiders', contrasting them with 'the stability and health of the insider community' (Wykes 2001, cited in Conboy 2006: 104). Typical news coverage of youth, frame young people as 'unruly, anti-social delinquents', and exacerbate fears of this social group, as the media portray them as 'powerful' and 'irrational threats' to society (Glover 1984; Curran 2002).

As a direct result of the news-making process, there emerges 'a world of us and them, of insiders and outsiders, a world of fear' (Schissel 2006: 42), with 'dramatic and morally charged representation of the latest outbreaks of deviancy' by contemporary youth (Bessant and Hil 1997: 1). Crime reporting, through representations, labelling and stereotypical images of young people, guides the audience or readership to form opinions on youth in contemporary society, based on distorted and exaggerated information. In affecting society's attitudes and perceptions of crime and offenders, the media also impact on societal reaction. This impact on social reaction has been explored by labelling theorists and critical criminologists, in their development of the concept of 'deviancy amplification'.

Labelling theorists, building on the tradition of social interactionism, were concerned with how and why particular people come to be defined and labelled as 'deviant' (Downes and Rock 2007: 134; Newburn 2007: 210). The focal point of labelling theory was on the impact of social reactions to deviance (Regoli et al. 2011: 164), with theorists emphasising 'the role of interaction in the construction of social labels' and exploring 'how individuals apply and react to labels' (Franzese 2009: 70). In the 1950s and 1960s, Lemert (1951, 1967), Becker (1963), Cicourel (1968) and other labelling theorists, 'were the first to approach the social reaction to deviant behaviour as a *variable*, not a constant' (Downes and Rock 2007: 134, original emphasis). Further, the perspectives of the labelling theorists impacted on social constructionist approaches to understanding crime and deviance, which 'attempt to understand meanings involved in social interaction' (Newburn 2007: 211–212).

In particular Lemert (1951, 1967), Erikson (1962, 1966), Kitsuse (1962) and Becker (1963) assert that crime and deviance is not 'inherent in any action' but through the process of labelling it is viewed and portrayed as criminal and deviant. As Kitsuse (1962: 253, cited in Taylor et al. 1973: 144) states, 'it is the responses of the … conforming members of society which identify and interpret behaviour as deviant which sociologically transforms persons into deviants'. Becker (1963: 9, original emphasis) presents a similar view, when he asserts that, 'deviance is *not* a quality of the act the person commits, but rather a consequence of the application by others of rules and sanctions to an "offender"'. Both Kitsuse (1962) and Becker (1963) emphasise the key role the audience plays in labelling actions as deviant. These theorists argue that it is 'the social audience rather than the individual actor' who 'eventually determines whether or not an episode of behaviour … is labelled deviant' (Erikson 1966: 11, cited in Newburn 2007: 212). Through social judgement certain social groups or individuals become 'the very essence of what is being complained' (Muncie 2006: 229).

Focusing on the role of societal reaction and the impact of social judgement, Tannenbaum's work in the late 1930s on juvenile delinquency was concerned with social reactions to children and young people who had their behaviour labelled as 'delinquent', 'evil' or 'anti-social' (Regoli et al. 2011: 166). Further, his work explored 'the consequences' that the labelling process 'portends for young people who were formally processed by the criminal justice system' (Franzese 2009: 70). Tannenbaum argued that 'delinquents are not inherently different from non-delinquents' (Regoli et al. 2011: 166) and he rejected the 'individual pathology' argument. Rather, he argued that social reactions are pivotal in who does and does not become labelled as delinquent; delinquency is not due to inherent personality traits or predispositions, it is due to how society reacts. His focus on young people illustrates how the labelling by adults of this relatively 'powerless' social group, became a continuous cycle.

In his 'highly compelling set of insights on the definition, dramatization and objectification' of juvenile delinquency (Prus and Grills 2003: 77), Tannenbaum (1938) introduced the term 'dramatization of evil' to describe the way in which 'juvenile play may be redefined as delinquent evil which must be suppressed' (Farr 2001: 74). His analysis can be clearly compared to the contemporary setting, in particular to the impact of societal reaction in the UK towards children and young people, following the death of James Bulger; the impact of New Labour's Crime and Disorder 1998 legislation which followed and the raft of criminalising measures directed towards children, young people and their families, such as Anti-social Behaviour Orders (ASBOs), Parenting Orders, Child Safety Orders and Curfews (see also Haydon and Scraton 2000). Some 60 years prior, the importance of exploring community and societal responses to young people was highlighted in the following observation by Tannenbaum (1938: 17):

> In conflict between the young delinquent and the community there develop two opposing definitions of the situation. In the beginning the definition of the situation by the young delinquent may be in the form of play … mischief, fun … To the community … these activities … often take on the form of nuisance, evil, delinquency, with the demand for control … chastisement, punishment … This conflict over the situation gradually becomes redefined. The attitude of the community hardens … into a demand for suppression.

In the contemporary setting, Scraton (2008: 5) argues that the application of labels to children and young people and the criminalisation of this social group is a 'powerful weapon', which 'extends to "political containment" by mobilizing "considerable popular approval and legitimacy behind the state"' (Hall and Scraton 1981: 488–489). The demonisation of certain social groups and 'the vilification, dehumanization and dissociation' of children and young people, 'underpin the political management and differential policing of their perceived and promulgated identity' (Scraton 2008: 5).

Contemporary responses to children and young people relate to Tannenbaum's (1938) theorisation of the direct impact of societal and community reactions on the alienation of this social group and on how their subsequent behaviour is responded to. In addressing the issue of reaction, Tannenbaum (1938) created the phrase, the 'dramatization of evil', to describe the 'suppression' of 'the entire' social group, which must be changed in order to suppress the "evil"' (Farr 2001: 74). For the individual, the result is 'a gradual shift from the definition of the specific acts as evil to a definition of the individual as evil, so that all his acts come to be looked on with suspicion' (Tannenbaum 1938: 17).

According to Tannenbaum (1938: 20), 'delinquents' and 'delinquency' are created via 'a process of tagging, defining, identifying, segregating, describing … stimulating, suggesting, emphasising and evoking the very traits that are complained of'. The result is the young person 'becomes the thing he is described as being' (Tannenbaum 1938: 20). At the core of this theory is the assumption that once labelled a delinquent or as 'anti-social', children and young people are 'likely to accept the description and live up to it' (Regoli et al. 2011: 166). Labels ultimately have 'long-lasting, potentially devastating' consequences for those individuals who are the subject of labelling, in particular through 'a self-fulfilling prophecy' (Franzese 2009: 71).

Lemert (1951, 1967) as an early advocate of this theoretical approach (Newburn 2007: 213), was primarily concerned with the community responses towards those individuals labelled as 'deviant', and on the impact the responses had on the subsequent behaviour of those labelled (Prus and Grills 2003: 77). Lemert's analysis, 'distinguished between two types of deviance: primary and secondary' (Lilly et al. 2011: 144) and in doing so, 'envisioned deviance as a continuum' (Franzese 2009: 71). Primary deviance refers to 'a type of deviance that most of us have experienced'; it is 'infrequent behaviour' and most who engage in it 'do not think of or define themselves as a deviant, nor do others' (Franzese 2009: 71). In contrast secondary deviance 'refers to a special class of socially defined responses which people make to problems created by the societal reaction to their deviance' (Lemert 1967: 40). Further, Lemert (1951: 76) asserts that:

> When a person begins to employ his deviant behavior or a role based upon it as a means of defense, attack, or adjustment to the overt and covert problems created by the consequent social reaction to him, his deviation is secondary.

This illustrates the outcome of societal reaction on those labelled and alienated from a community. In drawing on Lemert's theory, Lilly et al. (2011: 145) argue that 'the offender solves this problem by accepting his or her "life and identity … around the facts of deviance"'. In showing how social reaction brings about more crime, labelling theorists, in particular Erikson (1962, 1966), Kitsuse (1962) and Becker (1963) employed Merton's (1968) concept of the 'self-fulfilling prophecy'. This refers to a process, whereby 'in the beginning, a *false* definition of the situation evoking a new behavior which makes the originally false conception come *true*' (Merton 1968: 477, original emphasis, cited in Lilly et al. 2011: 145). The self-fulfilling prophecy highlights the direct impact on those labelled and also sheds light on the significance of power to the process of societal reaction and secondary deviance.

In Becker's (1963) groundbreaking book, 'Outsiders', he 'set out to develop a systematic theory of labelling and deviancy' (Slattery 2003: 135). Becker (1963) highlights the role played by 'moral entrepreneurs' in shaping public perceptions and societal reactions toward marijuana users in the USA. Aggleton (1987: 58) states that 'moral entrepreneurs' push inaccurate ideas into the public domain, which result in consequences for those labelled as 'deviant', including criminalisation and social exclusion. What is critical to the process is the reaction of those in authority, as they have the power to define, label, and have the most access to present their condemnation and solutions via the media. The rejection and isolation experienced by those to whom labels are applied, creates 'outsiders', whose own perception of themselves and their social group, is shaped by the labelling process and often confirmed through 'self-fulfilling prophecy'. It is these consequences that interactionist studies of deviance have focused on.

Deviancy amplification theory, developed by Wilkins (1964), is closely related to Lemert's distinction between primary and secondary deviance and the work of other labelling theorists. Deviancy amplification refers to 'the process whereby media, police, public and political reaction to non-conformity acts … has the obverse reaction of increasing' (Muncie 2006: 127–128), both the 'amount' and 'frequency' of crime and deviance (Tierney 2010: 153). Through the process that arises out of secondary deviation, those labelled incorporate the negative deviant self-image, which 'has a knock-on effect of producing more reactions from control agents, as others … also become involved' (Tierney 2010: 153).

Information provided through the media 'influences the dynamics of the interactions between the agencies of social control and the deviant group' (Farnen 1990: 107). The impact can be identified in policing responses, the further ostracism of the labelled individual from the community, the extent of the public indignation and societal responses, as well as political and policy responses, as will be discussed in the next chapter. The media's role is central to the 'deviancy amplification spiral', in transmitting often highly distorted and exaggerated information about crime to the audience, which has the effect of influencing societal reaction.

As Jewkes (2004: 67) asserts:

> The media set in motion a 'deviancy amplification spiral' in which a moral discourse is established by journalists and various other authorities, opinion leaders and moral entrepreneurs, who collectively demonize the perceived wrong-doers as a source of moral decline and social disintegration.

The theory of deviancy amplification not only refers to the fact that the media frequently exaggerate what happens, but it also refers to a type of effect. This effect relates to the influence the media and moral entrepreneurs have in labelling and reinforcing stereotypes, which feeds back and impacts on the perception and behaviour of the individuals and social groups who are labelled. As Muncie (2006: 128) states, 'together with the labelling approach, the concept of deviancy amplification draws attention to the unintended consequences of public perceptions, police actions and social reaction'. When the deviancy amplification spiral is set in motion, the media and moral entrepreneurs assert that there is an increase in crime and deviance, thus confirming the stereotypes.

Both labelling theory and deviancy amplification theories reveal 'how processes of reaction are also processes of invention and creation' (Muncie 2006: 128). They are pivotal theories, which explore the media's influence on public perception and the media's role in impacting on societal reactions to crime and deviance. Wilkins (1964) pointed out that whilst most people do not have direct contact with those who are labelled as 'deviant', they might feel they know all about and need to be protected from the 'mugger', 'dope-fiend', or 'juvenile delinquent'. However, as argued earlier in this chapter, in essence this information is gained from the media, who exaggerate, distort and portray crime in a dramatic way. The media's role therefore, is central in maintaining the deviancy amplification spiral in contemporary society.

The theory of 'moral panics' and 'folk devils' emerged and developed previous theory and research on labelling, secondary deviance, self-fulfilling prophecy, outsiders and deviancy amplification. The three initial, classic accounts of moral panics were: Young's study of cannabis and 'hippies' in, 'The Drugtakers' (1971) situated in 1968; Stan Cohen's (1972) study of 'Mods' and 'Rockers' situated in 1964–1966, and Stuart Hall et al.'s study of the mugging panic, 'Policing the Crisis' (1978) situated in 1972. As Young (2008: 176) asserts, 'all seem to represent major structural and value changes in industrial society as refracted through the prism of youth'. Essentially these researchers argue that the media's 'amplification of deviance' contribute to the creation of 'moral panics'.

Drawing on Becker's (1963) analysis, Young (1971) illustrates how words used to describe drug takers and labels applied to this group, set them apart, as 'anti-social', 'amoral', 'disorganised', and outside society (Sheptycki 2003: 129). Young's (1971) research shows the application and fulfilment of labelling theory, secondary deviance and deviancy amplification. In line with Tannenbaum's conclusion, Young (1971: 215) argues that 'by isolating, alienating and exacerbating the social circumstances of the drug taker', society 'contribute[s] significantly to the criminality'. By separating or segregating young people from communities in which they live, there exists 'a greater risk of long-term social disorder' (McRobbie 1994: 198). Young's (1971) study also found that the police and the British news media's condemnation of drug taking not only led to more arrests but also resulted in a great sense of community and shared identity among drug users (Krinsky 2008: 1). Therefore, negative responses can be internalised by groups or individuals and can result in undesired or unintended consequences.

Similarly in focusing on the impact of societal and media reaction, Cohen's (1972) pivotal study of the reactions to 'Mods' and 'Rockers' at the seaside resort of Clacton during Bank holiday weekends in the mid-1960s, emphasises the connection between media representation, societal reactions and the treatment of youth. In his study, Cohen (1972) was the first to develop the concept of 'moral panic' both theoretically and empirically. His original analysis states that a 'moral panic' occurs when:

> A condition, episode, person or group of persons emerges to become defined as a threat to societal values and interests; its nature is presented in a stylized and stereotypical fashion by the mass media; the moral barricades are manned by editors, bishops, politicians and other right-thinking people; socially accredited experts pronounce their diagnoses and solutions … at … times it has more serious and long-lasting repercussions and might produce such changes as those in legal and social policy or even in the way society conceives itself. (Cohen 1972: 9)

As the above definition asserts, the media and moral entrepreneurs are central to the creation and maintenance of 'moral panics' and in fuelling societal reactions to 'folk devils'.

Cohen (1980: 40) argues that a word or label 'becomes symbolic of a certain status (delinquent or deviant); objects (hairstyle, clothing) symbolize the word; the objects themselves become symbolic of the status (and the emotions attached to the status)'. Labels become defining terms of abuse, rejection and judgement. In applying Cohen's (1972) theorisation to the contemporary setting, the demonisation of children and young people involved in perceived anti-social behaviour and the labelling, and treatment of youth who wear the contemporary fashion item – a 'hoodie', are applicable examples. They are also reminiscent of Albert Cohen's (1955) study on 'delinquent boys' and Young's (1971) study on 'drug takers'. What Cohen's (1972) study of the reactions to 'Mods' and 'Rockers' reinforces, is how central media exaggeration; distortion; amplification; symbolisation; societal judgement and reaction, are to the process of creating, fuelling and maintaining 'moral panics' and to the treatment of 'folk devils'.

Employing Cohen's (1972) analysis, Goode and Ben-Yehuda (2009: 33) argue that it is 'moral panic' that 'divides society' into 'them' and 'us', 'deviants' and 'folk devils' versus 'law-abiding citizens'. It is typically the most marginalised social groups in society, such as young people, who are most frequently the subject of 'moral concern' and subsequently emerge as, or 'become the folk devils'. Goode and Ben-Yehuda (2009: ix) state that, 'the intensity of concern … takes on a special urgency' when the 'folk devils' are introduced. 'Folk devils' are 'one or more persons supposedly responsible for and/or representing exaggeratedly fearful conditions' (Goode and Ben-Yehuda 2009: ix). As Poynting et al. (2004: 2, 12) assert, '"Folk Devils" serve as simple, readily digestible apparent causes of the problem' and 'provid[e] an object of hostility which concretises and focuses' existing 'social anxieties'.

Societal reaction is closely linked to the media's portrayal and treatment of individuals and groups labelled as criminal and deviant. The media are central in transmitting to wider society, the urgency and moral concern presented by moral entrepreneurs, who gain society's support by framing their concerns via 'a strong sense of righteousness' and in whipping up 'heightened emotion, fear, dread, anxiety, hostility' (Goode and Ben-Yehuda 2009: 35). What is pivotal to the success of this process is that agreement must be reached at grassroots or ground level, with the majority of adults united in their crusade against the latest epidemic of youth crime and delinquency. It is in such an atmosphere that punitive responses flourish. The product of this process is the creation and maintenance of a 'moral panic'.

Cohen (1972) concludes that 'moral panics' and the creation of 'folk devils' have long-lasting consequences for how contemporary problems are dealt with. Particular social groups are significantly affected, young people being one such example. The process of 'moral panics' can produce long-term consequences beyond the initial societal reaction, in particular changes to, or the creation of legal and social policies. As Scraton (2004: 12) observes, what follows is the promotion of the use of 'discipline', 'surveillance' and 'punishment', to deal with children and young people 'in conflict with the law'.

Cohen and Young (1981: 429) argue that as a result of the one-way process of media communication, 'moral panic' is not a process everyone can 'democratically' join in. It is the official view that is most likely to be aired. In contrast the public are rarely given the first-hand accounts of those labelled 'deviants', instead their behaviours and motivations are explained to the public by moral entrepreneurs, who define what is 'natural' and 'acceptable' in society. If first-hand accounts do feature, they are framed and are limited by the primary definers. This is what Becker (1963) has described as a 'hierarchy of access', with those whose behaviour is most frequently reported, holding the least rights over what is said (Barrat 1994: 38). This results in a 'one-dimensional' view, based on 'official' views, which see 'deviance' as 'obviously wrong' and 'something to be controlled and eradicated' (Barrat 1994: 39).

Further to this, adults define and label 'the problem', 'what is anti-social', 'what is delinquent' and 'what is socially unacceptable', and they then react by relegating young people to 'a zone of exclusion where they represent the problem' (Brown 1998: 27–28). Persistently, via popular and media discourse adults 'seek to explain why these young people stand "outside" of society: without, of course, authenticating the voices of young people themselves' (Brown 1998: 27–28). West (1976) observes the reoccurrence of this continuous cycle of concern that revisits the younger generation, arguing that the media play a key role in maintaining this cycle. He asserts that, 'the press and television, echoed all too often in official pronouncements by authorities … find news value in reports of a wave of crime and hooliganism, concentrated among teenagers' (West 1976: 33).

This was evident in Hall et al.'s (1978) study into 'the law and order' panic concerning 'mugging'. The study illustrates the role of the press in 'an ideological overreaction', which serves ruling class interests at a time of economic crisis (Glover 1984: 40). It also illustrates how the press claims to speak on its reader's behalf and at the same time, serves to confirm the policies and actions of the control culture (Glover 1984: 40). Chibnall (1977: x) acknowledges this when he argues that, 'crime news may serve as … a chance not simply to speak to the community but to speak for the community, against all that the criminal outsider represents', providing 'a chance for a newspaper to appropriate a moral conscience for its readership'. Hall et al.'s (1978) study emphasises that 'the rhetoric of police statements, and courtroom verdicts is passed back and forth by the press', which focuses and 'channels popular opinion' by supplying the 'link between those in the control culture who define and deal with social problems and the public' (Glover 1984: 40).

In further assessing the outcomes or implications of 'moral panics', Thompson (1998: 37–38) argues that the 'most important interface in the control culture is that where state control in the form of legislation and legislators meets pressures of public opinion' as 'channelled by claims-makers and moral entrepreneurs'. This is particularly important when the moral entrepreneurs are themselves politicians (Thompson 1998: 37–38). Cohen's (1972) research illustrates how initial reactions, were shaped by local spokespersons or moral entrepreneurs, who defined the young people's actions as 'hooliganism', in media discourse. What followed were calls for quick government responses to the problem, for laws to be 'tightened up', for the courts and the police to be given more powers. As McRobbie and Thornton (2002: 70) succinctly conclude:

The studies of Cohen, Young and Pearson show moral panics as acting on behalf of the dominant social order. They are a means of orchestrating consent by actively intervening in the space of public opinion and social consciousness through the use of highly emotive and rhetorical language which has the effect of requiring that 'something be done about it'. The argument about deviancy amplification is precisely that where strategies are indeed followed by social and legislative action, they also reassure the public that there is strong government and strong leadership.

A major focus of that 'something', 'typically entails strengthening the social control apparatus of ... society', with reactionary responses including 'tougher or renewed laws', 'more intense public hostility and condemnation', 'more laws', 'longer sentences', 'more police', an increase in arrests, and 'more prison cells' (Goode and Ben-Yehuda 2009: 35). In high profile cases, which receive extended coverage in the media, heightened emotion tends to impact on the type of 'quick', 'reactionary' responses that follow. The media plays a key role in whipping up public concern and in calling for the government to act in punitive legislative terms, the police to respond on the ground and judges to set long prison sentences. As Goode and Ben-Yehuda (1994: 139) argue:

> Professional associations, police departments, the media, religious groups, educational organizations, may have an independent stake in bringing an issue to the fore – focusing media attention on it or transforming the slant of new stories covering it, alerting legislators, demanding stricter law enforcement.

Amplifying issues to such a level that only punitive, swift and tough policies appear to be the best option to deal with such events, is a recurring feature of 'moral panics'. For instance, Young (1971: 182) illustrates this very process, whereby an initial concern over drug taking in Notting Hill, London prompted the police to set up specialist drug squads, thereby ensuring that the 'problem' was amplified by increasing the number of drug-related arrests.

As outlined above, Cohen's (1972) research and writing has been key in theorising the role the media plays in influencing the wider public's negative perception of children and young people in conflict with the law. That said, the validity and applicability of Cohen's (1972) theory of 'moral panics' has been the subject of criticism and has been challenged by other academics. Waddington (1986), Beck (1992), Cornwell and Linders (2002) and Waiton (2008) each have criticised Cohen's (1972) theory. Goode and Ben-Yehuda (2009: 73–87), in analysing each of these main critiques, state that the arguments can be divided into two main criticisms: the validity of the concept, and its currency.

Expanding on this, it is evident that Cohen's (1972) conceptualisation of 'moral panics' has been criticised for over-emphasising ideological constructions at the expense of material conditions. McRobbie and Thornton (1995) suggest that Cohen's portrayal of the 'Mods' and 'Rockers' as having no freedom in their actions and as powerless victims in the face of media distortion and public condemnation focuses on the structural aspects of society. Rather, McRobbie and Thornton (1995: 568) argue that in contemporary society young people as 'so-called folk devils' now produce their own media to counter the mainstream. Their argument appears not to consider how significant consensus and dominant ideology are to the overall treatment of young people; in light of their position in contemporary society, they remain a group with limited agency. Further, their analysis fails to assess whether the production of alternative forms of media, have any impact on mainstream media representation of youth, and societal reaction.

Significantly Cohen (1980: 1) asserted that 'the processes by which moral panics and folk devils are generated do not date', as 'more moral panics will be generated and other ... folk devils will be created'. His prediction has been realised. As Barrat (1994: 41) asserts, in the contemporary setting:

> A gallery of ... folk devils is assembled for our inspection and edification ... although individual exhibits may change the show goes on. All ... relatively powerless ... just the visible symptom of deeper and less obvious disagreements and conflicts in society.

The process is continuous as 'moral panics' continue to emerge, linked to adult-defined and created issues or 'crises' surrounding youth. The concept of 'moral panic' and in particular 'its constituent components – the dynamics of hostility, denunciation, and disproportion – remain intact' (Goode and Ben-Yehuda 2009: 86).

The media, in defining, framing and continuing to focus on the 'problem' behaviour of children and young people, play a central role in maintaining the process of blaming and demonising youth in order to cloak or avoid addressing structural inequalities (Box 1983: 13). In exploring the implications of 'moral panics' for 'folk devils', it is asserted that one of 'the most pernicious social consequences' of the process 'is the manner in which it narrows the debate about youth crime and the position of youth in society generally' (Simpson 1997: 15). As Simpson (1997: 15) concludes, the theory of moral panics must continue to expose the process; 'unless this is done we face the prospect of living in a society where the marginalisation of youth continues to produce the devils we fear'.

Conclusion

In exploring the significance and pervasiveness of the media in contemporary society, this chapter has argued that media content is created as a direct result of a production process that occurs within an institutional, organisational, politically and economically conscious framework. Journalistic custom and practice and news values are central elements, which shape the media content that the public receive. This analysis of newsworthiness established why certain topics such as youth crime are newsworthy, as they fit with several of the 'news values' outlined. Further, this chapter has explored the impact of the 'hierarchy of access' to the media. This process ensures that moral entrepreneurs maintain the dominant ideologies, while marginalised members of society, in particular those labelled as 'anti-social', 'criminal' or 'deviant', have little means of challenging negative stereotypes or labels ascribed to them. The pivotal literature, previous studies and key theoretical concepts explored, provide the theoretical foundation on which the empirical research can assess whether the voices of children, young people and their advocates are regularly included or excluded in print media coverage in Northern Ireland.

Drawing on critical criminological analyses, this chapter has also discussed the long-established focus on youth as a 'problem' and the impact of labels applied to perceived anti-social behaviour. Framed as 'folk devils', children and young people in conflict with the law are continuously relegated to the margins of society and excluded. As noted above, Cohen's (1972) theory of 'moral panics' highlights the significance of media representations in establishing 'us' (the 'law-abiding members' of society) and 'them' (children and young people). The analysis has argued that the process and consequences of 'moral panics' are significant. In particular, the tangible consequences of social reaction are particularly evident when policy-makers and legislators take into account or set out to meet the demands of public opinion, often fuelled by moral entrepreneurs, opportunistic politicians and the media (Thompson 1998). This process of social reaction is explored further in the next chapter, which assesses the impact of social reaction on contemporary policy responses to children and young people internationally, as well as specifically focusing on the UK and Northern Ireland.

Notes

1. It has long been acknowledged that the media are difficult to capture and define (Craig 2004: 3). As outlined in Chap. 1, the terms 'media' or 'mass media' refer to the traditional definition of the media, as consisting of newspapers (the print media), radio (broadcast media) and news bulletins and programs (televised media). While choosing to focus on the contemporary media, this book acknowledges from the outset that there is an extensive body of work existing on the historical origins of the media; mass communication and its impact, and the role of technological development (see Downing 1980; Frost 2000; Curran 2002).

2. There has been much criticism of pluralist theories on the media, including the arguments that pluralism is an ideological justification for the media and that the basis of the theory is not grounded in evidence. Rather the pluralist model assumes that the content of the media is diverse, without presenting evidence to reinforce or prove this theory (see Blumler and Gurevitch 1995).

3. Rupert Murdoch's ownership of a range of media outlets in the United Kingdom (UK) and United States (US) is a prime example of the concentration of power and the influence of owners on media content (see Golding and Murdock 1991; Horrie 2003; Cole 2005). Further to this, academics such as Barker (1999: 46) argue that conglomeration has aided a general concentration of media ownership, with research such as Bagdikian's (2004) stating that the US media were controlled by 50 corporations in the 1980s, and by 2003 this had been reduced to five controlling the majority of the 178,000 media outlets. Significantly as Tait (2012: 518) observes, the 'scale and intensity' of the phone hacking scandal in 2011, saw the resignation of the chief executive of one of the UK's most influential newspaper groups, the resignation of one of the UK's most senior police officers, the arrest of Andy Coulson, who had acted as the then Prime Minister, David Cameron's head of communications, the resignation of two senior executives from key companies in the Murdoch empire, as well as the collapse of the takeover deal in relation to BSkyB and the closure of the *News of the World* (see also Keeble and Mair 2012; McKnight 2012; Watson and Hickman 2012).

4. As Barrat (1994: 61) notes, the majority of media organisations are influenced by 'a variety of commercial influences', including the need to be profitable and also obtaining revenue through 'advertising'. Some media outlets are part of the public sector, such as the BBC and they have the requirement 'to provide a public service', by 'informing, educating, and entertaining audiences' (Barrat 1994: 61).

5. Tait's (2012: 520) analysis of the phone hacking scandal asserts that it has 'revealed some fundamental issues in British political communications, the political system and the practice and regulation of journalism'. His analysis also

documents 'a secret history' between Murdoch and British politics (Tait 2012: 520–523).

6. Semiology provides a suitable vehicle for studying the meanings behind media content (see O'Connor 1989; Hall 1997; Berger 1998; Barker 2000; Schirato and Yell 2000). In contemporary literature it is now referred to as semiotics and was first developed by the Swiss linguist, Saussure, who proposed that meaning was 'produced through … language systems' (Schirato and Yell 2000: 19). He focused on the 'linguistic sign', which he divided into the 'signifier', 'the signified' and the 'sign' (Schirato and Yell 2000: 19).

7. As the findings of a number of content analysis studies highlight, the media exaggerate the levels of crime, in particular violent crime in the UK (see Ditton and Duffy 1983; Schlesinger and Murdock 1991; Williams and Dickinson 1993; Callanan 2005; Greer 2005; Reiner 2007).

8. Dorfman and Schiraldi's (2001) research found that 76 percent of the public said they formed their opinions about crime from the media, whereas 22 percent reported that their knowledge of crime was formed through their personal experiences.

3

The Impact of Social Reaction on Contemporary Policy Responses to Children and Young People

According to Goldson (2005: 266) '[i]f we hold a mirror to contemporary policy responses to children in trouble … it returns a particularly ugly image'. In society, the process of social reaction reflects the relationship between the labelling and demonisation of children and young people, punitive societal and political responses directed towards them and their criminalisation by the 'justice' system. The impact of social reaction is evident in policy responses, which as Goldson (2005) notes, continue to legitimate the social control of 'problem' youth, in punitive, repressive, disciplinary and retributive forms. As Chap. 2 has outlined, pivotal studies on labelling, 'moral panics' and 'folk devils' illustrate how societal reaction to atypical events lead to public demand for punitive, tougher law and policy creation or reform. As Goode and Ben-Yehuda (2009: 36, original emphasis) assert, 'the question of the appropriate social and legal control of ['folk devils'] … *almost inevitably* accompanies the moral panic'. At the core of social reaction are tangible consequences that emerge when labels are embedded, reinforced and maintained in popular discourse (Hall and Scraton 1981). As Scraton (2007: 232) asserts:

> Moral panic[s] … emanat[e] from state institutions that mobilise surveillance, containment and regulation. Tangible and material, they are reactive, involving concrete strategies, techniques and resources with social, political and economic consequences.

Such tangible consequences play out in particular communities to impact on certain targeted and identifiable social groups, who experience the sharp end of policies, both formally and informally (see Scraton 2008).

© The Author(s) 2018
F. Gordon, *Children, Young People and the Press in a Transitioning Society*,
Palgrave Socio-Legal Studies, https://doi.org/10.1057/978-1-137-60682-2_3

A combination of media sensationalism and political opportunism allows those in powerful positions to seek public support for regulatory interventions. In turn, this impacts on police responses, court proceedings and sentencing. Social reaction is therefore pivotal in the construction of images legislators and policy-makers have of children and young people.

This chapter explores the tangible consequences of social reaction. The chapter is structured into two related parts, which critically analyse contemporary policy responses to children and young people in Britain and in Northern Ireland specifically. Each part considers the proposition that there has been a progressively punitive shift in criminal justice and youth justice policies, driven by social, political and media reactions internationally and nationally, to crises concerning children and young people. This chapter also examines policy transfer and the United Kingdom's (UK's) recent legacy relating to children, young people, anti-social behaviour and crime. It considers whether new criminal justice and youth justice policies in Northern Ireland are inheriting the UK's legacy, by maintaining the punitive ideologies and practices promoted under periods of direct rule.

Contemporary Policy Responses: Britain

As a social group, 'youth regularly appear as the cornerstone of a number of key concerns about a disordered present' (Muncie 2009: 41). As Hall et al.'s (1978) study on mugging as a 'moral panic' demonstrates, the label 'problem youth', along with the reactions of politicians, police, judges and the media, fuel a general hostility towards all young people. These observations can be applied to the contemporary debate about anti-social behaviour being synonymous with children and young people and the subsequent legislative and policies responses, such New Labour's Crime and Disorder Act 1998 (CDA). It is evident that generalisations about youth; 'moral panics' and 'respectable fears'; adult anxiety about the rising trend of young people's involvement in crime and harking back to an elusive 'golden age', are not new phenomena, but rather are persistent responses (see Roberts 1971; Pearson 1983).

Adult anxiety and moralising remain a central and enduring focus of contemporary British society. They are elements particularly evident in social reactions directed towards children and young people, such as the well-rehearsed response that 'something needs to be done' to constrain youth and maintain societal order. This raises the question of whether there is a clear correlation between popular discourses, social reaction, the consolidation of public anxieties and punitive criminal justice policies directed towards youth.

Juvenile justice since its inception in the early twentieth century has fluctuated between a preoccupation with 'care and welfare' and 'control and punishment' (Crawford and Burden 2005: 1). Regardless of the political party in power in Britain, contemporary policies, however conceived and constructed, cloak the punitiveness that is at the core of criminal justice legislation and policy. As Goldson (2002: 128) notes, by the end of the 1970s the concepts of 'welfare' and 'treatment' had become 'almost synonymous with excessive intervention and intensified control'. This was evidenced in the shift in the use of language, from the 'child in need' to the 'juvenile criminal' (Whyte 2007). As Franklin (1996: 5) asserts, 'instead of policies to protect children in the community, the government and media have preferred to promote policies to protect the community from children'. Such policies are contrary to the United Nations Convention on the Rights of the Child (UNCRC) (Arthur 2010: 39) and have been driven more by social reaction and politics, than by any knowledge of the reality of youth involvement in crime (Elrod and Ryder 2005).

Following the 1979 election of the Conservative Government and the introduction of the New Right agenda, policy-makers immediately set out to deliver the pre-election promises of social authoritarianism (Davis and Bourhill 1997: 31). Prime Minister, Margaret Thatcher had made 'crime' the Conservatives' primary election mandate by attaching it to a general concern to re-establish 'Victorian values' and to overturn the supposedly 'permissive' culture of the 1960s (Muncie 2009: 144). During this period the emphasis was on individual pathology and personal responsibility, rather than social conditions and structural contexts of crime. The 'crisis' in law and order was a powerful rhetoric focusing on the decline of the family. 'Crime', 'lawlessness' and 'disorder' were portrayed as illustrative of a decline in traditional values, with children and young people depicted as lacking personal responsibility and not knowing right from wrong (Davis and Bourhill 1997: 31–32).

Newburn (1997: 642) asserts that the 1979 Conservative Manifesto 'promised, among many other measures, to strengthen sentencing powers with respect to juveniles'. Authoritarian promises were fulfilled in the legislation that followed, such as the Criminal Justice Act 1982. These policy and legislative responses had consequences, such as 'net-widening' through an increased use of police cautioning, 'tough' regimes in youth detention centres (Pitts 1988) and punitive community-based measures, such as intensive intermediate orders, night restriction orders and supervised activity orders, each of which was directed towards young offenders. Academic critiques of this legislation assert that the policy changes were based on political and ideological elements of the New Right agenda, rather than informed by rigorous research (Morris and Giller 1987; McAra 2012).

Against this backdrop, events such as the inner-city uprisings/riots of 1981 and 1985, 'public disorder and violence' at football matches and the miners' strike of 1985, were catalysts for the introduction of further reactive policies and legislation such as the Police and Criminal Evidence Act 1984 and the Public Order Act 1985 (Gabriel 1998). This legislation, inter alia, strengthened police powers of stop and search and gave police officers more discretion in dealing with disorderly behaviour. Although these measures were not specifically directed towards young people in conflict with the law, they were symptomatic of a wider political and public concern with 'law and order'. Inevitably, such legislation added to an existing climate of intolerance towards young people and impacted on the levels of police surveillance and control of youth.

The Conservative Government's 1980s 'return to Victorian values' and the New Right's rhetoric which championed a 'back to justice' approach over 'soft welfare' responses (Muncie 2004), was superseded by the 1990s 'back to basics' initiative and John Major's 'rallying call in the war of yob culture' (Scraton 1997: vii). Authoritarian policies that advocated a 'just deserts' approach in particular saw 'persistent young offenders' routinely targeted by police, with specific examples of 'joy-riding' and 'bail bandits' (Newburn 1995; Brown 2005; Smith 2003), providing vivid imagery on which successive Conservative administrations could legitimate their punitive stance on law and order.

In 1993, when two-year-old James Bulger was abducted and killed by two ten-year old boys in Liverpool, the demonisation and criminalisation of children took on a new momentum. This single event has been characterised as a turning point in the history of juvenile justice in England and Wales (Collins and Cattermole 2006: 9). As Scraton (2005: 76) argues, 'James Bulger's death had become a catalyst for the consolidation of an authoritarian shift in youth justice'. It was a shift, which in legal reform and policy initiatives, was replicated throughout institutional responses to children and young people. It carried media approval and popular (adult) consent.

According to Hendrick (2006: 397), following the killing of James Bulger in 1993, public and legal attitudes towards children 'hardened', reflecting John Major's assertion as Prime Minister that 'society needs to condemn a little more and understand a little less' (*Mail on Sunday*, 21 February 1993). As Ball (2004: 29) argues, the killing was 'allied to an intensive media focus' on young people, which fuelled 'the perception of a rise in the number of persistent juvenile offenders'. What followed were 'progressively more punitive, legislative responses' (Ball 2004: 29), including the then Home Secretary, Michael Howard's proposals for 'tougher' measures to deal with young offenders. In particular he evoked the sound-bite 'prison works' whilst outlining a 'zero tolerance' approach, the need for an increase in the use of custody for children and young people, alongside a renewed emphasis on individual responsibility and early intervention. 'Howard's Way' was consolidated in the punitive Criminal Justice and Public Order Act 1994 (Allen and Cooper 1995).

At the time of James Bulger's death, Tony Blair coined the 'realist' slogan, 'Tough on Crime, Tough on the Causes of Crime', attracting considerable public support. The language used was pivotal in New Labour establishing itself in the public's mind 'as the party best equipped to introduce tough and effective measures to deal with offenders' (Morris and Gelsthorpe 2000: 20). New Labour's 1997 Election Manifesto promised to introduce a system of fast-track punishment for persistent young offenders, a crackdown on petty crimes and neighbour disorder, reform of the Crown Prosecution Service (CPS) so that more criminals could be convicted, to have more police on the beat and proactive policing of public spaces (New Labour 1997).[1]

The Conservative Government was criticised for forgetting the 'order' part of 'law and order'. New Labour argued that a different approach was necessary, targeting 'the unacceptable level of anti-social behaviour and crime on our streets' and 'petty criminality among young offenders', by taking a 'zero tolerance' approach (New Labour 1997). New Labour won the election with a landslide victory in 1997, which was taken as public endorsement of its punitive 'tough on crime' approach. Blair had displayed intuitive 'political opportunism' rather than 'analytical awareness' of the reality of children and young people's involvement in crime (Scraton 2005: 76).

The new Government's early policy initiatives included establishing a Social Exclusion Unit to develop strategies and draft policies to deal with the consequences of 'inadequate parenting', the 'lack of training and employment', 'unstable living conditions', 'drug and alcohol abuse', 'high rates of teenage pregnancy', 'school non-attendance' and 'neighbourhood decay' (Smith 2003: 50–51). The Audit Commission's (1996) report 'Misspent Youth' paved the way for criminal justice reform. What was not acknowledged was that the 'use of custody for 10–16 year olds', had 'dropped from a high of 7,700 in 1979 to 1,600 in 1991' (Ball 2004: 29). In line with its election manifesto, New Labour viewed the low custody rates under the Conservatives as not efficiently tackling the problem of youth crime. New Labour responded with proposals in, 'No More Excuses - A New Approach to Tackling Youth Crime in England and Wales' (Home Office 1997b), which alongside the Home Office's Narey Report and Graham and Bowling's research[2] on the aetiology of youth crime, provided the impetus for reform (Fionda 1999: 36). It also placed the 'crimes' and actions of youth as a major social issue, emphasising particularly the impact on communities and victims (Smith 2003).

Reforms came, with the enactment of the Crime and Disorder Act 1998 and the Youth Justice and Criminal Evidence Act 1999. The ethos of New Labour's 'Third Way', which set the party apart from the approaches taken by the Conservatives and also previous Labour policy, introduced more restorative, alternative responses to youth crime. Measures included referral orders, which allowed for the diversion of youth from the justice system to more restorative, community-based alternatives. However, in practice a wide range of retributive measures underpinned such 'restorative' measures (Morris and Gelsthorpe 2000: 18). Morris and Gelsthorpe (2000: 18) argue that the restorative justice element of the CDA 1998 is 'just one theme in a broadly punitive and controlling piece of legislation'.

The 1998 Act introduced punitive measures such as the removal of *doli incapax*, anti-social behaviour orders, local curfew orders, child safety orders and these measures clearly indicate New Labour's hard-line approach towards society's most vulnerable (Fionda 1999: 37; Franklin 1999: 4). In effect, these measures widened the net and subsequently led to significant increases in the number of children and young people brought into contact with the criminal justice system. The rhetoric and the measures themselves, collectively indicate the emphasis placed on 'punishment':

> Within our youth justice system, punishment is important to signal society's disapproval of criminal acts and deter offending. It is the appropriate response to children and young people who wilfully break the law. (Home Office 1997b: 12)

Measures introduced such as, 'new guidance on cautioning ... removed acknowledgment of the vulnerability of young people ... discouraged the use of more than one caution ... [and] led to a rapid rise in court appearance and ... custody' (Ball 2004: 29). The reforms replaced the use of cautioning with a statutory system of reprimands, warnings and referral orders, forming part of the clear message that the Government was 'committed to the use of detention for young offenders' (Ball 2004: 29–30). A concern expressed in 'Tackling Youth Crime' (Home Office 1997b) was 'the need to encourage young offenders to accept responsibility' and as noted above, it was proposed that the presumption of *doli incapax* be abolished, in order for younger children to be held accountable (Fionda 1999: 38; Bandalli 2000: 82–84). The Home Office 'took the view that the presumption 'flies in the face of common sense' (Fionda 1999: 38) and it was abolished through Section 34 of the CDA. According to Ball (2004: 35), this added to the 'discernable erosion ... of the well-established differential treatment' since the early 1990s with 'regard to younger children' who offend. In effect:

Child-centred principles and practises which acknowledged … children as 'lacking competence' … [were] replaced … with policies and procedures which treat children as, 'fully competent' … and mature enough to accept responsibility … in the form of … punishment. (Ball 2004: 35)

These policies promoted new interventions, legitimated through the ethos of responsibilisation, which had consequences for the criminalisation of children and young people. Further, this was evidence of New Labour's 'low-flying authoritarianism', especially in relation to children and young people (Hall 1998: 13).

The promotion of 'the third way', which Blair employed to distinguish his policies from those of his predecessors, emphasised how 'critical' criminal justice policies were to establishing New Labour's 'break … from the view that social considerations weakened personal responsibility for crime and disorder' (Blair 1998: 12–14). The 'third way' promoted 'individual responsibility', via restorative justice processes. As McAlinden (2011: 387) highlights, 'while there are strong restorative elements within the revised legislative framework, there are also many punitive measures'. Ball (2004: 29–33) argues, following the enactment of the legislation, 'the relative social deprivation of children and young people within the criminal justice system remains constant', resulting in 'breach of treaty obligations under the UNCRC'. Punitiveness and punishment appeared to be successfully validated under the cloak of a restorative justice ethos.

Labour's policies, with their 'new' emphasis on notions of risk, restorative justice practices, victim perspectives and rehabilitative ideals, in practice had 'an overtly punitive orientation' (Hendrick 2005: 206). Behind the restorative justice 'guise', the approach taken has been retributive in nature, with increased labelling and stigmatisation of children and young people, through the emphasis on responsibility and blame (Morris and Gelsthorpe 2000: 24). As Morris and Gelsthorpe (2000: 24) conclude, the CDA 1998 and the 'Third Way' approach in general, promoted the use of 'blaming rather than restorative processes', by 'fuel[ling] public expectations that crime can be controlled effectively by a policy of deterrence through punishment' (Brownlee 1998: 313; see also McAlinden 2011).

Koffman (2006: 593) argues that Section 1 of the 1998 CDA, which introduced anti-social behaviour orders (ASBOs), 'generated heated debate at its inception' (Rutherford 2000; Scraton 2007; Squires 2008; Donoghue 2010). ASBOs, which are civil orders, were directed towards those over the age of ten, whose behaviour was 'thought likely to cause alarm, distress or harrassment' (Muncie 2009: 318). Critics Ashworth et al. (1998, cited in, Ramsay 2004: 908) in a combined analysis, argued that their introduction would allow police and local authorities to 'bring people into the grasp of the criminal law on a discretionary basis' giving them a 'vast power to create a new breed of outcasts and outlaws'. It was a criminal offence to break the conditions of an ASBO and in a process that further 'net-widened', a breach could lead to incarceration for a period of up to five years (Koffman 2006: 593).

In England and Wales, legislation including the Anti-Social Behaviour Act 2003 and the Serious Organised Crime and Police Act 2005, promoted the policy of 'naming and shaming' those who had breached the conditions of an ASBO. This removed the anonymity of children and young people and revealed their identities, names and photographs, both locally and nationally. The 'anti-social behaviour agenda' and its legacy, is therefore a stark example of the negative impact of social reaction on contemporary policy responses to children and young people.

The impact of the demonisation of youth is summarised by the former Children's Commissioner for England, Sir Al Aynsley-Green, in his assessment of contemporary youth justice policies and practices in Britain:

> Demonisation and lack of empathy for young people is a major issue … It causes anger and alienation … It is driving policy … we have a youth justice system dominated by a punitive approach. It doesn't focus on children's needs. (Gaines 2007, cited in Maruna and King 2008: 129)

What this sequence of events demonstrates is that social reaction fuelled by moral entrepreneurs and the media, significantly impacts on the policy responses of governments and policy makers and more widely criminal justice agencies, namely the police, courts and prisons. It is important to consider whether the processes in England and Wales have impacted on contemporary policy responses to children and young people perceived to be involved in anti-social or criminal behaviour in Northern Ireland.

Contemporary Policy Responses: Northern Ireland

As noted previously, when exploring current criminal justice and youth justice policies and practices, it is important to place contemporary analysis in the context of historical and long-established responses to targeted social groups, such as children and young people. Buckland and Stevens (2001: 6) assert that, 'despite being a universal problem, policies and practices to deal with juvenile delinquency are related to the social, political, historical and cultural context of the countries in which they are located'.

In a society that has experienced conflict and is now in transition, it is imperative to understand location and context. The 'special circumstances' of Northern Ireland, given the legacy of the Conflict, provide added dimensions central to critical analysis of contemporary policy and practice development, and its impact particularly on the most marginalised. What follows considers the importance of the structural, social, political, cultural, economic and material contexts in which contemporary criminal justice policies and societal reactions towards children and young people have emerged in Northern Ireland. It explores the legacy of the Conflict in terms of poverty, the impact of paramilitaries, differential policing and the treatment of children and young people and grounds a critical analysis of contemporary policy in its specific context by exploring the historical legacy of criminal justice policy transfer from Britain to Northern Ireland.

Impact of the Conflict on Children and Young People

In contrast to England and Wales, Northern Ireland is a society emerging from a 30-year period of conflict. Although it appears as 'a small dot on the world map – some 5,452 square miles in all' (Cairns 1987: 11), its contested history, the partitioning of the six counties of Northern Ireland and its position within United Kingdom, make it one of the most contested pieces of land in the world. There exists a wealth of academic literature, research and debate on the Northern Ireland Conflict or the 'Troubles' (see Loughlin 1998; Fraser 2000; Arthur 2000; Hennessey 2000; McGarry and O'Leary 2004; Aughey 2005; Tonge 2006). As McGarry (2001: 1; see also Whyte 1981) asserts, perspectives on the Conflict are diverse:

> For many people like the editorialists of the *Belfast Telegraph* or the audience of John Hewitt's poem, Northern Ireland is a place apart, its conflict the result of some unique pathology. This view was particularly dominant from the outbreak of the troubles ... it is still subscribed to.[3]

During the Conflict (1969–1998), around 3,700 people were killed and at least a further 40,000 injured (Gaffikin and Morrissey 2011). Hillyard et al. (2005: 190) record that 557 people under the age of 20 were killed due to the Conflict and seven of the sixteen deaths caused by rubber and plastic bullets, were of children under the age of 18. Young people's experiences of the police, police accountability, the lack of redress and the impact of differential policing in Northern Ireland are well documented (see Ellison 2001; Hamilton et al. 2003; Quinn and Jackson 2003; Kilkelly et al. 2004: 216–256; Scraton 2007: 153–161; Haydon and Scraton 2008: 67–70).

Many young people have been exploited and used by the police as 'informers' (Haydon and Scraton 2008: 70). Children and young people have also experienced police use of baton rounds, plastic bullets used during times of public disorder or riots.[4] This tactic has been heavily criticised locally by children and youth sector organisations, the Northern Ireland Children's Commissioner (NICCY 2005) and internationally by the UN Committee on the Rights of the Child (CRC) (October 2008: 7), particularly in light of the fatalities and injuries many, including children, have sustained. Generations of children and young people have grown up 'under the spectre of … trauma … bereavement … displacement and violence' and have experienced harsh and differential policing, with little 'recognition of the longer-term consequences of trans-generational trauma', segregated living and sectarianism (McAlister et al. 2009: 4). As Haydon and Scraton (2008: 60) observe, although much has been written about the Conflict, 'the full impact across three decades has not been fully identified … or accommodated'.

There is a 'strong … relationship between poverty and the conflict' in Northern Ireland (Hillyard et al. 2005: xx; see also Save the Children and ARK 2008). In Northern Ireland, with 100,000 children living in poverty and 44,000 living in severe poverty (Kenway et al. 2006; Monteith et al. 2008; Save the Children 2011), it is a significant issue. It results from social inequality and fuels social exclusion. Convery et al. (2008: 247) note, 'poverty is a defining factor in the lives of many children and their families', its impact is wide-ranging and it influences 'health and well-being, education and employment opportunities and access to quality accommodation'. Poverty exposes children and young people to multiple deprivations, with unequal access to health care services, including specific services for mental ill-health (Haydon and Scraton 2008: 64–65; see also Horgan 2005). Suicide rates are high, particularly in socio-economically deprived areas, coupled with inadequate mental health provision and support for those who self-harm or are suicidal. Tomlinson's (2007a: 5; see also Tomlinson 2007b) research on suicide notes the impact on families and communities, emotionally, socially and financially in Northern Ireland.

Significantly, while Northern Ireland has the youngest population of any UK jurisdiction (Save the Children and ARK 2008; see also Cairns 1987: 11), the impact of the legacy of the Conflict on children and young people has been ignored on a number of levels. The Belfast/Good Friday Agreement 1998 represented a key political development in the Peace Process and it failed to directly address 'the situation of children and young people' (Hillyard et al. 2005: 190). In communities, the State has failed to provide adequate resources and facilities and has 'neglected to ensure the psychological recovery and protection of children', who are the survivors of such brutality (Kilkelly et al. 2004: 242). In 1999, the UK Chief Medical Officer estimated that more than 20 percent of young people in Northern Ireland are suffering 'significant mental health problems' by their eighteenth birthday (Bamford Review 2006: 5).

The allocation of funds for children's mental health services has been recorded at just four and a half percent of the total health budget (see O'Rawe 2003). This lack of adequate mental health service provision has been highlighted in reports such as the Bamford Review (2006), the CRC's Concluding Observations (2008; 2015), as well as many of the children and youth sector organisations, who continue to lobby government on this issue (see Haydon 2008: 28; Include Youth, March 2009; Children in Northern Ireland 2010). This is one element in the continuation of the 'historic under-funding of children's services in the region, particularly when compared to neighbouring jurisdictions' (Children in Northern Ireland 2010: 4). As a direct consequence there are high levels of self-harm and suicide among children and young people. A recent report on suicide outlines the relationship between the high rates of suicide, poverty and social exclusion:

> The largest difference between suicide rates in Northern Ireland and other UK countries was in young people ... 332 suicides occurred in people under 25 during 2000–2008 ... Young people who died by suicide were more likely than other age-groups to be living in the poorest areas'. (Appleby et al. 2011: 18)

Previous critical qualitative research has emphasised the inter-generational implications of the Conflict. With research indicating that in the context of Northern Ireland children and young people as well as their parents suffer from 'conflict-related trauma'; a large proportion are the victims of social exclusion and experience 'extreme economic marginalisation' (Scraton 2007: 150). Many parents were part of the generation, which in light of 'the civil policing deficit ... experience[d] ... violence extended to informal "policing" by paramilitaries', in particular punishment beatings for 'those involved in alleged "unacceptable" behaviour in their communities' (Haydon and Scraton 2008: 61; see also Hamill 2011). As Haydon and Scraton (2008: 61) assert, 'while the cessation of punishment beatings and shootings were part of the agreed withdrawal of paramilitary presence in communities, threats and intimidation directed towards the "antisocial behaviour" of children and young people persist'.

Many children and young people were recruited by Loyalist and Nationalist paramilitaries during the Conflict and were used as messengers, distractions, as stone-throwers and as shields in riot situations and for planting bombs (Brocklehurst 1999). Paramilitaries' control of, and violence against, children and young people has been and has remained 'endemic' within both loyalist and nationalist communities. Children and young people have been 'refugees, exiles for anti-social behaviour' and the 'victims of punishment beatings' (Hillyard et al. 2005: 190; see also Smyth 1998; Kennedy 2001). Recorded numbers indicate that between 1988 and 2002, 496 young people under the age of 20 were the victims of punishment beatings and 388 were the victims of punishment shootings (see Children in Northern Ireland 2010: 3). PSNI statistics of recorded 'paramilitary-style' shootings and assaults, outline that between 1999 and 2009, there were 1,958 victims of such attacks (Children in Northern Ireland 2010: 3; PSNI 2011; Hamill 2011).

As research indicates, punishment beatings and shootings render many victims incapacitated or disabled and impact on children and young people, psychologically by affecting their mental health (Smyth 1998). As one community worker summarises, there are a range of 'emotional effects', which impact heavily on 'children's education, their mental health and their ability to participate in society' (cited in Scraton 2007: 149). Smyth (1998) states that children and young people's experiences of the Conflict have led to them developing a number of 'negative coping strategies', such as substance misuse, use of drugs and alcohol and also silence. Similar concerns were raised in a later study by Smyth et al. (2004: 43), who note that those children deeply affected by the Conflict have 'difficulties in concentration and the aggressive behaviour that followed their traumatisation was misinterpreted by others, being seen as deliberately disruptive behaviour'.

The legacy of the Conflict persists and impacts on children, young people and their families, who witness and experience violence, poverty, economic difficulties and inadequate service provision (see Kilkelly et al. 2004; McAlister et al. 2009). As Scraton argues (2007: 148), 'several generations have endured pervasive sectarianism, hard-line policing, military operations and paramilitary punishments'. While media and political discourses frame contemporary Northern Ireland as 'leaving the past behind' and 'moving on' (Convery et al. 2008: 246), qualitative research indicates that due to sectarianism, for many children 'the notions of post-conflict or transition are distant possibilities' (Kilkelly et al. 2004: 245; see also Scraton 2007; McAlister et al. 2009). This is evident particularly at interface areas where segregation of communities persists through physical barriers, such as peace walls to mark division between Protestant/Unionist/Loyalist areas and Roman Catholic/Nationalist/Republican areas. At interfaces, sectarianism fuels tensions and results in confrontations and violence such as rioting between the Protestant/Unionist/

Loyalist and Roman Catholic/Nationalist/Republican communities.[5] Many interfaces and peace walls ensure segregation; sectarianism, and that the legacy of the Conflict and its consequences remain constant features in the lives of children, young people and their families (see Leonard 2010a, b, 2011; Leonard and McKnight 2010, 2011).[6]

Criminal Justice Policy in Northern Ireland

Devolution of decision-making and powers from the UK Government to Stormont has been viewed as a defining moment in Northern Ireland's contemporary history, with popular and media discourse describing it as the main success of the 'peace process', marking an end of 'the Troubles'. As Brocklehurst et al. (2001: 89) acknowledge, 'in the shadow of political violence' transitioning societies have the major task of 'manag[ing] a diverse society through transformed public policies and new institutions of governance'. An example is 'the restructuring of the police service' in line with the Patten Commission's recommendations (Northern Ireland Office (NIO) 1999). However progressive the apparent advances are in terms of public policies and newly developed institutions or restructuring of existing institutions, this advancement is rarely experienced directly by people in communities. Recent critical research with children and young people highlights how many consider that the 'peace process' has 'made no difference' to their lives (McAlister et al. 2009: 69). Transition from conflict is not instantaneous, but a 'gradual', 'slow and complex' process (see Scraton 2007: 148; Convery et al. 2008: 247).

Given the Northern Ireland Assembly's relationship to the UK Government, directly through periods of direct rule or post-devolution, policy transfer and the impact of British policy on Northern Ireland communities, is significant when exploring the impact of contemporary policy development on children and young people. As Rose (1993, cited in Newburn 2002: 172) argues, given 'ideological proximity' between administrations, such as the UK Government and the Northern Ireland Assembly, it is to be expected that political parties would 'borrow' policies. Newburn (2002: 172) states that this has been a 'key facilitating factor in the spread of policy transfer' and 'in the rise of the new right'. Policy transfer can be considered 'one of the most tangible drivers' in facilitating and promoting punitive and retributive responses to offending and offenders (Muncie 2009: 358) and in this instance, young offenders who are the main target of measures to tackle anti-social behaviour.

Particularly regarding preventing crime and reducing re-offending, it has become common for governments to look 'worldwide' to discover 'what works' (Muncie 2009: 358), then to transfer and adapt policies in their entirety or partially. This has led to the promotion of authoritarian and punitive policies and responses, particularly within criminal justice. As Jones and Newburn (2002: 174) argue, there exists a 'growing convergence between aspects of criminal justice and penal policy in different nation states'. Literature on criminal justice policy transfer has placed the United States' (US) influence as central to many developments in crime control policy under New Labour, particularly as noted above, Blair's punitive 'soundbite' 'tough on crime, tough on the causes of crime' (Jones and Newburn 2002: 178). Examples include the transfer of 'zero tolerance' policing strategies, privatisation within the criminal justice system, harsher sentencing policies and growing incarceration rates (Jones and Newburn 2002: 174). Parenti (1999, cited in Scraton 2008: 6) notes the impact of such policies on targeted individuals and social groups in the US and argues that the 'law-and-order crackdown', with its 'masterful orchestration of disparate social forces', consisted of, 'multiple layers of public and private social control – from press to jails – acting in concert to form a totalising net of surveillance, enforcement and intimidation'.

Policy 'borrowing' or policy transfer[7] predates New Labour, as it has long been evident in the UK, particularly during post-1979 Conservative administrations (Jones and Newburn 2002: 178). As noted above, the CDA 1998 made fundamental changes to the youth justice system and it is evident that changes were informed by policy developments in the United States (Newburn 2002: 167–168). The parenting order, child safety order, the anti-social behaviour order (Newburn 2002: 168), the 'naming and shaming' of young offenders, community courts, parental sin bins,[8] 'boot camps' for a short period in the 1990s (Muncie 2009: 358) and child curfew orders (Newburn 2002: 168), were modelled on US responses to children and young people in conflict with the law.

Just as ideology and policies have been transferred from the US to Britain, Northern Ireland has long been associated with the transferral of British Government policy. As Birrell and Murie (1980: 65) observe, the Northern Ireland parliament has had a long history of following UK procedures and practices, particularly evidenced in 'the general policy of the Stormont parliament [which] was to keep in step with legislation enacted for Great Britain' (Dickson 1989: 4–5). During periods of direct rule, the British Government 'moved from a passive to a positive form of direct rule' and was 'mainly concerned with bringing Northern Ireland into line with British policies and legislation' (Birrell and Murie 1980: 88). This was clearly evident in relation to policies concerning children and young people, with the Northern Ireland 1968 Children and Young Persons Act, 'essentially a mixture' of the Westminster Children Act 1948 and the Children and Young Persons Act 1963 (Pinkerton 1994).

Dickson (2001: 8) comments, 'during the period of direct rule between 1974 and 1999 the process of assimilation between the content of the law in Northern Ireland and that in England was, if anything, fortified'. Pinkerton (1994: 28–29) argues that in relation to policies concerning children and young people, the legislative pattern and the process of 'policy transfer', has been one of 'delay and quasi-imitation' in Northern Ireland. The approach taken does provide 'a significant degree of local control' and 'an expression' of Stormont's 'desire to be in control of its own affairs', along with the creation and adoption of local legislation that maintains its consistent and shared relationship with the British Government (Pinkerton 1994: 29). Pinkerton (1994: 29) also argues that Northern Ireland has adopted British policies, such as 'its own version of the Welfare State', 'a version that met its own strategic political needs' but was nonetheless modelled on and influenced by British policy.

During periods of direct rule, the implementation and consequences of criminal justice policy in Northern Ireland, have been referred to by critical criminologists as 'evidence of the growing power of the "authoritarian state"' (Mulcahy 2002: 277, see also Hall and Scraton 1981; Sim et al. 1987).[9] In Northern Ireland the impact of criminal justice policy reforms and their implementation have been far-reaching. As Brewer et al. (1997) argue, the Conflict was significant in the 'management' of 'ordinary crime' in Northern Ireland. During a period of direct rule in the 1970s and 1980s under the Conservative Government, Northern Ireland experienced British 'criminalisation' policy. As Cox et al. (2006: 48) assert, in particular 'Thatcher, implemented policies designed to redefine the problem of Northern Ireland as one of criminal activity, not one of political or constitutional struggle'.

The Civil Authorities (Special Powers) Act (Northern Ireland) 1922, repealed by The Northern Ireland Emergency Provisions Act 1973, was enacted in order to re-establish 'law and order' on Northern Ireland's streets (see Mulholland 2002; Tonge 2006; Dickson 2010). As a result of direct rule, the Royal Ulster Constabulary (RUC), as it then was, and British Army policed the streets. There was a deployment of the Special Air Service (SAS), and policies included censorship, curfews, arrests without warrant on grounds of suspicion, broad powers to stop question, search and detain, the 'supergrass' trials whereby informers received immunity in return for giving evidence, internment without trial and the Diplock courts, which were judge-led trials, with no jury present (see Croft 1991; Whitman 1992; Thompson 2001; Cox et al. 2006; Neocleous 2008). Such policies emphasised Prime Minister Thatcher's ethos that 'Crime is crime is crime. It is not political' (October, 1981, cited in Coogan 2002: 281) and the promotion of the use of the term 'terrorism' to refer to Northern Ireland (Walker 2011: 8).

The punitive stance taken by successive Conservative administrations is clearly evidenced in the authoritarian policies implemented in Northern Ireland. Heightened criminalisation was at the core of the policies and 'special powers' legislation, such as the 1973 Emergency Provisions Act (updated in 1978) and the 1974 Prevention of Terrorism Act (updated in 1976), which impacted on communities, through the heavy presence of the RUC, British Army and SAS on Northern Ireland's streets, raids on homes and incarceration of many people without trial (see Croft 1991; Moore 1997). Tonge (2006: 68) asserts that 'the rhetoric of the authorities concerning the need to uphold the rule of law overlooked the abnormality of the law' in Northern Ireland.

Reflecting on the long-term impact of such policies and practices in Northern Ireland, researchers argue that while such powers originally were extended for what was deemed an 'emergency situation', these 'special powers' have been 'normalised' and made 'permanent' (see Hillyard 1987, 1988, 1993; Neocleous 2008). Therefore, they have been viewed and employed as part of the 'ordinary' legal and criminal justice 'landscape' (Mulcahy 2002: 277). The 'normalisation' period in Northern Ireland occurred post-ceasefires (1990s), with attempts to 'normalise' policing and regulation. During this period further policy transfer from Britain occurred. In the contemporary setting, the transferral and impact of such social control policies is evident in the raft of measures such as curfews, police surveillance of young people in public places, the removal or restriction of young people's movement and agency, 'anti-social behaviour orders', as well as media 'naming and shaming' and the prison systems responses to children and young people who are incarcerated by the courts.[10]

Following the pivotal Belfast/Good Friday Agreement 1998, a review of the criminal justice system in Northern Ireland was established. The report of the Criminal Justice Review Group, published in March 2000, was the impetus for the reforms to youth justice in Northern Ireland that followed, with the recommendations proposing a restorative justice approach (see NIO 2000: 219–250). The Northern Ireland Assembly's suspension between 2002 and 2007, mainly due to Sinn Féin's refusal to support the new policing arrangements (Walker 2011: 12), saw the adoption of criminal justice policies and legislation, which had 'clear implications for the administration of youth justice' (Convery et al. 2008: 254). Similar to the CDA 1998, the Justice (NI) Acts 2002 and 2004 (s.53) emphasise the need to 'protect the public by preventing offending by children' (NIO 2002: 21).[11]

The legislation introduced Reparation Orders (s.54), Community Responsibility Orders (s.55), Custody Care Orders (s.56), Youth Conferences and Plans for children aged 10–14 (s.56) and Youth Conference Orders (s.60) (see NIO 2002: 21–29). In the 2002 and 2004 Acts, the emphasis on 'responsibility' echo New Labour's 'self-styled model of "respect" and "responsibility"' (see Walters and Woodward 2007: 5). As Walker (2011: 12) states, the main objective of the legislation was 'to update the [Northern Ireland] system in line with English modes'. This is an example of contemporary transferral of an 'ideological and legislative mix [of policies] prescribed on punitive notions of individual responsibility and justice' (Walters and Woodward 2007: 5). Significantly, by emphasising 'responsibility' over 'rights', this legislation 'fail[s] to recognize children's rights explicitly' (Convery et al. 2008: 254).

As outlined above, while traditionally in Northern Ireland perceived anti-social behaviour has been policed, regulated and punished by paramilitaries (see Whitman 1992), it was not until 2004 that official policy and legislative 'measures' were proposed. Following the ceasefires in the 1990s, concern was expressed that there would be 'a possible future increase in anti-social behaviour among young people [who have] grown used to civil unrest' (McGrellis 2004: 3; see also Heskin 1980; Jarman 2005). This was highlighted in official discourse, which noted that young people are 'regarded with fear, suspicion and mistrust' (see NIO Statistics and Research Branch 2003, cited in Hamilton et al. 2003: 13) and viewed as threatening and intimidating, as perpetrators of anti-social behaviour and as instigators of sectarian tensions, disorder and social disruption (see Jarman and O'Halloran 2001; Jarman et al. 2002). As Hamilton et al. (2003: 13) have discovered, such feelings and suspicions may arise from little more than having groups of young people hanging around on street corners or marginal spaces.

Against this backdrop, in 2004 the NIO published a consultation document entitled: 'Measures to Tackle Anti-social Behaviour in Northern Ireland'. The media showed support for the measures, with typical commentary featuring quotations from those promoting the implementation, such as the Chairman of the Housing Executive, Sid McDowell, who called on the Government to introduce the legislation in Northern Ireland:

> We owe it to residents of those neighbourhoods to change things for the better. In the rest of the UK Anti-Social Behaviour Orders (ASBOs) have become an important tool in tackling the problem and they should be available in Northern Ireland.[12]

As Convery et al. (2008: 246) state, the 'several high profile incidents of serious violence, including rape and murder, have been represented by politicians and the media as inevitable outcomes of escalating "crisis"' of youth criminality. This placed 'pressure ... on legislators to address the "problem" of lawlessness among children and young people' in Northern Ireland (Convery et al. 2008: 246).

In contrast, children and youth sector organisations/non-governmental organisations (NGOs) (such as the Children's Law Centre; Include Youth; Children in Northern Ireland) presented their opposition to the proposed measures in written consultation responses and the Northern Ireland Children's Commissioner applied for a judicial review, challenging the introduction of ASBOs on several grounds (see NICCY 2004). The NIO had not consulted children and young people, the legacy of the Conflict had not been considered and the NIO had failed to conduct an Equality Impact Assessment, as required by Section 75 of the Northern Ireland Act 1998. In dismissing these arguments and in refusing leave, Justice Girvan stated that:

> Consultation... with interested parties who are in a position to put forward measured and meaningful responses ... one wonders ... what meaningful response could be obtained from children unless they were in a position to understand the legal and social issues to anti-social behaviour, the mechanisms of dealing with it, the shortcomings of existing criminal law and effectiveness ... of the English legislation and its suitability for transplant to ... Northern Ireland ... and the interaction of Convention and international obligations.[13]

The Anti-Social Behaviour (Northern Ireland) Act 2004 was enforced. The British Home Office Minister for Criminal Justice, John Speller, who had overseen the introduction of the legislation, stated that: 'It ... lets those who act in an anti-social way know that they will face firm sanctions' (NIO Press release, 25 August 2004, cited in Scraton 2007: 162).

Official, popular and media discourses illustrate how the NIO, politicians and the media promoted punitive legislation as an appropriate response. In doing so, they failed to acknowledge the legacy of the Conflict. As Scraton (2007: 163) argues, the anti-social behaviour of children and young people in Northern Ireland cannot be 'analysed in form or content alongside similar manifestations in Liverpool, Glasgow, Birmingham, Dublin or Limerick', as the behaviour is 'rooted in recent history of the Conflict'. Legislators and the media did not realise or report that the use of ASBOs carried 'potentially serious consequences' in light of the 'paramilitary punishments of children' (Scraton 2007: 162). The introduction of such measures, specifically the policy of 'naming and shaming', to a place where 'naming, shaming, beatings, shootings and exiling already existed', placed children and young people's lives in serious danger and breached the right to life (Scraton 2007: 162).

The added dimension of the legacy of the Conflict provides another level of concern surrounding policies that promote the 'naming and shaming' of children and young people. 'Naming and shaming' relates to the publicising of details belonging to those who have been granted an ASBO.[14] According to Yates (2008: 239), the practice in England and Wales included the 'posting [of] pictures of young people on local authority websites, leafleting local areas and releasing photographs and details of children and young people to the press'. New Labour maintained that such measures reassured the public, by providing evidence that 'something is being done' or deterring others. This retributive stance was emphasised by the then British Home Secretary, Charles Clarke, who stated:

> Many offenders think that they are untouchable and above the law. If they thought that there will be a news blackout of their actions then they must now think again. Publicising ASBOs has been tested in the courts and we are making the position clear: your photo could be all over the local media, your local community will know who you are and breaching an ASBO could land you in prison. (Home Office 2005, cited in Stephen 2006: 224)

Home Office guidelines on, 'Publicising ASBOs' (Home Office, October, 2005), are presented in an equally punitive tone. The guidelines outline that publicity 'should be the norm', as 'obtaining the order is only part of the process; its effectiveness will normally depend on people knowing about the order' (Home Office 2005: 1). There is no mention or suggestion from the Government that 'naming and shaming' will 'reform' or help 'rehabilitate' children or young people involved in what is perceived to be anti-social or criminal behaviour.

Similarly, as Pratt (2000, cited in Squires 2008: 137) argues, the practice of publicising ASBOs with names, addresses and photographs of recipients, adds an 'expressive', 'humiliating character' to 'the punitive experience', which not only affects the child or young person, but affects the entire family (see also Evans 2004; Scraton 2005). Recognising this, the European Commissioner on Human Rights, Alvaro Gil-Robles, heavily criticised 'the aggressive publication of ASBOs, through, for instance, the door step distribution of leaflets containing the names and addresses of children subject to ASBOs' (Gil-Robles 2005: 37). As Scraton (2005: 18) notes, Gil-Robles' observation in 2005 that 'the main selling point of ASBOs' is that communities can become involved in the process, is followed by his questioning of 'the appropriateness of empowering local residents to take such matters into their own hands'.

The 'naming and shaming' of children and young people in England and Wales has painted a clear picture of how retributive, punitive and dangerous such policies actually are. Children and young people, who are already vulnerable, are put at further risk. 'Naming and shaming' can encourage or stir up further anger, resentment and retaliation in communities. Rather than reducing 'harm' and 'distress' in communities, 'naming and shaming' may actually have the opposite effect. As Scraton (2007: 162–163) states, 'within a month of the introduction of ASBOs a poster produced by Loyalist paramilitaries appeared throughout East Belfast', warning and threatening those to 'STOP FORTHWITH' or the paramilitaries will 'DEAL WITH THE SITUATION AS [they] … DEEM NECESSARY'.

In England and Wales, local and national media have played a key role in 'naming and shaming', with certain children and young people held up as 'the worst' 'teen thugs' in Britain (see *Daily Mail*, 5 November 2010). The chapters that follow do examine and assess the extent to which the media in Northern Ireland have employed similar strategies. In light of paramilitary punishment beatings, the size of Northern Ireland's population and its tight-knit communities, 'naming and shaming' places children and young people at serious risk of harm, as well as the possibility of exiling them from their homes and communities. NGOs predicted that the policy would in effect place 'some of the most vulnerable children in our society directly in the firing line' (Include Youth 2004). Further, the consequences have the potential to breach the UNCRC, Article 6 (the right to life, survival and development) and Article 19 (protection from abuse and neglect). Publishing a young person's information in the public domain would be particularly 'dangerous … given the influence of non-state forces in Northern Ireland and past connotations with "anti-social behaviour"' (Haydon 2008: 46–47).

The NGO Alternative Report drawing on PSNI statistics notes that, during the period when Northern Ireland's ASBO policy was being developed, 13 children were shot and 25 were assaulted by non-state forces for allegedly engaging in anti-social behaviour (Haydon 2008: 47). NIACRO's[15] (2009: 9) 'collective experiences' of working within communities in Northern Ireland highlights that there is 'very clearly the need for resolution of disputes and differences between people in the communities'. However, it asserts that 'naming and shaming' is not the correct policy for this, as it only has negative consequences resulting in 'increased levels of victimisation, social exclusion and family breakdown' (NIACRO 2009: 9).[16]

In transferring controversial legislation from England and Wales to Northern Ireland, the Minister did not take into consideration 'the special circumstances', the legacy of the Conflict, the impact of punishment beatings and the practice of exiling of children and young people from their communities, as well as the policing deficit (Haydon and Scraton 2008: 71). This is one of most illustrative contemporary examples of policy transfer, which has not taken into account the circumstances and history of a country to which policy is being transferred. As Muncie (2009: 359) argues, the logic of assuming we can learn 'what works' from others is certainly seductive, but what is not always considered is the assumption that 'policies can be transported and are transportable without cognisance of localised cultures, conditions and the politics of space'. This emphasises the detrimental impact the transferral of policies and practices has on communities and specifically targeted social groups, such as children and young people.

ASBOs granted in Northern Ireland have not been used as regularly as in some authorities in England and Wales. A total of 122 have been issued in Northern Ireland from 2005–2009 (Department of Justice Northern Ireland (DOJ NI), January 2011: 17). Yet in 2008 the Criminal Justice Inspectorate (CJI) promoted them as a useful tool (CJI Report, October 2008). It is evident that the transferral of British criminal justice policies to Northern Ireland has left behind its own legacy of promoting and maintaining punitive policies, which have no evidence of successfully reducing the levels of crime in society. By ignoring the legacy of the Conflict and the context of the lives of children and young people living in Northern Ireland, the implementation of punitive policies have the potential to feed in to the existing responses (Scraton 2007), which as outlined, extend to community-based punishment beatings and exiling of children and young people.

Prior to the devolution of policing and justice, NIO consultation documents such as 'Together. Safer. Stronger' (NIO and Community Safety Unit, October 2008), provide consistent evidence that in the broad sense 'ideas, ideologies, practices and policies' (see Newburn 2002: 165) continue to be transferred from England to Northern Ireland (Gordon et al. 2009). The timing of the consultation document's publication was opportune on the part of the Minister and the NIO, particularly as devolution of policing and justice at the time had not occurred, but was planned. As Gordon et al. (2009: 5) argue, such policy development should be made by locally elected political representatives, in consultation with Community Safety Partnerships and local communities, in order to agree local priorities and ways of solving problems at local levels, with appropriate Government funding and support. In contrast, the NIO consultation document proposed further transfer of British policies to Northern Ireland, including the introduction of individual support orders, parenting support orders and a pilot of parental compensation orders (NIO and Community Safety Unit, October 2008).

Similar to the transfer of ASBOs and 'naming and shaming' policies, such proposals do not address the underlying problems of poverty, marginalisation and social exclusion, experienced by communities (see Gordon et al. 2009: 3). Further, policy proposals place the 'responsibility' on children, young people and their parents through proposals that impose economic sanctions. This has the potential to exacerbate the economic hardship and deprivation already experienced by families. The proposal and implementation of such policies under the umbrella of 'crime prevention', 'community safety' strategies and the management of 'risk', highlight how in the contemporary setting, social policy has become 'crime led [and] incorporated as another element of criminal justice policy' (Muncie 2004: 242–244). The title of the document: ''Together. Safer. Stronger' suggests collectiveness within communities working towards a 'safer' living environment. In reality this cloaks the consequences of such proposed policies, which have the potential to further alienate, punish and exile children, young people and parents, both socially and financially.

In ignoring the legacy of the Conflict and the impact of poverty, contemporary policy development in Northern Ireland has followed the same neo-liberal punitive penal policy trends as Britain. This is evident both in terms of the implementation of policies, but also in gaining public consent, particularly by emphasising the social construction of 'us', the community, versus 'them', children and young people. In July 2012, the Minister for Justice announced investment of 20 million pounds over a period of five years, to address 'the challenges of crime, disorder and the fear that communities face' (DOJ NI, July 2012). The strategy entitled, 'Building Safer, Shared and Confident Communities',[17] emphasised the fears of the community and the proposed approaches further reinforces 'us' and 'them'.

As outlined above, following the Hillsborough Agreement (NIO 2010) the devolution of policing and justice powers to Stormont in April 2010, enabled the local administration to exercise powers over policing, criminal justice, the courts, the prisons and other local security issues. The Hillsborough Agreement (NIO, February 2010: 7) outlined the need for: '[a] review of how children and young people are processed at all stages of the criminal justice system … to ensure compliance with international obligations and best practice'. The Minister announced a team to review youth justice. The concept of a Youth Justice Review offered the opportunity for a newly devolved Department of Justice and local legislators to develop policies and practices that take into consideration the legacy of the Conflict, the impact of poverty, the impact of paramilitaries and the policing deficit. Concern has focused on whether devolution would 'lead to more punitive responses, as locally accountable politicians attempt to appear responsive to community calls for action and media-fuelled moral panics' (Haydon and Scraton 2008: 73). The reality, which has not been fully acknowledged by criminal justice policymakers, continues to be one of social exclusion and marginalisation for many children and young people, whereby the unaddressed legacy of the Conflict continues to result in negative experiences of sectarianism, paramilitary punishments, attacks and shootings, as well as the constructed 'normality' of violence.

Conclusion

This chapter has explored the progressively punitive shift in criminal justice and youth justice policies in the last 40 years. Through its analysis of British criminal justice policy and the transfer of such policies to Northern Ireland, it has demonstrated how policy-makers continue to legitimate the social control of 'problem' youth in punitive, repressive, disciplinary and retributive forms. The chapter has established that 'tough measures' and punitive responses have resulted in policy and law reform that criminalises children and young people for anti-social behaviour, which may consist of merely 'hanging around street corners'. Building on the previous chapter, which established how media representations fuel and maintain such representations of children and young people, this chapter has demonstrated how negative reporting and ideological constructions are closely allied with contemporary political reactions and criminal justice policy and legislative developments.

As noted above, the resonance of punitiveness that surrounds contemporary criminal justice and youth justice policies emphasises individual pathology and responsibility. These are aspects that are continuously employed by opportunistic politicians, policy-makers and the media, to deflect away from the larger, more complex questions. In particular, such questions relate to the structure of society, why material and social inequalities exist, and why certain sections of society remain marginalised. For children and young people in Northern Ireland, their lives are impacted on daily by the legacy of the Conflict, high levels of poverty, the effects of social exclusion and marginalisation, the fear of punishment beatings and the blame placed on them, fuelled by media representations. As Scraton (2007: 165) asserts:

> Perhaps the greatest challenge is to change a collective mindset, fuelled by irresponsible media coverage, portraying children in conflict with the law as products of individual pathology blended with social dysfunction … the rhetoric of exiling and punishment is reprehensible, whether scrawled on the gable-end wall or written in the statute-book.

Against this backdrop and in exploring the role of the media further, Chaps. 4 and 5 that follow, both extensively analyse media content, as well as policy and legislative responses directed towards children and young people in a specific period of transition, following the devolution of policing and justice.

Notes

1. New Labour's 1997 Election Manifesto, 'New Labour because Britain deserves better', see: http://www.labour-party.org.uk/manifestos/1997/1997-labour-manifesto.shtml (accessed on 17 March 2010).
2. Graham and Bowling's (1995) research (published by the Home Office), focused on why people desist from crime. Their analysis of household surveys completed by 2,529 young people, conclude that females 'grow out of offending', while young males continue to offend. The authors argue that young people must realise that their offending behaviour was wrong and take account of the consequences. They highlighted the related factors of general maturity, responsibility and moral development. This emphasis on individual realisation and responsibility was employed in New Labour's policies, in particular 'rights and responsibilities' (see The Labour Party 1996).
3. McGarry (2001) in his opening critique of the range of perspectives surrounding the Conflict, argues that the dominant view is that Northern Ireland is 'a place apart'; a result of its own 'pathology'. McGarry (2001) quotes the Northern Ireland poet, John Hewitt's (1907–1987) poem 'Conversations in Hungary', in which the Ulster poet depicts the usual attempt to 'explain' Ireland to the foreigner (Nairn 1981: 213) and also draws on a number of contemporary newspaper headlines, to illustrate his argument that in the contemporary setting this dominant view still exists.
4. The use of baton rounds and other responses police can use at times of public disorder and rioting are outlined in guidelines issued by the Association of Chief Police Officers (ACPO), see: http://www.acpo.police.uk/ (accessed on 23 March 2010). Also, the PSNI must adhere to Section 3 of the Criminal Law Act (NI) (1967), which outlines the use/standard of force for the prevention of crime; the Police and Criminal Evidence (Northern Ireland) Order 1989; the Police and Criminal Evidence (Amendment) Order 2007, No. 288 (N.I.2) and the PACE Codes of Practice 2007, which outline the power of police officers and regulate the practice of the police in their application of the legislation. The Police Ombudsman's Office investigates complaints and has published a number of reports. See: http://www.policeombudsman.org/Publicationsuploads/PONI_BATON_REPORT_2005.pdf (accessed on 25 March 2010).
5. There is a wealth of research and literature on the impact of segregation and living in interface areas: see Jarman (2002, 2004, 2005, 2006, 2008); Conway

and Byrne (2005); Byrne et al. (2006); Leonard (2006); Shirlow and Murtagh (2006); Hamilton et al. (2003); Heenan and Birrell (2011).

6. One example is the Holy Cross Primary School dispute, Ardoyne, North Belfast. In 2001 pupils and their parents experienced intimidation and violence by loyalist paramilitaries and required armed police escorts when making their daily journey to and from school. The Holy Cross dispute has been written about extensively, see Cadwallader (2004); Cox et al. (2006); McEldowney et al. (2011).

7. 'Policy Transfer' is defined generally as 'a process in which knowledge about policies, administrative arrangements, institutions etc in one time and/or place is used in the development of policies/administrative arrangements and institutions in another time and/or place' (Dolowitz and Marsh 1996: 344, cited in Newburn 2002: 166).

8. 'Sin bins' refer to family intervention projects. As media commentary outlines, they can include monitoring and visits to the family home, to ensure that children and young people attend school, go to bed on time and eat proper meals (see SIN BINS FOR WORTH FAMILIES, *Daily Express*, 23 July 2009), or the policy can include families being taken into care and placed in residential blocks dubbed 'sin bins' (see THOUSANDS OF ENGLAND'S WORST FAMILIES TO BE PLACED IN 'SIN BINS' TO IMPROVE BEHAVIOUR, *Daily Mail*, 22 July 2009).

9. As Reiner (2000: 68) and Mulcahy (2002: 279) note, senior British police officers visited Northern Ireland, in order 'to discuss riot control and learn from their "success"'. The punitive measures and responses employed during riot and public disorder situations in Northern Ireland were replicated during the uprisings in Britain in the 1980s.

10. Extensive research reports on the conditions of imprisonment in Northern Ireland outline the routine breaches of a number of international standards, including the UNCRC, the Beijing Rules (1985), Havana Rules (1990) and Riyadh Guidelines (1990) (see Kilkelly et al. 2002; Convery and Moore 2006; Scraton and Moore 2005, 2007). Collectively this research concludes that many of the children incarcerated should not be in custody. This is further highlighted in reports by the Criminal Justice Inspectorate of Northern Ireland, who have emphasised that placing children and young people in custody, 'breach[es] international safeguards, and inappropriate use of custody … remains a more pronounced problem in Northern Ireland than elsewhere in the UK'. See: http://www.cjini.org/CJNI/files/74/743c0eb6-5bc1-4a27-b08f-e0d17ad490e3.pdf (accessed on 27 April 2010).

11. See: http://www.nio.gov.uk/justice_ni_act_2002_expanatory_notes.pdf (accessed on 19 April 2010).

12. See: http://www.4ni.co.uk/northern_ireland_news.asp?id=19675 (accessed on 20 March 2010).

13. For the entire judgment, see: http://www.courtsni.gov.uk/NR/rdonlyres/705ED37E-0CC3-46CA-8D89-3B0B3CB9E372/0/j_j_GIRF4194.htm (accessed on 20 March 2010).

14. The current practice breaches the rights of children and young people – such as Article 40(2) (vii) of the United Nations Convention of the Rights of the Child (UNCRC), Article 8 of the European Convention of Human Rights (ECHR), as enshrined by the Human Rights Act 1998, which provide for privacy of children and young people in the justice system 'at all stages of the proceedings', and uphold the right to promote and protect family life. As outlined in Chap. 1, the most recent concluding observations of the Committee on the Rights of the Child (October 2008) note that the government has not taken sufficient measures to protect children, in particular those subject to ASBOs and those who are targeted by negative media representation and 'naming and shaming' (para 36(b)) (see 2015 Concluding Observations also). They were also concerned 'at the general climate of intolerance and negative public attitudes towards children, especially adolescents, which appears to exist in the State party, including in the media' (para 24).

15. The Northern Ireland Association for the Care and Resettlement of Offenders (NIACRO) is an organisation who works with children and young people who offend, offenders and ex-prisoners, and prisoners, their families and their children. See: http://www.niacro.co.uk/about-niacro/ (accessed on 1 March 2010).

16. Young men have been 'named and shamed' in their local communities, having been accused of burgling houses, as Baroness Blood (2008: 8) has commented: 'Recent events being played out on our streets of naming and shaming young men as thieves is not the way forward' for Northern Ireland, a society which is in transition from a period of violent conflict.

17. The strategy, 'Building Safer, Shared and Confident Communities' can be accessed here: http://www.dojni.gov.uk/index/media-centre/ford-announces-20m-community-safety-strategy.htm (accessed on 30 July 2012). See also: http://www.dojni.gov.uk/index/publications/publication-categories/pubs-policing-community-safety/css-july2012.pdf (accessed on 30 July 2012).

Part II

**Media Representations, Social
Reaction and the Impact**

4

Print Media Content Analysis: Language, Imagery and Prominent Themes

As outlined in the previous chapters, the powerful impact of the print media is evident in its ability to de-contextualise, select and shape representations of children and young people in conflict with the law. Brown (2005: 50) observes that:

News stories and young people have rarely made happy reading since the advent of print media ... Mass media, from their inception, have been closely associated with mass anxiety about young people.

As research in other jurisdictions illustrates, news items about 'youth crime' are 'highly selective, often distorted and routinely exaggerated' (Bessant and Hil 1997: 1). How people in society therefore 'come to see ... and respond to' children and young people is influenced and impacted upon by media reporting, which typically presents this social group in a negative light (Bessant 1997: 4, 23; Schissel 2006: 19, 39, 45). This chapter critically analyses how newspapers in Northern Ireland represent children, young people and children and youth sector organisations. In doing so, this chapter presents an analysis of the language and imagery utilised by journalists and editors when reporting on children, young people and their advocates. It also outlines and analyses the significance of prominent themes that emerged from the large-scale study of print media content.

© The Author(s) 2018
F. Gordon, *Children, Young People and the Press in a Transitioning Society*,
Palgrave Socio-Legal Studies, https://doi.org/10.1057/978-1-137-60682-2_4

Content Analysis: Language and Imagery

Print media content comprises signs, including words, images, diagrams, illustrations and photographs, structured according to 'systems such as layout, typography, format and composition' (Nicholas and Price 1998: 8). Through the selection of words, 'underlying meanings and motivations' are presented, which enable journalists to 'express an opinion', 'attitude', 'judgement' or 'feeling' (Erjavec 2001: 707). They also make news items appear factual, natural and the reality. Significantly, headlines are 'part of news rhetoric', have 'textual and cognitive functions' (Erjavec 2001: 708), which summarise the most poignant pieces of information in a 'short, maximally informative' manner to 'attract' (Cotter 2010: 26), as well as orientate 'the reader to process the text in a predetermined direction' (Erjavec 2001: 708). The headlines and sections of media commentary included in the following analysis are representative of the media coverage analysed and have been selected as several similar news items featured in the data collected.

Use of Language in Demonising Youth

Analysis of 2,456 news items from newspapers sampled over six months indicates that words and phrases selected for headlines included language that, at its mildest, presented a clear general hostility towards and blame of youth for a range of social problems. Particularly, but not exclusive to news items on anti-social behaviour, crime and violence, this use of language extended to strong, outright condemnation, dehumanisation and demonisation, with headlines from the sample newspapers typically featuring words such as: 'YOBS'; 'YOBBISHNESS'; 'TEEN THUGS'; 'SICKOS'; 'EVIL'; 'UNRULY'; 'DISAFFECTED … YOUTH'; 'OUT-OF-CONTROL KIDS'; 'HOODS'; 'MOB'; 'TEARAWAY TEEN'; 'TROUBLED YOUTH'; 'CRAZY KIDS'; 'JOYRIDERS'; 'JUNKIE'.

In the main body of the news items the language typically employed was also profoundly condemnatory: 'young criminals'; 'child vandals'; 'young drug dealers'; 'child truancy'; 'running rampant'; 'young dupes'; 'young yobbos hurling abuse'; 'hoodie-wearing youths'; 'teenage-tearaway gang'; 'hot-headed youngsters'. Emotive language and descriptions printed in the form of Letters to the Editor and text messages, highlighted community responses. Language and stereotypical generalisations were employed to frame young people's behaviour as 'anti-social'; 'lawlessness'; 'drunkenness' and 'gangsterism'. This language was pivotal in the process of labelling and categorisation of youth as criminal and deviant.

It was the norm for journalists to alert the reader that the news item was about children or young people, by employing certain words, phrases and emphasising the specific age or age group, for example: 'Youth'; 'Kids'; 'Teens'; 'Teenagers', to describe children and young people. A typical headline was: 'TEENAGERS ROB WOMAN' (*News Letter*, 15 June 2010: 13). This is a common characteristic that has been acknowledged in other previous studies (see Heintz-Knowles 2000; Bucholtz 2002). Age was reinforced in examples such as: 'OUTRAGE ... 16-YEAR-OLD HAS COMMITTED 30 OFFENCES BUT HE'S BACK OUT' (*Andersonstown News*, 27 March 2010: 3), which not only emphasised the age of the young man, but also suggested the number of offences allegedly committed.

Language such as 'teenage thugs' (*Belfast Telegraph*, 22 March 2010: 1), 'tearaway teen' and 'young thug' (*Sunday Life*, 11 July 2010: 17), presented young people as 'symbols of trouble' (see Cohen 2002). As part of the process of creation and maintenance of young people as 'folk devils', journalists employed emotive language, thus amplifying alleged youth involvement: 'A senior police officer ... said a group of eight to 10 "hard core" male youths orchestrated a larger faction of up to 30 in the ensuing violence' (*News Letter*, 18 May 2010: 3). While specific labels presented negative connotations, the words accompanying 'teen', 'teens' and 'teenagers', such as 'out-of-control' (*North Belfast News*, 19 June 2010: 12) and 'tearaway' (*Andersonstown News*, 9 August 2010: 9), played a significant role in framing news items.

While young people were routinely portrayed as 'troublesome', it was evident that an additional layer of condemnation and outrage appeared in news items relating to children's alleged involvement in crime and violence. Age was highlighted in the use of language: 'THE RIOTERS AS YOUNG AS 10: OUR LOST GENERATION' (*Belfast Telegraph*, 14 July 2010: 4–5) and '"KIDS" BEHIND TROUBLE IN DUNMURRY, SAY SINN FEIN' (*Belfast Telegraph*, 1 March 2010: 5). Another headline: 'CHILDREN SET BARRICADE IN STREET ALIGHT' (*The Irish News*, 24 May 2010: 17), described how 'a group of up to 30 children, most said to be aged under 10, caused chaos'. The source of this information was not identified, with generalisations and speculation relating to the age and number allegedly involved. This was amplified by the inclusion of images and the caption: 'Child Vandals'. Further examples: 'spoilt brats' and 'horrendously demanding' (*Belfast Telegraph*, 8 June 2010: 14) reflected the application of broad generalisations.

The *Sunday Life* repeatedly used descriptions such as 'baby-faced defendant' (2 May 2010: 19), 'baby-faced ... schoolboys' (1 August 2010: 27) and 'baby-faced teen' (29 August 2010: 12), to highlight age and present an additional dimension of outrage. 'Baby-faced' evoked notions of childhood and emphasised how young the alleged perpetrators were perceived as being.

This was reflected in a caption beneath an image of young women smoking: 'OLD BEFORE THEIR TIME' (*Sunday Life*, 29 August 2010: 12–13). The description suggested that young people's behaviour was not what adults expect. Harking back to a time of 'tranquillity' (Pearson 1983), where children and young people had good behaviour and respect for their elders, is contrasted with contemporary adult responses to anti-social behaviour and 'hooliganism' and calls to 'return to the good old days' (see Chap. 3).

Throughout the news items there was a distinct difference in the representation of children and young people's perceived involvement in crime and violence. Previous research argues that 'the division between children and youth in Britain is associated with several other divisions', specifically 'sympathetic versus unsympathetic public perception' (Hall and Montgomery 2000, cited in Bucholtz 2002: 527). According to Fionda (2005: 27), it is only when children transgress adult defined boundaries by misbehaving, are they responded to in a similar manner as young people.

Labelling and Categorising Youth

Just as the social construction of age was reinforced by language and labels that infer particular meanings, class and gender were also, explicitly and implicitly, mirrored in media descriptions of youth in Northern Ireland. Hayward and Yar (2006: 15) note that certain areas have labels commonly used locally in popular discourse as derogatory terms to refer to working class young people, for example: '"Scallies" (Merseyside), "Neds" (Glasgow), … "Charvers" (North East), "Kevs" (London/Bristol)'. 'Hoodies' is a contemporary label that has been applied to children and young people in the United Kingdom (UK) (see Hall and Jefferson 2006; Marsh and Melville 2009; Coleman and McCahill 2011). As Robinson (2009: 132) asserts, 'the dominant reading of youths in hoodies is a negative one', with 'media-driven narratives' playing a central role in evoking fear, concern and reactions directed towards youth (see Pearson 2011). As discussed in Chap. 2, 'hoodies' is one contemporary example that can be applied to Cohen's (1972) theorisation of moral panics.

Similar to their application in other parts of the UK, the labels 'hoodie' and 'hoodies' featured in newspaper coverage in Northern Ireland and their use is an example of the transference of labels. The labels featured most regularly in news items relating to anti-social behaviour and crime and one example was: 'POLICE are searching for two teenage "hoodies"' (*News Letter*, 5 June 2010: 13). However, the label 'hoods' was more prominent, particularly with reference to children and young people in Belfast. As a label, the term featured most frequently in the *Andersonstown News* and was employed by the *Sunday World* and *Sunday Life*. Hamill's (2011: 8) research into punishment beatings and shootings, states that in West Belfast children and young people who are associated with 'anti-social behaviour' and 'crime' are 'known locally as hoods'. Language such as 'hood gang' (*Andersonstown News*, 9 August 2010: 2) and 'drugged up hoods', featured in a 'WE SAY' article written by the Editor (*Andersonstown News*, 24 May 2010: 15), in Letters to the Editor and text message sections.

Highly selective language was employed to create gender specific labels, such as 'young mum' (*Andersonstown News*, 14 August 2010: 4) or 'TEEN MUM' (*Belfast Telegraph*, 27 March 2010). As Bucholtz (2002: 527) argues, this language is 'socially meaningful' and authorises 'interpretation of biological chronology in social terms', that may shift according to the context or way in which journalists chose to frame the news item. It also constructs individuals as 'folk devils'. Cohen (2002: xviii) outlines that, '"welfare cheats", "social security frauds" and "dole scroungers" are fairly traditional folk devils', as are 'unmarried mothers'. The Conservative Government's 'goal of reducing ... expenditure with moral exhortation for people to take responsibility for their own lives', was evidenced in 'the 1993 "Back to Basics" campaign', which 'cynically constructed the single mother as a potent moral threat' (Cohen 2002: xviii). As Burbank and Chisholm (1998, cited in Bucholtz 2002: 534) assert, 'it is not adolescent pregnancy itself but the community's response to it that creates a social problem'. One example: 'FIVE 14-YEAR-OLD GIRLS BECAME MOTHERS IN 2009' (*The Irish News*, 2 March 2010: 6), highlighted the age of young women.

As Jamieson and Yates (2009: 80) argue, the 'highly emotive moral panic regarding the behaviour of young people [and] "feral children"' in the 1990s 'was intrinsically linked to right-wing concerns around the moral otherness of an "emerging British under-class"'. As Harvey (2007: 9) argues, 'in [the] rush to blame ... the politician-media complex has a field day stigmatizing and stereotyping an underclass', evident in the selection of language to refer to certain sections of society as 'idle wrong-doers, irresponsible single parents and feckless fathers ... welfare junkies, and much worse'. The 'damaging discursive power of the language of welfare dependency', presents 'stigmatising connotations' that make 'the problems of poor solo mothers and their children ... appear to be individual rather than social problems' (Fraser and Gordon 1994, cited in Lister and Bennett 2010: 1). Thus, the application of labels framed working class parents and children in pathological terms (see Kelso 1994; Chibnall 2003).

Similar discourse is reflected in contemporary Conservative party policy and publications from the Centre for Social Justice (CSJ),[1] in particular the concepts of 'Broken Britain' and 'Broken societies', which has been transferred to other parts of the UK (Mooney 2009; Hancock et al. 2010), including to Northern Ireland (Gordon 2010). In the build up to the publication of the 'Breakthrough Northern Ireland' (CSJ, September 2010) document, news items typically featured quotations from the then Director of the Centre, Iain Duncan Smith. The language and concepts presented in the document, such as 'worklessness' and 'welfare dependency' (CSJ 2010: 6–21); 'drug addiction' and 'alcoholism' (CSJ 2010: 26–31); 'educational failure' (CSJ 2010: 46) and 'family breakdown' (CSJ 2010: 36–40), were reflected in the news items. Headlines such as: 'EX-TORY LEADER: ESTATES A GLOOMY GHETTO FOR POOR' (*News Letter*, 1 March 2010: 6), included discriminatory language and stereotypical representations to describe selected neighbourhoods in Northern Ireland.

As part of the 'broken societies' discourse, the label 'disaffected youth' was employed to present young people as disillusioned and not satisfied with life or accepting of societal values. This perspective was reflected in news items and in Letters to the Editor. One example of a printed letter written by a member of the Conservative party, employed language such as 'second and third-generation unemployment, indebtedness and hopelessness' (*Belfast Telegraph*, 16 July 2010: 38), to place blame at the individual level. The author labelled members of society as having 'no sense of community', with 'negative attitudes to education', which was 'no surprise', as 'people have come to develop an in-depth knowledge of the benefits system rather than a trade or profession'. The title of this news item: 'TACKLE CAUSES OF VIOLENCE, NOT JUST SYMPTOMS', presented a stereotypical view of violence and made unsubstantiated claims that there was a relationship between 'unemployment', 'welfare dependency' and violence. Young people were presented as a specific problem: 'The fundamental issue here is disaffected youth' with 'too many … growing up with worklessness, lack of … education, no positive male role models … severe addictions'.

As Presdee's (2009: 283) analysis of rioting in England in the 1990s argues, 'the popular press, are always eager to promote the evilness of people'. Research in the UK illustrates this and asserts that journalists employ 'highly emotive' language when referring to children and young people in conflict with the law, which serves to 'dehumanize' and 'bestialize' (Jamieson and Yates 2009: 80). Throughout the six months of data collection, descriptions of children and young people in animalistic terms were evident in news items on antisocial behaviour, crime and violence. Examples included the headline: '"EVIL"

KILLER' (*The Irish News*, 26 March 2010: 24) and descriptions such as: 'monster Michael Gilbert ... was only 15 when he broke into a woman's house ... battered her with a hammer and raped her' (*Sunday Life*, 27 June 2010: 6). Other dehumanising descriptions such as, 'herd of howling jackals' (*Andersonstown News*, 8 May 2010: 6), presented young people as animalistic and their behaviour as 'wild', 'unruly' and violent.

The media's application of such dehumanising labels placed the focus on perceived inherent defects or individual wickedness. As Eschholz (2003: 62) argues, media representation of crime typically ignores 'endemic social problems' and 'tends to focus on individual pathology as the reason for crime'. Examples including a Letter to the Editor printed in the *Belfast Telegraph* (28 August 2010: 25), highlighted how such descriptions were employed in society: 'Until we realise that ... it is ... feral children's own fault that they are just plain bad, and no one else's, we will never get anywhere'. Blame placed at the personal level was compounded by the media's consistent failure to acknowledge or refer to existing social and structural inequalities. DeLisi's (2003: 28) analysis argues that, the media's approach in choosing to enhance 'the idea that the ultimate driving force of crime lies within the individual', results in 'the claims of individual pathology ... like self-control and psychopathy [appearing] more believable' to media consumers.

The words 'blame', 'blames' or 'blamed' were typically employed to frame children and young people as perpetrators and the cause of social problems, for example: 'YOUTHS BLAMED FOR "SINISTER ATTACKS" ON COMMUNITY' (*News Letter*, 19 May 2010: 11). Journalists routinely reinforced blame to evoke outrage concerning the alleged behaviour, by linking examples of alleged incidents to previous incidents and news reports. This reinforced and validated blame, heightened tension and legitimated the chosen interpretation and representation of the situation. One example was: 'another brutal murder ... inflicted on this community by young criminals' (*Andersonstown News*, 3 May 2010: 16). How journalists framed news items on gorse fires in March 2010 and May 2010, were prominent examples of blame-laying accusations being directed towards young people. Even when the word 'suspected' was employed in headlines, for example: 'TEENS SUSPECTED OF STARTING HILL FIRES' (*The Irish News*, 12 March 2010: 21), the main text of the news item chose to firmly place the blame on young people.

Language employed to reflect 'moral' attitudes and condemnation was closely related to the reinforcement of blame. Typically journalists and moral entrepreneurs described children and young people's behaviour as 'a disgrace': 'MLA Caral Ni Chuilin [said] ... "For them [Fire Service] ... to be stoned and spat on by anti-community thugs is utterly disgraceful'" (*North Belfast News*, 21 August 2010: 4). As Aldridge and Cross (2008: 203) observe, 'in the case of so-called "antisocial" children and young people, news values and moral values have entwined', with 'moral concerns ... never far from the surface of press reporting on children and young people' in the UK.

Headlines such as: 'GCSE STUDENTS' NIGHT OF SEX AND DRINK SHAME' (*Sunday Life*, 29 August 2010: 2), described young people's behaviour as an 'orgy of booze and sex'. Typically words such as 'SHAMELESS' and 'SLEAZY' were employed to describe images (*Sunday World*, 8 August 2010: 42–43). This use of language presented adult judgement to frame young people as not ashamed or embarrassed by behaviour that adults deemed to be unacceptable. This is consistent with findings from other jurisdictions, as sex and sexuality are typically placed 'in the context of adult activities and concerns', with adult definition and reactions towards youth creating and framing both as 'risky' behaviour and social problems (Bucholtz 2002: 534).

Clear examples of the categorisation of youth demonstrated journalists' selection of language which highlighted negative characteristics and presented them as if they were attributable to all children and/or young people in Northern Ireland. Throughout the data collection period, language employed by journalists to form stereotypical representations and make sweeping generalisations, took two distinct formats. First, more subtle generalisations and stereotypes were evident, such as: 'HALF OF THE YOUTHS IN ARDOYNE USE DRUGS, MUM TELLS JUDGE' (*Belfast Telegraph*, 5 March 2010: 16) and 'hundreds of booze-up teens' (*Sunday Life*, 29 August 2010: 12–13). Whilst the most specific and poignant examples included: 'Young men are horrible creatures ... if you know nothing else about the offender, it is a safe bet that it was someone male and young' (*Belfast Telegraph*, 2 August 2010: 29). This is consistent with findings from both existing historical and contemporary research. As Brown (2005: 55) notes, Hall et al.'s (1978) study of the mugging panic 'demonstrated how the image of problem youth was locked by the media into a generalized "climate of hostility to marginal groups"'.

The media's use of language to whip up concern or panic surrounding children and young people's perceived 'risky' behaviours was particularly evident in news items on anti-social behaviour, crime, drug taking, violence and youth suicide. Regularly journalists employed words and phrases such as 'crisis', 'epidemic' and 'urgent action', to frame the news item. Examples included: 'USE OF DRONE EPIDEMIC AMONGST KIDS ACROSS NORTH BELFAST' (*North Belfast News*, 6 March 2010: 1–2) and 'CRISIS MEETING' (*The Irish News*, 23 April 2010: 7). This use of language created a sense of urgency and immediacy regarding particular identified issues. Reflective of

Cohen (1972) and Young's (1971) pivotal analyses, Wood's (2010) research acknowledges the consequences of such reporting. Wood (2010: 97) argues that contemporary 'media portrayal of, and government response to, the "knife crime epidemic" has created a distorted image of the reality on the ground'. This illustrates how the use of language and the sustained focus on particular issues, can heighten concern and present issues as requiring immediate or 'urgent action'.

As Chibnall (1977: x) asserts, 'crime news may serve as … a chance not simply to speak to the community but to speak for the community, against all that the criminal outsider represents', providing 'a chance for a newspaper to appropriate a moral conscience for its readership'. Hall et al.'s (1978, cited in Glover 1984: 40) study emphasises that 'the rhetoric of police statements, and courtroom verdicts is passed back and forth by the press', which 'channels popular opinion' by supplying the 'link between those in the control culture who define and deal with social problems and the public'. Headlines such as: 'JUDGE REFUSES BAIL IN "OUTRAGEOUS CASE"' (*News Letter*, 20 July 2010: 6); 'JUDGE HITS OUT …' (*The Irish News*, 31 July 2010: 5); 'RIGHT SENTENCE FOR CRUEL KILLER' (*The Irish News*, 26 March 2010: 10) and 'POLITICIANS WELCOME … SENTENCE' (*Andersonstown News*, 29 March 2010: 9), emphasised support for longer sentences and punitive responses.

Representations of Children's Rights and 'Alternative' Voices

Journalists and editors employed similar language to describe the children and youth sector organisations and children's rights discourse. Throughout the six months period, 34 news items made reference to children and youth sector organisations in Northern Ireland and children's rights. This figure was low in comparison to the overall number of news items identified and emphasised how marginalised this sector was within media discourse. The news items established how journalists typically employed language to present negative descriptions of the work of the children and youth sector organisations. The office of the Northern Ireland Children's Commissioner (NICCY) was typically referred to as a 'quango' (*News Letter*, 8 June 2010: 8). Criticisms focused on the cost of running the office: 'the £2 million a year local kiddie-quango' (*The Irish News*, 17 July 2010: 32). News items also presented criticism of non-statutory children's sector and youth sector organisations and typically did not include the voices or responses of those organisations. The most extreme examples focused on individuals, with journalists including harsh, personalised comments. An example of a news item that criticised a children's sector organisation and its director, framed the story with the headline: 'THIS WOMAN SAYS PLAY IS THE SIMPLE SOLUTION TO OUR COMPLEX PROBLEMS. IS THIS ANOTHER EXAMPLE OF QUANGO SPEAK?' (*Belfast Telegraph*, 30 March 2010: 12).

The implications of the 'backlash against children' and children's rights discourse following the Bulger case in England, has had long-term consequences (Haydon and Scraton 2000: 448; see also Franklin 2002), as evident in the most recent Concluding Observations of United Nations Committee on the Rights of the Child (CRC) (October 2008). Media reporting and politicians' statements emphasised 'a fear of children's rights as challenging adult authority and, ultimately, adult power' (Haydon and Scraton 2000: 448). Blame placed on children's rights for constraining adults in their reactions towards children and young people's perceived misbehaviour was evident throughout the news items. One example posed the question: 'WHY DO TEACHERS HAVE TO ENDURE MENTAL TORTURE?' (*Belfast Telegraph*, 4 May 2010: 25) and argued that:

> We've stripped teachers of the right to use corporal punishment, so what action can they take … ? … Have a chat with … parents? Yeah right … they're raging on about their little one's 'rights' … we send our teachers naked into the classroom – and the kids know it … With no effective method of discipline.

Letters to the Editor sections also featured contributions that questioned the basis of children's rights discourse and proposed and supported punitive measures for responding to children and young people. One such example entitled: 'BRING BACK THE CANE TO SORT OUT UNRULY CHILDREN' (*Belfast Telegraph*, 21 August 2010: 26), criticised 'THE University of Ulster's Goretti Horgan' who 'says that "the rights of young people must always come first" and that "a child rioting needs help"'. The letter went further in its criticism: 'Goretti Horgan's words epitomise what is wrong with our community and this society'. The author argued: 'For your information Goretti, a child rioting does not need help. What they … need is … strong punishment, no matter how un-PC that may be'. Criticising children and children's rights, the author stated: 'Feral Kids roam around … all saying "You can't touch me. I know my rights"' and asked: 'What about the rights of ordinary, decent law-abiding people to go about their daily lives without fear of attack?' The author concluded that, '[This] current PC fad … is yet another example of children having all of the rights with none of the responsibilities'. Another Letter to the Editor was equally as forceful: 'Suggesting that the solution … is "giving people human rights" does not help, as human rights are theoretical whereas what is needed is practical' (*Belfast Telegraph*, 16 July 2010: 38).

Impact of Visual Images

Similar to the media's selection of language, visual images were included to attract readers and 'bring to life' stories. As Simpson (1997: 13) notes, the 'visual opportunities' available play a key 'part in deciding whether … and how [a story] is reported', as images created or selected, communicate a particular message (see also Davies 1997: 56; Lacey 1998: 5). The relationship between imagery and language is significant, as 'a picture … waits for language to unsettle it … text directs us how to read the picture, and the picture can act to externalise [and] … pull meanings … together' to make them 'appear natural' (Holland 1992: 10).

A total of 2,204 images featured either as part of news items or as single items with or without text captions and were in the form of photographic imagery or cartoon drawings. 1,095 images included children and young people. 877 included adults who were commonly referred to as 'victims', 'parents', 'residents', 'community workers' or 'members of the general public'. 410 images presented scenes of crime, damage and debris, graffiti, weapons and other items included to illustrate the contents of the news items. There were 297 images that included the Police Service of Northern Ireland (PSNI); criminal justice agency representatives; politicians (Councillors, Members of the Legislative Assembly in Northern Ireland (MLAs), Government Ministers)[2]; Northern Ireland (NI) Prison Service representatives; religious representatives; the Army; Emergency Services; Community Wardens; academics and other professionals. 48 images included youth workers and representatives from children and youth sector organisations.

As Simpson (1997: 13) asserts, 'acts of vandalism, graffiti and brawls … readily … captured by the lens' serve to reinforce headlines and visually illustrate the main text. This was particularly evident in news items on antisocial behaviour, crime, youth involvement in violence and youth suicide, with images often central to the media's presentation of the news item. Images of children and young people were often repeated in sustained coverage of particular issues, with large images and in some cases full-page images of children and young people, dramatically included as powerful visual representations.

The images of children and young people consisted of a range of photographs and cartoon drawings. Examples included: police and young people (*South Belfast News*, 13 March 2010: 20); young people with their faces blurred (*Andersonstown News*, 13 March 2010: 1); images taken from social networking sites of young people who have committed suicide (*Belfast Telegraph*, 17 March 2010: 7); Closed Circuit Television (CCTV) images of young people (*Sunday World*, 11 April 2010: 20); the PSNI arresting a young male (*The Irish News*, 13 May 2010: 12); 'hooded and masked youth' (*The Irish News*, 18 May 2010: 1); 'Hoodies' (*Belfast Telegraph*, 18 June 2010: 8) and 'Gangs of Youths' (*The Irish News*, 12 July 2010: 5).

Captions played a central role in presenting and interpreting the images in certain instances. Representative examples of this included a photograph of debris and graffiti with the caption: 'As unrest in St James' grew ever more heated, local thugs turned their attention to the Republican Plot at Milltown Cemetery' (*Andersonstown News*, 21 August 2010: 30). Another image of a group of young people, had the following caption positioned next to it: 'BOOZED-UP: Revellers in 24-Hour Square' (*Sunday World*, 8 August 2010: 42) and an image of a young male leaving court bore the caption, 'LOWLIFE' (*Sunday Life*, 8 August 2010: 27). News items on riot situations employed images that included both riot police and young people. These images were routinely accompanied by captions that highlighted violence on the part of young people: 'The images of hoodie-wearing youths throwing missiles at police' (*News Letter*, 19 July 2010: 10–11). This use of imagery reinforced the language employed in headlines. Collectively the language and imagery framed youth as 'out of control' and rebellious towards adult and state authority.

Content Analysis: Themes

In addressing several of the research questions, part two of this chapter explores a number of the most prominent themes that have emerged. Themes are defined as 'recurring typical theses that run through' news items (Altheide 1996: 31, cited in Green 2008a: 200), which emerge through the news-making process (see Cohen et al. 2007). The table below details the prominent themes, with column one outlining the broad themes and column two outlining specific themes that have emerged (Table 4.1).

Table 4.1 Content analysis themes

Themes		March	April	May	June	July	August	Total
Crime and Criminalisation	Crime	147	194	236	248	439	287	1,551
	Intergenerational: crimes against the elderly	11	8	16	22	11	17	85
	'Gangs'	3	4	18	9	33	28	95
	Anti-social behaviour	57	21	31	29	66	44	248
	Anti-community behaviour	0	0	3	2	5	3	13
	Alcohol and 'Underage' drinking	36	24	37	31	52	49	229
	Drug taking and Smoking	71	47	41	49	50	53	311
	Other 'risky' behaviours and Truancy	7	4	13	33	57	57	171
Youth involvement in Violence	Violence/Violent Acts	101	92	132	137	375	201	1,038
	Rioting and Interface Violence	36	12	19	23	262	97	449
	Youth Suicide, Attempted Suicide and Self-Harm	29	30	28	18	21	28	154
Demand for Punitive Responses	Calls for Punitive Responses	54	39	44	35	99	64	335
Conflict and Legacy of the Conflict	Conflict and Legacy of the Conflict	31	30	56	77	211	100	505
Other	Children's Rights and Children and Youth Sector	4	1	3	4	15	7	34
	Parenting and Family Life	6	5	2	30	58	19	120
	Gender and Sexuality	1	19	20	24	15	39	118
	Social Media and Networking Sites	2	4	6	5	38	29	84

Crime and Criminalisation

Criminal Acts

Children's and young people's perceived involvement in crime and criminal acts was a prominent theme in 1,551 news items. The types of crime and criminal acts described in news items ranged in nature, with journalists presenting a close relationship and links between anti-social behaviour, crime and violence. Children's and young people's alleged involvement in crime was typically reinforced by descriptions that framed them as perpetrators. Language and labels such as: 'YOUNG vandals' (*Andersonstown News*, 5 July 2010: 8) and 'teenage thief' (*Andersonstown News*, 23 August 2010: 4) were age-specific descriptions employed by journalists to frame children and young people as offenders. Blame was clearly placed on children and young people: 'LAY THE BLAME ON JOYRIDERS NOT THE SYSTEM' (*Belfast Telegraph*, 30 June 2010: 28) and 'SDLP councillor Danny O'Connor … was thankful that no one was hurt during the incidents which he put down to "dangerous youths"' (*News Letter*, 18 June 2010: 11).

Descriptions of incidents of crime were prominent features, with a wide range of criminal acts evident throughout the six months of media coverage. Typically headlines featured the words, 'YOUTHS', 'KIDS' and 'TEENS' to immediately alert the reader, alongside a description of the crime. Headlines included: 'UDA YOUTHS RIP-OFF KIDS CHARITY CASH' (*Sunday World*, 7 March 2010: 8); 'TEEN ON RAPE CHARGES' (*The Irish News*, 9 March 2010: 11); 'TEEN ARMED WITH KNIFE ROBS SHOP' (*News Letter*, 11 March 2010: 6) and 'YOUTHS HIJACK VAN' (*News Letter*, 22 March 2010: 4).

Similar emphasis was placed on PSNI responses, investigations and the arrests of suspects: 'POLICE are searching for two teenage "hoodies" who robbed a young woman' (*News Letter*, 5 June 2010: 13) and 'TEEN ARSONIST GETS CAUGHT ON … CCTV' (*Andersonstown News*, 22 May 2010: 4). Descriptions of court hearings, judicial decision-making and sentencing, further emphasised criminal justice system responses to 'offenders'. Examples included: 'YOB IS FINED FOR ABUSING POLICE' (*Belfast Telegraph*, 9 March 2010: 17); 'ARSON ACCUSED TEENAGER IS DENIED BAIL' (*News Letter*, 2 April 2010: 6) and 'TEENAGE CAR THIEF IS JAILED' (*Belfast Telegraph*, 11 August 2010: 10). In presenting additional layers of condemnation, journalists' descriptions of court appearances, such as: 'The 16-year-old sauntered from the court, smiling and clicking his fingers as he was led to the cells' (*Sunday World*, 4 July 2010: 4), presented young people as 'disrespectful'.

Criticisms of criminal justice responses were evident in news items relating to bail procedures and court decision making processes, with headlines such as: 'ARRESTED TEEN FREED ON BAIL' (*The Irish News*, 3 March 2010: 16). Further examples included moral entrepreneurs who questioned the court's decision to grant bail in particular cases:

TELL US: HOW DID THIS ONE GET BAILED? ANSWERS DEMANDED AFTER ACCUSED TEEN IS FREED; HE'S CHARGED WITH 27 CRIMES, WHICH INCLUDE … AGGRAVATED ASSAULT, POSSESSION OF OFFENSIVE WEAPON, CAR THEFT, BURGLARY AND RIOTIOUS BEHAVIOUR. MLA DEMANDS ANSWERS OVER BAILING OF TEENAGER. (*Andersonstown News*, 15 March 2010: 1, 3)

Another example: 'JUSTICE ROW OVER FAILURE TO TAG TEEN OUT ON BAIL' (*The Irish News*, 11 May 2010: 12), quoted a Sinn Féin MLA, who criticised the court's failure to ensure that a young male was tagged to enable the implementation of curfew conditions. The politician argued that there has been 'an increase in "anti-community behaviour and criminality"' as a direct result, with 'prolific offenders … making life unbearable for communities'.

Similarly, images and descriptions of victims were a common feature, with the 'innocence' of the victim emotively juxtaposed to the 'guilt' and 'inherent evilness' of the perpetrator. One example employed language and images of victims alongside images of those labelled as 'thugs'. This positioned blame at the level of the individual as well as the system that 'freed' them: 'THE MURDER VICTIMS WHO WOULD BE ALIVE TODAY IF THEIR KILLERS HADN'T BEEN GIVEN BAIL … AND THE THUGS WHO WERE FREED TO TERRORISE' (*Belfast Telegraph*, 14 April 2010: 4–5). This was common practice in news items relating to high profile cases. Journalists criticised initial responses to 'offending behaviour' and proposed that had, 'TROUBLE … BE[EN] NIPPED IN THE BUD' (*News Letter*, 31 July 2010: 22), then it might not have 'escalated'.

Criminal records and previous convictions were highlighted as further evidence of individual pathology. Further, they played a significant role in framing perpetrators as 'persistent offenders'. Representative examples included: 'CROSSAN IS BACK IN COURT' (*Andersonstown News*, 17 April 2010: 14) and 'BOY HAS TEN COURT DATES' (*Sunday World*, 4 April 2010: 26). In ongoing coverage of individuals, journalists made reference to previous convictions or similar behaviour to emphasise the relationship between crime and youth involvement in violence. One example was:

RAPIST QUINN IS OUT OF CONTROL, 21-YEAR-OLD ADMITS STRING OF OFFENCES MONTHS AFTER BEING RELEASED FROM JAIL, REVOLVING DOOR: MICHAEL QUINN AT AN EARLIER COURT APPEARANCE WHEN HE FACED CHARGES SURROUNDING THE SHOCKING RAPE OF A TEENAGE GIRL IN 2005. (*Andersonstown News*, 5 June 2010: 1)

Reference to previous media coverage indicated that this young man had been the focus of sustained media attention. It also indicated to the reader that the newspaper had been tracking and 'exposing' the alleged behaviour and crimes, as well as the impact on the community.

Intergenerational: Crimes Against the Elderly

The theme of intergenerational crimes against the elderly was prominent in 85 news items. Typically within headlines the age-specific words 'PENSIONER', 'OAP' and 'ELDERLY' were employed to alert the reader of the age and the presumed vulnerability of the alleged victims. One example was: 'TEENAGERS ARE MAKING LIFE A MISERY FOR OUR PENSIONERS' (*Andersonstown News*, 24 April 2010: 8), which highlighted journalists' juxtaposition of the vulnerability of the victim and the impact of the alleged behaviour of young people. It also employed the word 'our' to create a sense of ownership and solidarity amongst the readership and the victims. The emotive description evoked an immediate sense of sympathy for those referred to as 'PENSIONERS'. It also emphasised 'them' and 'us', whereby the victims were portrayed as being part of the 'inner community' of the readership (see Conboy 2006: 100). In direct contrast emotive language, such as 'TEENAGERS' and 'MISERY' was employed to firmly place young people outside of the 'law-abiding' community.

The term 'vulnerable' was consistently used to describe victims and this description was juxtaposed to labels such as 'thug' or 'teen', which framed the alleged perpetrator as 'guilty'. Juxtaposing vulnerability with criminal acts and violence, added an additional layer of vilification of youth: 'THUG IS JAILED FOR DRUG-FUELLED KILLING OF VULNERABLE OAP (71)' (*Belfast Telegraph*, 8 May 2010: 14). Images of alleged victims alongside headlines personalised the news item and presented a visual representation of the victim. Similarly the headline: 'OAPS TORTURED BY DRINKING, DRUG TAKING YOUTHS: GANGS OF YOUTHS GATHERING IN LOCAL ESTATE HAS EVEN FORCED LOCALS

FROM THEIR HOMES' (*North Belfast News*, 1 May 2010: 9), employed sensationalist language to describe young people as a 'gang'.

News items routinely emphasised the impact on victims, one example: 'GRANDMOTHER "LIVING IN NERVES" AFTER LATEST ATTACK ON HER HOME' (*North Belfast News*, 14 August 2010: 9), incorporated a direct quotation in the headline. News items typically featured direct quotations from those presented as victims, which emphasised the impact of crime. Headlines included: 'PENSIONER TELLS OF GANG ATTACK ON HIS FAMILY' (*News Letter*, 5 May 2010: 5); '"OPEN SEASON ON THE ELDERLY"; Seventy seven-year-old victim speaks out after crowbar robbery' (*South Belfast News*, 21 August 2010: 1–2) and 'OAPS "TORTURED" IN HOME: Pensioners the target of drug taking, foul mouthed youths outside their homes' (*North Belfast News*, 28 August 2010: 10). The inclusion of direct quotations personalised news items and intensified the juxtaposition between the representation of victims and perpetrators. One emotive example featured in several of the sample newspapers, with the *Belfast Telegraph* placing on its front page the following headline:

HOW TEENAGE THUGS ROBBED RUBY (82) OF THE WILL TO LIVE; TRAGIC RUBY BROKEN BY TEEN THUGS: PENSIONER DIED SOON AFTER BEING TARGETED BY MASKED ROBBERS; "MY MUM WAS 82 AND SO FULL OF LIFE … UNTIL THEY TOOK HER AWAY FROM ME". (*Belfast Telegraph*, 22 March 2010: 1, 4, 5)

Three images of Ruby and family members, accompanied the news item. One image was enlarged and printed on the front page; the size of the photograph of the victim covered the front page and was given prominence. Further images of the victim and the victim's family were presented in the double page news item.

Journalists reporting of another high profile case discussed the ongoing court case and framed the case commentary with a headline: 'TEEN KILLED OAP FOR £80 … AND THEN WATCHED TV, COURT HEARS' (*Belfast Telegraph*, 8 June 2010: 1). In transferring information from the courtroom to the public domain, the journalist labelled the accused as 'evil'. Similar to the above example, an image of the victim was prominent and descriptions reinforced vulnerability: 'partially-blind pensioner was stabbed and strangled in his own home by a teenager'. The journalist employed emotive language, such as 'the violent and brutal circumstances' and integrated selected words from the prosecution: 'The court was told that the accused claimed in a "fantastical tale" that he arrived after Mr O'Neill had died'.

'Gangs'

The label 'gangs' typically featured in news items relating to alleged crimes and anti-social behaviour, with 95 of the news items including 'gangs' as a prominent theme. Headlines typically employed the label alongside descriptions of 'victims' and details of the alleged act or behaviour. Examples of headlines included: 'THIRD NIGHT OF VIOLENCE AS GANGS CLASH WITH POLICE' (*Belfast Telegraph*, 14 July 2010: 5) and 'GANG HASSLING LOCAL PENSIONERS' (*South Belfast News*, 22 May 2010: 13). Words that accompanied the labels 'GANG' or 'GANGS' heightened tension and evoked notions of fear in relation to groups of young people. This was also evident in the main text of news items, with typical descriptions of young people as, 'gang of unruly youths' (*News Letter*, 28 May 2010: 10); 'rival gangs' (*Belfast Telegraph*, 18 June 2010: 18); 'gang of thugs' (*The Irish News*, 15 July 2010: 10); 'gangs of youths attacked police with missiles including fireworks and petrol bombs' (*The Irish News*, 12 July 2010: 5). Moral entrepreneurs framed 'gang activities' as 'drug-taking' or 'racketeering' (Lord Trimble quoted in, *The Irish News*, 9 June 2010: 6). Further descriptions such as, 'a rat pack gang of thieves and hoodlums who stole cars for high speed car thrills' (*Sunday World*, 4 July 2010: 4–5), made reference to 'vermin' and dehumanised young people.

Journalists also reinforced continued 'gang activity', by referring to previous news items or alleged incidents: 'Each year gangs of coat-trailing youths festoon the town with bunting and flags irrespective of the views of local residents' (*Sunday World*, 4 July 2010: 31). Similarly a Letter to the Editor entitled: 'BONFIRE GANGS ARE AT IT AGAIN' (*Andersonstown News*, 26 June 2010: 28), emphasised the perceived ongoing behaviour and problems. Not only were intergenerational relations emphasised in news items relating to 'gangs' and adult community members, but several news items stated that young people's behaviour negatively impacted on children: 'Gang of teenage girls … holding social meetings inside slide towers, rendering them out of order for younger children' (*News Letter*, 28 August 2010: 11).

Fitch (2009: 5) asserts that research studies such as Young et al. (2007) indicates that the label 'gangs' was imported from the United States (US) to the UK. Drawing on Aldridge et al. (2007) and Smith and Bradshaw's (2005) findings, Fitch (2009: 5) argues that in the contemporary setting the media, politicians and policy makers have adopted the label 'gangs' and have applied it to generalise and describe groups. Thus, the label 'gangs' is employed to refer to 'informal groups of young people who spend their leisure time assembled in the street' and it extends to descriptions of 'organised gangs' (Fitch 2009: 5; see also Batchelor 2001, 2009).

The *Andersonstown News* has produced sustained coverage of the 'IBA gang'. One journalist stated that the newspaper 'is aware of what IBA stands for but will not print the obscene name in full' (17 July 2010: 4). Typical representations referred to the 'IBA' as a 'notorious gang of around 12'. The following example illustrated that the young people were part of a distinct 'gang': 'rioting, involving about 100 anti-socials, including the St James' IBA gang' (*Andersonstown News*, 17 July 2010: 4–5). Another news item posed the question: 'SO JUST WHO ARE THE IBA ANYWAY?' (*Andersonstown News,* 17 July 2010: 4) and labelled the young people as 'St James' criminal gang', 'anti-social gang' and a 'mob' who were 'a dozen notorious youths … aged 17 to 23 … all from the St James' area [and] … well-known to locals'. Strong dehumanising language was employed: 'They are street rats … born and reared in St James' … their parents have either abdicated responsibility for their actions or, even worse, support them'. Two images of 'Bebo pages' were labelled as: 'EMBARRASSING: The IBA Bebo page gives an insight into the minds of the notorious gang'. The young people were described as 'a bunch of despised hooligans who have been terrorising the once pleasant and quiet neighbourhood for at least the past five years'. Quotations from anonymous adults, in particular residents, were given prominence:

> "They were up to no good when they were younger but now they are involved in proper crime from drug dealing to car theft and burglaries … drunk or on glue or drugs … fighting, giving abuse to residents and urinating in the streets".

Highlighting the age of the young people, the journalist stated that 'the gang has begun to gather a group of younger followers', with residents, 'want[ing] to put a stop to this … before they pollute the younger ones and lead them down the same path'.

Sustained coverage focused on descriptions of 'anti-social behaviour' and 'criminal activity', with the 'IBA', also referred to as 'the infamous criminal gang' who have 'defaced local businesses … on a graffiti rampage … terrorising the St James' area' and in doing so, have 'left their mark with paint and spray cans' (*Andersonstown News*, 19 July 2010: 8). The journalist positioned photographs of graffiti beside criticism and derogatory comments: 'Those behind the graffiti are uneducated and possibly even dyslexic – one slogan contains the letters "IAB" instead of "IBA"'. Previous media coverage was also referenced: 'The Andersonstown News also got a mention following our report on the history of criminal gang last week'. Politicians, in particular a local Sinn Féin Councillor, Breige Brownlee was quoted as calling for immediate action: 'This crowd of hoods need to be brought to book and parents need to seriously question what they are getting up to at night'.

Following a series of similar news items, a front page headline: "IBA GANG GIVEN 36 HOURS TO GET OUT: MASKED MEN FROM OGLAIGH NA HEIREANN ISSUE WARNING AFTER MARCHING THROUGH ST JAMES" (*Andersonstown News*, 31 July 2010: 1), presented the responses of an adult paramilitary group. The incident was also mentioned in other sample newspapers: 'a teenager narrowly avoided injury after being targeted in a suspected paramilitary-style attack ... in the St James's area' (*The Irish News*, 24 July 2010: 8). It was asserted that: 'Antisocial behaviour has reached an all-time high ... in recent months ... the emergence of a gang culture among youths has led to the upsurge'. Significantly existing academic commentary asserted that groups of young people, who spend their leisure time on the streets, were now labelled as 'gangs' in Northern Ireland (McAlister et al. 2011). However, the use this label is highly contested by research such as McAlister et al.'s (2011: 96) analysis, which describes its current use as an 'over-simplified application of the gang label'.

Anti-social Behaviour and Anti-community Behaviour

Anti-social behaviour was a prominent feature in 248 news items and the description 'anti-community' featured in 13 news items. Children and young people were regularly referred to in news items as: 'ANTI-SOCIALS' (*North Belfast News*, 1 May 2010: 4) and 'anti-social youths' (*Belfast Telegraph*, 1 July 2010: 12). In addition, themes such as alcohol and 'underage' drinking, drug taking, 'gangs' and crime were present. One example: 'it is attracting the usual anti-social element of drinkers and glue-sniffers ... harassing and intimidating passers-by' (*Andersonstown News*, 19 June 2010: 13), emphasised to the reader that this was a regular occurrence. A Letter to the Editor employed similar language: 'the realism is that gangs of young people, many ... full of drink or drugs attacked a respite home for disabled children and robbed businesses' and asked readers to 'support the community in the fight against these anti-social elements' (*The Irish News*, 23 July 2010: 24).

Descriptions of particular areas as 'anti-social hotspots' was a regular feature in news items, one example: 'PARENTS WARNED AS YOUNG PEOPLE GATHER WITH IRON BARS GANGS DISPERSED FROM RESIDENTAL AREA BECOMING AN ANTI-SOCIAL HOTSPOT' (*North Belfast News*, 29 May 2010: 15). Similarly new items that referred to the numbers of anti-social behaviour orders (ASBOs) issued in particular areas, labelled areas and communities as 'top of the list': 'BALLYMENA AT TOP OF PROVINCE'S ASBO TABLE' (*News Letter*, 28 April 2010: 4).

Moral entrepreneurs commented on the statistics: 'DUP councillor Sam Gaston says the figure comes as no surprise ... "Personally, I have heard of people getting these ASBOs and it didn't cool them down one bit"'. News items also typically featured imagery of young people in groups, with reference to areas and communities (for example: *Sunday World*, 21 March 2010: 17).

Journalists presented anti-social behaviour as a central concern within communities. Further, news items that featured the PSNI at local and managerial levels, considered tackling anti-social behaviour as one of their main community policing priorities. A news item that included an interview with the PSNI's Chief Constable, Matt Baggott, was an example: 'THE CHIEF CONSTABLE ON ... ANTI-SOCIAL BEHAVIOUR' (*News Letter*, 6 April 2010: 3). Further surveillance, regulation of children and young people in public spaces and the use of ASBOs, were measures typically promoted in news items. Examples of headlines included: 'HARASSED LOCALS HOPE ... CCTV IS ANSWER TO THEIR PRAYERS' (*Belfast Telegraph*, 12 March 2010: 24) and 'COMMUNITY SAFETY WARDENS TO TACKLE ANTI SOCIAL BEHAVIOUR' (*North Belfast News*, 8 May 2010: 10). ASBO's have been referred to in news items as punishment options: 'RIOTERS WARNED THEY WILL RECEIVE ASBOS' (*North Belfast News*, 26 June 2010: 11), with individual examples employed to reinforce community support for the measures: 'NOTORIOUS FALLS TEEN ... FINALLY HIT WITH ASBO' (*Andersonstown News*, 22 May 2010: 13).

News items that featured individual children, young people and their families, typically employed descriptions that condemned and sensationalised, for example: 'IT'S MUMMY'S LITTLE ASBOY; Judge lets young thug visit mother' (*Sunday Life*, 8 August 2010: 27), mocked the young man's application to visit his mother, in relation to his right to family life. In 'naming and shaming' the young male, the journalist labelled him: 'ONE of Ulster's worst thugs', who 'has had the conditions of his ASBO altered – so he can visit his mummy'. The journalist then proceeded to outline previous convictions and in doing so, employed descriptions such as, 'convicted drug dealer'; 'yob'; 'dozy thug' and 'cocky'. The news item stated that with '70 convictions' he 'terrorised the Co Antrim town' and 'broke his ASBO'. Printed photographs of the young male were referred to:

> As our picture shows McCrory celebrated outside Belfast Crown Court six years ago – when he was just 17 – after escaping jail when he was convicted of running a 'drugs supermarket'.

Reference made to previous news items indicated that the *Sunday Life* have sustained coverage of this young man.

Specific to Northern Ireland the term 'anti-community' was employed with reference to children and young people. The label featured in journalists' commentary and direct quotations by moral entrepreneurs, examples included a journalist labelling young people as being involved in 'anti-community activity' (*Andersonstown News*, 2 August 2010: 12) and a direct quotation from Sinn Féin MLA, Gerry Kelly, who stated that young people's behaviour was 'anti-community' (*North Belfast News*, 14 August 2010: 12). It explicitly presented children and young people as separate from the rest of the 'law-abiding' members of the community and against the community, in terms of rules, regulations and wellbeing.

Typically included alongside the term anti-social behaviour and criminality, the label 'anti-community' was employed by several of the sample newspapers. In 11 of the news items, journalists employed anti-community behaviour to refer to, and condemn children and young people's behaviour: 'Their actions are anti-social and anti-community. The only thing that they achieved was to cause further harm to this community' (*South Belfast News*, 17 July 2010: 2). Harm to the community was highlighted, with an emphasis on descriptions of the alleged incidents and perpetrators, juxtaposed to descriptions of the 'harm' caused to 'law-abiding' members of the community. The following example was representative of journalists' application of the label:

> Highly active cabal of anti-social elements and criminals so estranged from their community and so far beyond parental control that they are capable of the most appalling acts of anti-community behaviour.

The application of the 'anti-community' label firmly placed children and young people outside of their community and framed their perceived behaviour as acting outside of adult defined norms and established boundaries. As a label it is specific to Northern Ireland and its application positioned children and young people as contemporary 'folk devils'.

Alcohol and 'Underage' Drinking

Alcohol and 'underage' drinking featured as a prominent theme in 229 news items. There was a consistent link made between this theme and drug taking, anti-social and crime. The use of residents' quotations within the headline, presented a personalised reaction, with typical headlines incorporating words and phrases from adults: 'ANOTHER WEEKEND OF "TORTURE" AT

THE BONE: KIDS' TOYS AND RESIDENT'S CAR TARGETED BY TEENS DRINKING AT "RAVE" SITE' (*North Belfast News*, 27 February 2010: 11). Typically news items included references to 'groups' or 'gangs' of young people drinking alcohol: 'Teenage boys and girls … congregated in large groups with many drinking heavily … young people shouted and blasted horns' (*The Irish News*, 13 July 2010: 15).

Age was highlighted in both references to the age of the child or young person and other descriptions, typically the word 'underage', which made reference to 'not of legal age'. One news item, with the headline: 'UNDERAGE DRINKER "12 YEARS OLD"' (*News Letter*, 10 March 2010: 13), indicated the young age of the child. Similarly in an opinion piece about young people and rioting, written by a Queen's University academic, the description of children added to the condemnation:

[L]ook at how many young people are drinking alcohol at a Belfast Twelfth parade. I have routinely watched children who are barely teenagers carrying bottles of beer, apparently unchallenged. (*News Letter*, 19 July 2010: 11)

'Binge drinking' was a term employed in media discourse to suggest high levels of alcohol consumption and drunkenness. One example employed statistics to raise concerns about young women: 'the biggest growth group in terms of binge drinking and overdoses are among girls between 11 and 15 years old' (*The Irish News*, 20 August 2010: 14). An additional layer of shock, concern and condemnation existed in news items that referred to children and alcohol. Typically journalists highlighted the PSNI response: 'BINGE DRINKING WARNING' (*Belfast Telegraph*, 12 March 2010: 26) and 'ALCOHOL SEIZED FROM TEENAGERS' (*Belfast Telegraph*, 25 May 2010: 12).

Alcohol was typically associated with anti-social behaviour, crime and violence. Quotations from moral entrepreneurs emphasised the role alcohol played: 'JUDGE CLAIMS 80% OF CASES BEFORE HIM ALCOHOL RELATED' (*The Irish News*, 15 April 2010: 11). Adult condemnation and warnings to young people were evident, with one example that called for young people to: 'TREAT ALCOHOL WITH RESPECT' (*The Irish News*, 5 July 2010: 10).

Drug Taking and Smoking

Drug taking and smoking was a prominent theme in 311 news items. There was a close relationship in the media coverage between alcohol and 'underage' drinking and the theme of drug taking and smoking. As outlined above, while 'underage' drinking and young people's alcohol consumption was presented in the news items as a central concern, this adult concern appeared amplified with regard to drug-taking: 'Drink is the main problem, but they are standing on street corners sniffing drugs and taking pills' (*Belfast Telegraph*, 19 July 2010: 22).

Descriptions of children and young people smoking featured in news items relating to 'underage' activities. One headline: 'CALLS TO BAN CIG MACHINES' (*Sunday Life*, 11 July 2010: 27), presented how 'easy' it is for children and young to access cigarettes. However, the most sensationalist language was employed by journalists to describe alleged drug taking. Typical representations included: 'young drug dealers' (*North Belfast News*, 29 May 2010: 1); 'young wannabe dealers' (*Sunday World*, 11 July 2010: 28); 'drugged-up hoods' (*Andersonstown News*, 24 May 2010: 15), to describe groups of young people. Individuals have been described as, 'the drink-and-drugs loving thug' (*Sunday Life*, 25 July 2010: 27); 'HIGH AS A KITE … STONED OUT OF HIS HEAD … ' (*Sunday World*, 28 March 2010: 21) and locations described as a 'drugs den' (*Sunday Life*, 27 June 2010: 31). Typically, residents were quoted in news items, linking 'underage' drinking and drug taking to anti-social behaviour and crime: 'Young ones are outside drinking and taking drugs … [you] can't go out and reprimand them because the abuse they give is just obscene' (*North Belfast News*, 28 August 2010: 10).

Headlines such as: 'PARENTS ARE FEARFUL OF DRUGS MORE THAN GUNS' (*Belfast Telegraph*, 10 August 2010: 7) and 'TEENAGE youths across the West are turning towards a dangerous new craze of sniffing fumes from gas cylinders' (*Andersonstown News*, 7 August 2010: 10), evoked a sense of panic and indicated high levels of concern. This was also evident in news items featuring parents, particularly in relation to calls for assistance, for changes to be made to the law and for other parents to be vigilant in monitoring their children's behaviour:

EXCLUSIVE: MOTHER FEARS FOR HER OTHER CHILDREN … "I KNEW I'D LOSE MY SON TO DRUGS BUT WHEN I HEARD … I FELT MY HEART WAS RIPPED OUT". (*Sunday World*, 14 March 2010: 4–5)

Other examples included calls for the government to ensure that young people received adequate assistance: 'TEEN DENIED DRUG SUPPORT DESPITE OVERDOSING TWICE' (*South Belfast News*, 29 May 2010: 1). While news items typically exposed the ineffectiveness of the support available and concern for young people's safety, they also included another dimension to them. For instance, news items emphasised the relationship between drug taking and crime: 'BOY (15) IS ON THE RUN FROM DEALERS, DISTRAUGHT PARENTS TELL US HOW THEIR ONCE NORMAL TEENS ARE NOW STRANGERS' (*Andersonstown News*, 17 April 2010: 1). This news item included descriptions of a young man allegedly stealing money from his parents. Similar links were made in relation to drug taking and violence: 'BAP'S KILLER WAS SO HIGH HIS "EYES WERE POPPING"' (*Andersonstown News*, 22 March 2010: 2).

Prominence given to concerns surrounding the drug mephedrone was a significant feature throughout the data collection period, with a high level of news items printed in the month of March. Sustained coverage and the use of language provoked panic surrounding mephedrone. News items linked mephedrone to youth suicide and attempted suicide: 'DEATH FEARS OVER MEPHEDRONE USE: YOUNG PEOPLE ARE TAKING THEIR LIVES IN THEIR HANDS: WARNING' (*Andersonstown News*, 27 March 2010: 16) and 'DRUG LINKED TO DEATH IS A "GROWING THREAT"' (*News Letter*, 18 March 2010: 10). Journalists' selection of language included 'warning' and 'threat', which heightened concern and panic. Headlines included: 'WARNING TO PROTECT OUR YOUTH FROM PARTY DRUG' (*Belfast Telegraph*, 26 March 2010: 14), which juxtaposed adult concern with what was framed as youth 'recklessness'. Some of the sample newspapers highlighted their role in 'revealing' and campaigning for the drug to be banned: 'LAST NOVEMBER THE NORTH BELFAST NEWS REVEALED THAT THE LEGAL DRUG DRONE HAD HIT THE STREETS OF NORTH BELFAST ... DRUGS CLAIM ANOTHER LIFE' (*North Belfast News*, 27 March 2010: 1).

Amplification of children and young people's alleged drug-use was evident in headlines such as: 'MORE CHILDREN USE COCAINE' (*Belfast Telegraph*, 2 March 2010: 15); 'MORE YOUTHS ON COCAINE' (*The Irish News*, 2 March 2010: 8) and 'USE OF DRONE IS NOW AN EPIDEMIC ... AMONGST KIDS' (*North Belfast News*, 6 March 2010: 1–2). Journalists employed direct quotations from parents and moral entrepreneurs to call for increased surveillance of children and young people: 'JUDGE "DISMAYED" BY DRUGS PROBLEM' (*News Letter*, 5 March 2010: 11) and 'MORE NEEDS DONE' (*Andersonstown News*, 22 March 2010: 2). Further, this use of language called for punitive criminal justice responses to be directed towards those found in possession of the drug.

Other 'Risky' Behaviours and Truancy

Children and young people's behaviour was also defined as 'risky' and as 'truancy'. In some incidents these descriptions were positioned next to descriptions of anti-social behaviour and crime, such as 'child truancy ... and anti-social behaviour' (*North Belfast News*, 5 June 2010: 12), to suggest a relationship between truancy and anti-social behaviour and crime. In other examples, 'risky' behaviour and truancy were distinct descriptions. Overall, 171 news items featured 'risky' behaviours and/or truancy as a prominent theme.

Regarding the traditional definition of truancy, a number of the headlines referred to children's absence from school without permission. One news item entitled: 'ACTION DEMANDED ON SCHOOL TRUANCY', relied on comments from one politician and stated: 'Corner boys: Truancy can lead to a cycle of deprivation, according to UUP Assemblyman for East Antrim Roy Beggs' (*Belfast Telegraph*, 18 June 2010: 8). This news item focused on proposed long-term consequences of truancy and argued that 'action' should involve closer surveillance and regulation of children and young people, particularly those from 'disadvantaged areas'. It also asserted that parents' legal obligations and 'responsibilities' should be enforced.

The media's portrayal of children's and young people's behaviour as 'risky' took two distinct forms. Children and young people were either presented as 'at risk' or as posing a 'risk' to others or themselves (see Cottle 2001: 35; Brownlie 2005: 510). 'Risky' behaviours were typically linked to crime, for example: 'Social Services have said that they will intervene if young people are involved in "risky or criminal behaviour"' (*Belfast Telegraph*, 17 July 2010: 4). Young people's behaviour was presented as posing a 'risk' to themselves and others, within news items on 'fatal car accidents' and 'car crime'. One high profile example that received considerable media coverage related to a car accident in which seven young men and one man in his sixties died following a road traffic collision. The Priest's plea: 'PLEASE LIVE WITHIN THE RULES OF LIFE', was presented within the headline (*Belfast Telegraph*, 16 July 2010: 14), as a central element of the news item, to emphasise that adults 'were implor[ing] [young people] to live life "on its terms, within its rules and boundaries"'.

Further, 'risk' was also a central theme within news items on 'joy riding' or 'death driving'. Headlines and the main text reiterated the 'risk' young people placed themselves and others in and the potential consequences: 'HIGH-RISK, HIGH-SPEED CRIME WITH FATAL ALLURE' (*Belfast Telegraph*, 29 June 2010: 6). Within the main text of this news item the journalist stated that this 'risky' behaviour indicated that:

There is huge defiance of ... authority, towards ... the IRA – who once ruled these areas with an iron fist and kneecapped 'death drivers' – and the PSNI, particularly the dedicated Auto Crime Team.

Children and young people were portrayed as 'at risk' of manipulation, particularly in news items relating to rioting. The following description: 'Young people are ... the most at risk because dissidents are using them as cannon fodder' (*Belfast Telegraph*, 2 June 2010: 14–15), was echoed in other sample newspapers (*News Letter*, 17 July 2010: 6, 11; *The Irish News*, 17 July 2010: 13). Such descriptions related closely to the label 'disaffected youth'. In addition, journalists made reference to the Conflict, with one headline that described children and young people as: 'A NEW GENERATION AT RISK: YOUNG, ANGRY ... AND BACK ON THE STREETS' (*Belfast Telegraph*, 20 July 2010: 25). The journalist employed imagery that emphasised Northern Ireland's history. Further, this asserted how the actions of contemporary 'folk devils' evoked notions of 'history repeating itself'.

Other news items employed images of the violence of the Conflict to suggest that the actions of the current generation of children and young people could impact negatively on the process of transition. One journalist employed descriptions of youths rioting to reinforce the argument that children and young people had a lack of knowledge and hold, 'MISH-MASH' views which 'HINDER THE HEALING PROCESS' (*Belfast Telegraph*, 21 July 2010: 26). The journalist focused on children and young people's role, to argue that 'it is all too easy for generations born after the Good Friday Agreement to become embroiled in violence relating to the conflict'. The news item framed Northern Ireland as 'a society which does not learn from the mistakes of the past' and 'is doomed to repeat them'.

Youth Involvement in Violence

This theme relates to violence against others or violence against the self, which refers to suicide and self-harm.

Violence and Violent Acts

Youth involvement in violence and violent acts was a prominent theme in 1,038 news items. Typically, journalists employed sensationalist language to describe violence, with specific focus placed on descriptions of the acts, a focus on the perpetrator and the impact or potential impact on victims and the community. Media descriptions of children and young people's alleged involvement in violence against others were at the sharp end of the continuum of demonisation and vilification of youth. Headlines included: 'YOUTHS WERE "OUT TO KILL" ON A NIGHT OF HORRIFIC VIOLENCE' (*Belfast Telegraph*, 1 March 2010: 4–5); 'YOUTHS FIGHT WITH BATS AND KNIVES' (*News Letter*, 17 April 2010: 12); 'BOY THIEF PUNCHES PENSIONER' (*Belfast Telegraph*, 22 March 2010: 13) and 'WOMAN PUNCHED ... BY TEEN MUGGER' (*The Irish News*, 22 March 2010: 21). Descriptions of the acts, weapons and victims were prominent. The words 'violence' or 'violent' regularly featured within headlines, such as: 'TEENS ARRESTED AFTER VIOLENCE FLARES' (*Andersonstown News*, 21 June 2010: 8), and 'NO "CAUSE" CAN JUSTIFY VIOLENCE' (*Belfast Telegraph*, 1 March 2010: 28). These representative examples presented dramatic descriptions of violent acts and criticised any proposed alternative explanations other than individual pathology.

News items framing young people as the perpetrators of violence directed towards the PSNI, was a common feature. Representative examples included: 'POLICE COME UNDER ATTACK FROM YOUTHS' (*News Letter*, 8 April 2010: 4); 'YOUTHS ATTACK POLICE' (*News Letter*, 18 June 2010: 12); 'BRICK HITS POLICEWOMAN AS SHE DEALS WITH YOBS' (*Belfast Telegraph*, 1 July 2010: 12) and 'YOUTH "ATTACKED POLICE WITH POLE"' (*News Letter*, 3 August 2010: 11). Exaggerated language and imagery was routinely employed to emphasise individual wrongdoing. One headline: 'SICK 4AM ATTACK, PSYCHO KILLER: SNEERING TEENAGER THROWS CONCRETE BLOCK AND KILLS FAMILY'S TREASURED CAT' (*Sunday World*, 27 June 2010: 22), included images of the accused. Alongside images of the young male, the journalist stated: 'THIS ... snarling teenager from hell ... hurled a breeze block'.

High profile cases involving violent acts and murder received sustained coverage. Journalists referred to 'previous criminal convictions' in order to amplify the alleged involvement of young people in violence. One example was: 'TWO juveniles ... charged with attempting to murder a 30-year-old man ... one ... has 38 previous criminal convictions' (*Sunday World*, 1 August 2010: 7). In particular the *Andersonstown News*, reported regularly on two murder cases that occurred in the West Belfast area. The murder of Frank McGreevy received sustained coverage, with headlines focusing on the court case and sentencing. Descriptions included direct quotations from members of the victim's family: 'FAMILY CONTENT "EVIL" KILLER WILL SERVE AT LEAST 17 YEARS' (*The Irish News*, 26 March 2010: 24). A focus on the young male's 'CRIMINAL RECORD' was prominent in news items (*Andersonstown News*,

29 March 2010: 1, 6, 8). Moral entrepreneurs commented by welcoming the length of the sentence. Another case was presented in a similar way, with a focus on the perpetrator and emphasis on the PSNI investigation: 'SEAMUS FOX MURDER WILL BE A TEST FOR BAGGOTT AND THE PSNI' (*Andersonstown News*, 3 May 2010: 16).

It was usual for journalists to refer back to case examples when discussing a new case. This reinforced how the media sustained coverage of cases involving young people. One example: 'VALLIDAY TERM COMPARED TO OTHER KILLINGS, ALLISON MORRIS COMPARES THOMAS VALLIDAY'S 17-YEAR SENTENCES IN OTHER RECENT HIGH-PROFILE MURDER CASES IN WEST BELFAST' (*The Irish News*, 26 March 2010: 24), compared the perpetrators and prison sentences. Retribution was outlined not only in news items that directly proposed punishments and called for punitive responses, but was evident in news items that followed the sentencing and imprisonment of young people, with one headline stating: 'THEY GOT WHAT THEY DESERVED' (*Andersonstown News*, 8 March 2010: 1, 3).

Rioting and Interface Violence

Rioting and interface violence featured as a theme in 449 of the news items, significantly with the highest concentration in July and August. Typically the focus was on the alleged acts and behaviour of children and young people; the impact on communities; parental responsibility; criticism of police responses and a call for punitive responses directed towards children and young people. Chapter 5 will analyse in greater depth the July and August media coverage and the political, societal and criminal justice responses.

Details of interface violence made reference to sectarianism: 'Young people wielding machetes, meat cleavers and iron bars … scaling a "peace wall" … in order to get involved in sectarian rioting' (*North Belfast News*, 5 June 2010: 1). The location was labelled as a '"no go" area … as teenage rioters take over' (*North Belfast News*, 5 June 2010: 1). This further emphasised the impact on 'the community' and reinforced the 'outsider' status of young people (see Becker 1963). Similar news items focused on the responses of adults: 'RECREATIONAL RIOTING AND STAGED VIOLENCE BRINGING MISERY TO GLENGORMLEY RESIDENTS' (*North Belfast News*, 1 May 2010: 8) and 'KIDS TURN ON THEIR OWN COMMUNITY AFTER INTERFACE RIOT FAILS TO MATERIALISE' (*North Belfast News*, 6 March 2010: 8).

Quotations from moral entrepreneurs repeatedly featured in the main text of news items and in the composition of headlines. Examples included: 'SF URGES KIDS: STOP THIS RIOT NONSENSE' (*Belfast Telegraph*, 26 May 2010: 11), which described children and young people's behaviour as 'senseless' and 'SDLP "DISAPPOINTED" WITH YOUTHS AS POLICE USE CS GAS' (*The Irish News*, 19 April 2010: 15). Both articles condemned children and young people's alleged behaviour, highlighted in words selected, such as: 'DISAPPOINTED'. The focus remained on the behaviour of young people and whilst 'CS GAS' (Tear Gas) was mentioned, the latter news item clearly framed its use by the PSNI as a necessity.

Journalists and moral entrepreneurs quoted, condemned and directed blame at parents, which emphasised parental responsibility. Headlines included: 'WHERE ARE THE PARENTS WHEN THESE KIDS ARE RUNNING RIOT?' (*North Belfast News*, 6 March 2010: 6) and a Letter to the Editor stated, 'PARENTS HAVE TO TAKE RAP FOR THEIR CHILDREN' (*Andersonstown News*, 28 June 2010: 16). Similarly the following news item 'warned' parents: 'PARENTS' RIOT WARNING: YOUNG PEOPLE THROWING PETROL BOMBS AT CARS AND THE POLICE' (*Andersonstown News*, 13 March 2010: 12).

In emphasising the need for surveillance, discipline and control of children and young people, journalists referred back to prior reported incidents and used words such as 'more' and 'ongoing' to amplify children and young people's persistent involvement in rioting. In doing so, journalists heightened tension, as the following headlines demonstrated: 'MORE RIOTING ON THE SPRINGFIELD' (*Andersonstown News*, 6 March 2010: 9) and 'CONCERNS GROW OVER INTERFACE RIOTING' (*North Belfast News*, 5 June 2010: 2). Similarly journalists' use of the word 'warning' framed the location as a point of 'trouble': 'WARNING AFTER YOUNG PEOPLE CLASH AT FINAGHY CROSSROADS' (*Andersonstown News*, 7 June 2010: 6). Calls for 'something to be done' were evident, with proposed responses in the form of punitive measures: 'RIOTERS WARNED THEY WILL RECEIVE ASBOS' (*North Belfast News*, 26 June 2010: 11).

Youth Suicide, Attempted Suicide and Self-Harm

Violence against the self was a prominent theme, with 154 news items on youth suicide, attempted suicide and self-harm. Alcohol, under-age drinking and drug misuse typically featured in news items on youth suicide, attempted suicide and self-harm. One news item: '18,000 YOUNG PEOPLE IN

ULSTER "HAVE FELT SUICIDAL"' (*News Letter*, 24 May 2010: 9), linked 'youth employment' to suicidal feelings and included direct quotations from one charity representative: 'While some young people respond through being hostile, angry and volatile – often bolstered by alcohol – others withdraw into themselves'.

Age was highlighted in news items, particularly the young age of children and young people was included to evoke shock, with examples drawing on direct quotations from councillors: 'KIDS AS YOUNG AS FIVE HAVING SUICIDAL THOUGHTS' (*North Belfast News*, 24 July 2010: 1). A similar news item emphasised: 'FEARS OVER SUICIDE BIDS' (*News Letter*, 29 July 2010: 15), with age highlighted: 'Some of these people are as young as 16'. 'Boy', 'girl' and 'young' were words also employed to indicate age: 'YOUNG MUM TAKES OWN LIFE 8 MONTHS AFTER TWIN SISTER' (*The Irish News*, 31 March 2010: 1) and 'EXCLUSIVE … Boy who nearly drank himself to death tries to take own life' (*Sunday Life*, 8 August 2010: 8). The latter news item also included descriptions of alcohol consumption and drug taking.

Drug taking and youth suicide were prominent particularly in March, when there was the highest volume of news items relating to mephedrone.[3] News items, such as: 'DRUG "IS PUTTING KIDS IN COFFINS"' (*Belfast Telegraph*, 25 March 2010: 1) and 'PARENTS BLAME LEGAL DRUG FOR TEEN'S SUICIDE' (*News Letter*, 26 March 2010: 4), framed mephedrone as a major contributory factor. Sustained coverage was central in the media's amplification of young people's drug-use. This is consistent with well-established research (for example, Young 1971), reinforced in contemporary analyses (Bessant 2003), asserting that there is news-value in conflating young people's drug taking.

Personal accounts of young people featured in the media coverage. One example, based on personal experiences of a young man, included direct quotations: "DRUG LEFT ME SO DEPRESSED I TRIED TO KILL MYSELF" (*News Letter*, 14 April 2010: 20–21). The journalist stated that 'the true effects of so-called "legal highs" become chillingly obvious', 'WHEN a 20-year-old … with his whole life ahead of him, looks you in the eye and tells you he "doesn't mind" if he dies, that's when you know drugs have taken over'. Details of violence against the self were included: 'he admits to putting a knife to his throat' and 'leaving harrowing messages all over the walls'. Another example included direct quotations and listed 'crimes' the young man allegedly committed: 'HELP ME … PLEADS SUICIDAL TEEN DRUG ADDICT: BOY'S CATALOGUE OF CRIME BEFORE HE FINALLY TRIED TO HANG HIMSELF' (*North Belfast News*, 20 March 2010: 1–2).

It was more prominent for families and community workers to be quoted, with journalists including several images of family members holding photographs of the deceased. Headlines such as, 'FAMILIES AIR GRIEF TO END SUICIDE' (*Sunday Life*, 11 April 2010: 17), presented personalised experiences and called on other young people not to 'waste' their lives. Several news items included calls for support and funding: 'SBN OVERDOSE STORY "HIGHLIGHTS NEED FOR YOUTH FACILITY"' (*South Belfast News*, 12 June 2010: 1). In addition, several news items exposed the lack of facilities and the treatment of suicidal young people: 'TEEN SUICIDE PARENTS CHALLENGE MINISTER, 19-YEAR-OLD TOOK HIS OWN LIFE FOLLOWING 8-HOUR HOSPITAL WAIT' (*The Irish News*, 27 August 2010: 4–5).

It was usual for journalists to compare and refer to previous youth suicides and news items. One example: 'MEOW MEOW DEATH NO5' (*Sunday Life*, 11 April 2010: 16–17), referred to five incidents of youth suicide and included images of the young people. The journalist included descriptive information such as: 'Tragic drug-user Ryan Strachan slashed his wrists' and 'turned to drugs in 2008 after a drug-crazed father and son almost battered him to death in an unprovoked attack'. The suicide of one young male received considerable media attention and was referred to in relation to other suicides. One example: 'A LIFE LOST TO "LEGAL HIGHS", BAN MEOW NOW TRAGIC JAMIE FOUND DEAD AFTER BATTLING AN ADDICTION TO MEPHEDRONE' (*Sunday Life*, 28 March 2010: 6–7), directly called for mephedrone to be banned. Sustained coverage placed mephedrone as a central concern. Phrases such as 'epidemic' and panics relating to drug-use in previous decades were referred to: 'In the 1980s a lot of people ... died from heroin use. Then in the Nineties there were a lot of drug related deaths and suicides' (*News Letter*, 14 April 2010: 20–21), and heightened concern.

The media's use of quotations and images of young people accessed from social networking sites such as Facebook and Bebo was a regular feature. Images printed were typically of the deceased, as well as their family and friends. Images selected of young people socialising with their peer group, were typically framed as part of the 'drug culture' and 'party scene'. This reflects Critcher's (2003) analysis of the amplification and stereotypical representations of 'the rave/ecstasy culture' of the late 1980s and early 1990s. In addition, copies of comments written by young people were printed within the main text of news items, one example: 'SHOCKED PALS SHARE THEIR GRIEF ON WEB' (*Sunday Life*, 28 March 2010: 6), was based on comments shared between young people on their social networking sites.

News items proposed responses, many of which suggested closer surveillance. One example: 'MP BACKS MOVES TO CRACK DOWN ON SUICIDE WEBSITES' (*Belfast Telegraph*, 26 June 2010: 14), referred to the 'irresponsible' role of internet websites, with the Member of Parliament (MP) stating that he 'support[s] every effort to investigate ... clamping down on this kind of behaviour'.

Demand for Punitive Responses

Demand for punitive responses appeared as a prominent theme in 335 news items and related to 'calls for something to be done' about children and young people's involvement in anti-social behaviour, crime and violence. Typically, such calls were presented in the form of direct quotations from adults, such as members of the community, victims or the families of victims and moral entrepreneurs. Further, journalists' commentaries and their use of language included direct calls for community, criminal justice, legal and policy responses.

Responses at community level were emphasised in news items, such as: 'LOCALS HAVE A DUTY TO BANISH MINDLESS THUGS' (*Belfast Telegraph*, 15 July 2010: 30). Direct questions posed by journalists, such as: 'SO WHAT'S BEING DONE ABOUT ALL THE ANTI-SOCIAL BEHAVIOUR?' (*Andersonstown News*, 20 March 2010: 8) framed anti-social behaviour as a major issue that required a direct response. Similarly headlines such as: 'MORE NEEDS DONE TO COMBAT "MEPH" MENACE' (*Andersonstown News*, 22 March 2010: 2); 'POLICEWOMAN'S DAD: "I WANT TOUGHER ACTION AGAINST THESE THUGS"' (*Belfast Telegraph*, 15 July 2010: 4) and 'IT IS NOW TIME TO COME DOWN HARD ON RIOTERS' (*Belfast Telegraph*, 24 July 2010: 26), called for quick, punitive responses directed towards children and young people.

Calls for the PSNI to respond regularly featured: 'ANTI-SOCIAL ATTACKS WILL ONLY GET WORSE UNLESS TACKLED BY PSNI SAY LOCALS' (*South Belfast News*, 17 April 2010: 18) and 'POLICE CALLED ON TO RESPOND BETTER' (*The Irish News*, 1 March 2010: 9). Accompanying descriptions such as: 'CLAMPDOWN AS POLICE MOVE IN TO CLEAR PARKS' and 'GET-TOUGH POLICY' (*Andersonstown News*, 7 June 2010: 1) emphasised calls for quick and firm responses from the PSNI. Specific responses, such as increased 'arrests' and surveillance of children and young people were prominent, for example: 'RESIDENTS WANT POLICE TO ARREST RIOTERS' (*News Letter*, 15 July 2010: 5).

Criticisms of PSNI responses reinforced the call for more punitive measures to be employed. One journalist stated that: 'there is a strong feeling in the law-abiding community that police could have done more … particularly with … children involved' and asserted that, 'questions are being asked … why police snatch squads were not utilised … why … baton rounds were not used to bring the violence under control?' (*News Letter*, 16 July 2010: 20). A news item written by the Editor of the *Belfast Telegraph* presented a similar opinion, reinforced in the headline: 'TIME FOR ACTION ON YOB CULTURE' and argued that: 'It is high time … the PSNI made a more comprehensive and high-profile attempt to eradicate yobbism … Actions … speak louder than words' (23 August 2010: 26).

In response, the PSNI regularly outlined the measures available and 'warned' children and young people. One journalist stated that: 'The PSNI … have urged young people to be aware of the consequences of their actions', as 'culprits could … find themselves subject to Acceptable Behavioural Contracts and ASBOs' (*North Belfast News*, 26 June 2010: 8). Similarly, comments of individual judges and the judiciary also appeared as authoritative voices presenting condemnation and reinforcing criminal justice responses. The media focused on particular cases and positioned them as being significant issues. Typically, what followed was a focus on specific crimes and strong messages that they would not be accepted: 'COURT VOW TO TRAMPLE ON SECTARIAN CRIMES' (*Belfast Telegraph*, 27 May 2010: 16) and 'COURTS "WILL NOT TOLERATE HATE CRIMES"' (*News Letter*, 27 May 2010: 11).

Retributive criminal justice responses were proposed regularly in news items, with high levels of media support given to Judges who issued 'long' prison sentences. Typical headlines such as: 'GUILTY DUO "SHOULD NOT BE FREED"' (*Belfast Telegraph*, 8 May 2010: 10), included calls for the imprisonment of two young males, indefinitely. Similarly, news items, such as: 'THE EVIL KILLERS LEFT TO FESTER IN OUR JAILS' (*Belfast Telegraph*, 12 May 2010: 7), described several high profile cases and prisoners in Northern Ireland, listing examples of young men currently imprisoned. Prison sentences were deemed 'not long enough', with headlines such as: 'CONTROVERSIAL CASES WHERE SENTENCES CAUSED ANGER' (*Belfast Telegraph*, 19 June 2010: 5) and 'PENSIONER BLINDED IN ONE EYE SAYS ATTACKER SHOULD GET LONGER JAIL SENTENCE' (*The Irish News*, 30 June 2010: 19). Journalists included direct quotations from victims or their families, to evoke notions of innocence, vulnerability and sympathy on the part of 'undeserving' victims (see Greer 2007). This added to the intense descriptions of perpetrators, with emphasis on individual pathology and notions of evilness and guilt.

Calls for changes to the law and the introduction of legislation to 'tackle' issues, was a regular theme. News items directly proposed reasons as to why legislation should be introduced: 'WHY WE NEED TO PUT NEW LEGISLATION IN PLACE' (*Belfast Telegraph*, 14 April 2010: 5). Proposed measures were typically 'tough' and punitive in nature, with journalists emphasising this in the use of language employed: 'TOUGH LAWS NEEDED FOR KNIFE CRIME' (*Sunday World*, 15 August 2010: 18); 'DANGEROUS DRUG MUST BE OUTLAWED' (*News Letter*, 26 March 2010: 18) and 'MLA CALLS FOR TOUGHER ACTION' (*North Belfast News*, 27 March 2010: 10). Each example included a call for immediate action and directly outlined proposed responses.

Pressure placed on the Department of Justice (DOJ NI) and the Justice Minister, David Ford, regularly featured throughout news items. Headlines included: 'FORD NEEDS TO GET HIS ACT IN GEAR' (*North Belfast News*, 15 May 2010: 6) and the following example that employed an emotive case to reinforce calls for punitive responses:

REMEMBER KATIE, AS THE KILLER OF THIS YOUNG WOMAN GETS JUST 14 YEARS BEHIND BARS, THERE'S A SIMPLE MESSAGE FOR THE JUSTICE MINISTER AS HE CONSIDERS NEW ANTI-CRIME MEASURES. (*Belfast Telegraph*, 19 June 2010: 1)

Juxtaposed to the emotive description of the young female victim, was harsh language to emphasise that: 'Life [sentences] should mean life'. Another example stated that it 'is time for the Executive and Justice Minister to consider if parents should have a legal ... obligation to control the behaviour of their children' (*Belfast Telegraph*, 17 July 2010: 24). Letters to the Editor also proposed the implementation of punitive responses such as 'jail time' and the use of 'tasers', with a forceful title: 'ASSEMBLY MUST TAKE TOUGH LINE ON RIOTING' (*News Letter*, 20 July 2010: 18). The author argued that 'this mindset of ... today's youth on the streets stems from the lack of ... discipline' and proposes the implementation of 'a much more severe penalty ... (hard labour in jail)'. In criticising the government, the author argued that 'the present laws are a laugh ... rules must be changed' (*News Letter*, 23 July 2010: 20). In line with Pearson's (1983) analysis, the letter concluded that: 'It's time our leaders remembered their old school days and the cane' (*News Letter*, 23 July 2010: 20).

Criticisms were directed towards the government for not taking direct action on certain issues. One example: 'DEPARTMENT CRITICISED FOR LACK OF ACTION ON "LEGAL HIGH DRUG"' (*The Irish News*, 26

March 2010: 16), reflected the media's stance on mephedrone and placed pressure on the government to 'ban' the drug. The then Health Minister was an example of a 'moral entrepreneur' who had access to the media to respond: 'BANNING MEPHEDRONE PRAISED BY MCGIMPSEY' (*The Irish News*, 30 March 2010: 19).

Conclusion

This chapter has analysed the print media's representation of children and young people in Northern Ireland. The content analysis findings illustrated how 'meaning' is produced and constructed. In line with the literature on 'news values', 'newsworthiness' and 'crime reporting' (Galtung and Ruge 1965, 1982; Chibnall 1977), the analysis of language and imagery confirmed Wyke's (2001) argument that in the contemporary setting, broader cultural relations around gender, ethnicity and in particular age, need to be considered. The analysis clearly acknowledged that headlines have 'important textual and cognitive functions' and 'ideological implications' (van Dijk 1991: 50) for the ways in which children and young people were represented and subsequently responded to. Further, the analysis reinforced how images and photographs gain some of their meaning from the context and language that frames them (Bignell 1997).

Consistent with previous research, negative ideological constructions were prominent in the media coverage (Glover 1984; Briggs and Cobley 2002). The 'hegemonic function' of the published language and imagery, identified, categorised, demonised and criminalised children and young people (Lacey 1998). The analysis demonstrated how overgeneralisations reduced children and young people's perceived behaviours to exaggerations, by focusing on negative 'character traits' (Barker 1999) and emphasising individual pathology. Representations were stereotypical and were reinforced by 'official' views from moral entrepreneurs, which is consistent with previous studies on the media's representation of crime (Kidd-Hewitt 1995; Bessant and Hil 1997). The evident marginalisation or exclusion of 'alternative voices' and the rights discourse, confirmed that news items represented only 'partial account[s] of reality' (McNair 1994: 34). This is significant as the news items analysed provide for most people their primary source of information on 'crime', 'offenders' and punishment (Erikson 1966). As the content analysis demonstrated, there are aspects that are consistent with academic literature and studies from other jurisdictions.

In addition, there are elements of the analysis that are specific to Northern Ireland. Poignant examples included journalists' use of language and labels such as 'anti-community' and 'hoods' and the prominent crosscutting theme of the legacy of the Conflict. The theme of the legacy of the Conflict was referred to explicitly in 505 news items and implicitly featured within a number of other themes, such as the media reports of rioting and interface violence. Typical descriptions such as, 'clashes reminiscent of the dark days of the Troubles' (*News Letter*, 15 July 2010: 4), compared contemporary rioting and interface violence to the Conflict. A prominent quotation from the First Minister, Peter Robinson, reinforced condemnation: 'We are particularly disappointed when we see young people involved and the baton of hatred being handed on to another generation'.[4] Exploring the impact of this media and political discourse further, the chapter that follows will focus on the media representation of what has been framed as 'sectarian rioting' and interface violence in July 2010.

Notes

1. The Centre for Social Justice was set up by Iain Duncan Smith MP in 2004 and describes itself as 'an independent think tank'. Further information can be accessed here: http://www.centreforsocialjustice.org.uk/ (accessed on 3 April 2011).

2. This finding demonstrated that editors and journalists included quotations from the different 'levels' of government/governance in Northern Ireland. Councillors are locally elected representatives based in local Councils in Northern Ireland (26 Councils in Northern Ireland) and MLAs are Members of the Legislative Assembly at Stormont. Government Ministers typically included Ministers from the Government in the United Kingdom (UK) and Government in the Republic of Ireland (ROI), as well as Government Ministers based at the locally elected Assembly in Northern Ireland.

3. Mephedrone was banned in the UK from 16 April 2010 onwards, with the ban receiving cross-party support. See: http://www.direct.gov.uk/en/Nl1/Newsroom/DG_186993 (accessed on 27 April 2010).

4. See: http://www.bbc.co.uk/news/uk-northern+ireland-politics-10636126 (accessed on 14 July 2010).

5

Reading the 'Riots'

Cohen (1972: 198) argued that:

> The manipulation of appropriate symbols – the process which sustains moral campaigns, panics and crusades – is made much easier when the object of attack is both highly visible and structurally weak.

In Northern Ireland, children and young people's 'visible presence on the streets and their confrontations with paramilitaries, vigilantes or the police are part of their recognition of space and identity', in a climate of 'limited opportunities' (McAlister et al. 2011: 106). Historically, riots have been a recurrent feature in Northern Ireland (see Fields 1977; Evelegh 1978; Darby 1986; Farrell 2000). In official discourse, Northern Ireland has been set apart, with Northern Ireland Office (NIO) reports strongly emphasising that: 'riots … differ from … those which occur in other parts of Europe, having gone well beyond problems of crowd control' (cited in, Human Rights Watch 1991). However, Leonard (2010a: 38) observes that, 'despite this long history, the practice remains under-researched and under-theorised'. In relation to children and young people, existing qualitative studies focus on their perceptions and experiences of rioting (see Jarman and O'Halloran 2001; Jarman 2002; Byrne et al. 2005; Leonard 2009, 2010a, b). While studies such as Leonard (2010a) refer to media discourse, there has been no existing content analysis of the media's representation of rioting and interface violence in Northern Ireland.

This chapter, structured as a case study, focuses on the media's representation of rioting in Northern Ireland in July 2010.[1] The chapter contextualises the case study by reviewing literature on the contestation of space and

© The Author(s) 2018
F. Gordon, *Children, Young People and the Press in a Transitioning Society*,
Palgrave Socio-Legal Studies, https://doi.org/10.1057/978-1-137-60682-2_5

conflicting identities in Northern Ireland. It also uses content analysis to establish how local, national and international newspapers framed youth involvement in rioting. Further, it explores the Police Service of Northern Ireland's (PSNI) initiative, Operation Exposure. This involved the dissemination of images of children and young people accused of 'sectarian disorder' in Derry/Londonderry (PSNI 2010) and the publication of images following major disturbances in Ardoyne, Belfast, in July 2010. The chapter reflects on the case study as the first opportunity post-devolution, to explore the media's representation of, and the PSNI's response to civil disorder involving children and young people.

Contestation of Space and Conflicting Identities

Contestation of space was explored in the previous chapter with reference to adult regulation of young people in public places, via criminal justice measures such as anti-social behaviour orders (ASBOs), curfews and dispersal zones. In contrast to England and Wales, there is another dimension with regard to the contestation of space in transitioning societies such as Northern Ireland. In light of 'its divisions', 'particular circumstances' and the 'politicisation of space', the existence of contested spaces and the impact of conflicting identities remain 'a lasting feature' of the legacy of the Conflict (McAlister et al. 2010: 69).

In Northern Ireland, the 'sectarianization of space' (Jarman 1998: 84, cited in Harnett 2010: 74) is evident in 'residential segregation' and 'territorial control' (see Shirlow 2008), which is 'most acute in working class' communities, in particular interface areas where Catholics and Protestants live in 'close proximity' (Harland 2010: 2–3; see also Lysaght 2008: 151). As well as the presence of physical 'peace walls' or 'interface barriers', space is 'labelled and politicised … by flags, murals and symbols', which symbolise 'specific cultural identity, territory and "ownership"' (McAlister et al. 2010: 69; see also McGarry and O'Leary 2009). These impact on 'the functions of space' and 'control' or 'influence' the 'activities of individuals and social systems' (Graham 2011: 88; see also Bairner and Shirlow 2003). The legacy of the Conflict heavily influences how children and young people negotiate space (Haydon and Scraton 2008: 63; McAlister et al. 2009: 5).

Conflicting identities is one of the 'central dynamics of political and cultural conflict' in Northern Ireland (Bean 2007: 158; see also Taylor 2001; Fahey et al. 2005). McAlister et al.'s (2010: 70) exploration of 'how identity is linked to place', observes that it 'serves to create feelings of inclusion or exclusion', with versions of 'historical constructions of space ... passed down ... to children and young people'. Similarly 'rituals' and 'ceremonies', as a 'means of perceiving and displaying difference' (Graham 2011: 88) reinforce the contestation of space and the expression of identities. Parades are one 'illustration of traditional repetition of social memory, relied on to stimulate loyalism and nationalism', whereby 'historical and mythical figures anchor identities and play an important role' (Brocklehurst 2006: 98).[2]

Parades remain 'an idiom of contestation' (Ross 2007: 88). As Brocklehurst (2006: 97) argues, 'Orangemen's marches visually illustrate the ... traditional symbolism of historical conquest' and the physical 'routes ... may be perceived as statements of territorial claims' (Farren and Mulvihill 2000: 31, cited in Ross 2007: 88). The Orange Order's '"marching season" is the period between Easter Monday and the end of September, when more than 3,500 parades, many of which are seriously disputed, are held' (Harland 2010: 17). Rioting typically occurs 'in areas where tensions have risen in response to disputes over parades and in particular in ... interface areas' (Jarman 2002: 1). Examples of 'conflicts between marchers ... and aggrieved residents' have 'marred' towns and cities 'for over a century' and conflicts at 'the local level' still represent the ongoing resistance to marches (Kaufmann 2007: 149).[3]

McAlister et al. (2010: 76) observe that for young people 'rioting and sectarian clashes ... assert cultural identity while symbolising resistance towards perceived inequalities'. Similarly, Grattan (2008: 255) asserts that 'for many young people ... conflict and violence against the perceived "other" ... [is] in "defence" of community, identity ... [and] culture'. Although typically framed by adults as 'recreational' (see Jarman and O'Halloran 2001), research findings assert that for young people rioting is 'considered ... to have a firm political basis' (McAlister et al. 2009: 98) and is a means of expressing identity and 'defending space' (McAlister et al. 2010: 76; see also Leonard 2010a, b; Meadows 2010).

The British Government has played a major role in making decisions regarding parades and in responding to parading disputes in Northern Ireland. The Public Order (NI) Act 1951 and the Flags and Emblems Act 1954 are both examples of legislative interventions (Kaufmann 2007: 150).[4] The Royal Ulster Constabulary (RUC) traditionally were given a prominent role in decision-making and the policing of parades (see Cochrane 1997). Following the high profile Drumcree dispute and nationalist disputes over the RUC's role (see McGarry and O'Leary 1999), an Independent Review chaired by Dr Peter North published a report in 1997. The 'Report of the Independent Review of Parades and Marches' recommended that an independent body should be created to make decisions on parades.[5] Following the enactment of the Public Processions Act 1998, the British Government established the Parades Commission to 'independently' regulate, 'ban' or 'allow' parades and mediate 'parading disputes' (Smithey 2011: 120, 124).[6]

The Parades Commission has 'responsibility for making decisions on parades' (McCrudden 2007: 255). The complexity of the parading issue involves 'conflicting rights', in particular 'cultural rights' (McCrudden 2007: 255; see Lysaght 2008; Dickson 2010). Responses to the Parades Commission reflect this and it is described by 'many Orangemen and loyalists ... [as] an illegitimate body that violates their democratic right to parade' and 'some nationalists claim it is a biased instrument of the British government' (Smithey 2011: 124). The issue of parades and the annual expressions of disagreement 'provide a microcosm of the overarching' impact of the contestation of space and conflicting identities in Northern Ireland and is 'an example of the impact of history on the present' (Little 2008: 68).

'Worst Rioting in Years': Case Study of Northern Ireland

Intense local, national and international print media coverage in July and August 2010 represented rioting in Ardoyne (North Belfast); Derry/ Londonderry; Donegall Road/St James' (West Belfast); Lurgan (County Armagh) and Ormeau Road (South Belfast), as 'the worst rioting in years' (see *Financial Times*, 12 July 2010; *The New York Times*, 13 July 2010).[7] Historically, rioting and interface violence has occurred at each place (see Elliott and Flackes 1999; Wood 2006; Bell 2007; Kaufmann 2007; Kelly 2011). The existence of boundaries, conflicting claims over territory and identities, continue to impact on the lives of children and young people (see Kilkelly et al. 2004; Haydon and Scraton 2008; McAlister et al. 2009). Context, such as the legacy of the Conflict and 'underlying causes', were omitted from or marginalised in the reporting of the 2010 riots.

Media Content Analysis

Darby (1986: 11) notes that rioting in Northern Ireland is 'predominantly a summer activity', typically coinciding with annual Orange Order marches.[8] This is consistent with findings in the previous chapter, as the highest concentration of news items on rioting and interface violence were printed in July and August 2010. The following content analysis explores coverage from eight local sample newspapers, as well as international news items accessed from online newspapers and national news items accessed in hard copy from United Kingdom (UK) and Republic of Ireland (ROI) newspapers in July and August 2010 (see Appendix 2). The news items cited and analysed are representative, as further examples exist in the data collected.

Framing Youth Involvement: Orchestration of Violence

As outlined previously, the outcome of the news-making process is typically a 'selected' and 'constructed representation constitutive of "reality"' (Barker 2000: 260). This is evident in the language employed and in 'other signs like photographs' and images, which 'frame' news items in a particular way (Bignell 1997: 81). Journalists' selection of language depicted the rioting in July 2010 as orchestrated, planned and premeditated: 'ARDOYNE CHAOS PLANNED' and 'FEARS OVER INVASION OF … THUGS … [with] DEADLY INTENTIONS' (*Sunday Life*, 11 July 2010: 2, 6). Several journalists blamed 'dissidents' for orchestration in headlines such as: 'RIOTERS LURED KIDS OF 8 INTO THE FRAY' (*The Sun*, 14 July 2010: 1) and descriptions of children as 'cannon fodder' (*News Letter*, 1 July 2010: 6) and human 'shields' (*News Letter*, 15 July 2010: 5). However, it was more common for young people to be solely blamed for orchestration: 'the good news is … adult involvement was minuscule … The bad news is that youthful participation was extensive and widespread' (*The Sunday Times, Comment*, 18 July 2010).

Mobile phones and social networking websites were described as a contemporary medium used by young people to organise riots, fuel violence, boast and celebrate.[9] News items described young people as: '"YouTube rioters" of a new generation' (*The Irish News*, 23 July 2010: 10, see also *The New York Times*, 14 July 2010), who 'PUT VIOLENT CLIPS ON INTERNET', which 'show the disorder to be a source of entertainment' (*News Letter*, 29 July 2010: 10–11). Another journalist described: 'Children as young as 9 … attacking … lines of riot police, while … youths … take photos for display on social networking sites' (*San Diego Union-Tribune*, 14 July 2010). Journalists and moral entrepreneurs alleged that text messages aided orchestration: 'SUMMONED BY TEXT TO THE ARDOYNE RIOTS' (*The Irish Times Weekend Review*, 17 July 2010: 3); 'the most exciting event in their alienated young lives: they text their pals to … join them' (*The Economist*, 17–23 July 2010: 32) and the Chief Constable condemned 'text rioting', whereby young people 'text[ed] each other to come … [and] have a go at police' (*News Letter*,

14 July 2010: 4). Such representations portrayed the use of social networking sites and mobile phones as a mark of the current generation of children and young people, as opposed to previous generations.

Comparisons to the Past

When comparing the 2010 rioting to the Conflict, local journalists blamed youth for 'dragging' Northern Ireland 'back through the horrors of the past' (*The Irish News*, 15 July 2010: 11). Levels of violence were described as: 'reminiscent of the dark days of the Troubles' (*News Letter*, 15 July 2010: 4) and 'JUST LIKE OLD TIMES' (*Sunday Life*, 18 July 2010: 10). International and national journalists described the rioting as: 'one of the worst outbreaks … in the last decade' (*The Hindu*, 13 July 2010); 'a throwback to the violence that erupted regularly … before … 1998' (*The New York Times*, 13 July 2010) and 'levels of mayhem not seen since the Good Friday peace agreement' (*The Sunday Telegraph*, 18 July 2010: 17). These descriptions strongly amplified the levels of violence and presented clear comparisons between the Conflict and contemporary riots. Further comparisons presented the riots as 'a worrying sign for the future' (*The Irish News*, 17 July 2010: 32), with one comment piece written by the then Secretary of State, describing it as 'shocking … to see children younger than 10 rioting in the same streets that saw death and destruction in August 1969' (*Belfast Telegraph*, 19 July 2010: 29). He also asserted that: 'we cannot see that repeated for generations to come'.

Journalists employed examples to reinforce the intergenerational aspect of rioting:

> "This is the sort of stuff my grandad did … he wrote out the recipe for the cocktails for me… told me it was OK to riot as long as I didn't get arrested". … his mother … wept … "When I was wee, our house was always being raided … because … da' was always rioting … Now my son is bringing the same trouble to my door". (*The Sunday Telegraph*, 18 July 2010: 17)

Also within the above news item the journalist relied on observers' accounts, which included descriptions of young people engaging 'the police in battle … taunt[ing] … with shouts of "SS-RUC"'.[10] This journalist referred to the 'slogan' as 'an indication of how some … are stuck in the past, however young'. Similar news items stressed that: 'despite being born into peace, violence became a part of … children's life last week' (*Sunday Life*, 18 July 2010: 10).

These strong comparisons to the past, heightened concern and evoked 'panic' surrounding the current generation of children and young people. They also presented the notion of 'history repeating itself'.

'Lost Generation': Language and Labels

The current generation of children and young people were framed as: 'OUR LOST GENERATION' (*Belfast Telegraph*, 14 July 2010: 4–5). References to the past and future also reinforced this generalisation:

> We … talk about the next generation being different, freeing themselves from the bigotry of the by-gone age. Yet there can be nothing more chilling than the laughter of the young men who threw petrol bombs last night … Without the education to question, to self-examine, this part of the next generation is long lost. (*Belfast Telegraph*, 13 July 2010: 4–5)

Similar themes to those analysed in Chap. 4, particularly the use of language, labels and stereotypes, were presented in the newspaper coverage of the riots. Headlines such as: 'CHILDREN AT HEART OF BELFAST BATTLES THAT LEFT 82 HURT' (*Daily Mail*, 14 July 2010: 19), positioned children at the centre of the riots. Another journalist stated: 'ULSTER'S TROUBLED YOUTH – WHY CHILDREN RUN RIOT'; 'these "hard men" are in fact children … "Why do … some as young as eight, who should be playing with toys … feel the need to riot?"' (*News Letter*, 19 July 2010: 10–11).

In framing young people as 'the lost generation', several journalists employed sensationalist language such as: 'swarming mobs' (*Daily Mail*, 14 July 2010); 'VICIOUS Youths'; 'youth thugs'; 'young rioters' and 'hooded youths', involved in 'an orgy of violence' (*Daily Mirror*, 14 July 2010: 4–5) and 'intense clashes' (*The Irish News*, 13 July 2010: 11). Such sensationalist language was typically accompanied by large images. As outlined in Chap. 2, the relationship between language and imagery in news reports can often be significant, with photographs gaining 'some of their meaningfulness from the … context in which they appear', often functioning as 'proof' that the media message is 'true' (Bignell 1997: 98–99).

Age was emphasised to evoke shock: 'the disturbances had enticed kids as young as EIGHT to join a hate mob hell-bent on injuring cops' (*The Sun*, 14 July 2010: 1) and 'Northern Ireland's top policeman … told reporters … some of the rioters were as young as 8, 9 and 10 years old' (*Global Post*, 21 July 2010). An additional layer of condemnation was evident in news items that focused on children: 'CHILDREN BEHIND WORST RIOTS IN NORTHERN IRELAND, SAYS POLICE CHIEF' (*The Hindu*, 13 July 2010); 'Police … and former militants … struggled to contain, and make sense of … rioting by crowds that included children so young' (*The New York Times*, 14 July 2010) and 'even more shocking was the age of the young people involved' (*News Letter*, 14 July 2010: 5). Images were accompanied by bold captions: 'PATHETIC … rioters were children' (*Daily Mirror*, 14 July 2010: 1).

News items labelled young people as 'hoodies' (*News Letter*, 13 July 2010: 4–5) and 'anti-community': 'COMMUNITY DISOWNS TEEN RIOTERS' (*South Belfast News*, 17 July 2010: 1). Intergenerational relations were high-lighted: 'OAP FOILS 12TH RIOT BY CHASING OFF YOBS' (*Sunday World*, 11 July 2010: 15). Journalists employed dehumanising language to describe young people: 'a mob … [that] can only be described as animalistic' (*The Irish News*, 14 July 2010: 10); 'circling the Land Rover like wolves around a meat wagon … a pack of cannibals' (*The Sunday Telegraph*, 18 July 2010: 17) and 'a nihilistic act by … "feral gangs" … wild youth' (*The Irish Times Weekend Review*, 17 July 2010: 3).

Descriptions reinforced individual pathology: 'the chilling response … "F**k 'em, let 'em burn" a young man [said] … as he poured a can of diesel through the window of the train' (*The Irish News*, 15 July 2010: 1); 'RIOTING IN IRELAND HAS SINISTER EDGE' (*Global Post*, 21 July 2010) and descriptions such as: 'ferocity of … attacks … the rage of … rioters … their callousness … how young many … were … fired up in their attempt to kill or … injure officers' (*The Irish Times Weekend Review*, 17 July 2010: 3). Blame was routinely placed at the level of the individual: 'rioters can … be identified … from early childhood … "behaviour … is attributable not to the parades issue or … political motives, but … pathways to poverty"' (*News Letter*, 19 July 2010: 10–11). 'EVIL' was emphasised in language and imagery: 'WE REVEAL EVIL FACES BEHIND BLOODY RIOTS', which described pho-tographs of youth as: 'snarling faces of hatred' and 'hate filled thugs' (*Sunday World*, 18 July 2010: 9–10).

Gender stereotypes were evident in quotations, particularly from Father Donegan, who was routinely quoted: 'The behaviour of … young girls was deplorable … that is a worrying new development' (*North Belfast News*, 17 July 2010: 4; see also *The New York Times*, 14 July 2010) and 'girls, many of them dressed for a night out – "it looked like a Milan catwalk"' (*San Diego Union-Tribune*, 14 July 2010). Journalists stated that: 'It's a me Tarzan, you Jane situation … "the young lads playing up to the girls"' (*News Letter*, 19 July 2010: 10–11); 'acting it up for the girls' (*The New York Times*, 14 July 2010) and 'desperate to impress the girls who goaded them on, the violence became a macabre mating ritual' (*The Sunday Telegraph*, 18 July 2010: 17).

'Recreational' Rioting

The media further demonised youth by presenting children's and young people's motivations as 'fun' rather than political: 'A DEADLY GAME FOR YOUTH OUT FOR "FUN"' (*Belfast Telegraph*, 13 July 2010: 3). Headlines portrayed youth as seeking entertainment, with no regard for the consequences: 'THUGS AGED EIGHT PUMMEL POLICE IN "RECREATIONAL" RIOT … THAT LEAVE 82 HURT' (*Daily Mail*, 14 July 2010). Jarman and O'Halloran (2001: 3) define 'recreational rioting' as 'violent interchanges … a social activity, undertaken through boredom and bravado rather than having a more political basis'. This label was employed throughout the media coverage, with examples such as: 'local youths want to attack the police … because they consider it fun … "Recreational rioting is the term … like a Disney theme park for rioting"' (*San Diego Union-Tribune*, 14 July 2010).

International headlines presented similar descriptions: 'RECREATIONAL RIOTING: A YOUTH FAD IN NORTHERN IRELAND: A decade after peace … teenagers throw Molotov Cocktails – this time in the name of fun' (*Global Post*, 21 July 2010). The news item described young people's actions as 'stemming not from political ambition' but rather, 'daily skirmishes' that 'now have a catchy name: recreational rioting … the extracurricular activity of choice for youths in the poorest parts … fueled on alcohol, drugs and boredom'. Another news item stated: 'There are people who have genuine objections to the contentious issue of parading, that has been totally hijacked now by youths running riot, holding the community to ransom' (*Belfast Telegraph*, 14 July 2010: 4–5). This approach taken by several editors and journalists clearly framed youth involvement as 'non-political'.

The label 'recreational rioting' was also used to portray youth involvement in criminality, with journalists' descriptions of the riots as: 'a combination of "recreational rioting and lawlessness"' (*News Letter*, 19 July 2010: 10–11). Several news items argued that the label 'recreational rioting' did not reinforce strongly enough the 'sinister' element of young people's behaviour. One comment piece written by Nelson McCausland DUP MLA, asserted that: 'Some … call it "recreational rioting" but this was no ritual stone throwing [it is] … criminal thuggery … attempted murder … those responsible must face the full rigour of the law' (*North Belfast News*, 17 July 2010: 13).

In line with Jarman and O'Halloran's (2001: 3) definition, the media's application of the label 'recreational rioting' stressed that young people 'engaged in violence … had little or no political point' (*The New York Times*, 14 July

2010) or 'no political agenda' (*The Irish Times Weekend Review*, 17 July 2010: 3). Moral entrepreneurs stated that: 'I don't believe they had a political motivation' (Conall McDevitt, SDLP MLA, in *South Belfast News*, 17 July 2010: 1) and 'it's like a game to them ... There is more politics in a box of cornflakes' (Father Donegan, in *News Letter*, 19 July 2010: 10–11). This was further emphasised in another headline: 'NO CAUSE, NO EXCUSE, JUST BRUTAL INSANITY' (*Belfast Telegraph*, 13 July 2010: 1), which proposed that:

> Today we stand again in the eyes of the world as inexplicably tribal, undeveloped, brutal and harsh ... Take another look at the picture ... the price we pay for thuggery dressed up as historical grievance.

In contrast, one journalist asserted that: 'it would be foolish to dismiss those young men ... as a homogeneous mass of apolitical yobs', as 'recent history teaches ... out of this mass of disaffected and the ... nihilistic will come the foot soldiers of the next generation of republican terrorism' (*The Observer*, 18 July 2010: 32). The application and maintenance of labels such as 'recreational rioting' in the media marginalises or excludes 'young people's own view of what they are doing' and it 'imposes an adult (and middle class) judgement' (Meadows 2010: 251). In choosing to portray young people's 'motivations' as 'fun' and not 'political', the media do not acknowledge the alienation of children and young people from the political processes in a transitioning society, such as Northern Ireland.

Impact on Transition

Journalists emphasised the 'timing': 'Irish youths have picked the wrong time of year to riot for kicks' (*Global Post*, 21 July 2010) and 'the rash of street fighting comes at a critical time for Northern Ireland's peace process', with the devolution in April of 'policing and justice powers ... symbolizing the final "jigsaw piece" of the peace process' (*Global Post*, 21 July 2010). News items amplified concern: 'the country's moving forward as everybody thinks, but it makes you think, you know, is it?' (*Belfast Telegraph*, 15 July 2010: 4) and 'the new justice minister whimpers on about "shared future" strategies', but 'does he really believe that those out rioting ... care one iota about integrated schools, shared sports facilities and community picnics in the park?' (*The Irish News*, 19 July 2010: 10).

The riots were framed as 'a step back' for Northern Ireland's transition: 'SECTARIAN RIOTS SHAKE NORTHERN IRELAND' (*Financial Times*, 12 July 2010) and 'POLITICAL RIFTS REAPPEAR' (*The New York Times*,

13 July 2010). Quotations from the First Minister reiterated that: 'nobody ... who has "more than two brain cells to rub together wants to go back to the bad old days of the past"' and 'we need to treat as pariahs those who would seek to take us there' (*Belfast Telegraph*, 6 July 2010: 12). Similar descriptions included: 'a new generation of "out of control" children and youths at the frontline' (*Belfast Telegraph*, 14 July 2010: 4–5) and 'YOUNG IRA REBELS ... TO DESTROY NORTHERN IRELAND PEACE PROCESS' (*Daily Mail*, 15 July 2010), which stated that: 'Ministers are concerned that the younger generation appear no longer to be under the control of the Sinn Féin old guard ... Former terrorist Gerry Kelly ... sent packing by younger hard-liners'. Another news item employed an alleged quotation from a young person to form the headline: 'SINN FEIN ARE YESTERDAY'S MEN' (*The Sunday Telegraph*, 18 July 2010: 17). The journalist quoted an alleged conversation between young people:

"Shove off, old man ... you sold out your community ... so that the likes of Gerry Adams and Martin McGuinness could parade about in posh suits and sit up in Stormont. What do they care about the Ardoyne now? You lot don't speak for us any more. Why don't you just f—— off".

"We need to be better organised next week ... Adams and McGuinness can whine all they like. They're yesterday's men. They have no stomach left for the fight. Neither have our fathers. They are old, tired men, ground down by 30 years of war. We are just being blooded for the next 30".

This journalist employed the alleged conversation to propose that young people were 'disillusioned' and a 'threat' to Northern Ireland's transition. Thus, such representations contribute to the 'panic' surrounding youth and the future political stability of Northern Ireland.

In light of legacy of Conflict in Northern Ireland, Brocklehurst (2006: 110) asserts that 'the continuation of violence by children is also to some extent placing a focus on children as agents of change within their communities'. This was clearly evident in journalists' repeated reference to 'the lost generation' and the representation of children and young people as 'out of control'. In describing children and young people in this way, it feeds into what the literature describes as 'the process of control', whereby adult responses and reactions seek to deter 'unwanted outcomes' like riots (Such et al. 2005: 302). Barry's (2005: 2) conclusion that, young people 'are the perceived threat to an already precarious status quo and are ... often scapegoated as a result', applies to children and young people in Northern Ireland.

PSNI, Political, Judicial and Community Reactions and Responses

PSNI responses employed strong language: 'WE'LL NAIL RIOT YOBS: BAGGOTT VOWS TO IDENTIFY THUGS ON CCTV'; 'POLICE chief … vowed … rioters … will be prosecuted' (*Daily Mirror*, 14 July 2010: 1) and *'Top cop … vowed to "bring to book" all those rioters caught on CCTV – some … primary schoolkids aged just eight'* (*Sunday World*, 18 July 2010: 10, original emphasis). Support was emphasised in quotations from the Chief Constable, who described 'the complex goals of the police operation', praised his colleagues and stated that: '[what] you saw last night that you will not have anywhere in the world' (*The Hindu*, 13 July 2010). Political support was evident in quotations from Michael Martin, Ireland's Minister for Foreign Affairs: 'I would like to pay tribute to the PSNI for their professionalism and restraint in policing the unacceptable violence' (*The Irish News*, 15 July 2010: 11). The British Prime Minister: 'lauded the Police … for exercising restraint in the face of potentially deadly attacks' (*San Diego Union-Tribune*, 14 July 2010). The journalist juxtaposed this comment to the opposing viewpoints of 'residents … calling for more aggressive tactics to scatter mobs and arrest … hooligans'. The reliance on and prominence given to quotations from 'moral entrepreneurs' further emphasised the hierarchy of access to the media and the promotion of a dominant discourse (Becker 1967: 241; Hall 1986; Allan 1999).

News items demanded swift, punitive responses. Political reactions included: 'unionist politicians complained about the police's policy of containing the violence and called for a more proactive approach' (*The Irish Times*, 2 August 2010: 6) and 'Stormont Justice Committee chairman Lord Morrow … call[ing] for police to use Tasers and CS spray to tackle rioters' (*Belfast Telegraph*, 15 July 2010). Further representative headlines included: 'ROBUST POLICING NEEDED, NOT EXCUSES' (*News Letter*, 19 July 2010: 16); 'POLICEWOMAN'S DAD: I WANT TOUGHER ACTION AGAINST THESE THUGS' (*Belfast Telegraph*, 15 July 2010: 4) and '1,000 MORE POLICE NOW' (*Daily Mirror*, 14 July 2010: 5). Community responses were evident in headlines such as: 'RESIDENTS WANT POLICE TO ARREST RIOTERS' (*News Letter*, 15 July 2010: 5) and several Letters to the Editor: 'SOFTLY, SOFTLY APPROACH TO RIOTING HAS TO STOP' (*The Irish News*, 27 July 2010: 20) and 'IT IS NOW TIME TO COME DOWN HARD ON RIOTERS' (*Belfast Telegraph*, 24 July 2010: 26). Such headlines strongly called for a range of harsh, punitive responses directed towards those rioting.

The PSNI responded to such criticisms by issuing strong warnings: 'There will be significant arrests … Individuals will not go scot-free' (*San Diego Union-Tribune*, 14 July 2010) and 'Baggott vowed … rioters … will be prosecuted' (*Daily Mirror*, 14 July 2010: 1). News items outlined details of the PSNI's investigation process: 'a team of 20 … officers … formed to try to identify … rioters … is to examine 100 hours of video footage and 1,000 photographs', 'so that arrests can be made' (*The Irish Times*, 17 July 2010: 6). Journalists referred to the rising numbers of young people arrested: 'those arrested range between 15 and 20 years of age' (*Andersonstown News*, 19 July 2010: 4) and 'youngest … charged … so far is aged 13' (*The Irish News*, 31 July 2010: 4–5). The PSNI 'signalled that a firm line would be taken with all those involved no matter how old they are. "Children will be treated as offenders"' (*The Irish News*, 31 July 2010: 4–5). Routinely the Chief Constable asked: 'the public [to] help police bring offenders before the courts'; 'the judiciary … [to] ensure tough sentences were handed to the guilty' (*Daily Mirror*, 14 July 2010: 1) and other senior officers called on the 'courts to ensure that those convicted … receive jail sentences' (*The Irish News*, 14 July 2010: 4–5).

Judicial responses and punishment were emphasised in headlines such as: 'CURFEW FOR RIOT CHARGE TEENAGER' (*Belfast Telegraph*, 22 July 2010: 26) and 'YOUTH IS CHARGED OVER PETROL BOMBING' (*Belfast Telegraph*, 16 July 2010: 10), which outlined the judge's decision: 'Bagnall … was not prepared to release him despite his young age' (*News Letter*, 16 July 2010: 4). Another headline: '"RIOT" TEEN ARRESTED "WHILE ROLLING JOINT": Court told boy, 16, at centre of Twelfth trouble' (*Daily Mirror*, 29 July 2010: 20), summarised courtroom commentary: 'Opposing bail, the officer claimed the youth could not be controlled with … his own mother said to be in … fear of him'.

Journalists focused on individual cases and printed photographs of the accused, with one such example: 'TEEN ON RIOT RAP' (*The Sun*, 2 August 2010: 20), describing how a '19-year-old … charged in connection with vicious riots … handed himself into cops … after images were released of people wanted over the attacks'. A lack of respect for the judiciary was highlighted: 'the teenager … entered the dock … limping – a friend wolf-whistled from the public gallery' (*The Irish News*, 16 July 2010: 8). A further layer of outrage existed in relation to young women's alleged involvement: 'schoolgirl … arrested' and '15-YEAR-OLD girl … among eight … arrested' (*The Irish News*, 16 July 2010: 5). As the literature acknowledges, young women's perceived involvement in crime receives further or an additional layer of condemnation, with young women presented as 'doubly deviant' (Berrington and Honkatukia 2002: 59).

Condemnation of Parents

Journalists portrayed the rioting as an indication of 'the collapse of parental responsibility ... not any deep-seated political agenda' (*San Diego Union-Tribune*, 14 July 2010), with descriptions of 'young children ... with no parental control lighting petrol bombs' (*News Letter*, 14 July 2010: 4). Calls for punitive responses were directed at parents: 'LEVYING THE BLAME: PSNI Chief Constable ... slams the parents of youths involved in ... rioting' (*The Irish News*, 14 July 2010: 4–5) and 'it is time for the Executive and Justice Minister to consider if parents should have a legal ... obligation to control ... their children' (*Belfast Telegraph*, 17 July 2010: 24). Journalists posed questions such as: 'WHERE ARE HIS PARENTS?' (*Belfast Telegraph*, 14 July 2010: 1, 4) and 'Where are the parents of these mini-terrorists?' (*News Letter*, 19 July 2010: 10–11). A Sinn Féin MLA argued that: 'parents ... must be challenged by their neighbours ... community and ... statutory agencies' (*North Belfast News*, 24 July 2010: 10) and expressed outrage that: 'One parent ... insisted her child had a right to riot'. This 'most ... revealing quote' (*Sunday World*, 18 July 2010: 10) was repeatedly printed: '"Mum, can I stay out for another half hour" ... "OK, just don't get arrested," she replied' (*Belfast Telegraph*, 13 July 2010: 3).

Reactions were punitive, with politicians 'want[ing] Social Services to take more responsibility ... step in and take action' (*North Belfast News*, 17 July 2010: 2) and strong warnings: 'PARENTS OF CHILD RIOTERS COULD FACE INVESTIGATION FOR NEGLECT' (*Belfast Telegraph*, 17 July 2010: 4) and 'WE'LL COME KNOCKING' (*Belfast Telegraph*, 17 July 2010: 1). Journalists outlined that: 'very young children ... face criminal charges while ... parents ... get off scot free' (*Belfast Telegraph*, 17 July 2010: 24). One Letter to the Editor proposed, 'if a child is convicted for rioting' then their 'parents should lose ... child benefit for six months', which 'might encourage a little more effort from ... those too lazy or incompetent to look after their children' (*News Letter*, 16 July 2010: 20).

Comparisons were made with 'the rest of the UK [where] ... parents can be prosecuted for letting their child truant ... parenting contracts can be taken out ... parenting courses ... [and] fines' (*Belfast Telegraph*, 17 July 2010: 4). The potential for policy transfer (see Newburn 2002) was emphasised in a comment piece,[11] which outlined the legal position regarding parental responsibility and stated that: 'People need to ... tell their representatives ... what laws they want ... to bring the situation under control' (*Belfast Telegraph*, 17 July 2010: 5).

This was a further call for policy transfer from the UK and emphasised the media's promotion of calls for further contemporary policies to be transferred.

'Alternative' Voices and Rights Discourse

Journalists routinely reinforced dominant ideologies by marginalising 'alternative' interpretations of the riots and criticising children's rights discourse. Examples included the *Daily Mirror's* 'Editor's Comment' entitled: 'STANDING UP TO YOBS' (14 July 2010: 10, original emphasis), which vigorously reflected:

> [Y]ou've got to wonder what would happen if one [sic] them was hit with a baton or a plastic bullet. *How long would it be before the cries would ring out of the young boy's human rights had been abused? Not long, you would imagine*.

Headlines presented the police as 'powerless' and 'constrained' by human rights: 'WHAT ABOUT THE HUMAN RIGHTS OF THE POLICE?' (*News Letter*, 21 July 2010: 19); 'A MURDEROUS MOB AND POWERLESS POLICE: THE IMAGES THAT SHAME US' (*Belfast Telegraph*, 14 July 2010: 1) and 'PSNI HAVE TO CONTROL MOBS WITH ONE HAND TIED BEHIND THEIR BACKS' (*Belfast Telegraph*, 14 July 2010: 2–3). Similarly an 'OPINION' piece entitled: 'SAFETY OF RIOTERS IS NOW MORE IMPORTANT THAN POLICE', written by 'A former PSNI officer who faced some of Ulster's worst rioting', criticised human rights and stated that 'he left the riot squads over "rioter-friendly" tactics' (*News Letter*, 16 July 2010: 5).

Journalists criticised the NI Children's Commissioner for taking 'four days to comment on children's involvement in the riots' (*News Letter*, 19 July 2010: 10–11). Youth workers voices were missing or marginalised. When quoted, their 'alternative' opinions were typically framed in line with the angle taken by the journalist. One such headline starkly juxtaposed differing viewpoints: 'THE FURIOUS FATHER AND AN APOLOGIST FOR RIOTERS' (*Belfast Telegraph*, 15 July 2010: 4–5). The dismissal of, or strong disagreement with 'alternative' viewpoints was evident in examples such as: 'Youthful rioting may … be a symptom of deep social and economic problems, but these occur in other areas where there is no rioting' (*The Sunday Times, Comment*, 18 July 2010) and other strong commentary:

> This isn't about social deprivation … No excuse can be made for the … rioting other than there are people who want to destroy … stability in Northern Ireland

or ... an element of youthful society has completely lost the run of itself. (*Belfast Telegraph*, 19 July 2010: 27)

Another representative example was condemnatory and punitive in tone:

As ink continues to flow over the Twelfth of July riots, one thing everyone seems to agree is that Ardoyne is over-run with juvenile delinquents. In Derry ... no half-brick is ever thrown without a poverty-related excuse. To dissuade young people from rioting the PSNI is publicising the case of a Derry youth denied access to America last year on a family holiday to Disneyland, due to a conviction for disorder. Holidaying in Florida may be dreadfully common but it is hardly a sign of economic deprivation. (*The Irish News*, 24 July 2010: 30)

The absence of contextual information and 'alternative' views was clearly insightful with regard to how the media chose to make one set of views prominent. In addition, the examples cited above illustrated the strong and direct dismissal of 'alternative' viewpoints or contextual information, when they were included in media discourse. Such information reflected the angle taken by the journalist. In news items on rioting and interface violence, strong and direct condemnation of those alternative views reinforced individual pathology and added an additional layer to the vilification of youth.

PSNI's Operation Exposure

Background and Context

As the above content analysis outlines, the views of politicians and victims' families were given prominence, with many criticising the PSNI for what they described as 'soft tactics'. In contrast, the PSNI continuously defended their 'tactics', presented strong assurances that those rioting would be identified and prosecuted and called for the judiciary to issue punitive sentences. The condemnation, marginalisation or exclusion of 'alternative' views and rights discourse clearly indicated that the climate was one of intolerance, with the media playing a central role in reinforcing and maintaining blame on children and young people. Further, this extended to two 'tactics' employed by the PSNI in Derry/Londonderry and in North Belfast – Operation Exposure in Derry/Londonderry and the release of images by North Belfast's PSNI, following the riots in July 2010.

The following analysis of newspaper coverage was collected from the eight sample newspapers and in addition, two local newspapers, the *Derry Journal* and the *Londonderry Sentinel*, as well as national and international newspapers. The analysis also includes documentary analysis of documents publically available via Freedom of Information requests; documents personally requested and received from the PSNI in Derry/Londonderry; documents provided by the Northern Ireland Human Rights Commission for use in this research, and contextual information gained from an interview with the main architect of Operation Exposure, PSNI Inspector Jon Burrows.[12]

As previously outlined, policing in Northern Ireland has long been contested. Studies demonstrate the 'hostility', 'suspicion', fear and negative associations young people, particularly from 'socio-economically disadvantaged areas', attach to the police (Horgan 2005: 8). Traditionally, the state and state agencies such as the police held a prominent role in decision-making and in policing parades (see Cochrane 1997; Jarman 1997; Kaufmann 2007). Police responses to rioting in Northern Ireland are extensively documented (see Ryder 1990; Ripley and Chappell 1993; White 1993; O Dochartaigh 1997; Ellison and Smyth 2000; Mulcahy 2006), as well as the negative impact of police responses on children and young people (see Ellison 2001; Kilkelly et al. 2004; Smyth et al. 2004; Horgan 2005; Scraton 2007; McAlister et al. 2009).

In 2010, PSNI responses 'on the ground' included several 'operational' tactics, such as the deployment of 'Tactical Support Groups'; 'Armed Response Units'; the 'Roads Policing Unit'; 'Water Cannons' (PSNI 2010); the firing of 'Attenuating Energy Projectiles' (AEPs) and the use of video recording equipment to record riot scenes (see Northern Ireland Policing Board, September 2010: 6).[13] Several members of the Policing Board, an independent body set up to ensure that the PSNI is 'accountable', 'effective' and 'impartial', voiced their concerns at a meeting in September 2010 and 'were alarmed … at the number of AEPs fired', with some members firmly 'opposed' to 'use of AEPs' (Northern Ireland Policing Board, September 2010: 6–7).[14] At this meeting the Board's 'Human Rights Advisor advised Members that the Operation Exposure had raised implications following the release of photographs of minors (under 18)' (Northern Ireland Policing Board, September 2010: 7).

Operation Exposure was 'piloted' by the PSNI in Derry/Londonderry in the summer of 2009 (see *Londonderry Sentinel*, 24 May 2010). Internal PSNI recruitment correspondence described the operational role as 'the management of CCTV images, from seizure by Police through various indentification [*sic*] methods', which included 'release to the media and subsequent collection and dissemination of intelligence back to investigating officers for action' (PSNI 2010). From the outset, the media were positioned as a key partner in one of the practical elements of the 'operation', with local newspapers such as the *Derry Journal* and *Londonderry Sentinel*, facilitating the PSNI by publishing 'unidentified' Closed Circuit Television (CCTV) photographic images 'of people they want to speak to in connection with crime' (*Derry Journal*, 27 September 2010). News items such as: 'COPS RELEASE CCTV IMAGES' (*Londonderry Sentinel*, 22 April 2010) and 'POLICE TO FOCUS CAMERAS ON "THUGS"' (*Derry Journal*, 3 September 2010), presented Operation Exposure as an ongoing 'feature' news item. The 'pilot' was described as 'a success', 'with 80 per cent of all images … positively identified by police in partnership with the community' (*Londonderry Sentinel*, 9 April 2010).

Relaunched to Target Youth

In April 2010, following a suspension of Operation Exposure, the local media announced: 'OPERATION EXPOSURE RELAUNCHED' (*Londonderry Sentinel*, 9 April 2010). The journalist described the operation as 'revamped following the trial run due to concerns over human rights issues … raised by some local politicians'. Inspector Jon Burrows was quoted:

> We have taken on board some concerns that were raised and … have reviewed the entire operation. We now have all the checks in place to balance the rights of victims with the rights of suspects who may appear in the paper.

The journalist outlined that 'the PSNI hope to enjoy the same level of success and public assistance they enjoyed with the pilot scheme which ran in the City last year'. Other local journalists reminded their readership that: 'OPERATION EXPOSURE CONTINUES' (*Londonderry Sentinel*, 17 May 2010). News items quoted the PSNI Area Commander, who described 'the willingness of the public to cooperate with police to identify criminals', as essential to the success and outcomes (*Derry Journal*, 27 September 2010), with headlines that directly called for public assistance: 'CAN READERS HELP THE POLICE IDENTIFY THEM?' (*Londonderry Sentinel*, 5 October 2009). The PSNI also indicated that there was a '"dramatic increase" in interface violence and sectarian attacks' in the Foyle district (*Derry Journal*, 27 September 2010) and proposed that tactical operations such as Operation Exposure were required to tackle this increase and 'to stamp out attacks on patrols by catching those responsible on camera', with the PSNI 'vow[ing] to up the ante on "thugs"' (*Derry Journal*, 3 September 2010).

Another facet of Operation Exposure in Derry/Londonderry included the printing of 35,000 leaflets, which were subsequently distributed in August

2010 (PSNI 2010; see also *Derry News*, 20 August 2010).[15] The leaflets contained 21 numbered images of 23 children and young people who the PSNI wanted to speak to regarding 'sectarian disorder at the Fountain/Bishop Street interface' (PSNI 2010). The leaflet called on the public not to 'turn a blind eye to violence … Help us tackle sectarianism in our City' (PSNI 2010). The PSNI included on the leaflet their assurance that while 'many of the images are of young people' they 'have exhausted all other reasonable means of identification and have taken this step after careful consideration' (PSNI 2010). Poster versions of the leaflets were also placed in local PSNI stations and included the images of children and young people.

Having been influenced by the 'success' of Operation Exposure, following the Ardoyne riots, on 30 July 2010, the North Belfast PSNI released 14 images of young men they wanted to interview as part of their investigations. The 14 photographic images featured in several of the sample newspapers; also on BBC Newsline NI (British Broadcasting Corporation) and UTV (Ulster Television), the two main televised news outlets in Northern Ireland, as well as both of the televised news websites and the PSNI's website. The PSNI also launched the images onto the national arena, via Crime Watch UK (BBC News, 9 September 2010).[16]

International and national news items made reference to the PSNI's 'tactic'. Several international news items described it as 'the unusual step … of releasing footage … which showed youngsters' (*The Hindu*, 13 July 2010). National newspapers, in particular the tabloids were clearly sensationalist in their reporting. Representative examples included: 'RIOT CAM 14' (*The Sun*, 31 July 2010: 8), which described the young people as: 'most … aged in their teens … The CCTV gallery was compiled while yobs attacked cops' and captions alongside the images state: 'WANTED … four of the suspects captured on CCTV'. Another news item: 'RIOT SQUAD? POLICE RELEASE PICS IN HUNT FOR THUGS BEHIND THEM' (*Daily Mirror*, 31 July 2010: 10), included photographs with bold captions such as, 'SNAPPED'.

News items in local newspapers were equally as sensationalist and condemnatory. Representative examples such as: 'EXCLUSIVE: RIOTERS UNMASKED' and 'WE UNMASK THE THUGS' (*Sunday World*, 25 July 2010: 1, 4), printed images released by the PSNI and also focused on one young male from Ballymena who allegedly travelled to 'Ardoyne while his girlfriend was … about to give birth'. The newspaper boasted that they 'saved several pictures as well as most of his profile information' from his social networking site and were able to identify the young male. Similar to findings in the previous chapter, the young age of those allegedly involved was routinely included for 'shock value' (see Black and Roberts 2011), for example:

'YOUNGEST HELD IN RIOTS PROBE "'JUST 13"' (*News Letter*, 31 July 2010: 6). With reference to the photographs released by the PSNI, the journalist stated that they 'have one thing in common – their baby faces'.

Community Support

In addition, the PSNI and the media consistently called for community assistance and support, with headlines such as: 'PUBLIC HELP WITH RIOT ARRESTS' (*News Letter*, 24 July 2010: 6) and 'TWELFTH RIOTS: DO YOU KNOW THESE SUSPECTED RIOTERS?' (*The Irish News*, 31 July 2010: 12–13), which directly asked the readers: 'DO YOU recognise these people? … all appear to be in their teens and early twenties'. Another news item stated that 'the photographs have been released as detectives step up their probe into … the violence' (*Belfast Telegraph*, 31 July 2010: 14). The young people were described as 'gangs – which included children as young as eight', with 'Detective Chief Inspector … Little appeal[ing] for assistance in identifying the suspects', which, 'the community will know'.

The PSNI presented Operation Exposure as a 'considerable success' (*Derry Journal*, 11 May 2010) and asserted that: 'when the public trust us with information … we deliver – putting criminals behind bars and making the city a safer place for all'. Praise for 'local media', who 'helped police to identify and prosecute those involved' reinforced the media's central role in dissemination (Derry District Policing Partnership, January 2010: 2). Further praise was directed at the public for showing 'strong … support for the measure' (*News Letter*, 18 August 2010). There are several comparisons that can be made to police 'tactics' in England, Scotland and Wales, in particular the 'naming and shaming' of children and young people who have been granted an ASBO; the dissemination of ASBO conditions and leaflets including photographs and 'wanted posters', which have been used by police forces in other parts of Europe (see Barry 2005; Scraton 2007; Yates 2008; Northern Ireland Human Rights Commission (NIHRC), 2 September 2010). The main architect of Operation Exposure, Inspector Jon Burrows, was 'formerly of the London Metropolitan Police' (*Derry Journal*, 25 October 2011) and this further suggests that Operation Exposure was a contemporary example of policy transfer that failed to acknowledge or consider the impact of the legacy.

Support for Operation Exposure and the publication of images in the media, has been reinforced in particular by Unionist politicians, who have spoken publically and at interview (see UTV, 26 January 2011[17]; 'HAY DEFENDS OPERATION EXPOSURE', *Londonderry Sentinel*, 23 August

2010; see also interview with DUP MLA).[18] In contrast, several children's sector, youth sector, human rights and equality sector organisations, as well as academics, strongly disagreed with the PSNI's publication of children and young people's photographs and held concerns relating to safety and the preservation of children's rights (see Boyce 2010: 67–71). Examples of criticisms printed in Letter's pages, such as: 'OPERATION EXPOSURE CHILD ABUSE' (*Derry Journal*, 20 August 2010) and 'YOUNG PEOPLE NEED TO BE LISTENED TO, NOT TALKED AT … SAYS PHIL SCRATON' (*Belfast Telegraph*, 14 October 2010), directly challenged the PSNI's 'tactic'.

Children's Rights v Public Interest

In a letter to the District Policing Partnership (DPP) in Derry/Londonderry, the Northern Ireland Human Rights Commission (2 September 2010) outlined several concerns in relation to human rights (European Convention on Human Rights (ECHR) and the Human Rights Act (HRA) 1998) and children's rights (United Nations Convention on the Rights of the Child (UNCRC)) and concluded that the 'PSNI's action in releasing images of children' was 'not … consistent with the state's obligations under the UNCRC'. Thus, 'any image that the police could have assumed to depict a child should not have been released to the media or distributed to households' (NIHRC, 2 September 2010). The PSNI argued that each individual case was 'risk assessed' prior to release of an image (PSNI: undated document).[19] In reality, the debate was reduced to the rights of the 'law-abiding' community and 'the public interest' versus the rights of children and young people who have had their photographs disseminated. The media have been central in reinforcing this, with headlines such as, 'THE FURIOUS FATHER AND AN APOLOGIST FOR RIOTERS' (*Belfast Telegraph*, 15 July 2010). This starkly framed the debate as 'victims' and 'perpetrators' and overshadowed children's rights discourse and denied children and young people due process of the law and the presumption of innocence (Article 6 of the ECHR).

Significantly, the family of one young person aged 14, who had his photograph printed as part of the Operation Exposure leaflet and dissemination in the local media, sought legal advice on the right to privacy. In September 2010, Mr Justice Treacy in the High Court granted leave for a judicial review application (BBC News NI, 28 September 2010).[20] The barrister acting on behalf of the young man sought 'an undertaking "that such an operation wouldn't be used until trial"' (BBC News NI, 29 September 2010).[21] However, the PSNI Commander's proposals that: 'Operation Exposure will be expanded shortly' (*Derry Journal*, 27 September 2010) saw the 'tactic' expanded by the PSNI to now feature photographic images of 'people failing to turn up to court', as part of Operation Relentless (UTV, 22 November 2011; see also BBC Newsline NI, 22 November 2011).[22] The PSNI restricted further information requested on Operation Exposure under the 'litigation privilege', due to the ongoing proceedings (see PSNI 2010).

Judgment

In March 2013, the Divisional Court dismissed the application. The court concluded that within the meaning of Article 8(2) of the ECHR, any interference with the applicant's rights was necessary for the administration of justice, for the prevention of disorder and crime and the protection of society. Following an appeal, on 1 July 2015, the Supreme Court gave its judgment in the matter of JR38.[23] The appeal considered two core legal issues. Firstly, did the publication of the image amount to an interference with the appellant's right to respect for a private life under Article 8 of the ECHR and, secondly, if there was an interference, was it justified?[24] The Supreme Court unanimously dismissed the appeal. The Lords agreed that, if there had been an interference with the appellant's Article 8 right, it was necessary for the administration of justice.

The Supreme Court's judgment is illuminating in further demonstrating the limits of privacy, particularly in the exercise of balancing the right to a private life and other specific societal values (Gordon 2016: 260). The judgment can be criticised for presenting a very one-dimensional view of Article 8, in the sense of it being a privacy right only (Gordon 2016: 260). The children's rights sector in Northern Ireland have also criticised the judgment for not being consistent with the UN Convention on the Rights of the Child (UNCRC). Lord Kerr is the only justice to refer to the UNCRC and the Beijing Rules (Gordon 2016: 260). At the 72nd session of the Committee on the Rights of the Child on 23 May 2016, the UN Committee made direct reference to Operation Exposure and asked for commitments that police policy in the future would not 'name and shame' children (Gordon 2016: 260–261). The concerns raised further emphasise issues regarding the safety, well-being and rights of minors to fair due process within the criminal justice processes.

Operation Exposure and the publication of children and young people's images by the North Belfast PSNI, demonstrate the impact of social reaction on contemporary policy responses to children and young people in Northern Ireland, as well as the legacy left by the UK government in relation to policy development responses and policy transfer. In addition, the courts' responses and case judgments indicate the far-reaching consequences of police tactics breaching children's rights and the maintenance of such punitive and damaging responses by the legal system.

Conclusion

This chapter has explored the media, political, governmental and societal responses to children, young people and rioting following a time of significant 'change' in Northern Ireland, with the devolution of policing and justice powers to Stormont. The case study has offered the first unique opportunity to explore the media's representation of, and the PSNI's response to children, young people and rioting in the summer of 2010. As outlined in previous chapters, the police are 'moral entrepreneurs (van Dijk 1991) and have easy access to the media. The PSNI's Operation Exposure initiative (Derry/Londonderry) and the publication of children's and young people's images following the Ardoyne riots in North Belfast, are stark contemporary examples, which clearly illustrate how close the relationship between the state, state agencies such as the PSNI and the media, are in a transitioning society.

As Muncie and Fitzgerald (1981: 422) poignantly note, 'in times of rapid social change … the ensuing public disquiet is resolved by the media identifying certain social groups as scapegoats or folk devils' and thus, as 'visible symbols of what is wrong with society'. As this chapter has demonstrated, the media's use of selective language and imagery to frame rioting and interface violence presents vivid representations of children and young people as perpetrators. This is consistent with national and international research, which asserts that 'the media reserves its most vociferous reporting for the apparent "crime waves" and "social problems" generated by certain sections of … youth' (Bessant and Hil 1997: 2). As the content analysis has established, children and young people are routinely portrayed as evil, which is a construction that typically 'absolves the rest of society of blame' (Green 2008a: 204).

This case study has demonstrated how the state and state agencies respond to this social group, without consideration of children's rights and the impact of the legacy of the Conflict. The following chapter builds on this analysis by exploring qualitative interview responses from those journalists and editors who wrote the news items analysed, the politicians who were heavily quoted and the architect of the PSNI's Operation Exposure. This will provide a unique insight into the procedures, reasoning and motivations of those who

were central to the creation and maintenance of negative ideological constructions and the responses that followed.

Notes

1. The rioting in Ardoyne in 2010 has been employed in existing academic literature as an example of contemporary violence, to question Northern Ireland's
   'political future' (Bean 2011: 154) and to assess the police's role in a transitioning society, from the perspective of the PSNI (Kay 2011: 151–152).
2. Farrell (2000: 62) refers to 'Orange' in relation to Orange Order parades and
   'Green' in relation to Nationalist parades. He also refers to parades on Saint
   Patrick's Day as part of the Nationalist community's expression of culture.
3. Jarman's (1997: 108) research notes the experiences of 'the Roman Catholic
   population' on 12 July, 'who … are in some cases virtually imprisoned for the
   day' and typically 'allowed no part in the proceedings'. Further, Kaufmann
   (2007: 150) notes that 'since the 1960s, British pressure, Republican agita-
   tion, and IRA violence have led to an expansion in Nationalist parading and
   resistance to Unionist parading through "Nationalist areas"'.
4. Kaufmann (2007) discusses the curtailment of republican parading, however
   not Orange parades as they had the status of 'traditional processions'. Thus,
   Kaufmann (2007) argues that in the past Orange parades have been supported by both the government and RUC. Legislative interventions, such as
   the Public Order (NI) Order 1987 is one such example. See: http://www.
   legislation.gov.uk/nisi/1987/463/contents/made (accessed on 1 June 2011).
5. For further information on 'The North Report', see: http://cain.ulst.ac.uk/
   issues/parade/north.htm (accessed on 20 August 2011).
6. For further information on the role and remit of the Parades Commission in
   Northern Ireland, see: http://www.paradescommission.org/ (accessed on 30
   July 2011).
7. McKeown's (2001) database, which records and analyses the 'patterns of
   politically motivated violence during the years 1969–2001' demonstrates the
   extent of violence and fatalities during this period. McKeown's (2001) findings are clearly not in line with the contemporary media's claims that the riots
   in 2010 were the 'worst' in years. See: http://cain.ulst.ac.uk/victims/mcke-
   own/index.html#intro (accessed on 21 August 2011).
8. Timing of the riots was a theme frequently highlighted by journalists. For
   example, news items described how 'wilful young adults', 'released from
   school… join their annual summer scheme for a bout of recreational violence
   and peeler taunting' (*The Irish News*, 5 July 2010: 10), as the 'flags, flutes and
   family combines with warmer weather for a recipe of literal and figurative
   Molotov cocktails' (*Global Post*, 21 July 2010).

9. Reilly's (2010: 1; see also Reilly 2011) contemporary study explores the use of social media in riot and interface situations in Northern Ireland and looks at the 'strategies being deployed by community groups and the … PSNI to prevent incidents of recreational rioting … with a particular focus on how they respond to suspicious activity on social networking websites'. The research is based on interviews with the PSNI and interface community workers and differed from Leonard's (2010a) research, which includes the voices of children and young people to gain a direct insight into young people's perspectives on rioting in Northern Ireland.

10. This is a label historically used to describe the police in Northern Ireland. The 'SS' relates to the name given to Hitler's police and the 'RUC' refers to the Royal Ulster Constabulary, which was the police force prior to the establishment of the PSNI (see Appendix 1).

11. Mrs Rosemary Craig writes this comment piece in her capacity as an Associate Lecturer at the School of Law, University of Ulster.

12. Interview conducted on 2 November 2010. The interviewee is referred to throughout the monograph as: PSNI1, however he did waive his right to anonymity (see Appendix 2).

13. AEPs were introduced by the PSNI as a 'less lethal replacement' for the 'L21A1 baton round', and there have been several concerns raised about the impact of AEPs on children and young people. For more information, see: http://www.nipolicingboard.org.uk/index/our-work/content-humanrights/content-lesslethal/content-aeps.htm (accessed on 30 July 2011).

14. For further information on the role, responsibilities and work of the Northern Ireland Policing Board, see: http://www.nipolicingboard.org.uk/index (accessed on 30 July 2011).

15. This news item, 'COMMISSIONER'S CONCERN OVER PSNI LEAFLETS' (*Derry News*, 20 August 2010) can be accessed online, see: http://www.derrynews.net/2010/08/20/commissioner's-concern-over-psni-leaflets/ (accessed on 21 August 2010).

16. This news item can be accessed online, see: http://www.bbc.co.uk/news/uk-northern-ireland-11249047 (accessed on 4 July 2011). See also the role of Crime Watch UK role in releasing the images: http://www.bbc.co.uk/crime-watch/appeals/2010/09/belfast_riots.shtml (accessed on 4 July 2011).

17. For more information, see: http://www.u.tv/news/Police-pictures-risk-childrens-rights/d2e7b577-d003-4da3-9e87-2a744216c202 (accessed on 4 July 2011).

18. Interview conducted on 5 November 2010. The interviewee is referred to throughout the monograph as: POL3 (see Appendix 6, Table 6).

19. This document was released to the researcher by the PSNI via e-mail, for the purposes of this research.

20. For more information, see: http://www.bbc.co.uk/news/uk-northern-ireland-11429160 (accessed on 4 July 2011). The local print media reports on

the judicial review include headlines such as: '"EXPOSURE" PHOTO BREACHED TEEN'S PRIVACY: COURT HOLD' (*Derry Journal*, 28 September 2010) and 'DERRY TEEN WINS PHOTO PRIVACY BID' (*Derry Journal*, 29 September 2010).

21. For more information, see: http://www.bbc.co.uk/news/uk-northern-ire-land-11435661 (accessed on 4 July 2011).

22. For more information, see: http://www.psni.police.uk/operation_relentless (accessed on 25 November 2011). For access to each news item, see: http://www.u.tv/News/PSNI-put-warrant-wanted-pictures-online/aab87fbd-f6ca-4743-ba73-19e2aa90b819 (accessed on 22 November 2011) and http://www.bbc.co.uk/news/uk-northern-ireland-foyle-west-15833297   (accessed on 22 November 2011).

23. [2015] UKSC 42.

24. Gordon, F. (2016) 'Publication of children's images, privacy and Article 8: judgment in the matter of An Application by JR38 for Judicial Review (Northern Ireland) [2015] UKSC 42' *Northern Ireland Legal Quarterly*, 67 (2), 257–261, 2016.

6

'It's the Nature of the Beast': Responses from the Media and Other 'Moral Entrepreneurs'

Contrasting opinions exist in relation to the power dynamics present in the news making processes:

> If you want to look at the portrayal of young people in the media, don't start by assuming a conspiracy. (Laidler 1997: 105)

> Institutional critiques … are commonly dismissed by establishment commentators as 'conspiracy theories', but this is merely an evasion. (Herman and Chomsky 1994: xii)

Academic research and critical analyses of the role, practices and content of the media, such as studies produced by the Glasgow Media Group, have been criticised by the media profession (see Harrison 1985; Winston 1986). However, as Herman and Chomsky (1994: xii) assert, such responses are 'an evasion', which attempt to deflect attention away from those in power. As outlined in previous chapters, there is very little existing or ongoing academic research on the media in Northern Ireland. Of the limited existing studies, few contain the voices of those working in the media. Academics have criticised research on 'moral panics' and media representations, for not including the voices of those who produce the news items (Lashmar 2010). In addressing this, this chapter presents the findings from 16 interviews with newspaper editors, journalists, broadcast journalists, politicians and an Inspector from the Police Service of Northern Ireland (PSNI).[1] The observations that Northern Ireland *'is a very media intensive place'* (JOURN1), has *'a large number of newspapers for such a small place'* and *'enjoys high levels of readerships'* (ED5), emphasise the importance of research on the print media.[2]

© The Author(s) 2018
F. Gordon, *Children, Young People and the Press in a Transitioning Society*,
Palgrave Socio-Legal Studies, https://doi.org/10.1057/978-1-137-60682-2_6

Rarely questioned on their role and the content of the news items they produce, several of those working in the media felt somewhat challenged or uncomfortable. For instance, one editor at the close of the interview asked: *'Did the rest of the journalists roughly answer the questions like mine or did they have different agendas?'* (ED5) and another editor stated: *'When I am talking to you everything is about defending our coverage'* (ED6). Interviewing those who are trained interviewers and perhaps more used to asking questions, than answering them, presented itself as an interesting dynamic. While defensiveness was the most common approach, one editor proposed that, *'it is a rather unusual industry in that we rely on academics and others to give us some view of whether we are on the wrong path'* (ED7).

This chapter's analysis compares and contrasts the views of the interviewees with regard to the key themes drawn from the literature review, as well as prominent themes that emerged from the content analysis and case study. Thus, reference to the findings in Chaps. 4 and 5, are included in the analysis that follows. This chapter is divided into three parts. Part I critically explores the role of the media in the 'new' Northern Ireland, focusing on the procedures and practices used by the media organisations in presenting the news items analysed in previous chapters. Part II explores the meanings and interpretations editors and journalists attach to media coverage of children and young people. It assesses the relationship between the state, state agencies and the media. Part III analyses the views of interviewees with regard to their current and future engagement with children, young people and advocates.

Role, Impact and Regulation of the Press

The empirical research explored the role and functions of the media from the perspective of those working in the journalism profession. When considering the role of newspapers in society, editors and journalists indicated that they have several important functions, which include: *'to inform as accurately as possible'* (ED1), *'to be balanced'*, *'report fact as opposed to speculation and comment … and not to sensationalise'* (ED4). One editor stated that it is a newspaper's role to *'expose'* and *'lift the stone'* in order *'to tell the public … about what other people like politicians don't think the public ought to know'* (ED2). Another editor stated that journalists must, *'hold a mirror up to society and reflect what society is like … what people do … and show it as more flawed'* (ED5). Such responses indicated the important role of newspapers in society. Further, the range of responses presented the existence of a myriad set of opinions on the media's role.

Journalism in a Period of 'Transition'

The literature review established the importance of analysing journalism in its social, cultural, political context. Interviewees clearly identified the transition from conflict as a significant contextual influence on the role of the media in the 'new' Northern Ireland. As one journalist suggested: *'this is contemporary Northern Ireland, the role of the media is situated in a particular time and space … and … is really quite complicated'* (JOURN2). Specifically focusing on the current ongoing transition, one politician stated that, *'the media has played a major role in bringing the province forward out of the violence'* (POL3). Several interviewees suggested that as a result of the *'very unusual set of circumstances'* (JOURN3) and *'form of government here'* (ED7), *'the media needs to be the opposition'* (JOURN3). Editors and journalists asserted that the transition from conflict has brought with it inevitable *'changes'* to the newsroom agenda and media content. As an editor described:

> *Now 17 odd years down the line since the ceasefires, I think the media is still coming to grips with it … when I started out in journalism … the Troubles[3] were still going and … basically filled papers … that's all gone now … The media are very much coming to terms with how it is replaced … it's sort of settling down to peace time, normal reporting.* (ED4)

The impact of *'the normalisation of media coverage'* is that newspapers appear *'more focused now on bread and butter issues than we used to be'* (ED5). Typically journalists argued that, *'because of the Troubles … so many different things … fell below the radar'* (JOURN3) and *'we should now be talking about them'* (JOURN2). Several interviewees proposed that *'crime'* and *'criminal justice issues'* were particularly prominent and have *'filled that vacuum'*, with journalists now *'look[ing] to … police … courts and … prisons to generate stories that would have previously been generated by the Troubles'* (ED4). One editor succinctly described this focus on *'criminal justice issues'* as *'feeding the beast'* (ED2).

Politicians also discussed the changing role and focus of the media. One politician stated that during the Conflict:

> *The situation was different, we weren't getting as many complaints then and people were saying: 'Bring back the RA,[4] they will sort it out for us' … More pressing matters, children and people getting shot by plastic bullets, was a headline. That was a more serious incident than people standing on a street corner drinking … so I think that was the reason, because we had better headlines.* (POL5)

This politician emphasised that children and young people *'standing on a street corner'* was not as much of a focus for the media during the Conflict, whereas it has become a focus now in this transitional period (POL5). The interviewee went on to state that while they did not think society *'has declared war'* on children and young people, *'in my own party room … young people are labelled badly … I think that's where adults and young people aren't in touch'* (POL5).

Three politicians discussed the impact of the devolution of policing and justice and one representative comment was:

> We have only had devolution for a small period of time but there are very few people in the political class speaking out about the causes of crime … rather people are happy to jump on the bandwagon and talk about crime and blame it on young people. (POL4)

This response emphasised prominent political responses to 'crime' and young people. It indicated the role politicians play in reinforcing punitive opinions and reactions, which are subsequently presented in media coverage. Further, it provided an insight into the role of political discourse and politicians in criminal justice policy making, post-devolution.

Journalistic Custom and Practice

The interviews considered journalistic custom and practice from the perspective of editors and journalists. In doing so, this empirical study addressed the call for academic research to explore 'the professional ideologies', 'work practices' and 'constraints' experienced by those working in the media (Curran et al. 1988). While Barrat (1994: 94) asserts that, 'journalists are probably the worst people to ask about news values', the interview responses provided an insight into newsroom culture, current practices and how such dynamics impact on media content. Those working in the media routinely raised 'accuracy', 'responsibility', 'pressures' and 'personalities', as key elements of journalistic custom and practice.

When discussing the accuracy of news items, several interviewees felt the need to defend media content. One typical response was: *'we are not reckless in our reporting'* (ED1). Accuracy was regularly linked to responsibility and as one editor commented, *'we have a responsibility … to … carry out the journalistic checks'*, so that *'the information we put out in the public domain is 100 percent accurate'* (ED4). Editors also emphasised the individual responsibility placed on journalists: *'you … thoroughly check stories as best you can, but you are relying on reporters to do their job'* (ED6) and *'all I … see is what the journalist hands me, I am not working on it'* (ED3). The pressures of the working environment were described as having an impact on accuracy of media content. As one interviewee highlighted, *'accuracy is not always possible'* (ED1).

A small number of editors and journalists stated that their role in producing news items *'can be very formulaic'* (JOURN3), as they work *'with the notion of the story too casually'*, producing *'interest stories and selling it that way'* (JOURN2). Several interviewees acknowledged that, *'you are taking the easiest options all the time … it is office-phone journalism now'* (ED6) and *'you cut corners, you go for the simplest explanation rather than the … complicated explanation'* (JOURN2). This element of current journalistic custom and practice was heavily criticised by two politicians. One representative response reflected on personal experience:

> *Journalists are quite lazy … they don't go out and look for a story … someone rings and tells them if there is a story … If it is something valuable and worthy of a news piece, then they should come out and do it.* (POL5)

Keeping the approach *'simple'* inevitably has an impact on media content (see Chibnall 1977; Poynting et al. 2004). One journalist was of the opinion that the readership is typically provided with, *'a partial story … a partial message'* (JOURN2). A unique response from a journalist outlined that in some instances this can include, *'a skewed and twisted story, where the newspaper … manufactures the truth'* (JOURN2). Further, individual personalities or *'inflated egos'* (ED1) were said to influence the approaches taken and one journalist was of the opinion that, *'the best journalists … play devil's advocate'* (JOURN1). In contrast, several interviewees were critical of some in the profession including, *'journalists who … push their own agenda or … individual prejudices or the editor's prejudice'*, which were described as *'quite surprisingly pro-establishment or quite right wing'* (JOURN3). In contrast two interviewees felt that, *'opinionated'* (ED1) journalists were *'a good thing'* in the profession and *'worth having'* in order, *'to engage the readers … provoke [and] … stimulate debate'* (ED1).

Technological developments were a significant factor which impacted on news production. As one editor observed, *'the whole business has changed dramatically … I don't necessarily think it's for the best'* (ED1). With the introduction of *'24-hour news'*, a perceived increase in readership expectation was described as an additional pressure. In addition, the impact of the economic recession has resulted in *'massive pressure … to hit deadlines'*, with *'fewer journalists on the ground'* (ED4). Inevitably *'pressure'* and *'less resources'* were said to have *'an effect on the quality'* of media content (ED7) and one editor predicted that, *'if the current climate continues … our ability to keep … quality up, will lessen'* (ED7). These responses were in line with the existing literature, which highlights how the 'news-making' process is influenced by 'personal whims', 'rules … of the office', time pressures and 'the need to make profit' (Barrat 1994: 92).

Newsworthiness and Crime Reporting

It is well established that the definition of 'newsworthy events' are typically 'determined by professional and social ideologies' and 'organizational routines' that operate in the newsroom (van Dijk 1991: 40). 'Newsworthiness' relates to the decisions that editors and journalists make about which stories to cover and how, and which to exclude (Newburn 2007). Those working in the media unanimously highlighted how difficult a concept *'newsworthiness'* was to define. Typically interviewees stated that: *'it's your own intuition'*, *'you make a judgement call'* (ED1) and *'it is the old, man bites dog test … you know in your head … what you have to do and … report on'* (ED3). These responses were reflective of Machin and Niblock's (2006: 1) observation that journalists typically 'describe their thinking as so instinctive that it defies explanation'.

Editors and journalists highlighted that in, *'play[ing] to the galleries … you reinforce what you think your audience wants to hear'*, by *'creating … a narrative'* that consists of *'an active drama'*, which will *'grab the public's attention'* (JOURN2). In line with Chibnall (1977) and Galtung and Ruge's (1965, 1982) analyses, interviewees acknowledged that the content of news was therefore predominantly *'negative'*. In defending this, one editor employed the following example: *'in the past people have set up good news newspapers and they've always closed'* (ED5). The *'narrative'* particularly in relation to *'crime'* was described as typically, *'sensational shock horror probe reporting'*, which *'is what people are buying them for'* (ED3). All of those interviewed agreed that *'crime'* and *'punishment'* was one of the most *'newsworthy'* and *'strong'* themes within newspapers (ED4).

Several interviewees stated that media coverage does not represent the actual amount of 'crime' in society. There were differing viewpoints, with some interviewees arguing that *'crime is hugely underreported'* (ED7). The interviewee representing the PSNI was of the opinion that, *'the news media …*

present to the wider public that crime and disorder is all prevalent … it does affect the fear of crime' (PSNI1). While the majority of those working in the media acknowledged that newspaper reporting of *'crime and the criminal justice system is bound to shape the public's perception'* (ED4), in contrast a small number described their role as *'reflecting people's beliefs'*, rather than *'influencing'* public perception (ED5).

Editors and journalists described *'tabloid newspapers'* as a clear example of *'an opinion former'* (ED6). As one tabloid editor acknowledged: *'we go out to have headlines that are biased or take a stance'*, by *'call[ing] people murderers … "string them up" … make sentences longer … jail them'* (ED6). Another editor felt that *'naming and shaming'* was justified as, *'part of the deal with the law, is if you break it … public shame is also a key part of punishment and rehabilitation'* (ED5). Significantly, several interviewees argued that language employed to describe *'offenders'*, as well as labels, such as *'monsters'*, were *'not … invented'* by journalists, but come *'from the professionals who work with them'*, or *'the relatives of the victims or … survivors themselves'* (ED2).

In contrast, one journalist was critical of this approach. In line with studies that demonstrate the existence of 'overgeneralisations' and 'oversimplifications' in crime reporting (see Bowes 1977), this journalist emphasised that editors and journalists, *'have a tendency to be a little bit black and white in … coverage of crime … the villain is the villain … cops and robbers … goodies and baddies'* (JOURN3). The journalist stated that, *'Jamie Bulger is a good case in point'*, with the media *'perpetuat[ing] … this myth that it is black and white and there is no background story'* (JOURN3). This response demonstrated how the lack of *'background'* or contextual information included in news items on crime, typically resulted in oversimplified representations. A similar observation was noted by Poynting et al. (2004: 50), who conclude that 'ideological explanation[s]' typically 'provid[e] a simple narrative of us and them, good and evil, victim and wrongdoer'.

One editor in strongly criticising the approach of one local tabloid newspaper, described it as *'useless'* and emphasised how, *'some bastard behind the hedge with a long lens camera … is just the dregs. You would be ashamed to be … associated with crap like that'* (ED1). This was a contemporary illustration of the practice of intrusion. Significantly, discussions 'over ways to reconcile freedom of expression by the media' and 'the respect for the private lives of individuals', has been a core part of 'a long process of debate' on the role and practice of the media in contemporary society (House of Commons 2003: 3). The direct impact of media intrusion will be explored further in the chapters that follow.

Readership, Sources and Influence

Editors and journalists emphasised the relationship between the commercial element of the newspaper industry and catering for the readership: *'we have to pay our way in the world … so we produce the products that people want'* (ED7) and *'tailor content to … meet … demands'* (ED4). While the readership do not usually play an active role in how media content is produced, they do play a key role in interpreting news items (Ang 1990a) and in the 'compliance', 'acceptance' and 'reproduction' of a dominant discourse (Teo 2000). Each editor and journalist demonstrated how the media's relationship with its readership *'is very close … in Northern Ireland [as] people … trust the press'* (ED2). *'Power'* to influence public opinion was highlighted by several interviewees who emphasised that, *'our news coverage tends to help shape opinions … change perceptions'* (ED4) and *'you do … colour people's views … no doubt about that'* (ED1).

One editor emphasised how central *'contacts'* were to the sourcing of content, as *'every newspaper … depends upon contacts, your stories come in through contacts'* (ED2). The use of sources is a central element in the 'news-making' process, as very few news events are directly observed by journalists, most are gathered from secondary sources and are 're-packaged' (Barrat 1994). Interviewees asserted that when reporting on *'crime'* and *'criminal justice issues'*, journalists *'go for elected representatives'*, *'professionals working in the field'* (ED2) and *'fairly right wing politicians'* (JOURN3). As a politician interviewed stated:

> *The media like a package … if the media want a lock them up and throw away the key voice on a debate, they'll ring [name] and get him on … he is going to give you this right-wing, punitive, all young people are bad perspective. They will … come to me and say well here's a liberal leftie … she could go up against him … she'll ding dong with him … That's what the media like … the black and white, here's one for and here's one against … Again no analysis, no understanding … or awareness about the issues … and what we are going to do to tackle those. (POL2)*

Consistent with the research reviewed in Chap. 2, there was a general consensus amongst those working in the media that they have *'a very close relationship with politicians'* (ED4). One editor described the relationship as *'a double edged sword'* (ED4), as *'politicians need the media, because politicians need the profile, the media needs politicians because we need that kind of source of information'* (ED4). While some interviewees suggested that, *'with some politicians … there are people having lunch or coffee with certain people from newspaper outlets and there is a certain schmoozing going'* (JOURN2), as *'politicians have a job to do, they want to get their message across in the most positive way'*

(JOURN1). One unique response from a journalist stated that their *'job is to cut through the spin and get to the accuracy of what they [politicians] are saying'* and ideally, *'there should be tension ... you have to be friendly but it doesn't mean that you are friends'* (JOURN1).

Several editors and journalists made the observation that, *'now ... we have a devolved administration that has to deal with justice issues ... politicians ... [are] much more sensitive to public opinion in that area'* (JOURN1). This 'closeness' with the media was also evident in responses from politicians and each politician interviewed highlighted the need for a relationship with media outlets. Typically, politicians outlined their personal experiences and relationships with editors and journalists:

> *There are certain journalists that you develop a relationship with ... I have a number of journalists that I would be very close to, that I am able to talk to off the record ... Politicians are always looking for headlines ... that is how we get our publicity ... that is how we get our PR.* (POL3)

Politicians utilise the media as *'a platform ... to get re-elected'* or *'to moralise and say this is what we should do'* (POL1). Several politicians were critical of their colleagues and one representative response was:

> *Politicians care more about getting media ... very often the relationship is too cosey ... it is unhealthy ... doesn't lead to good investigative journalism ... Some ... just prefer the airtime as opposed to the consequences of that airtime.* (POL2)

In contrast one politician emphasised political *'responsibility'* and stated that on certain occasions, *'you don't like to go to newspapers with issues because they do tend to make stories bigger that what they are'* (POL5).

In line with Chibnall's (1977) analysis of crime reporting, editors and journalists acknowledged that their relationship and *'ongoing conversations with the PSNI'* (ED4) played a significant *'confirmation'* role in relation to incidents of *'crime'* (ED6). One editor described the PSNI as, *'our touchstone ... they tell us that something happens'* (ED6). However, several interviewees indicated that *'the relationship is not as close as the media would like it to be'* (ED4), as *'the PSNI are exceptionally closed'* (ED7). One editor made reference to *'striking examples'* of *'things happening ... up to and including murder ... that we have no idea about'* (ED7). The PSNI spokesperson acknowledged that the PSNI operated *'a degree of caution, because the media aren't there to do us a favour'* (PSNI1). However, the interviewee observed that the PSNI *'have got much more media aware ... you see lots more interviews with police'*, as the media *'can be a very good way of getting the message across, whether it is an apology ... or intervention message'* (PSNI1). The PSNI spokesperson acknowledged that media coverage *'does make a big difference to the [public's] response'* and can be employed *'to convince people to trust you'* (PSNI1).

Editors and journalists considered that media content *'does influence government'*, which was evident *'whenever you see politicians courting certain newspaper proprietors'* (ED2) and as a result *'the government do introduce new laws ... probably on the back of media opinion'* (ED1). Interviewees also asserted that content did influence *'policy makers at Stormont'*, who *'do sit up and take notice if something is highlighted ... and run with in the media'* (ED5). Several politicians interviewed were critical of how media content and language can influence policy. One representative comment was:

> *What you end up with ... is a sensationalised press, who are fed it all too easy ... [and] vilify young people as a cohort ... turn them into the problem and then that ends up in government policy, [such as] ... 'The Cohesion, Sharing and Integration Strategy'.* (POL4)

There were differing opinions on whether the media impacts or has an influence on the legal process. Several of those interviewed stated that, *'on legal issues [it] ... is a much different ball game ... I don't think that there is that much of an impact'* (ED1). Notably, in contrast several other interviewees stated that media content could influence the legal process. As one editor commented, *'I have no doubt that ... stories have influenced judges, they are human after all'* (ED7) and another described how their newspaper had *'got private briefings from judges ... really upset that we would be criticising them ... and they do react by increased sentences on appeal'* (ED6). Several interviewees highlighted that, *'the media can certainly drive notable change'* but in their opinion it occured *'only if the public gets on board'* (JOURN2). Therefore, such viewpoints demonstrated the significance of the role of the readership, as well as the power of media representations in shaping the audience's or readership's understanding (see Croteau and Hoynes 2003).

Media Ethics, Regulation and Training

There has been limited research into the media's perspective on the current media regulatory bodies and guidelines (see Kieran 1998). Thus, the findings from interviewees were insightful in this respect. One editor described, *'journalistic ethics'* as *'a bedrock'* (ED6). A small number of journalists emphasised their personal, *'strong ethical views'* (JOURN3) and one commented, *'we all* have our own moral code, the court you have to face at night' (JOURN2). The current formal regulatory system for the press, while typically criticised by academics and others for *'not being independent'* (ED2), was in the media's experience, *'a very effective system'*, as the *'PCC are … very thorough … robust and … efficient'* when investigating complaints (ED4). Interviewees were keen to emphasise that, *'there is no sense of doing any favours'* (ED4). Editors stressed that although, *'the PCC … know us very well … it is a professional working relationship, it is not "pally pally", we don't get away with anything'* (ED2) and *'the fact that it does involve senior members of our industry, almost gives it more clout'* (ED4).

When discussing adjudications, interviewees typically described the process as *'we win some, we lose some'*, with the role of the legal profession central in responding to the Press Complaints Commission (PCC), *'our lawyer would write out huge responses'* (ED6). When discussing the impact of regulation on the profession, typical responses related to the outcome of PCC investigations. One editor stated that, *'we've only … got nailed about half a dozen times … generally we get the adjudication on our side … when we don't, we have to publish the adjudication'*, but explained that with certain cases, *'you do get narky about … things'* (ED2). Another editor commented that, *'papers like it … it saves … having to go to court'* (ED6).

One editor was critical of the PCC and described it as, *'a useless fucking organisation, might as well go to the Salvation Army … reactive … you get a rebuke … you carry an apology, so what?'* (ED1). Several other interviewees felt the PCC had become *'tougher'* and had *'more teeth recently … people are free to ignore it, but in practice no one does'* (ED5). Overall, the majority of editors and journalists interviewed held the *'belief that the media should be self-regulated'* (ED5), and felt that the current regulatory system was *'effective'* (ED4), as the *'PCC … keeps standards higher … if the PCC Code wasn't there, standards would be much lower'* (ED5).

One editor argued that, *'it is a question for them whether they help vulnerable members of society or not'* (ED7). Whereas other comments indicated that *'the PCC is free of charge'* (ED7) and *'accessible'* to members of the public (ED4). Another editor described the regulatory body as, *'very conscious of the issues surrounding children and young people'*, evidenced in *'the Code of Practice … guidelines'* and *'very strict rules'*, which ensured that *'the media is very closely policed'* (ED4). However, as another journalist pointed out, *'I wouldn't expect kids to know about OFCOM or the Press Complaints Commission'* (JOURN3). With regard to training in the area of *'child protection'*, interviewees acknowledged that the current *'journalism course wouldn't include that'* (ED4). In addition, several interviewees asserted that: *'I don't think we need any more people monitoring the media'* (JOURN2). Further, they noted that in addition to the PCC, their profession were also *'regulated ... in matters of accuracy and privacy ... under the European Law'* (ED5).

The politicians interviewed did not comment in depth on the current regulatory system for the press, as many had no experience of the PCC. However, one politician asserted that, *'regulation of the press is always difficult. The whole thing is about privacy laws'* (POL1). In contrast to the majority opinion of those working in the media, several politicians suggested that, *'NICCY or even OFCOM ... should start to monitor the media on how they portray children and young people'* (POL2). As one politician asserted, *'if you are relying on vulnerable groups to come to you to complain, often it does not happen'* (POL2). The findings emphasised that editors and journalists feel the current regulatory arrangements and guidelines are suitable. In addition, interviewees' responses outlined that media training did not include education or training in the area of children's rights and child protection. Further, those working in the media placed the onus on the regulatory bodies, particularly in relation to 'access' and how 'vulnerability' has been considered in regulatory and editorial guidelines.

Media Portrayal and Representations of Children and Young People

Language and Imagery

As the literature review established, the media's selection of words, phrases and images presents 'certain meanings', which 'define what is a social problem' and 'how an issue should be understood' (van Zoonen 1996: 38–39). Thus, language and imagery plays a central role in the construction and amplification of social problems, such as children and young people's perceived involvement in anti-social behaviour and crime. Consistent with Chibnall (1977) and Galtung and Ruge's (1965, 1982) analyses, editors and journalists routinely spoke in terms of *'positive'* and *'negative'*, as well as *'good'* and *'bad'*. One comment from a journalist was, *'we are in a negativity culture here ... we are reinforcing negativity constantly ... we cannot get a grip of positivity ... we are reinforcing it with young people'* (JOURN2). This was a unique response, as the majority of those working in the media forcefully emphasised examples of *'positive'* representations.

Editors and journalists typically asserted that *'newspapers are stuffed full of positive stuff'* (ED3). Representative comments described newspaper coverage of children and young people, as *'good'* and *'fair'*. As one editor argued, *'we are conscious that we want to portray a positive side of young people ... we often go out of our way to write positive stories'* (ED5) and another representative comment asserted that:

> *They get a fair win ... there is much interest in what young people do on the sports field ... young people tend to forget that when they start slagging off the press for giving them a hard time ... they get a fairly reasonably good press.* (ED1)

Two politicians criticised this focus on sports and educational achievement. As one politician commented:

> *May be it's a middle class media ... promoting a middle class notion of what children should be about ... A Level's, GCSE's ... may be it is something to do with class... and how they perceive how young people should act.* (POL2)

In contrast Bessant and Hil's (1997) assertion that 'youth crime' is deemed 'newsworthy' because of 'negativity' and its 'dramatic appeal', when the content of media coverage was discussed further, several editors and journalists were defensive. One editor asserted strongly, *'I haven't seen a... general, "young people are awful", kind of stuff in any of the papers'*, and further argued that:

> *Young people in trouble with the law ... for some reason there is a view that when it is reported ... that we are in some way denigrating that whole community. I think that sensible people can see that that is not the case.* (ED7)

Expressing a different opinion, a journalist referred to it as *'the nature of the media'* and asserted that:

> *If there is a small element who get pregnant ... that is what the media focuses on ... it is the 20 percent who get the headlines and the generation ... gets a bad name ... The media does distort but it's the nature of the beast ... I don't know how you'd get around that because going to school to see young people get prizes doesn't sell newspapers, but ... rioting does.* (JOURN1)

It was more common for editors to defend the news items they produce:

> *If kids are involved in crime ... the press are fair in their reporting and balanced ... There was a case yesterday ... nailing a guy about 18 or 19, he ... used a blow-torch to break into people's homes that ... is a very professional criminal job... he is a young person which makes it worse and whenever you go back to the Jamie Bulger*

killing … I think that it's fair to report that in the way it was. It was evil. If it is a crime, it really doesn't matter what age you are … it should be reported. (ED2)

Another editor firmly placed blame on *'the tabloids'*, which were described as, *'much more likely to stereotype children'* by employing language such as, *'hoodies … yobbos, young thugs terrorising estates'* (ED4). The editor also asserted that, *'as regards the rest of us … we certainly take a much more balanced view … because we are so closely policed by the PCC … we are less likely to indulge in … sensationalised or unbalanced reporting'* (ED4).

In contrast, a small number of those working in the media did acknowledge that *'demonisation'* and *'negativity'* featured in the daily newspapers and community newspapers in Northern Ireland:

We have to put our hands up and say sometimes we can demonise young people because … young people in this community … congregating … that is anti-community, sometimes that is … criminality … we have to report on that. (ED3)

This is consistent with the literature analysed in Chap. 2, which outlines that news coverage frames youth as 'unruly, anti-social delinquents'. In turn this presents children and young people as a 'threat' to the 'inner' community (Glover 1984; Curran 2002).

One editor emphasised how 'newsworthy' particular stories become:

In terms of bad press … young people go out to celebrate their exam results and are found laying drunk … they are going to get a bad media … If students … starting acting the maggot … you just say … How fucking pathetic and juvenile is that? If you have a choice between drunken students … causing mayhem … including [researcher's name] … or a young student who has been named musician of the year … the likelihood is that the students pissing up against the wall … are going to make the front page … A whole squad of kids cleaning the windows … for … pensioners, is that going to make the front page? Some wee bastard who has been spending the past two nights wrecking windows … is held up on front of a court … is more likely to make the news. (ED1)

Further, this interviewee made several comments in relation to the researcher, specifically in relation to presumed age and student status. The comments reflected this interviewee's prejudice and views, which were influenced by stereotypes.

The use of specific language and labels to describe children and young people were justified by several editors and journalists who asserted that, *'it is also the way people talk in real life'* (ED5); *'you see it … everywhere, young people as "smicks" and "hoods"'* (ED3). Further to this, several interviewees justified this *'bad press'* coverage (ED1) by asserting that: *'young people are taking part in crime. They are the hoodies … the people out rioting'* (ED6).

Another similar response was:

> *I don't see how a media should praise children for being good citizens. What we do highlight is when they are not … and some have to accept that the majority … of that kind of anti-social, minor crime is carried out by that age group.* (ED7)

One editor described newspaper coverage of *'anti-community … youths'*, as *'part of our community duty'* (ED3). The editor stated that newspapers *'have to report on it'*, especially as *'people expect to read about it'* (ED3). Another representative view further reinforced opinions on children and young people's position in society:

> *If you are going along to a children's play area it is not hard news… Young people … aren't particularly powerful … so often when you are going to interview them it is because they are causing trouble.* (JOURN1)

A number of politicians presented several observations, which are consistent with Tannenbaum's (1938) analysis of the role of society and societal reaction. One example was: *'the press for young people is more negative than for other age groups … that fits in with stereotypical views … reflects what society thinks'* (POL1).

The opinions of children and young people were dismissed by some of the editors and journalists. When discussing the potential stereotypical, symbolic nature of clothing and *'hoodies'*, one interviewee stated that:

> *The whole dress thing … is in their heads … 'Just because we wear jeans and trainers … have holes in our shoes, why are you giving us a hard time?' No we are not, I couldn't care whether you fucking go in your bare feet. So the dress thing … sorry, people are pathetic.* (ED1)

In contrast, two journalists reflected on the language and imagery employed and emphasised journalistic responsibility and ethical standards:

> *You could go to the next level and say that all students are binge drinkers … going out and getting the pictures of the kids as drunk as possible and throwing up on the street and wearing as little as possible if they are girls … that doesn't interest me, so I think the journalist has to have a certain amount of integrity and ethics around what they are doing.* (JOURN3)

Words like thugs or thuggery ... give a certain impression like a deliberate act ... We need to have a serious conversation with ourselves about how we do present ... particularly children ... in troubled circumstances. (JOURN2)

One politician interviewed held a similar opinion and stated that the media regularly focus on, *'disadvantaged young people ... mostly young males. When it is young females, it is even worse'* (POL2). Another politician employed a personal example to illustrate the implications of the use of particular words and phrases:

I actually did a thing with the 'Andytown News' last week and the journalist was trying to sensationalise it by saying he wanted to use the word significant and I said I didn't use the word significant. I said there was a lot of drug and alcohol issues in our community. I didn't say a significant number of issues, because that would have transformed his story into a headline story. So he didn't use the word significant, he used it in his part, but didn't use it as my quote. (POL5)

This example was particularly insightful, as it emphasised one politician's experience of the news-making process. It also indicated how central personal and political responsibility was to ensuring viewpoints were not manipulated in order to *'sensationalise'* (POL5) news items.

Media Content Themes

As part of the investigative element of the interviewing process, the interviewer presented interviewees with a list of preliminary themes that emerged from the content analysis of newspaper coverage. The main focus of their responses related to the themes of anti-social behaviour; crime; violence; 'gangs'; youth suicide and intergenerational relationships. Their comments reflected the differing views and approaches that exist among journalists in Northern Ireland in relation to the media's reporting on, and engagement with children, young people and their advocates.

Anti-social Behaviour

Editors and journalists used the phrases, *'anti-social behaviour'* and *'criminality'*, interchangeably when describing: *'kids ... out drinking ... sniffing glue ... the hoods ... running rampage through the streets'* (ED2). One editor also regularly employed the phrase *'anti-community behaviour'* and stated that the use of phrases such as, *'anti-social behaviour and anti-community behaviour'* were *'sort of a technical trick'*, employed by the newspaper to *'separate ... crime and what happens on the streets'* (ED3). Several interviewees asserted that *'anti-social behaviour clearly ... has been an issue for years ... these are the people who are taking part in criminal acts'* (ED5). Another editor posed several questions:

> *Are we saying that that minor criminal act should not be reported? Should be reported in a different way because there are young people involved? ... I think that most people are sensible enough in their opinion ... there are good and bad ... criminals and non-criminals ... you hear it time and again that the media somehow portray all young people as bad ... I am open to be shown.* (ED7)

While the above interviewee required evidence, another editor acknowledged:

> *[C]overage of young people is negative ... we have done stories about young people ... gangs ... anti-social behaviour, at time were ... 200 of them have gathered to play music and rave ... We've done all that stuff ... We try to contextualise it as well ... We mightn't be doing as good a job as we should be.* (ED3)

In discussing this further, the same editor went on to describe young people as a social group involved in, *'outrageous acts of anti-community behaviour ... vagrant criminality'*, which included *'street drinking ... hanging around street corners, urinating, screaming late at night, having sex ... leaving used condoms about ... taking drugs'* (ED3). The interviewee argued that:

> *Young people have to take their responsibility ... if you are a young person living down there, even if you are not engaging in it ... it is not as frightening or as hostile an environment ... because that is ... their peer group ... other people who were getting on to us, were absolutely terrified ... barring their doors ... So that is the balance we have to strike ... Clearly we have to report on it.* (ED3)

Significantly, several editors and journalists agreed that reporting of *'anti-social behaviour'* should involve an element of *'naming and shaming'*, which was typically described as *'legitimate'* (ED2). One editor asserted that, *'we do it consistently'* and provided reasons for this approach:

> *Those ... kids ... I don't have an answer of what you do with them ... they are outside the embrace of the law ... they take pride in beings hoods ... there is poison at the heart of a community ... It's back to parents and respect ... for the people who*

live in your community … Pensioners who are being intimidated … attacked … robbed … If I got the name of one of … those hoods, I would … put them in the paper. (ED2)

One politician highlighted public support for this media approach:

I can understand residents who want them to do it as well … you hear it every time you go to a residents meeting, they want to name and shame young people and put a letter around the doors. (POL5)

One journalist proposed that media coverage of *'anti-social behaviour and ASBOs'* becomes *'a badge of honour'*, as *'children like the attention'* and the *'sort of notoriety'* (JOURN1). This journalist also succinctly presented a point that several other interviewees also raised:

If the state is not prepared to ban the use of … names … then you can't blame the media … The media will go where the story is and if there is no barrier … then the media will report. (JOURN1)

The *'badge of honour'* or *'a badge of pride'* (POL2), and *'self-fulfilling prophecy'* (POL5) were highlighted by two politicians, who argued that the media play a central role in each process:

The media has a big influence … If they are portraying young people as bad [and] sensationalise … I have no doubt there are young people who would aspire to that and say, 'Sure well that's what is expected of us. That's how we are portrayed. So why not live up to the reputation?' (POL2)

These findings demonstrated how editors and journalists employed the phrases anti-social behaviour and anti-community behaviour, as well as their association with criminality and deviance in news items. Further, the interviewees' responses also provided an insight into the origin and application of the labels 'anti-community' and 'anti-community behaviour'. As noted in Chap. 4, these labels are specific to Northern Ireland.

'Gangs'

Routinely, editors and journalists made links between *'anti-social behaviour'* and what has described as *'gang activity'* (ED3). One editor focused on the *'exposure'* given, rather than the impact of the language employed to describe young people:

The IBA … I think we did things wrong … as a community worker pointed out to me … getting on the front page … became a badge of honour for those young people … hardcore criminals, beyond redemption or rehabilitation, they need to be behind bars … I would say we let them show off by giving them the front page. (ED3)

One politician who represents the West Belfast constituency, emphasised that:

The IBA stuff … is a perfect example, if you are going to get any thing blown out of proportion – that was it. Things were appearing in the paper and it just in the space of four weeks … spiralled into being a catastrophe … It then became a popular thing that people were latching on to … Something was made out of nothing, something that could have been resolved quietly, away from the media focus, with community groups … and then you have two young people shot … Once the 'Andytown News' covered it, it got bigger news coverage … everybody was jumping on it because it was a bad news story and it was gripping people. (POL5)

The responses from editors, journalists and politicians reinforced the application of the label 'gang' to describe children and young people's perceived involvement in anti-social behaviour, crime and violence. As discussed in Chap. 4, the sustained media coverage of the 'IBA Gang', amplified youth involvement in violence. The application of the label 'gang' in this context was one illustrative example of the transferral of labels from the US and UK, to Northern Ireland.

Intergenerational Relationships

Journalists and editors consistently referred to *'elderly people'* and *'pensioners'*. Only one journalist acknowledged that the media contributed to the *'fear of crime'* and outlined that when *'elderly people get a knock on the door from a young person … they are fearful … we are part of the reason why'* (JOURN2). One politician also commented on the media's role in contributing or *'perpetuating fear'*:

The media would more likely talk up crimes against older people, which are on the decrease … if crime against an older person was committed by a younger person … it instils fear within and between generations. (POL2)

Another journalist emphasised that when reporting on 'intergenerational crime' journalists must, *'filter out your own point of view … my personal point of view might be to slap the little brat who is torturing the pensioner'* (JOURN1).

Employing an example, one politician asserted that intergenerational crimes were given prominence, as *'some pensioner being beaten half to death … is a bigger news story than some young person who goes and helps'* (POL3). Another politician commented on the role of political representatives:

> *Quite often with older citizens politicians sympathise and … then fall into the trap that the media fall into about young people being bad and that really disappoints me … Politicians really have a responsibility to engage with young people, listen to their needs and their views … we are politicians for everyone … not politicians for an older generation.* (POL2)

As established in Chap. 4, the routine juxtaposition of the term 'vulnerable' to describe older citizens, with the description of young people as perpetrators, added an additional layer of vilification of youth. The interviewees' responses reinforced this juxtaposition. Further, the interviews with politicians provided an insight into the lack of opportunities for young people to be involved in political debate.

Violence

Several editors and journalists stated that they *'have to report'* on youth involvement in violence, as *'there is just no way of getting away from the fact that … young people can descend into criminality'* and were part of *'a very small hardcore … of hardened criminal elements, criminal minded … career criminals'* (ED3). One editor stated that, *'it's hard not to be negative about two kids who beat a lady to death'* (ED5).

Another interviewee employed high profile case examples to demonstrate his editorial line:

> *The Harry Holland case[5] … was … shocking … along with another one or two cases … because they are young, their crimes are relatively lightly punished … They don't get the book thrown at them in the way that perhaps the community thinks that they should and when they are released and come out, a lot of them go back to reoffending … In that instance, there is no question of excusing them or helping them or trying to offer them some way out of it, you just have to report the fact that that is the way they are.* (ED3)

Further to this, several other editors and journalists employed high profile case examples when discussing newspaper reporting of the rights agenda. One representative response was:

The Bill of Rights is where I think a lot of people felt very strongly ... In their discussion groups ... they were suggesting that we decriminalise the under 18's. I think that most sensible people would accept that that is a bonkers idea ... I would not like ... to be interviewing Megan McAllorum's mum and telling her that the guy who abducted, raped, murdered and abandoned your daughter's body can't be prosecuted because of his age ... I would not like to be telling the next mother who because he got off, went on to do the same to ... sorry there is a Bill of Rights ... I think most sensible people would see that as absolute bunkum. There are a whole series of cases ... were people under the age of 18 committed the most serious crimes ... I don't think anyone could support the idea that they simply go through youth diversion or something ... the victims would have to live through that. I don't think they are living in the real world really. (ED7)

One politician discussed the media's portrayal and perception of the rights agenda, at length and stated that:

I don't think the media is particularly interested in portraying any rights agenda ... Look at the debate around the Bill of Rights for Northern Ireland, the media is ... hostile to the concept ... and 'The Irish News' is a classic case in point ... because of the fact that it could leave the murderers of Harry Holland go free ... well it wouldn't ... it is a total ignorance and frankly a very dangerous sort of analysis ... The media find it too easy to generalise and to editorialise ... positions which are not just ill-informed but are potentially dangerous ... the lack of human rights agenda means that we send too many people to prison ... they treat them as if they are lost to society and that is it. (POL4)

The responses from interviewees reflected findings presented in Chap. 4, in particular the strong language employed by several editors and journalists and reference to high profile case examples. This reinforced that children's and young people's alleged involvement in violence was at the sharp continuum of the demonisation and vilification of youth. Further, several responses from those working in the media demonstrated how journalists employed high profile cases when criticising 'alternative' viewpoints and rights discourse.

Youth Suicide

Several interviewees discussed media reporting of youth suicide and as one journalist commented, '*there is a lot of issues around mental health, around suicide ... I'm not ... sure we necessarily do a good job*' (JOURN3). One editor employed a personal experience to illustrate the impact of news items:

The epidemic of suicide among young people … we've tried to down play it … three kids dead … in one week and it looks as if a tabloid newspaper like us are sensationalising that, but then you've got the politicians who come out and say … we want something done about this … After I made that mistake … the man hanging from the bridge, I put it in the front page … we went way, way over the top on it … We offered a quarter of a million quid's worth of free advertising [to charities] … you'd like to do more, but … we are a red top Sunday paper … looking for the next story, the next big story, and it's very hard to go in and do features. (ED2)

Another editor provided an insight into journalistic practice and described how journalists typically source information on the deceased:

The first thing any journalists do … like a reflex action, is to go straight on to Google Images and … search … Their lives are all there … things they are saying can be ridiculous of course … we would go on to … Facebook … take pictures and stuff and … contact parents. (ED6)

In discussing the media's reporting of youth suicide, one politician asserted that:

What you get in many tragic cases … the media … phone up families … and get comments and personally I wouldn't like that job … some things are just unsavoury and inappropriate. (POL1)

A similar practice was emphasised by an editor, who outlined that in relation to reporting on 'anti-social behaviour' and 'crime', journalists would:

Say to people this is what happened, then … interview people and ask them to make sure this doesn't happen again or ask what is going on, on the ground with young people or what are the Cops doing … We try to seed the story with those kinds of things … we … say to people what we can do about it … what are the solutions … options and to offer people a wee bit of hope as well. (ED3)

'Solutions', 'options' and 'hope' were stressed throughout this editor's response and that was unique among media opinions. In contrast, as one politician asserted:

The media play a useful role in highlighting problems, but they play a relatively little role in fixing problems. Public authorities spend many, many hours and money trying to prepare public relations strategies to manage information … may be you would be better off spending those resources fixing the problem, rather than managing the media. (POL1)

The findings assert that in slanting towards 'distortion', 'exaggeration' and 'misrepresentation' of children and young people (Schissel 1997; Simpson 1997), the media's preoccupation with portraying this social group 'as powerful and irrational threats to society', hides 'the root causes which lie in social deprivation' (Glover 1984).

Northern Ireland Context: Reporting, July 2010

In discussing the content of the news coverage of what was described in media and political discourse as 'sectarian rioting' in July 2010, typically editors and journalists referred to the events as *'shocking'* (ED4). Visual *'images'* (ED4) and *'pictures'* printed in newspapers were described as *'dramatic'* (JOURN1) and *'shocking'* (ED4). In describing the media as *'ambulance chasers'*, one politician argued that media outlets have *'vested interests'* in reporting on riots:

> *It soon gets around the world, which means that the media outlets who have taken the pictures ... make a lot of money if they get reproduced ... so it is in their vested interests to push the story out ... so this may not be the Conflict starting over again but ... they can pass it off as that ... It is highly irresponsible but it pays them to do so.* (POL4)

Those working in the media routinely referred to *'the angle'* of news stories and one representative comment summarised the approach taken:

> *If you are reporting the Ardoyne riots, clearly the angle is loads of people have rioted ... a lot more people aren't happy about it and it shouldn't be happening ... I think it is inevitable that the focus is going to be on, simply who are these people, why are they doing this, how do we catch them?* (ED7)

Politicians also reflected on this approach taken by editors and journalists. Representative comments included:

> *The media reporting on riots or shootings is easy peasy for the media, it doesn't require much investigative journalism ... If it bleeds, it leads ... but that is a symptom almost of our society that that's what they buy newspapers for.* (POL1)

> *Anyone involved in rioting, the media are going to zone in on who is the youngest ... That shows a lack of understanding of what is happening in deprived communities ... It is this middle class notion of my parents brought me up well and why are these parents not doing the same thing? It's too simplistic.* (POL2)

Several responses from those working in the media indicated an unwillingness to report on the issues facing 'deprived communities'. The following response was representative in that it placed responsibility on politicians and not on the media to address issues:

> The 'forgotten people' out there ... have been left behind ... Is that the media's fault? It is not the media's fault. Don't belittle or blame the media ... You say: 'Well why don't you spend more time on people who are disadvantaged ... living in poverty ... having a hard time' ... but ... we're trying to inform and... entertain people that's what we do ... you could spend so much time in deprived areas looking at the squalor and poverty and seeing real deprivation ... you can only do that for so long and so many times ... it is people in those areas ... their local councillor ... MLA ... MP, those are the people who should be ... driving those communities on ... but don't blame the media for society's ills ... The media are sometimes in a place where nobody else is and they talk the language that nobody else talks right ... They don't need to worry where their next meal is coming from. Do they have holes in their shoes? No. But don't blame the media because of what's happening is really bad in poor areas. (ED1)

A politician posed a question in relation to this issue:

> You need to ask yourself ... is it the role of the media to address that level of detail or is it the job of communities to address that level of detail? (POL4)

Reference to 'sources' and those prominently quoted were reflected on by several of those working in the media. As one editor commented, 'police went on the record ... various statutory agencies flagged it up ... children as young as nine or ten ... involved in street violence' (ED4). Similarly, another interviewee made reference to the reliance on 'the Ardoyne priest', who 'was saying young lads were out rioting and the girls were all dressed up to the nines ... admiring and going to go out with the boy who could throw the stone or best petrol bombs' (ED6). Further, the majority of editors and journalists emphasised the 'fun' element of rioting for children and young people. As one representative comment asserted, 'someone come up with that saying ... "recreational rioting"... and it is absolutely perfect' (ED6). As discussed in Chap. 5, the term 'recreational rioting' presents youth involvement as 'fun', rather than having any 'political basis' (McAlister et al. 2009: 98) or representing an expression of identity or defence of space (see also McAlister et al. 2010; Meadows 2010). Politicians held similar views on young people's involvement:

It is recreational rioting … not the same as rioting for a political or a social reason, they are rioting because there is nothing better to do with their time. They see where they can cause destruction and they go and do it. (POL5)

In contrast, one journalist criticised the media and political responses and stated that:

The media doesn't want to know about the social history … get a few people hauled out to condemn it and then they move on without maybe tackling why. (JOURN1)

A further two interviewees working in the media criticised the content of news items printed in July 2010. One editor who had, *'an unashamedly Republican/Nationalist viewpoint'*, argued that:

Young people are carrying the can for this … problem that is generations … old … The press just report it every year in exactly the same way – these kids are running wild … there is no analysis … tabloids and the national press … go for the easy headline … that's why we have the demonisation of young people … With depressing regularity you are going to get the same headlines, which will be pasted from last July onto next July … How can that be right? (ED3)

Similarly one journalist stated that:

We like clichés because we have a deadline … It's easier to type a cliché than think of something responsible. Recreational rioting … thuggery is a cliché, these are clichés, stereotypes, which reinforce problems but we need a wake up call in journalism to think about what these words mean. (JOURN2)

The majority of editors and journalists stated that the 2010 media coverage included several additional elements, which had not been present in previous years. *'Dissidents'* were described as one new *'focus'*, with several editors and journalists emphasising that they *'are getting a foothold of … young people'*, who are *'being recruited'* (JOURN1). Similarly, several interviewees stated that the *'focus on the age of the people involved'* was *'slightly more'* evident (ED4). Placing the *'focus on youth'* (JOURN2) and highlighting the *'age'* of children and young people was described as *'justified'*, as it was a *'striking'* element (ED4) and was *'the shock factor'* (JOURN2).

In addition, several of those working in the media emphasised the 'past' and 'transition' in a number of significant comments. As one journalist commented, *'that violence would have been considered par for the course a couple of years ago ... may be it got a lot of focus because it is more unusual now'* (JOURN1). Further representative comments made similar observations:

> *Why are we experiencing this in the context of a peace settlement? Is now a question we didn't ask in the past ... We are supposed to have left this behind us, why are we seeing this? It is like we've signed a peace agreement and therefore everything is fixed ... so there is a certain naivety in our coverage and the public's understanding.* (JOURN2)

> *Any time up until this stage you could use the excuse, well look what they grew up with ... soldiers interning their fathers, or ... policemen ... killed ... The climate was so negative that it meant that you could excuse some of the things away ... I've heard it talked about in our newsroom, you look at the kids who are ten ... born after the Good Friday Agreement, what could they possibly know about sectarianism and about the real Troubles?* (JOURN3)

Several politicians interviewed held similar opinions and positioned young people's involvement as central to the orchestration of the riots:

> *There is a generation now that hear the stories about 'the war' ... they missed out, so they are determined to go and do it again ... In the Ardoyne ... Bobby Storey and various other heavy weight Republicans confronting people. In days gone by they would only have looked sideways and that would have been enough, now you get a different generation coming through, with no respect for their older generations, so it is a young person's activity coming through.* (POL1)

One politician was critical of what is described as *'some excuse'* in relation to the legacy of the Conflict:

> *I think it is an all too easy political excuse to say that the reason we have a juvenile justice problem is because we have had a conflict in our past ... it services some political leaders to perpetuate that myth ... trying to pass off some excuse that because you were born in community X and community X ... [was] particularly affected by the Troubles, that people who were born after the ceasefires and there was no life memory ... of the Troubles are somehow caught up in them, I just don't accept that.* (POL4)

News items were referred to as consisting of *'factual'* information (ED2) and *'photographic evidence'* (ED6). As one editor asserted, *'a lot of that weren't just us, there was photographic evidence ... people in the area saying these people were young and where are the parents?'* (ED6). Further representative examples included the following responses:

I was there ... in Ardoyne over the Twelfth ... there were youngsters on the streets ... it was ... a wrecking campaign ... Your responsibility is to report what's happening ... If it's factual and accurate ... then you have an obligation to report it. (ED2)

I don't think we should make any apologies for drawing attention to the facts ... Newspapers ... had a right to draw attention to the concerns that young people ... were involved ... we would be abdicating our responsibility if we sweep that under the carpet. (ED5)

When discussing the content of news items, one editor initially stated that the media could *'possibly ... be more explicit in saying that the vast majority of young people in the area weren't involved'* (ED5). However, the editor concluded by stating, *'it's straightforward, it's self-evident from the story'* that not all children and young people were involved (ED5). Another editor presented a strong and defensive response:

We are not the ones here who are cheerleading for those fuckers ... getting young kids ... out doing some job for the Real IRA ... children ... corrupted by fucking losers. We didn't put them there, it wasn't our influence ... so don't blame us. (ED1)

Ardoyne was described by the same editor as *'a shit hole'* and the PSNI were praised for having to *'deal with these fucking eejits throwing stones and petrol bombs'* (ED1). Further, those rioting were described as *'a crowd of fucking losers, going nowhere, achieving nothing and doing nothing but causing trouble'* (ED1).

In addition to this criticism, several other editors and journalists argued that children and young people were not 'demonised', instead it was their parents who received criticism in the media coverage:

Kids of nine ... on the streets, well you are not really demonising the kids in ... that reporting, what you are doing is asking the questions about the parents. (ED2)

Sometimes it is quite ... middle class ... where are the parents? When the reality is that the parents may well be pissed somewhere ... or ... part of the rioting ... or dead ... That is the reality ... The shock factor is ... a reminder to some of the parents ... I don't think it's a simple case of the middle class demonising children, I think there is a kind of genuine ... paternalistic concern for kids getting involved. (JOURN3)

A small number of those working in the media made referenced to, *'people saying there wasn't enough analysis'* (ED1) and in discussing this further, representative comments included: *'there wasn't any analysis because ... we are past*

that … we are past that stage' (ED1) and *'it is very hard to analyse trouble …
when you have analysed it once, it is very hard to analyse it again'* (ED4).
Another editor stated that, *'analysis is … very hard to get'* and it is common
practice to:

> *[E]nd up ringing people … the local priest for analysis and he would say, 'Yes these
> kids, the parents aren't looking after them', or the analysis was coming from … the
> Cops … they are the kind of quotes … rather than separate analysis pieces.* (ED6)

Other journalists stated that some elements were evidently missing from
media content, such as the voice of the Children's Commissioner and also
stronger outcomes in relation to arrests by the PSNI. As one journalist
asserted, *'I don't think I've seen the Children's Commissioner on about it … and
… she should have been on'* (JOURN1). These findings reinforce Ericson
et al.'s (1987: 9) observation that journalistic custom and practice, shapes and
restricts what is reported, how it is reported and whose voices are included.

In calling for stronger responses directed towards children and young
people, a journalist stated: *'It does astonish me why they don't arrest more people, it is frustrating … If I lived in a community where there was regular rioting
… it would drive me completely nuts'* (JOURN3). Post-devolution of policing
and justice these findings provide the first insight into the media's portrayal
of rioting, the reaction from politicians and the way in which both the media
and moral entrepreneurs framed youth involvement. In particular, the analysis demonstrates the impact of social reaction on contemporary criminal
justice policy.

PSNI's Operation Exposure

A further unique insight into the responses directed towards children and
young people was gained through interviews with the PSNI, media and politicians. As discussed in the previous chapter, the PSNI's Operation Exposure
was re-launched in order to 'tackle' what was framed by the media, politicians
and the PSNI, as sectarian rioting. The main architect of the PSNI's Operation
Exposure outlined that, *'primarily to pilot it … was just a brainwave'* and having completed a range of unsuccessful *'problem solving techniques'*, the PSNI
'had 70 unidentified images of kids involved in quite nasty disorder' (PSNI1).
The interviewee stated that this *'was the background to me saying we need to
consider releasing the images of these children to the media'* (PSNI1). The PSNI
interviewee also described how:

The media was absolutely essential to Operation Exposure ... that was the form of releasing the images, it was important that we got the local papers on board because that it what the local people read ... We couldn't have done it without the media, it was important ... for persuading the public on why it was important to ring us. (PSNI1)

In light of the *'public clamour for ... people to be caught and pay a price for'* the riots (ED7), each editor and journalist interviewed showed support for the PSNI's Operation Exposure and the publication of photographs of children and young people. A considerable number of those working in the media described the PSNI's tactic and *'efforts'* as *'pretty successful'* (ED7) and *'effective'*, particularly *'because ... parents came forward to turn some of them in'* (JOURN1). The *'public view'* was described as supporting the PSNI's *'tactic'*, as *'a message needs to be sent out that this will not be tolerated anymore'* (ED7).

While this was a 'new' PSNI tactic in Northern Ireland, several interviewees noted the similarities between the PSNI's release and publication of images and what tabloids newspapers routinely print. As one tabloid editor highlighted, *'we put pictures of young people in our paper, who are engaged in crime, robbing shops, on CCTV for instance ... we have done that and will continue to'* (ED3). Another editor, in making reference to newspapers in England, emphasised the relationship between police forces and the media:

It is not unusual ... Cop forces in Manchester ... in London ... do it regularly and I thought it was great for us because you get 30 photographs and it would make a great page and ... readers love it too, because they are looking to see if they know anybody ... When we are fed it, we will certainly put it in the paper. (ED6)

The PSNI also indicated that this 'tactic' had been employed in parts of the UK and the following response highlighted policy transfer and implementation:

The tactic of releasing images has been done before and you can see it on 'Crime Watch' ... I worked outside London ... in 2001 ... we had a major riot ... we released dozens of images to the newspapers and most of those people were caught. What Operation Exposure has done, has taken the best practice of releasing images on an ad hoc basis, on an infrequent basis and put it into an ongoing coordinated ... operation. (PSNI1)

In supporting what was generally referred to as a new PSNI *'tactic'*, previous responses to rioting were referred to by several editors and journalists:

What we had before was hand to hand fighting ... water cannons ... petrol bombing ... it is a really dangerous place to be ... They obviously decided this year that they were going to change tactic ... I think it is probably a good idea. (ED1)

Typical responses often emphasised a view of 'the end justifies the means'. Editors asserted that young people *'should be brought to book'* and the PSNI should employ *'whatever means it takes to do that'* (ED2). Another editor posed the following question: *'from a children protection way ... is it not better that they are apprehended and go into the legal system, before they are involved in further rioting ... [and] paramilitary groups?'* (ED5). Similarly the PSNI representative asserted that publishing the photographs, as a *'deterrent'* was required:

I have watched children grow up from the age of ten, throwing stones, to the age of 15 or 16 were they are engaged in paramilitary groups and at 17 or 18 they are now terrorists. You need to nip that in the bud. (PSNI1)

Several interviewees acknowledged that, *'some of the pictures, people would say certainly they are under 18'* (ED7) and mentioned the 'legality' of publishing children and young people's images. Typically editors and journalists stated that *'the police believe it is legal ... and an effective way of apprehending offenders'* (ED5) and thus, *'there are no legal ramifications'* because it *'[was] the police ... providing us with the pictures'* (ED3). One journalist provided an insight into newsroom practice:

We had a discussion ... should we really have been putting the pictures out given that we wouldn't be able to identify them in court and someone made the point that it is not us putting them out, it's the police putting them out and ... we are entitled to report it. (JOURN1)

Another journalist emphasised that it, *'isn't going to be much of a moral dilemma for journalists ... whether you use'* the images, as they are of people who are in *'a public arena ... engaged in criminal activity'* (JOURN2). The journalist described the *'images'* as *'absolute gold dust for an editor'* and stated that *'it would be irresistible for the media not to use those images ... pictures speak a thousand words ... they sell a thousand newspapers'* (JOURN2). This response reflected Barrat's (1994: 97) observation that if news items are accompanied by 'vivid photograph[s]' or images, these 'aesthetic' components 'heighten the impact' and thus, the news item is typically given 'higher priority' or greater prominence.

Several of those interviewed challenged rights discourse. One representative, moderate response was, *'the human rights stuff can go too far'*, as the images printed *'in the paper ... or ... the TV footage ... [is] a matter of public record'*

(ED2). One of the most disparaging viewpoints from an editor in relation to rights discourse, was the following comment:

> *There will be those people who say, listen this isn't in line with their rights or that Bill of Rights … go fuck yourselves and you can quote me as saying that … I don't remember any protests on the streets … mass demonstrations … rallies or petitions saying how this is awful … in this climate? I couldn't give a fuck … will they be back rioting in Ardoyne next year? No, I don't think so … You can't say journalists shouldn't be biased … should be very objective … Crap … So do I support the police on this? Yes, I do … let's not pussy foot around things, this isn't the time for to try and reason with people.* (ED1)

Significantly, one journalist who had previously described their approach and beliefs as *'liberal'*, stated that *'society'* is:

> *[N]ow … so interested in talking about rights that we forget about rights and responsibilities … 'I have the right not to be published in the paper', but what about your responsibility as a citizen and when do those rights get given up?* (JOURN3)

In strongly disagreeing with criticisms of Operation Exposure voiced by children and youth sector organisations, one editor argued:

> *If you were a child … rioting in Ardoyne or Londonderry and there is an image of you in the paper, I don't think anybody is going to be giving you a punishment beating for it … or there is going to be domestic violence … I think that the people who are likely to be handing out punishment beatings are more likely to be applauding you … The bottom line is that if you weren't on the streets rioting you wouldn't be in any danger.* (ED4)

The PSNI officer also presented similar responses:

> *Children's groups … were telling me there is a real live risk, but I researched that, there have been no examples of an image being released by the police that was then used by the paramilitary groups to … target that individual. I argue that the reverse is the case, when the community know the police have taken action … it narrows the potential for other groups to fill that vacuum.* (PSNI1)

> *Thirty-two were not charged and that is something that the human rights lobby have struggled with … I have given them the facts … I was accused of was demonising … [and] criminalising young people … when in actual fact I had evidence to charge … them but I said, 'Don't … take them to youth diversion, tell social services … their parents and let's help'.* (PSNI1)

Similarly several politicians, in supporting Operation Exposure and the PSNI, criticised those who questioned this 'tactic'. One typical response launched an attack on the work of advocates:

> *The police did the right thing ... what is being dealt with was young thugs who were out throwing stones, creating mayhem ... Don't ... criticise ... police ... If these young people had been sitting doing their homework ... the police wouldn't have been looking for them ... I hear what the do-gooders say ... those people are usually very out to the left ... You know they too are running industries at the end of the day ... it is about them and ... their employment, as well as they always err of the side of this human rights legislation and ... to a large degree anti-police and anti-everything establishment.* (POL3)

The architect of the 'tactic' concluded that, *'Operation Exposure is one of the greatest examples of ... [how] the ... power of the media has been harnessed ... [and] the community reliance on the media has been harnessed to identify criminals and solve crimes'* (PSNI1). The responses from interviewees built on the analysis in the previous chapter, to explore the motivations behind the PSNI's Operation Exposure and the publication of the images of Ardoyne. The analysis further demonstrated the close relationship between the state, state agencies such as the PSNI and the media and their unwillingness to acknowledge or address the legacy of the Conflict.

Engagement with Children, Young People and Their Advocates

Becker's (1967: 241) conceptualisation of the 'hierarchy of credibility' confirms that those 'at the top' of institutions have their views 'regarded as the most credible account available' (see Hall 1986; Allan 1999). Thus, prominence given to the views of 'primary definers' sets the news agenda (Becker 1967) and establishes 'the boundaries' of debate on social issues (Barrat 1994). This was reflected in the content analysis and case study, which established that the voices of children, young people and their advocates were excluded or marginalised in media discourse. Thus, interviews with the 'primary definers' explored their views on 'access' to the media and current and future engagement.

The central theme to emerge from the interviewees' responses was one of perceived *'difficulties'* in relation to engagement with children and young people. Interviewees indicated that in society, *'there is so much more cotton wool surrounding children'* (JOURN3), *'it is not just like an open access'*, media outlets *'have to get permission from the adult'* and *'sometimes the job doesn't appear because it is too much hassle to get the consent'* (JOURN1). Several journalists stated that, *"'don't work with animals or little children", kids are hard to interview… you get like one word answers'* (JOURN1) and another journalist stated that, *'children don't like to be interviewed'* (JOURN2).

Several politicians also indicated that it is *'difficult'* to engage with children and young people. One representative comment described young people as follows:

> *They don't have any experience … haven't finished their neurological development … don't really engage … don't vote … are very egocentric in their viewpoints … It is … quite difficult for politicians to go and represent these people.* (POL1)

Another politician asserted that young people's *'voices are definitely missing'* and this is *'because people don't know how to engage with young people… as they have gotten older'* (POL5). Similar opinions were voiced by those working in the media, who asserted that *'young people … don't have a PR machine'* (JOURN1) and it is *'not easy'* to engage with this social group (ED1). As one editor argued, *'they are coming from a world that's far removed from a world that I live'* and further stated that:

> *Do you expect … 16-year-olds to come knocking on your door and saying [name] you are never going to believe we've wrote a story … that's not their gift … Now some 30-year-old PR person will knock you down to get the story out.* (ED1)

Several editors and journalists provided examples of how their media outlets included the voices of children and young people: *'we do pretty well in terms of including young people's voices when they are needed'* (ED4); *'most [newspapers] … do what we do … sections for young children … for teenagers, college sections for people in their teens and twenties'* (ED7) and some *'newspapers will involve children in writing'* (JOURN2). A small number of editors and journalists described this approach as *'slightly patronising'* (ED4) and *'it is … like we are acknowledging that you exist rather than weaving the experiences of children and young people into the output'* (JOURN2). One editor described young people as not having *'a stake in society'* and as *'they don't buy our products … we don't chase 15-year-olds'* (ED5).

One editor employed a created analogy to describe why he has had limited engagement with children and young people:

Lets face it ... I'm more interested in ... some businessman ... entrepreneurs or ... politicians, than some 19-year-old girl who is doing her first year degree in languages at Queen's ... what could she tell me? ... Unless she's got something going on in her life ... you know they are only coming out ... It's like an analogy ... like springtime, you can see the buds are out and what do you see, buds, that's all you see ... maybe in ... May ... you have a nice flower out there ... and it's ready for picking ... and that's a bit like the student ... I don't want to hear any self-pitying students – 'Oh we are getting a hard time from you the press' ... That's bullshit ... we don't care because you haven't got to the stage in your life were it really matters. (ED1)

In relation to the media's engagement with children and young people's advocates, editors and journalists placed a lot of emphasis on the Children's Commissioner, who was routinely criticised. Several interviewees stated that the, *'role ... has not helped as much as we all thought'* and described it as *'very much behind the scenes'* and *'not a very public role fighting on children's behalf'* (JOURN3). One politician, while acknowledging that the *'Commissioner does some good work'*, stated that, *'I wouldn't be giving her full points'* and described the office as *'a quango'* (POL3). One editor presented stronger criticism of the role and also of the children and youth sector as a whole:

The Children's Commissioner, what a pointless job is that? Sounds great right, but it has as much relevance as... an empty Heineken bottle in the middle of a church ... They get a hard time when they deserve it in my view ... and I'll make no apologies for it and I don't want to hear any fucking left winger or some doo dah. (ED1)

Several other interviewees working in the media criticised children and youth sector organisations. One representative viewpoint was:

There is a huge young person's lobby ... programmed to look out for bias ... pre-programmed to only see the negative things and may be because they are dealing a lot with problems ... they are seeing the negative things but there is a lot of positivity out there. (ED6)

Another editor strongly dismissed the views of advocates:

If you ask any interest group, do you feel you are adequately portrayed in the media, every single one ... will ... say, 'No' ... That is not reliable, that is anecdotal evidence, the amazingly colourful cannot be used to draft policy upon. (ED5)

A small number of interviewees stated that those *'in youth work ... don't really get a fair shake'* and the reason for this was, *'it is true, bad news sells newspapers'* (ED2) and that *'the channels of communication are open ... but ... are not used that much'* (ED4). Several recommendations were made by the media and representative suggestions included:

> *Rather than local youth groups trying to contact the press directly to get a quote through, make sure that their local representative knows ... so that local representative can say ... their message.* (ED6)

> *If youth organisations ... are concerned about this representation ... do what disability groups and sexual identity interest groups have done ... become more of a lobby for that interest and to not let go of it and to get the bit between their teeth.* (JOURN2)

In providing examples of personal engagement with children and youth sector organisations, one journalist stated that certain organisations that had, *'quite ... negative experiences with a different media organisation'*, subsequently hesitated in having further contact with the media and *'it did take me a long time to ... talk them round and explain myself'* (JOURN3). The same journalist criticised some non-governmental organisations (NGOs) who:

> *[E]xpect you to deliver almost exactly what they want ... there is an expectation that ... they would get an easy time ... that their views will be unchallenged ... that is not only unrealistic ... but it shows a lack of maturity on their part as well ... sometimes they do need to be challenged.* (JOURN3)

In contrast two politicians acknowledged the 'difficulties' or 'barriers' experienced by advocates. The following representative comment was particularly insightful:

> *Instead of trying to get on with advocacy work ... they are starting from a position were they have to try and improve the image that the media has portrayed... every time they are meeting with politicians or ... on radio ... or TV, they are always starting from the position, look that's what the media portray, that is not the reality ... here is an example of one of these young people and what they are having to deal with ... It doesn't always go down well, particularly with politicians ... or a media that are very populist ... These groups are portrayed as defenders of young people who behave badly ... in many respects they are defenders because they understand the issues ... these young people are grappling with ... [and] what needs to be done to address those issues.* (POL2)

The responses established that while politicians and the PSNI have 'easy' access and can utilise the media for their own purposes, this was not the case for children, young people and their advocates, who routinely struggled to have their voices heard. The findings also provided an insight into the existence of dismissive attitudes on the part of editors and journalists, in relation to the views and media produced by children and young people.

Conclusion

This chapter has confirmed that through selected language, editors and journalists present their role as speaking for, and on behalf of the 'insider' community of their readership (see Wykes 2001). Consistent with findings from previous studies, editors and journalists placed importance on meeting the needs of their readership and highlighted the prominence given to 'negative' or 'bad news' (see Galtung and Ruge 1965, 1982; Chibnall 1977; Ang 1990a). Instructively, several editors and journalists refused to acknowledge that children and young people are represented in a negative light. Their responses reinforced the importance of the evidence-base provided by the content analysis of media content in previous chapters.

However, several responses did suggest that some individuals working in the media were critical of the language and imagery employed in news items on children and young people in conflict with the law. As one journalist predicted, *'the bigger challenge will be for journalists to check what they are doing, as they are typing that on to the screen … this is more complicated than a four letter word'* (JOURN2). This journalist described how negative representation, *'adds to the sense of dislocation'* among young people and *'now the media is just another bully in the playground'* (JOURN2). As the analysis demonstrated, those working in the media concluded that such outcomes were due to *'the nature of the beast'* (ED3). Such responses removed responsibility from individual editors and journalists, by presenting the issues as part of the overall *'nature'* of the mass media.

A number of new insights also emerged from the analysis of the primary material. While the literature asserts that there is a decline in the readership of newspapers (Franklin and Murphy 1997; Meyer 2009), editors and journalists in Northern Ireland stressed the *'high'* readership levels. Significantly, the impact of change and transition was identified and explored by interviewees. The economic recession, the pressure of 24-hour news and changes to technology emphasised the increase in *'desk'* journalism and the decrease in investigative journalism. A new insight was gained into the use of social media and networking sites, which have impacted on journalistic custom and practice. This new practice of sourcing information and imagery on children and young people is a contemporary form of surveillance of children and young people.

The findings provide a unique insight into the impact of transition from conflict on both journalistic custom and practice and on the focus of media content. Editors and journalists stated that the Conflict had previously dominated news coverage and now they were trying to come *'to grips with'* how to replace such coverage. They outlined how *'crime'* and *'criminal justice issues'* are addressing and filling this *'vacuum'*. This new finding emphasised the amplification of crime (see Barrat 1994). Moral entrepreneurs also placed an emphasis on devolution and as one politician asserted:

> *Until devolution of policing and justice, the only public discourse that was taking place on a lot of these issues was through the media and so it was sensationalised ... I think devolution is critically important to youth justice.* (POL4)

Thus, devolution of policing and justice was described as a significant dynamic in the 'new' Northern Ireland. This change of focus clearly illustrated that the Conflict provided *'better headlines'*, but now in a period of transition children and young people's leisure time on the streets is a dominant headline news story (POL5), framed as anti-social behaviour. The next chapter explores the 'hidden' voices and views of children, young people and their advocates.

Notes

1. The PSNI Inspector presented his personal reflections as the architect of the PSNI's Operation Exposure initiative and as the officer responsible for the implementation of the 'official policy'. During the interview the Inspector referred to several policy documents, which he subsequently gave the researcher access to, via e-mail.
2. For reference key see Appendix 2.
3. As outlined in Chap. 1, 'the Troubles' is a reference to the Conflict in Northern Ireland.
4. This is a colloquial term for what is most commonly known as the Irish Republican Army (IRA).
5. This interviewee refers to the high profile case of the murder of Harry Holland in West Belfast, see: http://www.belfasttelegraph.co.uk/news/local-national/family-seeking-tough-sentences-over-harry-holland-murder-14359177.html (accessed on 12 August 2009).

7

'The Hidden Voices' in the Media: Responses from Children, Young People and Their Advocates

As established in Chap. 2, 'the news-making processes' ensure the maintenance and centrality of dominant discourses in the mainstream media. Hall's (1986) analysis asserts that 'the hierarchy of access' to the media and the perpetuation of negative representations of certain social groups are intertwined. He argued that:

> Profoundly … some things, people, events, relationships always get represented: always centre-stage … in the position to define, to set the agenda, to establish the terms of the conversation. Some others sometimes get represented – but always at the margin … responding to a question whose terms and conditions have been defined elsewhere: never 'centred'. Still others are always 'represented' only by their eloquent absence, their silences, or refracted through the glance or the gaze of others. (Hall 1986: 9)

Hall (1986: 9) explores 'how things, people, relationships are represented', alongside the prominence of certain voices and the absence or marginalisation of 'hidden' voices. The main focus of this chapter explores 'what and who regularly gets left out' (Hall 1986: 9) of media reporting and impact this has on the experiences of those 'hidden' voices.

The content analysis findings affirmed the proposition that children, young people and their advocates' voices were hidden, marginalised and most commonly excluded from print media coverage (Chaps. 4 and 5). Their absence in the mainstream media and in the political sphere has been well documented in international and national research (Crane 1997; Bentley et al. 1999; Brown 2005; Hunt et al. 2010). As one Australian study observes, 'the most striking fact about the coverage of social issues relevant to young people is how few times a young person's, or even a youth worker's view is included in

© The Author(s) 2018
F. Gordon, *Children, Young People and the Press in a Transitioning Society*,
Palgrave Socio-Legal Studies, https://doi.org/10.1057/978-1-137-60682-2_7

the analysis' (Youth Bureau 1994: 32, cited in Crane 1997: 95). Routinely, where young people are 'unfairly generalised', it is 'rare to see a correction of the facts provided by young people themselves, or those who represent them' (Youth Bureau 1994: 32, cited in Crane 1997: 95). Although attempts are made to challenge the 'distortion', 'exaggeration' and 'misrepresentation' (Glover 1984; Simpson 1997; Schissel 2008), the media's unwillingness to provide 'alternative' voices with the same access as 'moral entrepreneurs', ultimately impacts on media content.

An in-depth focus on the impact of negative media reporting on the experiences, lives and work of children, young people and their advocates in a transitioning society, is absent from academic research. The previous chapter addressed the call for contemporary academic studies to include and critique the voices of those working in the media (Lashmar 2010). What follows addresses the call by McRobbie and Thornton (1995) to explore whether 'folk devils' play a role in the 'moral panic' process. Further, it addresses McRobbie and Thornton's (1995: 568) proposition regarding young people's own forms of media as a means of challenging the mainstream media. A true exploration can only be attempted through an inclusion of the voices of children and young people.

This chapter addresses the key themes, particularly the consequences of negative media reporting for how children and young people perceive themselves and their peers and the perceived impact of negative representations on advocates and on service provision. Children, young people and their advocates provide first-hand accounts of their experiences of media intrusion and the impact of negative media reporting. Further, the chapter explores the perceived impact of negative media representations on official discourses and on the creation of policy and law, along with perceptions and experiences of the current regulatory system. The analysis compares and contrasts the views of the interviewees and focus group participants regarding the key themes drawn from the literature and those that emerged from the content analysis in previous chapters. The chapter specifies three core themes: media portrayal and representation of children and young people; the impact of negative media representations, children's rights and media regulation; the engagement of children, young people and their advocates with the media.

Media Portrayal and Representation of Children and Young People

The central role the media plays in the processes of demonisation, criminalisation and punishment of children and young people has been well documented in academic literature (Schissel 2006; Scraton 2008). When asked about *'the role of the media'* in society, children, young people and their advocates held similar views and suggested that it *'should be … inform[ing] people accurately and factually'* (YW1), in particular *'about current issues'* (Focus Group 1, aged 15–19). There existed a consensus amongst advocates that newspapers *'should be … a lot more investigative'* than they currently are, as *'the whys are as important as who and what'* (YW1). Similar to the views expressed in the previous chapter, interviewees acknowledged that there existed a *'close'* relationship between newspapers and their readership. As one children's advocate stated:

> *People still read their local paper and they are very, very local in Northern Ireland, so there is a real opportunity, about trying to have a conversation … we need to find a way to have a public conversation with the public about its children and how it treats its children.* (YS2)

In analysing the media's reliance on the concept of *'the freedom of the press'*, several interviewees argued that *'children's best interests are paramount'* (CS3). One interviewee criticised the media's approach and argued that, '*I don't think freedom of the press means you can sensationalise the activities of a minority of young people … [it] is not about writing whatever the hell you want, whatever way you want*' (YS1).

Consistent with findings in the previous chapter, interviewees and focus group participants routinely spoke in terms of *'positive'* and *'negative'*, as well as *'good'* and *'bad'*. The prominent opinion was that the media's portrayal of youth is excessively *'negative'* and journalists present children and young people as *'bad'*. This is in line with Galtung and Ruge's (1982, 58–59, original emphasis) analysis that '*negative news … enters the news channel more easily*'. Children and young people felt that, *'There isn't coverage about the good side'* (Focus Group 1, aged 15–19) and anything *'good'* or *'positive'* they were involved in, was not reported:

> *We did a programme … called 'Giving Back' … to show to 'The Andytown News' that we've done something good … We got our photos took … they said it would be in the paper … and it wasn't.* (Focus Group 6, aged 14–16)

One young person noted the responses of those working in the media: *'Nolan [British Broadcasting Corporation (BBC) Radio Presenter] said, "A young person doing a good thing was a waste of airtime"'* (Focus Group 2, aged 17–21). As these quotations indicated, issues and concerns existed surrounding both the media's representation of children and young people in terms of language, imagery and associated negativity, as well as issues in relation to the media's willingness to engage with children, young people and their advocates.

Language and Images

As the content analysis findings demonstrated, the media's selection of language and images to portray children and young people, presented clear 'underlying meanings and motivations' (Erjavec 2001: 7070). In particular, this 'meaning-making process' is influenced by, and reflective of adult 'attitudes', 'judgements' and 'feelings' directed towards children and young people (Erjavec 2001: 707). Discrimination was noted by focus group participants, who highlighted the derogatory language employed by journalists, such as, *'Yobs'* (Focus Group 4, aged 16–20); *'Hoods'* (Focus Group 6, aged 14–16); *'they call you scumbags … and mad … whether you are good or bad, you are a scumbag'* (Focus Group 5, aged 17–23) and *'troublemakers … criminals'* (Focus Group 3, aged 15–21).

Advocates highlighted the impact of similar *'negative, patronising terminology'* (YW1) and language on how children, young people and adults view this social group. As one advocate asserted, *'the media … is really demonising young people and has picked young people as like the evil of our society … everything they do is wrong and bad'* (YW2). Further representative comments referred to the discriminatory language employed by journalists to describe young people as *'louts', 'a hoodie generation', 'demonic children'* (CS3), *'scum', 'rats', 'thugs'* and *'feral'* (YW3).

Advocates presented their concerns in relation to the impact of *'these connotations'* (YW3). As one advocate stated, *'what worries me is how children themselves start to classify themselves in the same sort of language'* (CS3). A youth worker who argued that this use of language *'dehumanises those young people'*, observed that, *'it [this use of language] is very prominent even within practitioners who will say, "We will not work with those eight, they are the wreckers"'* (YW3). These responses are examples of the application and internationalisation of labels, whereby social judgement and reactions play a significant role in how adults and young people themselves perceive and refer to certain behaviours. One young person described how labelling in the media amplified perceptions of anti-social behaviour and crime: *'they are always … using negative language … whenever you put it any other way it wouldn't be half as frightening'* (Focus Group 1, aged 15–19).

Representative responses from children and young people highlighted the categorisation of youth in the media and also their personal frustrations. Reflecting Cohen's (1980: 40) original analysis, which asserts that, 'objects (clothing) symbolize', 'a certain status (delinquent or deviant)' and those 'objects themselves become symbolic of the status', young people described a dominant common perception as, *'oh you are wearing a hoodie … you must be a hooligan ... thug'* (Focus Group 2, aged 17–21). Young people also argued that, *'the media shouldn't be writing in a stereotypical way ... generalising and labelling all young people'* (Focus Group 3, aged 15–21). Consistent with Cohen's (1972, 1980) analysis, such labels become terms of abuse and judgement. As demonstrated in Chap. 4, when describing children and young people, editors and journalists applied labels such as 'hoods' and 'anti-community', which are specific to Northern Ireland.

Young people proposed that there exists a clear distinction between children and young people in media coverage:

> *We are put under the same heading as disruptive and they put wee kids under the toddlers' pictures. They don't get anything serious and we don't get anything good.* (Focus Group 1, aged 15–19)

In addition to the evident discrimination in terms of *'age'*, specific words and phrases employed by the media were also described as stereotypical and discriminatory in relation to *'class'* and *'place'*. One young person stated that, *'how badly you are portrayed ..., depends of where you are from'* and if you are from *'certain communities'*, this can impact on *'getting a job'* (Focus Group 4, aged 16–20). Advocates also emphasised the media's representation of young people from particular *'areas'* or *'communities'*:

> *Half a dozen young people get drunk on the Falls Road and start causing a nuisance, that is big news ... Half a dozen ... on the Malone Road get drunk and it is 'high spirits' ... There is a class factor in terms of how the media is portraying young people ... again it is back to that issue of language.* (YS1)

One youth worker described how journalists and in particular *'columnists'* take *'a dry cynical look at the world'* and in turn they chose to *'perpetuate the view of the underclass ... the pyjama wearing peroxide dyed blonde, unemployed single parents ... kids running around the streets',* which *'has a perpetuating effect ... people think that is what West Belfast is'* (YW3). The youth worker also stressed the impact of such stereotypical representations:

> *The media doesn't realise ... the extent to which it actually shapes opinion and mood ... The series of really negative headlines on the front of a local paper can really have a massive impact on the mood in that area.* (YW3)

Those working in the youth sector asserted that the language employed by the media *'whips up hysteria ... antagonism'* and *'hostility'* (YS1). While this *'element of whipping people up'* and *'courting the extreme view',* produced news items that *'people want'* (YS1), advocates argued that as a result, *'there isn't a good perception of other young people … even amongst young people'* (YW4). Several interviewees emphasised how *'stories from the media … have a big part to play'* (YW4) in how other members of the community refer to, and treat children and young people. In particular one youth worker argued that:

> *There is a barrage of adults who are using this … very negative language to describe young people … that goes for local politicians … community workers … interface workers … [who] are not actually taking the time out to stop and have a conversation with them, so they don't know them.* (YW4)

Just as the media select particular words and phrases for headlines, images printed in newspapers are usually there for 'visual impact' (see Davies 1997; Lacey 1998). The specific selection and the impact of imagery was something that was widely acknowledged by children, young people and their advocates. Many of their opinions were in line with the literature, in particular the assertion that 'vivid photograph[s] … heighten the impact of the news item' (Barrat 1994: 97). Typically, children and young people emphasised how images were *'used'* for effect and to add to a story. In particular they stated that: *'we are used … a picture of a young person to sell a story'* (Focus Group 1, aged 15–19) and *'they always look really, really mad in the photo … it is not as if it is a proper photo … they find the one that makes them look most like a lunatic'* (Focus Group 1, aged 15–19).

Several young people referred to the repeated use of the same image and one representative comment was:

> *Our local paper … always use the same photo of young people drinking outside … from about like five years ago … They use it over and over again … four wee lads … in tracksuits … and they talk about young people out drinking again this week.* (Focus Group 2, aged 17–21)

Contemporary examples of Tannebaum's (1938) 'dramatization of evil', were evident in descriptions of the media's selection of imagery and the impact of such images printed in newspapers. As one youth worker stated:

> *A picture speaks a thousand words … if you are an elderly person looking at a newspaper … and you see this image, a menacing, grainy image of young people I think it filters through … even though you might not think it does and … it brands all young people as dangerous.* (YW1)

Several interviewees emphasised the use of emotive images in the media:

They pick a one off incident and that is blown up and … they … put photographs of Jamie Bulger along beside it … What it is trying to do is to frame the readers' mindset. (CS3)

As Green (2008a: 198–199; see also Green 2008b) asserts, cases such as 'the Bulger case' have left a 'lasting impact', and in particular 'the now iconic CCTV image of James Bulger's abduction by the two boys remains powerfully evocative today'. Thus, placing such an image alongside contemporary descriptions of the perceived involvement of children and young people in anti-social behaviour and crime, can have a significant impact on the perception and responses directed towards this social group.

Media Content Themes

Participants were presented with a list of themes that emerged from the content analysis of newspaper coverage. Typically children, young people and their advocates were *'not surprised'* (CS3) by the themes and noted that *'they are all negative'* (YW1). The main focus of their responses related to the themes of anti-social behaviour; 'gangs'; crime; violence; youth suicide and intergenerational relationships. Children and young people also highlighted a range of adult responses or reactions, which they felt the media promoted in its coverage.

Anti-social Behaviour

Children, young people and their advocates routinely emphasised the notion of *'blame'* and questioned the adult meaning or interpretation of what constitutes anti-social behaviour. They also provided examples of direct personal experiences of *'naming and shaming'*. Children and young people described various examples of media coverage, which emphasised how in their opinion the media present it as if *'all young are involved'* (Focus Group 6, aged 14–16). As children and young people explained, *'the [newspaper] keep going on about my street … but nothing ever goes on in my street'* (Focus Group 2, aged 17–21). Further representative comments included:

You'd read about a group in the park … people ring the police straightaway … they might have been doing nothing … then it's in the media and it's just a vicious circle. (Focus Group 3, aged 15–21)

After our results it was all smeared over the 'Sunday Life' … this is what happens on results night and look at the state of our young people … We are like, no, that is a couple of people … and they take a picture of it. (Focus Group 1, aged 15–19)

Several advocates argued that the media portray *'all young people as anti-social and as hoods'* (YW2). A number of interviewees stated that anti-social behaviour is now commonly *'referred to as anti-community behaviour'* by the media (YS1). This label is routinely used in West Belfast. Interviewees asserted that the application of this label framed them as *'wreckers'* of community safety and well-being (YW3) and further emphasised the separation of young people from their communities. Although the label 'anti-community behaviour' is specific to Northern Ireland, the media's role in separating children and young people from 'the inner community' has been acknowledged in previous research (Conboy 2006). Advocates stated that *'because justice wasn't devolved'* to Stormont, the *'tendency to lift and bring across'* legislation and policies from the UK, such as *'ASBOs'*, as well as calls for the introduction of *'parenting orders'*, was overshadowing *'more preventative stuff'* (CS3).

A number of children and young people described personal experiences of being *'named and shamed'* and the impact this tactic had on their lives and interactions with adults (Focus Group 1, aged 15–19). Children, young people and their advocates were of the opinion that *'the media tends not to worry about naming … young people … it is money in their pocket'* (Focus Group 4, aged 16–20). One children's sector representative stated that working in the media *'is very competitive … there is that killer instinct'* and asserted that:

It is who can get the headline … the best and biggest to out the youngest thug. It is an industry where … there is … very little consideration for people behind the news story. (CS2)

A youth worker stated that, *'newspapers putting young people's faces in the papers before they have even committed a crime … is really very damaging'* (YW2). In particular much information used by journalists *'can be speculative'* and it was clear from the images and details printed that, *'people know who they [young people] are'* (YW2). Similar observations have been made in previous literature. As Scraton et al. (1991: 112) assert, there exists 'an unhealthy competiveness' among journalists and media outlets have 'become reliant on speculation' and 'the persistent emphasis on the statements of those in authority'.

Several young people outlined the *'damage'* of *'speculative'* reporting (YW2) and emphasised how it had contributed to them or their peers being *'blamed'* for *'damage'* they had not committed:

Me and him were away to a summer camp ... so we weren't at the riots ... but someone's car was burnt and we got the blame ... and it was all over the [newspaper's name] like ... saying that we burnt the wee man's car ... The lads came round and said, 'I'd crush you into the ground' ... because [they] thought it was us who burnt the car. (Focus Group 6, aged 14–16)

Further to this, in line with findings contained within previous research on this area (Pratt 2000; Evans 2004; Scraton 2005; Squires 2008), interviewees and focus group participants discussed in great detail, the impact of *'naming and shaming'* and the implications for the safety and lives of children and young people. As one young person stated, *'my mate got put in the paper ... she got branded ... that could lead to her getting beat up ... you only get one side of the story'* (Focus Group 3, aged 15–21). Further representative views included references to personal experiences:

We used to get the blame of absolutely everything ... There was 13 text messages about us in one week and there was this man ... he came down with a brush and chased us ... The text messages was the 'TWO SPECKIES' ... people know it is us and that is their code word ... This has been going on ages ... More people recognised us ... because the papers ... you just seen us walking down the street and we were 'the speckies' ... that's what people referred to us as ... They wouldn't let us take part [in] ... a barbeque ... we were banned from the summer scheme. (Focus Group 6, aged 14–16)

Youth workers highlighted the physical injuries children and young people had sustained and they emphasised the central role the media played in *"whipping up a media frenzy ... in St James"*:

A group of young people portrayed in the ... media as some rampaging criminal thugs ... then half of the community saying, 'We need to respond ... by getting the PSNI' and half of the community going, 'They are not going to do anything about it anyway'. The PSNI come in unable to do what they do ... Then dissident groups came in ... threatening, going into the houses saying, 'You have 24 hours or we are going to kill you' ... The residents' view was that was great. In the middle of a media frenzy ... without an understanding of the wider political context, what you have is this group of young people extremely vulnerable involved in their anti-social activity and they are to be shot or killed and ... people thinking that was the way to deal with it. (YW3)

There is a young person in hospital … When things are appearing in the press, there is always going to be a risk that there will be some kind of retribution. (YS1)

Another youth worker indicated the conflicting media representations of one young man prior to, and following a punishment attack and blamed the local newspaper for creating the climate in which the shooting took place:

On the front page … is a photograph of a young man who had a punishment shoot-ing … laying in the bed with his bandages on… a couple of weeks ago they were calling that same young person a thug, a hood, anti-social … and now it is, 'God love him, he has got shot' … They just constantly use them. (YW4)

'Gangs'

Several interviewees working in the youth sector noted the adoption of the label and concept of *'gangs'* and this reflects several arguments put forward by a number of academics (see Batchelor 2009; Fitch 2009). They stated that the media's use of the label *'gangs'* amplified the behaviour of children and young people and associated it with premeditation and *'criminality'*:

When I think about criminal gangs, I think about people who are sitting down … organising things or … planning … [the media] are at the minute constructing that around groups of fluid young people who are running around housing estates involved in very, very minor nuisance behaviour. (YW3)

Young people also discussed the transferral of the word *'gangs'* and its introduction into Northern Ireland news coverage. As one young person asserted, *'it was like they were complete gangs from America or something … The IBA … they were made out to be a full gang'* (Focus Group 5, aged 17–23). One youth sector manager highlighted the potential ramifications of *'por-traying groups of young people as gangs and gangsters'*, as *'there is almost a romanticism to that'* and *'a kind of notoriety, which is something to aspire to … among young people who have not had the same life chances'* (YS1). These responses from children and young people reinforced Fitch's (2009) argu-ment discussed earlier (see Chap. 4). Fitch (2009: 5) asserts that in the con-temporary setting the media and politicians have adopted the label 'gangs' from the US and have applied it to describe and generalise groups of chil-dren and young people.

Crime

Representations of children and young people's perceived involvement in 'crime' emphasised how the media chose to present them as 'big scandals', with 'our young people ... out of control' and how it is practice for journalists to 'sensationalise it to sell newspapers' (YW4). Gender was specifically highlighted by each focus group and there was a consensus that young men were the 'target' of the majority of the media's reporting on 'crime'. One focus group felt that while, 'boys get it worse ... if they get their claws into a story where a girl is ... they make it ten times worse' (Focus Group 1, aged 15–19). In addition, the Northern Ireland Children's Commissioner emphasised her concerns on how 'information' was presented about 'young ones in conflict with the law' and she made the observation that:

> It is very often as much that they can drag up about that young person ... that will help put them in as negative light as possible ... I just think there was no need for that information to be released. (NICCY1)

As Chap. 4 demonstrated, editors and journalists made reference to criminal records and previous convictions and presented such examples as further evidence of individual pathology. The representative news items analysed, outlined how the media frame perpetrators as 'persistent offenders', by making reference to previous convictions or similar behaviour.

Violence

Young people's perceived involvement in violence was strongly linked to crime. It was most common for interviewees and focus group participants to highlight how 'high profile' cases involving youth were presented in a different way to adult's involvement in violence. Previous chapters have referred to high profile cases and the sustained coverage they have received in the print media. As existing literature demonstrates, reference to high profile cases plays a key role in the continuum of criminalisation of children and young people (see Scraton 2005; Collins and Cattermole 2006). Significantly, advocates asserted that the media's continual reference back to 'high profile' cases, connected new cases with older examples, thus adding to the continuum of demonisation and vilification of youth:

There was a couple of incidents very close together and … really hyped up by the media to the point where people won't even go out if there is a group of young people standing at the corner … After Harry Holland was killed … that was really sensationalised … If it had of happened by adults, they wouldn't have been connected or lumped together … It has become high profile … taken on a new life. (YW2)

Youth Suicide

There has been no existing research into the media representation of youth suicide in Northern Ireland and the impact such coverage has on the bereaved. The Samaritans (2011: 5) submitted a report to the Leveson Inquiry, outlining the impact of 'widespread national media attention' in 2007 and 2008 of 'a series of … suicides involving young people in the Welsh county of Bridgend'. Similar to the views of children, young people and their advocates in Northern Ireland, the Samaritans' (2011) report described 'intrusion' and indicated how negative and inaccurate media reporting is, as well as the direct long-term consequences on friends and families bereaved by suicide. As the following analysis will reinforce, there were serious issues identified in relation to the media's treatment and representation of youth suicide.

The Northern Ireland Children's Commissioner observed that, *'recently with the death of a young girl … we've seen the perception in the media was … she was a hopeless case anyway and it was a drug thing'* (NICCY1). Youth workers emphasised how the media, *'don't always see the young person as the victims … while it is portrayed, "God help these young people"'*, in reality *'there is always a negative undertone'* to the reporting (YW2). The *'link'* made between drugs and youth suicide in the media, was described as *'scaring a lot of people'* (YW4). One youth worker emphasised that following the deaths of young people by suicide, *'the way the media cover that type of story is … sensationalising this young person's death'* and as a result *'death … becomes a scandal'* (YW4). A youth worker asserted that the print media *'are not talking about the affect drugs is having on … everyday life'*, but rather their approach *'is selling newspapers on the back of young people dying'* (YW4).

Young people held similar opinions and one focus group involving young people who had been bereaved by the suicide of their friend emphasised how *'completely wrong … the media portrayal of it was'* and described how:

The media done it in such a way … to suit itself … the first news article about it that came out, stated that he was 19, so that they could legally use it, but in actual fact he was 17. (Focus Group 4, aged 16–20)

Further, young people described how their friend's death, *'was plastered all over the newspapers'* (Focus Group 4, aged 16–20). They described how the *'newspaper chose to run with the story of drugs'*, with *'front page'* headlines such as, *'MEOW, MEOW KILLS TEENAGER'*, which framed the suicide in an inaccurate way (Focus Group 4, aged 16–20). The level of publicity *'nation-wide'* was due to the ongoing call at that time for *'a ban'* on the drug *'meth-adrone'* and the young people felt the death of their friend was reported *'on the front page of every newspaper'* and *'publicised more'* in order to pressurise the Government into introducing legislation (Focus Group 4, aged 16–20). As the young people concluded, *'they said it was banned because of him'* (Focus Group 4, aged 16–20).

Young people considered that the use of images of young people who had taken their own lives was highly inappropriate. Their discussion of how the media *'actually posted the picture of the suicide in the paper'* (Focus Group 2, aged 17–21) concluded that the media should not print such images. Other young people described how the media selected and printed *'party pictures'* of their deceased friend, *'rather than nice ones that were on the same page of Facebook'* (Focus Group 4, aged 16–20). Young people clearly stated that they felt this was an intrusion into their privacy and that they had not given per-mission for such images to be printed in the newspaper. This also extended to comments they had left on Facebook pages:

> *They just quoted everything off Facebook, they didn't ask us any questions but any wee notes we'd put up on Facebook, they just took that as if we'd said that to them.* (Focus Group 4, aged 16–20)

Young people argued that this *'intrusion'* directly fed into media representa-tions and in addition it extended to journalists accessing phone numbers and telephoning the young people directly:

> *After the suicide … the means that they [the media] get their information on young people … that affected us. One of our experiences was, a journalist rang me and the only people I had spoke to was the police and friends and I don't think any of my friends would have passed my number on to a journalist … personally I think it come from the police.* (Focus Group 4, aged 16–20)

As outlined in the previous chapter, the media's use of Facebook and Bebo images is an example of a contemporary journalistic practice that is consis-tently utilised. While children and young people maintained that images and comments were private and should not have been printed, as discussed in the previous chapter, those working in the media described searching on social networking sites and contacting parents, as a *'reflex action'* (ED6).

The young people felt that as a result of *'the media's sensationalism'* of youth suicide, important contextual information was typically omitted from media reporting: *'they never mentioned the fact that he was bullied for … years … he had family problems … the health service didn't do anything'* (Focus Group 4, aged 16–20). Advocates strongly emphasised that service provision was affected as a direct impact of the current predominant approach taken by journalists:

> We have young people who have seen … their friends after they've taken their own lives. So you are dealing with all of that and trying to help and support them and then you are dealing with this … negative portrayal. (YS1)

There was a consensus that *'suicide needs to be dealt with'*, however currently *'with the media … out to get young people … they are not prepared to do something about the problem that they keep bringing up'* (Focus Group 2, aged 17–21). Young people felt the reason was, *'it is too much work'* for the media (Focus Group 4, aged 16–20).

Based on their direct experiences, the responses of children, young people and their advocates raised similar serious issues and concerns in relation to the media's representation of suicide and the treatment of the bereaved. The impact of media intrusion by journalists and photographers in Northern Ireland had long-term consequences for several of the young people who had been bereaved by the suicide of their friend.

Intergenerational Relationships

Children, young people and their advocates emphasised the impact of negative media reporting on intergenerational relationships between young people and older citizens. Several interviewees stated that, *'the media has a lot to answer for'* (YW1) with regard to the 'fear' of crime. Interviewees and focus group participants emphasised how the media's amplification of *'minor stuff'* was typically *'blew up into, "ANTI-SOCIAL THUGS TERRORISING WEE PENSIONERS"'* and as one youth worker commented, *'we knew it wasn't, we know the kids'* (YW3). Several youth workers emphasised how the media maintained *'this impression of old people standing behind closed blinds, peeking out and afraid to leave their houses'* (YW1). Young people also emphasised this and felt that while, *'you hear of these attacks … in the media … they are few and far between'*, but appeared more frequent *'because the media drag it out … as if it is happening all of the time'* (Focus Group 2, aged 17–21).

Chapter 1 has made reference to this disparity between the perception and reality of children and young people's involvement in crime. Significantly, the Department of Justice Northern Ireland (2012a) outlines the stark difference between the existing 'high levels of worry' and 'fear' of crime, compared to 'the lower prevalence of crime'. This reinforces the media's role in amplifying children's and young people's alleged involvement in anti-social behaviour, crime and violence. Further, this finding is consistent with existing international research (see Poynting et al. 2004: 219; Schissel 2006).

Demand for Punitive Responses

Those who work with children and young people consistently highlighted the impact of dominant 'calls for something to be done about young people'. As one youth worker stated, the media presented young people as *'the demons within our community … [who] … we need to do something about it'* (YW2). Youth workers also emphasised how media representations impacted on the community's expectations of youth workers and their role. As one youth worker stated, *'we are not the police, the PSNI are'* (YW4). A number of youth workers in West Belfast noted how, *'in the aftermath'* of *'high profile'* case examples, such as *'the Harry Holland murder'*, newspaper's printed *'a series of editorial lines … text messaging and letters around lock them up and throw away the key'* (YW3). In line with Goode and Ben-Yehuda's (2009: 36) analysis of the reactionary 'social and legal control' directed at 'folk devils', advocates argued that punitive responses and approaches were reinforced in Government policies and legislation. As one representative comment highlighted, *'the Government … are driven by the media … that is how policy is made on the hoof … in a very reactionary manner and not evidence-based'* (CS2).

Media Reporting, July 2010

As noted in Chaps. 4 and 5, a further prominent theme absent from previous research was the media's representation of children and young people's perceived involvement in what has been portrayed as 'recreational' rioting and interface violence. Children, young people and their advocates indicated that the extended and intense media reporting of what was labelled as 'sectarian rioting' in July 2010, was in reality *'not as bad as it was portrayed'* by the media (Focus Group 1, aged 15–19). In asserting *'it happens every year'*, young people questioned why the media *'say that one year was really bad'* and *'why is it being pumped up?'* (Focus Group 1, aged 15–19). There was consensus among young people and their advocates that the media coverage amplified the rioting and the following question posed by one youth worker was representative:

> *When you look at those headlines around the Twelfth and ... look at how young people were reported on back then [during Conflict], which is it, have young people got worse or has the media decided to portray them as it?* (YW1)

One young woman argued that the media *'brainwashed people into thinking this was so bad that it needed three week's worth of coverage'*, and she was critical of journalists as they did *'not ... balance it out with plenty of good things ... involving young people'*, that took place on *'the week of the Twelfth'* (Focus Group 1, aged 15–19). Several young people stated that the focus on the alleged young age of rioters was a clear pattern in the print media coverage and as one young person stated, *'see the way people read a ten-year-old was out rioting, that was every ten-year-old was out rioting'* (Focus Group 3, aged 15–21).

Several youth workers asserted that while *'there is always going to be a bit of trouble ... the media just feeds bad feeling among young people'* and instead *'we need to look at what is behind it'* (YW1). Similarly, young people felt that the media chose to ignore the context of rioting and disputes in relation to Orange Order parades. As a young person stated, *'where do they think the hate is coming from? ... They are not looking at the source of the problem ... sectarianism in this country ... is such a taboo'* (Focus Group 2, aged 17–21). This has been reinforced by contemporary critical research, which indicates that for many children and young people 'sectarianism entrenches hatred for the "other" physically as well as psychologically and culturally' (Kilkelly et al. 2004: 245; see also Scraton 2007; McAlister et al. 2009). However, this contemporary research does not explore the media's role in ignoring and perpetuating this ongoing dynamic present in a contemporary transitioning society, such as Northern Ireland.

Most of those interviewed discussed the ongoing transition from conflict to peace and the dominant view was that, *'because we are in a transition period ... you are in that transitional period where young people will be demonised for political reasons'* (YS1). The viewpoint of those advocates related closely to Young's (1971, cited in Goode and Ben-Yehuda 2009: 90) observation that there exists 'an institutionalized "need" for moral panics'. Another interviewee asserted that:

> *Because the Troubles aren't there per se to take over all the coverage ... their focus is now on young people and labelling them as the lost generation and a new generation of hate, that is just asking for the Troubles all over again ... If the media would stop doing it ... it would make a huge difference, it wouldn't transform everything ... but it would be a huge factor.* (YW1)

Advocates routinely described young people as a target or a scapegoat for *political* purposes and one representative comment put forward reasons why children and young people were demonised in July 2010:

Things like another generation of hate or recreational rioting ... are really in a sense designed to stir up ... hostility towards the young people ... There is ... a political dimension ... because we are in this transition phase ... people are trying to negoti-ate how ... we deal with interface rioting when before it was acceptable ... There is a political context and unfortunately young people are in the middle of all that ... It is necessary to actually demonise the young people or criminalise them, than to give some kind of rationale. (YS1)

Young people also referred to the Conflict and a large number of the focus group participants discussed how the Conflict still impacts on their lives. One representative comment was:

Northern Ireland was a war zone and ... still is in bits and pieces ... it has always been for people ... to fight and drink ... The media are portraying our generation as fighting for the sake of fighting ... previous generations are looking down at us and saying, 'At least we were fighting for a cause'. (Focus Group 4, aged 16–20)

Similarly another young person put forward reasons why children and young people were *'blamed'* for *'dragging Northern Ireland back to the past'*:

We are expected to be the perfect generation because we haven't had it as bad as our parents ... but because we are the post-conflict generation ... we are supposed to be the perfect kids ... They expected after the peace process that everyone would get along and they set such high expectations and hopes for the next generation and they decided our fate and because we are not living in that there place ... it is like, 'Oh what have we done this for, they are throwing away all our work' ... but we are fol-lowing the example we have been set. (Focus Group 2, aged 17–21)

This view of young people *'following the example ... set'* by adults has been acknowledged in previous research and as noted in Chap. 3, concerns had been expressed following the ceasefires in the 1990s, particularly in relation to 'anti-social behaviour among young people [who have] grown used to civil unrest' (McGrellis 2004: 3). Such et al. (2005: 302) observe that, 'in exerting ... power, adults often prioritize the future of the child and society over the child's present well being: a stance of so-called "futurity"' (see also Prout 2000). This relates to the 'process of control' (Such et al. 2005: 302) ongoing in a transi-tioning society, whereby adult responses and reactions seek to deter 'unwanted outcomes' like riots, but the difficulty lays in dealing with the legacy of the Conflict. Barry's (2005: 2) conclusion that, young people 'are the perceived threat to an already precarious status quo and are … often scapegoated as a result', applies to children and young people in Northern Ireland.

Many of the children and young people who participated in three focus groups considered the media '*must think older people wouldn't riot but they do*', describing how, '*there was a good few adults there … all the older people wanted us to help*' (Focus Group 6, aged 14–16). Children and young people's advocates also argued that the media and politicians, rather than focusing on the exploitation of this social group by adults, in particular dissident republicans, chose to promote reactionary responses:

> *Young people … seen rioting at interfaces … [the] reaction to that is to clampdown harder … They will quote these examples … as a reason for being harder on young people … for longer sentences … to introduce more legislation … so there is a lot of politics that goes on as a result of how young people are portrayed.* (YS1)

This is a direct illustration of the analysis in Chap. 3. In particular it demonstrates how societal reaction to atypical events, lead to public demand for punitive, tougher law and policy creation or reform directed towards children and young people (Scraton 2007; Goode and Ben-Yehuda 2009).

PSNI's Operation Exposure

Existing research has not explored the relationship between the media and the Police Service of Northern Ireland (PSNI). The case study of the PSNI's Operation Exposure (see Chap. 5) is a post-devolution example of how the PSNI, the media and the state collectively responded to children and young people. The media's reporting and the PSNI's response in 2010 was typically described as '*different this year*', mainly with '*the Operation Exposure in Derry and the similar thing in Ardoyne*' (YW2). Youth workers observed how it '*became the focus*', with '*pictures … on a running loop and that brought young people into the focus a whole lot more*' (YW2). There was a consensus amongst children, young people and their advocates that this PSNI tactic was '*wrong*' and '*unfair*' (Focus Group 3, aged 15–21). Responses asserted that, '*if it happened anywhere else … like the Iraqi Police had put it out, everybody would be appalled*' (YW2); '*it was morally wrong … a major breach of the rights of young people*' (YW4) and '*violation of human rights*' (Focus Group 1, aged 15–19). Several youth workers described the PSNI's Operation Exposure as:

The same thing paramilitaries were doing about ten years ago … in … a nationalist community … there would have been a poster up in a local shop … pictures of young people … barred from this community or from services … for A, B, C. (YW4)

However, as one young person pointed out, there existed an unambiguous political divide on the issue:

The Nationalist view … they were just children, you can't put their faces in the news and the Loyalist view … if they are old enough to throw it, they are old enough to have their picture in the paper. (Focus Group 4, aged 16–20)

The fact that *'newspapers backed up the PSNI',* was criticised by advocates who argued that the media facilitated the PSNI in order *'to sell newspapers … which is really sad'* (YW1). One representative view emphasised how *'quick'* the *'media were … at publishing the photographs'* and emphasised that:

They just loved it … is so much easier … to actually have a face … it is money from heaven for them, particularly over the summer … It was also the police's way of saying we are doing something about it … it was more about PR for the police. (YS2)

The *'faces'* of children and young people were recognised by youth workers and other young people. As one youth worker stated, *'I was watching the news and I was seeing young people I work with'* (YW4). Similarly young people stated that, *'I recognise all of them'* and *'the police could just go one night and find … them'* (Focus Group 1, aged 15–19).

Children, young people and their advocates raised a range of implications for the safety, lives and well being of those children and young people who had their images released by the PSNI in leaflet, poster and print media format. Responses from advocates and young people emphasised the presumption of *'guilt'* even before due process of the law had been fulfilled, describing the reaction as, *'it was guilty without trial'* (YW4). As one young person stated, *'it is just accepted they are a bad person'* (Focus Group 1, aged 15–19). Similarly a youth worker asserted that:

Coming out from PSNI … looks very official, all these photos … on it, we want them for questioning … see really in the society we live in you are guilty until proven innocent and especially if that is being posted through people's doors, basically people are looking at them and going, 'Criminal' … It is not right … not the way to go about it. (YW2)

Children, young people and their advocates noted the impact of printing images of young people in the media. As one youth worker stated, *'[it] could damage a young person's life or could lead them to get shot or a beating or arrested* (YW4). As one young person highlighted:

> *They are going to have that for the rest of their life ... recognised as a troublemaker ... Every time they walk down the street, they will get, 'There is that young person who was in the front of the newspaper' and could end up getting beat up for it or looked down on.* (Focus Group 3, aged 15–21)

Further, one young person described her experience of another similar PSNI tactic referred to as *'Operation Snapper'*,[1] in Derry/Londonderry:

> *I was in the wrong place at the wrong time ... the next thing this big swarm of people in yellow jackets ... came ... with their video cameras ... starting taking our names ... names were on record for a year ... I was 15 ... It is scary ... to get branded like that ... I don't think it was right. It was on the BBC News at Six.* (Focus Group 1, aged 15–19)

While young people do acknowledge that they *'piss about'* (Focus Group 3, aged 15–21) and do *'silly things ... everyone does'* (Focus Group 1, aged 15–19), there was a consensus amongst young people and their advocates that the responses directed toward this social group were hostile and discriminatory. As the next section will illustrate, such reactions impact on the lives and rights of children and young people.

Impact, Rights and Regulation

> *If newspapers are looking for shocking stories to get people to buy their newspapers they should put some stories in about the impact of the media on young people, into the media.* (YW1)

The above quotation from a youth worker emphasised strong feelings that existed in the children and youth sectors in relation to the impact of the sensationalised media coverage. Personal experiences of 'naming and shaming' and media intrusion painted a collective picture of the extent to which the media's representation and the actions of journalists can impact on the lives of children, young people and advocates. Advocates routinely made reference to the negative impact on the perception of service provision and the work they are involved in.

Experiences of Negative Reporting and Media Intrusion

There was consensus among children, young people and their advocates that *'the media has a huge impact'* and *'a massive influence'* (YW1). Children and young people typically described the impact they felt negative coverage had on how they were viewed, treated and reacted to by adults. Young people stated that, *'old people are really scared of you'* (Focus Group 4, aged 16–20) and *'I don't like the feeling of someone being scared of you'* (Focus Group 3, aged 15–21). Young people also stated that restrictions were placed on them, for example, *'there is a shop in Belfast, they won't let you in ... that has come from media coverage'* (Focus Group 4, aged 16–20).

Several children and young people had been the subject of negative media reporting and *'naming and shaming'* by the print media. As the young people described it: *'I made the front page like'* (Focus Group 5, aged 17–23) and *'I've been in it a couple of times as well'* (Focus Group 5, aged 17–23). A further representative comment from a young person referred to the wording of a headline:

> I was in the paper and it said, *'HOOLIGANS WEAR MASKS'* and at the time it was only one person ... and they were only doing it for a bit of craic. (Focus Group 5, aged 17–23)

Their experiences highlighted the impact of negative media reporting on their lives, relationships within their communities, the fear of punishment attacks and also future prospects, including employment opportunities. Young people described how once ascribed a negative label or *'bad name'*, this status remained a constant feature in a young person's life, influencing how they were treated, policed and represented by the media:

> Once the COPs know who you are ... once an offender, always an offender. Me and my mates ... anytime something went wrong ... it was always, 'They did it or where were they?' ... We got a bad name ... [newspaper's name] gave us hell for everything ... was like, 'YOUNG HOOLIGANS CAUSE DAMAGE'. (Focus Group 3, aged 15–21)

Children, young people and their advocates described the impact of negative media reporting and argued that *'it becomes a self-perpetuating cycle'* (YS1). Many of the *'young people ... hearing all of this stuff they are supposed to be doing'*, were made to feel *'like they are just bad people'* (Focus Group 2, aged 17–21). As a result young people routinely stated, *'I am a hood ... this is what is expected of me'* (YS1) and some indicated that, *'if I am going to get blamed on this I might as well do it'* (Focus Group 2, aged 17–21). These experiences provide contemporary illustrations of Merton's (1968) theory of 'self-fulfilling prophecy', whereby 'folk devils … antisocial or offending behaviours are the self-fulfilment of ascribed negative status' (Scraton 2008:1) and actions become 'deviant' because they are labelled as 'criminal' (Becker 1963).

Based on their experiences, advocates stressed that negative media reporting and *'naming and shaming'* had serious consequences for the lives and well being of children and young people. Several interviewees strongly asserted that, *'it has a huge impact on young people who are the victims of that demonisation'* (CS1). In particular it can position them as *'outcasts'* (YW2) and *'disconnect them in terms of becoming stakeholders in society'* (CS1). Based on their experiences of *'working with young people over the years'*, advocates asserted that many *'young people … have not heard a positive … encouraging word'* and *'when they start to hear things that are positive about themselves'*, many young people *'think … I don't have to live up to … this negative stereotype … [and] turn their lives around'* (YS1).

Several youth workers described how young people *'are getting punishment beatings'* as a consequence of *'getting such a bad press'* (YW4). As one youth worker argued, *'the community is setting up their own kids for punishment beatings or criminal records'* (YW4). Another youth worker made reference to, *'the two kids in St James, "the speckies" … they are 14-year-olds'* (YW3), who have personally commented above on how they have been labelled by the local media in their community. The youth worker asserted that, *'everyone knows who they are … it leaves them extremely vulnerable to a vigilante attack, a paramilitary attack of some sort'* (YW3). There was a consensus that, *'there is nothing positive that can come of this for young people and their communities'* (YW2).

Children and young people's advocates also emphasised the impact of negative reporting and personal attacks by the media, on individuals working in the children and youth sector. One director of a children's sector organisation described her personal experience of being targeted by one newspaper: *'If you looked at the headlines … when they picked on me, "THAT WOMAN" and they had painted me as a complete and absolute do-lally person'* (CS3). Other children and youth sector managers and directors emphasised the negative impact such media coverage had on staff morale. This was something that the Northern Ireland Children's Commissioner emphasised:

> *The sad part about it is that you are always afraid that mud will stick, even though the mud is wrong … When you see some of those articles written … 'THE COMMISSIONER NEEDS TO GROW UP AND LIVE IN THE REAL WORLD' … People perceive out there that we are doing nothing all day long, twiddling our thumbs … It hurts me a bit … my worry is it de-motivates the staff because they've put all this hard work into it and somebody comes off with some snide comment …*

that really is because of their lack of interest in the office. Sometimes that might be personal to me because of my background ... it does de-motivate staff and I see that and staff get frustrated. (NICCY1)

Children and young people provided examples of what can be described as media *'intrusion'* and the impact this had on their lives. Young men and a young woman who participated in one focus group, discussed media reporting and the *'intrusion'* they experienced following the death of their friend and the impact this had on the grieving process:

They don't respect anything ... [name of journalist] contacted me 12 hours after [friend's suicide] ... I just told him straight away 'No', but there was quotes ... from what his family were meant to have said and his family hadn't released statements. (Focus Group 4, aged 16–20)

There was reporters outside their house [and] TV cameras ... the family had refused to give any pictures ... One of the journalists actually took a picture through their door of a picture of him and one of his sisters. (Focus Group 4, aged 16–20)

The young people noted how permanent the media representations were and described the permanent presence of printed newspaper articles in the public domain. Further, they described the impact of the lasting impressions created by negative representations. They also expressed their frustrations and anger at how their deceased friend had been unfairly and inaccurately reported on, following his death by suicide:

They just took it that he took drugs, he deserved to die ... For us ... the news ... made us a lot angrier ... his family wanted him to be held in a good light for the good things ... but it was definitely an intrusion ... because the family tried to keep it private. (Focus Group 4, aged 16–20)

The young people had formed a group and with support from bereavement counsellors and youth workers, were working on raising awareness of suicide, raising money for charity, providing training in suicide awareness and working to challenge media reporting.

Children's Rights

As Haydon and Scraton (2000: 448) note, media reporting and political rhetoric emphasise 'a fear of children's rights as challenging adult authority ... and power'. In line with the UN Committee's Concluding Observations (2008), there was consensus among children and young people's advocates as to the media's negative portrayal of children's rights. Typical responses included descriptions of children's rights as '*a very wishy-washy thing*' (YW2) and '*the notion of goodies for baddies*', particularly in relation to the rights entitlements of '*children and young people in conflict with the law or on the margins*' (YW3).

Interviewees felt that '*negative*' accounts presented in the media of children's rights, labelling it as '*problematic*' (YW3), were due to the '*lack of proper understanding of the rights agenda*' (CS2). As the Northern Ireland Children's Commissioner asserted, this perception was reinforced by '*parts of society in Northern Ireland [who] believe rights aren't something you should be given, you should earn them*' (NICCY1). Advocates highlighted that due to '*sensationalism*' in media representations, it is only those '*working with these young people*' (CS1), '*at the coalface day and daily*' (NICCY1), that '*know the reality in terms of the impact of a denial of their rights*' (CS1) and '*the difficulties … problems and horrendous situations some young people have been put in*' (NICCY1).

Advocates noted the descriptions of them as being '*wishy-washy liberals*' (YS2) or '*woolly liberals*' (YW3). Advocates were '*presented as a bunch of lunatics … group of do-gooders, who don't know the real world*' (CS3), '*are not in touch with reality*' (NICCY1) and responded to '*problems*' by '*hugging kids*' (YW3). One interviewee from the children's sector stated that advocates were routinely '*labelled as living in another planet … as one of the politicians accused one of our colleagues of last week*' (CS1). The Children's Commissioner stressed that in her experience the media and society in general viewed '*rights … as a really bad word … people feel threatened by the word*' and as a routine the media '*pitch adults' rights against children's rights*' (NICCY1). This was emphasised by other interviewees:

> *Oh these children's rights against everybody else's … There is a sense that we are really getting carried away and that is why we have the problems we have because children … are having these rights and holding them up and using them against others.* (CS2)

The Children's Commissioner highlighted that although '*lambasted for it*', she '*was not … afraid to use … the word … rights*', as '*that is my job*' (NICCY1). Other children and youth advocates expressed the difficulties they faced and one youth worker expressed reservations about engagement with the media: '*If you are engaging as the token lone liberal voice, what is the purpose of that other than to isolate your view? … I am not sure of the benefit of it*' (YW3). Another interviewee expressed similar concerns:

If you go on to talk about the rights of children who are detained in Hydebank Wood … it is very difficult to get a fair hearing and you will be juxtaposed with people who are not the most rational in terms of their views. (CS1)

A director of a youth sector organisation described an approach they had developed in order to be included in media debates on children and young people:

We have learnt to temper the word rights when we do this media, which when we started it … I thought it was a betrayal to the cause … what happened when we said about children's rights was we were being cut off … so what we do is we talk about services … best interests … talk about rights without mentioning the word rights … which is terrible but it is the only way we don't get cut off … These kids … as far as the media is concerned, have abdicated any right to rights, they are not deserving of rights only responsibility, so we have to play it a bit cleverer. (YS2)

The experiences of advocates and their views on how children's rights were portrayed by the media, reflects what Lansdown (1994: 42) describes as, 'the profound backlash against the idea that children have a right to greater levels of participation'. It has been well acknowledged that 'the case for children's rights is not uncontroversial' (Lansdown 1994: 42). The dominant argument is that 'the focus' should be 'on teaching' children 'about responsibility', rather than just giving them rights (Lansdown 1994: 42). This further emphasises the disregard and opposition to 'advances in children's rights' (Haydon and Scraton 2000: 448), which will be explored further in the concluding chapter.

Journalistic Ethics and Media Regulation

When discussing journalistic ethics and the current system of media regulation, children, young people and their advocates highlighted issues surrounding knowledge, understanding, effectiveness and accessibility. It was argued by advocates that children and young people need to be educated on the regulatory system and reform is required in the area of print media regulation.

The Children's Commissioner asserted that while *'there are ethical guidelines'* in existence, the print media *'come very close to the wire on them … They bring legal people into see how far they can go'* (NICCY1). Children and young people also concurred and one representative view was:

They just publish it and it doesn't matter … or whether it's legal … they will probably make enough profit from the story to cover any [legal] problems that they will have. (Focus Group 4, aged 16–20)

Other advocates held similar views that, *'local papers just seem to print what they want and there is nobody pulling them in … saying we want you to retract that'* (YW4). One advocate stated that, *'if you look at the PCC guidance around the reporting of children and young people, you couldn't argue with it'*, in relation to its content (YS2). However, the *'guidelines'* in existence were routinely described as *'not working'*, as *'it is clearly the case they [the media] ignore it'* and suggestions included the development and *'need'* for *'actual codified legally binding regulations for the media around children and young people'* (YS1).

In relation to the accessibility of regulatory bodies such as the Press Complaints Commission (PCC) and the Office of Communications (OFCOM), there was a consensus amongst those interviewed that, *'very few young people would know of their existence … or how to complain … it is not widely known and … is not accessible'* (NIHRC1). An advocate noted that, *'we know that this group of young people complain the least … they haven't got the skills or the faith or the confidence in the system to make complaints'* (YS2). While another interviewee concluded that, *'it is sad … young people … don't pick up the phone and contact the newspaper or … the Press Complaints Commission … it says so much'* (YW1). This was reinforced by comments from children and young people who typically had not heard of the regulatory bodies or the complaints mechanisms. Children and young people asserted that, *'adults … [would] have more courage to go forward and do something about it'* (Focus Group 6, aged 14–16). Further, children and young people considered that newspapers:

> [F]eel they can print what they want … about young people and get away with it because if they print lies about someone who is older, they know ways of going about and saying, 'No that's not true' … They can sue the paper, but someone who is 16 isn't even going to know where to start or that they can. (Focus Group 2, aged 17–21)

In discussing their individual experiences, advocates described incidences whereby they have tried to seek redress, however *'often it is after the fact when the damage has already been done'* and the regulatory bodies *'couldn't give us any redress'* (CS1). Such experiences reinforced their opinion that the system of *'self-regulation is not working'* (YS2) and reform is required in this area.

Engagement with the Media

The voices of children, young people and their advocates provided a unique insight into their experiences of engagement with the media in Northern Ireland. Further, the interviewees and focus group participants considered how meaningful engagement could be achieved in the future.

Experiences of Engagement with the Media

Due to children and young people's 'lack [of] … status, rights and power … in society', they 'have few legitimate means to having their voice heard' (Barry 2005: 1). Children, young people and their advocates reinforced this view when they asserted that this social group have limited opportunities to have their opinions included in news items. There was consensus among interviewees and focus group participants, that journalists did not consult or engage enough with them on issues that have affected the lives of children and young people. Rather, journalists chose to *'interview people who are going to … condemn'* (Focus Group 1, aged 15–19) and it was typically journalistic practice to, *'talk to a few upset adults and they've got a story'* (YS2). Young people also highlighted that:

> *Politicians have this foot in the door with newspapers and … 'This is a problem … we are doing this', so it makes them look as if they are actually doing something when they are not.* (Focus Group 2, aged 17–21)

Several young people questioned the prominence given to politicians in the media:

> *Youth workers should be in the papers … they spend more time with us. When does a councillor ever come round to us and say want to have a chat and all?* (Focus Group 5, aged 17–23)

Young people felt that, *'our voice doesn't matter on anything'*, even *'current affairs'* and while they had *'seen loads of people being interviewed, you never see a young person on'* (Focus Group 3, aged 15–21). Similarly advocates felt that, *'there isn't an opportunity for young people to have opinions'* (YW4) and this *'seems crazy … reporting on a story that involves young people without talking to young people'* (YW1). The representative from the Equality Commission asserted that in Northern Ireland, *'young people's access to media is not taken seriously … The "seen but not heard" mentality is very strong'* (EQ1). Children and young people felt that if their voices were included, *'the coverage would be more accurate'* and therefore, *'less negative as a result'* (Focus Group 2, aged 17–21).

In addition to the absence of their voices in the media, there was a consensus amongst children and young people that, *'there is no one to speak for young people'* (Focus Group 4, aged 16–20) and that youth groups did not receive enough media focus. As one young person observed, *'there is a lot of youth groups out there making a difference and you never hear about them'* (Focus

Group 2, aged 17–21). Young people considered that journalists *'should make more of an effort … have a feature with a youth group … and do a detailed interview with young people'* (Focus Group 2, aged 17–21). Routinely, youth workers emphasised that children and young people's engagement must not be *'tokenistic'* in nature and described how *'a column every week in [newspaper] written by a young person … that is so false'* (YW4). The following comment from another youth worker was representative in highlighting the sector's views on engagement with the media:

> *The media would … be looking for a pat on the back if they came … and chatted to our young people … the media needs to be going to young people … who are in the thick of being branded as troublemakers and nuisances … it is not enough to talk to some token young person.* (YW1)

In particular youth workers discussed their experiences of engaging with the media and they reported a range of predominantly negative experiences in relation to engagement with, and treatment by journalists: *'phone-in media … uses shock tactics … He … spent … half an hour attacking me'* (YS2). As one youth worker stated:

> *I have had experiences with [newspaper's name] and I know a youth worker was asked to do an interview … said he could meet them in a local park … to talk about young people … the park and the issues … whenever he arrived to talk to the reporter they were actually leaving and said look sorry we've missed each other … Whenever he opened the paper the next week there was an interview with him in it and he hadn't actually spoke to the reporter … so this is what you are dealing with … I know lots of people who have had these types of experiences.* (YW4)

These experiences bring into question the integrity and ethics of individual journalists, as well as the truthfulness and accuracy of media content. The existing lack of *'trust'* (YW4) was reinforced by other advocates who, based on their personal experiences typically described journalists as *'very manipulative'*, as they *'can turn things around … you say one thing and it turns out as another'* (YW2). Such experiences have left many youth workers *'suspicious of talking'* (YW2) and engaging with the media. As a result many of those interviewed explained that if their organisation *'wanted to run an article in … local paper'*, they would *'write the article … and our own stories … tag photographs and give it to them, because we didn't trust them'* (YW4).

Another youth worker, in describing the *'issues about engaging with the media'*, felt that *'it has gotten to the stage were youth workers are writing the article, taking the photographs and sending them in … and … not getting published'* (YW2). Similarly other youth workers described how staff, who *'aren't trained in writing press releases'* (YW1), were often left feeling frustrated when newspapers did not publish the materials they have written. One youth worker emphasised that the onus should not always be on organisations and that the media should make more of an effort, as in their experience, *'We sent in loads of stuff and it wasn't put in ... It takes a lot of time and there is two staff here ... It wouldn't kill them to come out and do a story'* (YW1). Similarly, the Northern Ireland Children's Commissioner stated that while *'people will turn the tables and say give us your good news stories'*, the reality is that *'lots of kids write good stories, which editors never cover or [they] ... get a wee snapshot'* (NICCY1). These news items *'were never highlighted in the same way as the negative stories are'* (NICCY1).

Although negative experiences had deterred many youth workers from engaging with the media, several organisations stated that although engagement can be *'difficult'* (CS2) and *'upsetting'* (NICCY1), they must continue to engage with the media in order to bring about change. The following representative comments reflected this viewpoint:

> *There is a constant uphill battle ... it is difficult to put people up there all the time and have to face a barrage of attack ... and yet you have to, someone has to take that on ... it is a very difficult task.* (CS2)

> *You have to keep doing it ... if it does us the power of good in our sector ... people feel you are mad but at least you are in there fighting ... you are losing the battle, but nobody can claim that you are not standing up and being counted for it. I have learnt not to take it personally, I don't get upset about it ... as long as I feel that I did the best then I move on to the next thing ... we actually think it is our responsibility to not just talk about how awful the media are but to do what we can to make it better.* (YS2)

Advocates also criticised particular organisations, such as *'the Equality Commission, Human Rights Commission and NICCY'*, who they felt *'have ... done nothing in terms of pulling the media ... and reining them in and ensuring that they do not demonise ... children and young people'* (CS1). There was consensus among advocates that more needed to be done, with those working in both the children and youth sector noting the responsibility placed on them to *'challenge'*, as well as *'engage'* with the media. They made several suggestions, including that, *'the Children's Commissioner needs to be much more of a presence or have somebody employed to look at the media'* (YW1). A further representative suggestion outlined that:

Organisations need to keep hammering the door of the press … it can get very discouraging when you don't get anywhere but the best thing you can do as an organisation is try and get to know a reporter that is sensitive to the issue you are dealing with. (YW1)

Young people, who develop and produce their own forms of media emphasised the positive impact of their work and its role in challenging the negative representations in the mainstream media:

We work on … representing young people who might not be in other forms of media … We … challenge all the bad press … report on all the good things … It is important for us to get young people's views on issues that affect them. (Focus Group 1, aged 15–19)

Typically, a youth worker acknowledged the scale and *'challenge'* of trying to *'get them [the media] to change their ways'*:

I realise … it is maybe not necessarily improving on a larger scale but … what we do here … is at least something in a big pot and hopefully eventually other people will feed into. (YW1)

Further, the youth worker discussed the benefits of employing the media as part of *'outreach work'* and provided the following example of *'young people who all they know is rioting in their area [and] … by giving them a voice through the media, it absolutely had a good effect on them'* (YW1). A director of a youth sector organisation, in describing a current *'piece of work … to educate young people how they can directly interact with the media'*, stressed the challenges of this type of work, as organisations *'have to change the way the media want young people, because what they want is specific, to expose kids'* (YS2). The predominant view was that while children and young people's own forms of media did have positive outcomes, on a *'larger scale'* (YW1), tackling the mainstream media should be the primary objective.

McRobbie and Thornton (1995: 568) argue that, 'so-called folk devils now produce their own media as a counter to what they perceive as the biased media of the mainstream'. While two focus groups discussed their work and own media, there was an overwhelming view that the mainstream media *'did not take seriously'* (Focus Group 1, aged 15–19) or acknowledge the media outputs created by young people. Based on such responses, it can be concluded that McRobbie and Thornton's (1995) argument does not fully consider the 'power' of the mainstream media and the existence of 'the hierarchy of access'. Thus, Cohen's (1972) conceptualisation of 'moral panics' has retained its analytical coherence.

In creating and disseminating their forms of media, children and young people in Belfast emphasised its 'consequences', some of which have been physical and have long term consequences for their lives. One example discussed at two focus groups outlined how one young person was the victim of a punishment beating and 'got big pins in his legs ... for making it [YouTube Video]', which had directly addressed and challenged the demonisation of children and young people in his area by a local newspaper (Focus Group 6, aged 14–16). While the 'policing' of young people and punishment beatings have been documented in existing research (see Whitman 1992; Hamill 2002, 2011), this finding in relation to retribution for creating a form of media to challenge stereotypes, has not been identified or explored in previous research.

The Future

While children, young people and their advocates described their frustrations at the media representations and the lack of meaningful engagement with the journalists, several interviewees and young people made suggestions that looked to 'the future' (YW1). A typical response called for an end to the demonisation of youth and stated that, 'the ideal would be to see a future were children and young people are not demonised. I'd like to see a future were the media tell a story how it actually is' (YW1).

Children and young people suggested that the media should engage with them 'not in a tokenistic way' but in meaningful way (Focus Group 4, aged 16–20). As one young person concluded, 'the only people who can understand youth, is youth' (Focus Group 4, aged 16–20). Others working in the children and youth sector suggested that there was 'an issue with the training of journalists' and a clear 'absence of children's rights' within current journalism training courses (CS1). A director of a children's sector organisation stated that:

> I came across an excellent project in South Africa that was doing intensive training to produce guidelines and booklets ... for the media and training in terms of children's rights and young people's rights ... I think there is merit in replicating that. (CS1)

Another advocate raised the following poignant questions, 'How do we bring media to book? How do we have ... unbiased, balanced, impartial reporting?' (CS3). Several interviewees were of the opinion that children and youth sector organisations 'are not doing enough challenging to be honest' and suggested that their organisations 'need to be all collectively challenging' negative media representations (CS3). Emphasis was placed on *the importance* of producing an evidence-base and as one director in the children's sector proposed, *'hopefully your research will be seminal in informing that work'* (CS3).

Conclusion

This chapter has drawn on the direct experiences of children, young people and their advocates to explore the role and impact of media representations in the processes of demonisation, criminalisation and punishment. Reflective of Chibnall's (1977) analysis, advocates described the typically negative and often simplistic approach taken by journalists. Children and young people outlined the negative impact of imagery and language, in particular derogatory terminology. Consistent with the existing literature, their responses reinforced the media's impact on social reaction, in particular in relation to official policy and community responses directed towards children and young people (see Cohen 1972; Erjavec 2001). Further, the application and internalisation of labels emphasised the impact of negative media representations on how children and young people perceived themselves and their peers. Contemporary examples of Merton's (1968) theory of 'self-fulfilling prophecy' were evident in the discussions of the impact of the application of labels, 'naming and shaming' and the subsequent behaviour of some children and young people.

A number of new insights also emerged from the analysis, several relating to changes in journalistic custom and practice and contextually concerning changes regarding the transition from Conflict. The media's use of content taken from social media and networking sites was discussed by children and young people, who felt that journalists accessing and publishing comments and imagery from Facebook, Bebo and Google Images was an invasion of their privacy. The impact was clearly evident in the responses from the young people who discussed the media coverage following the death of their friend (Focus Group 4, aged 16–20). Their responses described the impact of media intrusion, not considered in previous research in this area.

Reflecting issues raised in the literature review, this chapter has demonstrated that in Northern Ireland the voices of children, young people and their advocates are hidden and excluded. The findings reinforce the contemporary applicability of Hall's (1986) theorisation of 'the hierarchy of access' to the media. The chapter also considered children and young people's own forms of media and their experiences of the limited means they have to challenge negative media representations. Punishment attacks and exiling demonstrate the serious consequences for the lives of those young people. The findings also considered the impact of transition. In particular young people spoke of adults expectations following *'the peace process'* and how they were blamed for a range of social ills, such as riots and interface violence, without consideration of the legacy of the Conflict, or as one young person described it, *'the example we have been set'* by adults (Focus Group 2, aged 17–21). The overall contribution of the empirical research, in particular the original and new findings that emerged, will be explored further in the following, concluding chapter.

Note

1. The PSNI's Operation Snapper initiative targeted under-age drinking and drinking in public places in particular. See: http://www.psni.police.uk/operationsnapperfoylejuly (accessed on 1 July 2012).

Part III

Challenges and Future Policy Responses

8

Conclusion: Reading Between the Headlines – Demonising and Scapegoating of Youth in Transition

As a central 'part of the dramatic element', particularly within media reports on crime and anti-social behaviour, 'scapegoats and folk devils are located and … woven into the narrative' (Eldridge et al. 1997: 61). This monograph has been concerned with how children and young people are represented in print media coverage and responded to at a time of political, economic and social change in a post-conflict transitioning society. Children and young people are routinely 'presented as emblematic of a moment in society's socio-cultural history' (Scraton 2008: 1) and are 'treated as a key indicator of the state of the nation' (Griffin 2009: 229). According to Griffin (2009: 229), this is heightened at times of societal change and transition, whereby on one hand youth are 'assumed to hold the key to the nation's future' and on the other they are feared for their capacity to challenge both 'adult social identity' and 'a stable social order' (Fionda 2005: 27).

During the data collection period, devolution of policing and justice symbolised change and transition. In political and media discourse it was described as the 'final hurdle' for Northern Ireland.[1] However, this emphasis on leaving the past behind and moving on diverted attention away from dealing with the past. It was clear in the empirical study upon which this monograph is based, that images of children and young people in the media were severe. Journalists routinely objectified youth as the problem and presented punitive responses as the solution. Thus, the empirical findings confirm the proposition that children and young people are convenient scapegoats. As a social group, the blame that is placed on them invariably diverts attention away from structural and institutional issues that are inevitable in a society accommodating a gradual transition from conflict.

© The Author(s) 2018
F. Gordon, *Children, Young People and the Press in a Transitioning Society*,
Palgrave Socio-Legal Studies, https://doi.org/10.1057/978-1-137-60682-2_8

The research methods employed, enabled analysis based both on content and on reaction. The content analysis of six months of print media explored the language and imagery and extracted the key themes that were prominent. The qualitative interviews asked those who edit and report to explain and, if necessary, defend the newspaper content they produce. Interviews with politicians and the Police Service of Northern Ireland (PSNI) explored the relationship between the media, the state and state agencies. Children, young people and their advocates presented their experiences of the impact of negative media representations. As the following analysis of the primary research themes demonstrates, the critical theoretical approach and methodology employed, ensured that the empirical research was derived in a thorough and rounded examination of the relationship between media representation, children and young people's lives and the politics of a society in transition.

Significance and Role of the Media in Northern Ireland

In critically exploring the significance and role of the media in contemporary society, the Chap. 1 identified the absence of critical research on the contemporary media in Northern Ireland. The empirical research contained within this monograph sought to address the existing gap. Theoretically, in exploring the significance and role of the media, the primary research prioritised an exploration of the impact of the meaning-making processes of news production and the relationship between newspapers and their readership. The impact of 'change'[2] and transition on the role of newspapers emerged as a new theme from the empirical findings. Thus, the empirical findings have laid the foundation for future critical research on the contemporary media in Northern Ireland.

As established in Chap. 2, through their involvement in the production of media content, editors and journalists play a central contributory role in the meaning-making processes that define what constitutes reality. These processes have an impact on the type of information journalists select as newsworthy and how they chose to frame such information. Typically, when consuming media content the readership interact passively rather than critically (Surette 1998). Thus, while the readership does not play an active role in how media content is produced, it does play an active role in interpreting news items (Ang 1990a; Tolson 1996). In applying this broad analysis to Northern Ireland, the research specifically explored editors' and journalists' perceptions of their role and relationship with their readership. In line with the literature, editors and journalists routinely asserted the existence of a *'duty'* to their readership. This *'duty'* involved fulfilling particular functions through media content, such as informing, educating, socialising and entertaining their readership (see Perry 2002).

Beyond descriptions of their *'duty'*, those working in the media stressed that the content of the news items they produce closely *'reflected'* the views and opinions of their readership. Further, discussions of the news-making process included descriptions of journalists *'tailoring'* the content of news items in order to meet the demands and preferences of their readership. Acceptance on the part of the readership was further reinforced by several editors who described the act of regularly purchasing a newspaper as confirmation that the readership is *'happy'* with the content. This insight gained from the interviewees' responses reinforced their perception of the role of the media, as well as their readership's role in acceptance, compliance with, and reproduction of a dominant discourse.

The meaning-making process and the role of interpretation on the part of the readership emphasised the existence of an established relationship between newspapers and their readership. Despite academic analyses that record a recent decline in readership of newspapers (Franklin and Murphy 1997; Meyer 2009), editors and journalists chose to describe Northern Ireland as a media *'intensive'* society, that *'enjoys'* high readership levels (see Appendix 1 for NI readership figures). Those working in the media were eager to emphasise the existence of a *'very close'* relationship between newspapers and their readership. The perception that this constituted a relationship built on *'trust'* was further emphasised when editors and journalists reinforced that they *'know'*, *'live'* and *'work among the community'* (ED3).

Exploring the significance and role of newspapers in Northern Ireland, involved close consideration of the economic, social, cultural and political contexts in which news is produced. *'Change'* emerged as an unanticipated theme with reference to the *'business'* and *'economic'* functions of newspapers; constraints faced by editors and journalists due to the impact of the economic recession; the impact fewer resources has on the content of news items and the emergence of contemporary developments in journalistic custom and practice. More specifically with regard to social, cultural and political context, post-conflict *'change'* and transition was a prominent theme to emerge during interviews.

Editors routinely highlighted the *'business'* and *'economic'* functions of newspapers. Specifically they described the management of resources, the monitoring of market research and sales figures, as key aspects of their role. Inevitably, the economic recession has reduced the *'resources'* available and the number of journalists 'on the ground', which interviewees highlighted as having 'massively' increased the 'pressure' (ED4) they experience, coupled with the demands of the twenty-four hour news environment. Only a few interviewees stated that the 'pressure' of change has had 'an effect on the quality' of media content, with predictions that if the 'current climate continues' it will result in longer term consequences for the quality of media output (ED7).

Editors' descriptions of the economic constraints and pressures also emphasised the impact on the content of newspapers. Those working in the media acknowledged the prominence given to 'bad news', in order to 'sell newspapers'. Definitions of 'newsworthy' stories were also linked to the creation of an economic 'profit'. A prominent example discussed was the 'profit' generated by printing the images released by the PSNI's Operation Exposure and images of Ardoyne in July 2010. This insight is in line with the literature, which describes newspapers as profit-driven organisations (see Chap. 2; Murdock and Golding 1977; Glover 1984; Hart 1991; Curran and Seaton 1992; Hall 1997). The focus on profit had an effect on content, which specifically reflected a dominant discourse. As one editor described it: 'if we genuinely thought that by sticking six pages of young people's voices in the paper would sell newspapers, we'd be damn sure to do it' (ED5). Thus, economic 'profit' influenced whose voices are included, excluded, hidden or marginalised.

'Changes' in technology and the development of social media and networking have influenced 'new' journalistic practices. The content analysis and case study demonstrated that accessing images and information from young people's Facebook, Bebo, other social networking sites and Google Images has become common practice. Editors and journalists described the practice of accessing images and information from social networking sites, as an immediate 'reflex action' (ED6). As the content analysis demonstrated, one tabloid newspaper, the Sunday World, regularly described in news items how journalists accessed and stored imagery and text from social networking sites for use in future news items (see Chaps. 4 and 5). This journalistic practice was a form of 'surveillance' of young people, particularly those in conflict with the law, who were routinely targeted subjects of sustained media coverage.

While recent research suggests that journalists should consider the ethics of using information from social networking sites (Keeble 2009; Frost 2010), studies have not considered the impact of journalists publishing text or images that have been written by individuals for a private audience (see Foreman 2011). In contributing to existing research, this study explored the direct impact on children and young people. Young people described the practice as an invasion of their privacy, as the media did not ask for permission, often selected 'the worst photographs' and quoted the information as if young people had directly provided the journalist with the comments (Focus Group 4, aged 16–20).

Studies such as Wolfsfeld's (2004) comparative analysis, suggests that Northern Ireland's media played a 'peace-keeping' role during the Conflict. This was reflected in several responses from politicians. As one politician asserted, *'the media ... played a major role in bringing the province forward out of the violence'* (POL3). However, while several editors and journalists made reference to the *'complicated'* role of the media and how it was *'situated in a particular time and space'* (JOURN2), a role in 'peace-keeping' was not raised. This indicates that those editors and journalists interviewed did not perceive this as part of the role of newspapers in Northern Ireland.

The impact of political *'change'* and transition on the media's role in Northern Ireland, and on the content of news items, was a new theme that emerged from the empirical findings. Unique to the research context, *'change'* was strongly emphasised by editors and journalists in their discussions of the transition from Conflict in Northern Ireland. Previous research such as McLaughlin's study (2006: 60) predicts that the 'transition from conflict to peace' represented 'profound and political challenges' for the media in Northern Ireland. However, the direct impact of transition on journalistic custom and practice, on the focus of media content and on representations of specific social groups, had not been considered by previous studies.

Significantly, in describing the impact of transition on the role of the newspapers, editors and journalists pointed to the evident *'change'* in the focus of print media content. Those working in the media referred back to the content of news items during the Conflict. Typically, they described the Conflict as a prominent theme, which *'fill[ed]'* newspapers (ED4). It was significant that those working in the media described the profession as *'still coming to grips with'* the transition from Conflict following the *'ceasefires'* (ED4). The evident *'change'* to the focus of news coverage in Northern Ireland was described as reflective of *'the normalisation'* (ED5) and *'settling down to peace time, normal reporting'* (ED4).

Editors and journalists described the theme of the Conflict as *'all gone'* from media content. In addition, they emphasised how their profession is *'coming to terms'* with how the theme of the Conflict *'is replaced'* (ED4). The empirical findings demonstrated that the *'vacuum'* has been *'filled'* by news items that focus on *'crime'* and *'criminal justice issues'* (ED4). This change in focus outlined in the interviews with editors and journalists, was consistent with the print media content analysis findings. Collectively the interviews and content analysis demonstrated the reliance and prominence given to quotations from politicians, the PSNI and other moral entrepreneurs. As one editor commented, journalists now *'look to police ... courts and prisons to generate stories'* (ED4).

Several politicians interviewed also acknowledged the 'change' in the media's focus and the content of newspaper coverage. One example provided by a politician noted that during the Conflict, children and young people 'standing on a street corner drinking' was not a headline news story, as 'we had better headlines' (POL5). However, the quantitative and qualitative content analysis findings indicated that this was one of the significant focuses of media attention in this transitional period. Further, several politicians discussed the impact devolution of policing and justice has had on political debate. They emphasised that 'very few … [are] speaking out about the causes of crime', but instead 'are happy to jump on the bandwagon … talk about crime and blame it on young people' (POL4).

The empirical research findings reinforced the importance of considering the significance and role of the media in its social, cultural, political and economic context. In line with predictions made by academics such as McLaughlin (2006: 60), who asserts that editors and journalists in post-Conflict Northern Ireland 'must now adapt to mediating a difficult period of conflict resolution', the new theme of 'change' explored the impact of transition. Having to adapt to 'change' and political transition, as well as new technologies, the economic recession and readership expectations were significant concerns that editors and journalists outlined. Their descriptions of the 'pressure' and impact of 'change' provided a valuable insight into the 'changing' role of the media and the focus of media content in the 'new' Northern Ireland. The content analysis and interview findings demonstrated how an increased focus on 'crime' and 'criminal justice issues', coupled with sustained condemnatory political debate and discourse, targeted children and young people. As will be explored further, such severe media representations decontextualised children and young people's perceived behaviours, in particular by failing to consider the impact of the legacy of the Conflict.

Media Representations and Impact of Negative Ideological Constructions

The literature review established that editors and journalists play a central role in producing media representations of children and young people that typically slant toward 'distortions', 'exaggerations' and 'misrepresentations' (see Chaps. 1 and 2; Glover 1984; Simpson 1997; Schissel 1997; White 2002; Osgerby 2004; France 2007; Springhall 2008). As outlined previously, this study included quantitative and qualitative analysis of newspaper content in order to establish how children and young people were portrayed in Northern

Ireland. The quantitative findings established that over a six-month period, children and young people were the subject of 2,456 news items and 2,204 images. The qualitative content analysis examined the language and imagery employed by journalists. It also explored the prominent themes that emerged, in particular the portrayal of children and young people's perceived involvement in anti-social behaviour, crime and violence, and calls for punitive responses. From this analysis, several findings and themes were identified as new and specific to Northern Ireland. One example was the application and impact of labels, such as 'anti-community', 'hoods' and 'recreational rioting'.

The content analysis demonstrates that editors and journalists selected sensationalist language and severe imagery to represent children and young people in certain definite ways. Typically, media representations amplified the perceived involvement of youth in 'anti-social' behaviour, 'crime' and violence. Language and labels such as: 'YOBS'; 'UNRULY'; 'DISAFFECTED'; 'CRAZY'; 'young criminals'; 'child vandals' and 'teenage-tearaway', constructed youth as a 'problem'. Further, stereotypical generalisations and age-specific language framed children and young people's behaviour as 'anti-social', 'lawlessness', 'drunkenness' and 'gangsterism'. These broader themes were also prominent in the responses from politicians and other moral entrepreneurs, who typically employed similar language when expressing their opinions.

The most severe portrayals that referred to children and young people as 'SICKOS', 'EVIL' and 'monsters', were at the sharp end of the continuum of the demonisation of youth. When challenged on the severity of media representations, editors and journalists defended and justified their use of emotive language and labels, by asserting that *'professionals'*, *'survivors'* or *'relatives of the victims'* routinely referred to children and young people in this way. This extreme language also featured in the printed form of Letters to the Editor and text messages. While other studies have not analysed readership responses, a notable exception is Poynting et al.'s (2004: 3) study. In this monograph the analysis of such contributions highlight the severity of community reactions directed towards children and young people in Northern Ireland. The findings reinforce the role of language, labels and stereotypes in maintaining dominant negative ideological constructions of children and young people.

Significantly, analysis of imagery had often been overlooked in previous content based studies. As the findings demonstrate, the images of youth were visually dramatic and powerful. Thus, it was clear that as a social group, children and young people in Northern Ireland were represented in media discourse as visible 'symbols of trouble' (see Cohen 2002). While acknowledging that images *'speak a thousand words'*, editors also strongly justified their publication of images, by describing them as *'factual'*, *'realistic'*, *'evidence'* (ED6) and *'a matter of public record'* (ED2). Their responses reinforced findings that emerged in Davies' (1997: 56) study, in particular that photographs were 'presented as if offering a transparent record of the real'.

In this study it emerged that the interpretation of imagery was closely bound up with the specific historic, cultural and social context within which the images have been produced. Children and young people in their discussions of how journalists *'find'* or *'choose'* images, observed that media representations typically included the most extreme imagery, which framed youth as *'menacing'* and *'really, really mad'* (Focus Group 1, aged 15–19). Further, advocates discussed the impact of dramatic and powerful imagery on adult perceptions. Their responses described how negative imagery *'frame[s] the readers mindset'* (CS3), *'filters through'* and *'brands all young people as dangerous'* (YW1). Visual representations therefore played a key role in reinforcing negative ideological constructions of children and young people as *'troublesome'* and in severe instances, as *'evil'*, *'demonic'* and *'feral'*. Collectively the dramatic imagery, emotive language and criticism of any alternative explanations other than individual pathology, clearly impacted upon the images of youth that the readership received.

The journalistic practices of applying labels and naming and shaming singled out children and young people and separated them from 'law-abiding' members of their community. Labels employed by editors and journalists, such as 'anti-community', explicitly framed children and young people's perceived behaviour as *'against the community'*. This label was unique to Northern Ireland and the meaning attached to it was significant in reinforcing the separation of children and young people from the rest of the community. Children and young people's responses confirmed how ascribed labels became terms of abuse and judgement. One prominent example was the relationship between *'wearing a hoodie'* and being labelled a *'hood'*.

First-hand accounts of naming and shaming by *'community newspapers'* outlined the impact on children's and young people's lives, experiences and wellbeing. In defending this journalistic practice, editors typically described *'public shame'* as *'part of... the law'* and a core element in the *'punishment'* and *'rehabilitation'* of *'offenders'* (ED5). Their responses did not acknowledge ethical issues in relation to publishing details and images of children and young people. These findings provide a unique insight into how those working in the media justify their role in naming and shaming. Further, it provides those previously hidden voices the opportunity to describe the impact of having been targeted by the media.

The role of the media representations in amplifying youth as a threat to the stability of the adult 'inner community' was particularly evident in relation to children and young people's alleged involvement in 'gangs'. In line with existing literature (see McAlister et al. 2011), the findings show that media representations frame identifiable groups of young people who spend their leisure time on the streets, as 'gangs'. This study also built on McAlister et al.'s (2011: 96) findings, in that it provides evidence of the 'over-simplified application' of the label 'gang' by the media in Northern Ireland. This was particularly evident in the media's construction and sustained coverage of the 'IBA gang'. While young people did not classify the 'IBA' as a 'gang', it was evident from their responses that *the IBA were made out to be a full gang*' by the media (Focus Group 5, aged 17–23). These findings demonstrate the media's role in the construction of 'gangs' and the amplification of young people's perceived involvement in 'gangsterism'.

In their discussions of the impact of negative media reporting and 'naming and shaming', children, young people and their advocates asserted that media representations and *the judgement within*' (YW2) communities were central in positioning youth as *outcasts*'. While a small number of advocates described 'naming and shaming' as a *badge of honour*', typical responses outlined concerns that young people internalised negative media representations. In directly addressing one of the key research questions, the findings demonstrate that labels were internalised by children and young people. This negatively impacted on their perceptions of themselves and their peers. Significantly, youth workers emphasised the impact of negative media representations on the opinions formed by some *practitioners*', who refused to work with certain children and young people. This consolidated exclusion of children and young people who had been singled out and ascribed outsider status.

Advocates noted the impact of children and young people's internalisation of negative media representations on the subsequent behaviour of some children and young people. This behaviour confirmed the stereotypes and labels that were ascribed to them. Thus, confirming the existence of *self-fulfilling prophecies*' and a *self-perpetuating cycle*', through which children and young people when labelled do *what is expected*' (YS1). Children and young people's responses described the process of being made to feel *like … bad people*' (Focus Group 2, aged 17–21). The subsequent reaction of several young people was, *if I am going to get blamed on this I might as well do it*' (Focus Group 2, aged 17–21). In directly addressing one of the key research questions, these findings demonstrate the significance of negative media representations in contributing to acts of secondary deviance. Significantly, this insight into the direct experiences of children and young people and the descriptions of their subsequent behaviours provide a unique insight and contemporary application of Merton's (1968) theorisation. Merton's (1968: 477, original emphasis, cited in Lilly et al. 2011: 145) analysis contends that 'a *false* definition of the situation' evokes 'new' behaviour 'which makes the originally false conception' or construction 'come *true*'.

Naming and shaming and negative media representations also impacted on subsequent adult responses directed toward children and young people. Children, young people and their advocates provided examples of how *'punishment beatings'*, *'paramilitary attacks'* and *'vigilante attacks'*, followed sustained negative media coverage. They stressed that media representations clearly identified to *'everyone'* who the young people were within the community. One youth worker poignantly placed blame on *'the community'* for *'setting up their own kids for punishment beatings'* (YW4). This was also reflected in the earlier analysis of the media's reporting of the 'IBA GANG'. When questioned, the editor who allowed the publication of the news items acknowledged that, *'I think we did things wrong'* (ED3). However, as the content analysis demonstrated, the same newspaper continued to 'name and shame' children and young people in that particular community.

While previous studies have explored the relationship between media representations and the decontextualisation of children and young people's perceived involvement in 'crime' and 'deviance' (see Chaps. 1, 2 and 3; Durham et al. 1995; Davis and Bourhill 1997; Schissel 2006), this has not been considered by previous research in Northern Ireland. Analysis of empirical data has illustrated how media representations of children and young people removed such perceived behaviours from their socio-economic and political contexts. In particular, the interviews with advocates highlighted how media representations of children and young people's perceived behaviours were framed *'without an understanding of the wider political context'* (YW3). This decontextualisation was clearly present in the media coverage of July 2010, as journalists did not describe children and young people's behaviour as Conflict related, but defined it as 'criminal', 'deviant' and 'violent'. In particular, the repeated use of the label 'recreational rioting' framed their motivations as 'fun' rather than political.

In transitioning societies there exists a significant dynamic evident when those in power avoid or are reluctant to ask awkward political questions and address structural inequalities, but need to be seen as possessing strong leadership skills in order to ensure the stability of that society. In this study, advocates asserted that because of the *'transition period'*, children and young people were *'demonised for political reasons'* (YS1). This was evident in the content analysis of newspaper content, as the *'simple explanations'* diverted attention away from the larger questions and issues, in particular the legacy of the Conflict. This finding reflected Schirato and Yell's (2000: 77–78) study, which discusses how narratives and explanations in the media attempted to divert attention away from the conditions, as well as the political and economic realities that define and determine the lives of the most marginalised.

Published in 1972, Cohen's theorisation of 'folk devils' and 'moral panics' highlighted the reaction towards youth at a time of social change in post-war Britain. Cohen (1972: 192) asserted that:

> The Mods and Rockers symbolized something far more important than what they actually did ... [via] messages about 'never having it so good' ... Resentment and jealousy were easily directed at the young.

During focus groups, children and young people indicated their frustrations with adult responses and reactions directed towards them and this is reflected in the following comment from a young woman:

> *We are expected to be the perfect generation because we haven't had it as bad as our parents ... after the peace process ... they set such high expectations and hopes ... they decided our fate ... it is like, "Oh what have we done this for, they are throwing away all our work" ... but we are following the example we have been set.* (Focus Group 2, aged 17–21)

This description of the content of adults' responses was in line with 'explanations' and social reactions that emerged in both media and political discourse during and following the riots in July 2010 (see Chap. 5). The July 2010 case study illustrated how the media and politicians heightened tension and evoked notions of anxiety and resentment directed towards children and young people. News items that accused children and young people of 'bringing back the Troubles', firmly placed blame on them for 'dragging' Northern Ireland 'back through the horrors of the past' (*The Irish News*, 15 July 2010: 11). This constructed children and young people as a threat to the stability of contemporary society and positioned them as 'folk devils' in the 'new' Northern Ireland. Thus, Cohen's (1972) initial theorisation was useful in understanding the role and impact of media representations on social reaction and responses directed toward children and young people in a transitioning society.

Social Reaction, Policy and Legal Responses in the 'New' Northern Ireland

Previous research in Northern Ireland has described the impact of negative perceptions of youth and social reaction as 'not so clear' (McAlister et al. 2009: 15). Therefore, this study set out to explore this previously unaddressed issue. From the outset, the empirical research contained within this monograph identified the importance of considering the relationship between media representations of youth, negative ideological constructions, social reaction and policy and legal responses. Following a review of contemporary responses in Britain and Northern Ireland (see Chap. 3), the empirical research considered the images that legislators and policy-makers have of children and young people. The exploration of the impact of social reaction on policy and legal responses in the 'new' Northern Ireland, involved a consideration of whether the UK's legacy in terms of criminal justice would be inherited or contested post-devolution.

As outlined above, the call for punitive responses emerged as a key theme from the content analysis. This theme demonstrated how calls for 'something to be done' about youth involvement in anti-social behaviour, crime and violence, were given prominence in headlines and commentary. Significantly, the strong language employed reinforced the 'need' for legislators, policy-makers and the judiciary to introduce and implement 'GET-TOUGH POLICIES', 'TOUGHER LAWS', more police and 'longer' prison sentences. These reactions were amplified particularly in relation to high profile cases. While rare in number, high profile cases received sustained media attention and were often utilised by journalists when discussing 'new' cases. In defending this practice, editors and journalists referred to the reactions of victims and their families when justifying their proposals for punitive measures.

The impact of the amplification of youth involvement in high profile cases, in particular involving violence, was also explored in detail during the interviews with advocates. Youth workers in West Belfast referred to several alleged incidents that had been reported during the data collection period. Their responses argued that cases involving adults were not treated in the same way. They observed that high profile cases involving children and young people were 'connected or lumped together' (YW2). These findings reflected the central role of the media in exaggerating children's and young people's alleged involvement. It was evident that when the deviancy amplification spiral was set in motion and maintained by severe emotive representations, this influenced social reaction and the political responses that followed.

Theoretically, Cohen's (1972: 9) study identified the pivotal role of language, such as epidemic and crisis, in the process of deviancy amplification. As Cohen's (1972: 9) research demonstrated, media representations and political reactions were typically followed by serious and long-lasting repercussions in terms of legal and social policy. Core elements of Cohen's (1972) theorisation were reflected in the findings that emerged from the case study of children, young people and rioting in July 2010. Specifically, it was evident that anxiety and concern surrounding the stability of Northern Ireland was heightened by the media coverage. Journalists' descriptions of Northern Ireland as being 'dragged back' to 'the old times', amplified the level of violence and positioned young people as contemporary 'folk devils'. The selection of strong language, such as 'DESPAIR', 'DISGUST' and 'REVULSION', framed adult condemnation of youth. In defending their use of language, editors and journalists asserted that these descriptions *'reflected'* adult responses and societal reactions to children, young people and the rioting.

The severity of adults' responses was evident in the content analysis of readers' contributions or replies. This analysis was central in exploring the relationship between negative media representations and social reaction. The significance of the content contained within Letters to the Editor, comment pages and text message sections had not been the focus of existing studies. Therefore, as outlined previously, the analysis of readers' contributions or replies offered a unique insight into community reactions toward youth. In particular the content of 'WE SAY' sections of the sample newspapers, which condemned youth, further reinforced the 'outsider' status that was ascribed to children and young people. These findings highlight the central role the readership played in the acceptance, reproduction and maintenance of a dominant discourse that demonised and in extreme cases, vilified youth.

Significantly, children and young people discussed the direct impact of negative community reactions on their interactions with adults in their community. The negative impact of text message pages was discussed at length, in particular the volume of texts and their content. Young men, who had been the focus of a sustained 'campaign' in text messaging sections of the *Andersonstown News*, stated that they were easily recognisable from the messages printed. They considered that the labels imposed by the text messages were reinforced in the community, with the young men excluded from community events. Advocates also highlighted the impact, with a youth worker describing the content of the text messaging as clearly a form of *'bullying'* (YW2). This was one example among many that children, young people and their advocates raised. It demonstrates the severe impact of negative representations on social reaction and subsequently on children and young people's relations within their community.

In exploring the impact of social reaction during a unique period of transition, the research considered the legacy of direct rule and whether the transfer of UK criminal justice legislation, policies and practices have continued or have been contested post-devolution. The research timing represented a period of specific political transition. As McEvoy and Ellison (2003: 55–58) note, during periods of negotiation and transition in post-conflict societies, there exists potential for changes to the decision-making institutions. The findings in this research study establish that this was particularly evident.

Significantly, the content analysis noted repeated calls for the new Justice Minister, 'TO GET HIS ACT IN GEAR' and introduce new legislation in line with the UK (for example, parenting orders). References made to the use of such measures in England and Wales reinforced calls for their introduction in Northern Ireland.

The impact of the transferral of policies and practices from the UK to Northern Ireland was identified in the case study of the PSNI's Operation Exposure and publication of images of children and young people in Ardoyne in July 2010. The interview with the architect of the PSNI's Operation Exposure confirmed that the practice had been transferred from the UK to Northern Ireland. As the interviews with editors and journalists demonstrated, sample newspapers played a willing partnership role in printing the images of children and young people in Derry/Londonderry and Ardoyne. The tactic was hailed as successful by the PSNI, media and several politicians interviewed.

Subsequently, Operation Exposure has been developed by the PSNI, in particular through applications for protection orders, to gain access to the media's footage of riots, under the Police and Criminal Evidence (NI) Order 1989. This practice has been criticised within the media, who have been reluctant to comply. It has resulted in a court judgment (July 2011) ruling that the public interest in convicting those involved in rioting outweighed the potential or perceived danger to journalists, photographers and other media employees.[3] This case is significant, as it contrasts with the media's willingness to facilitate the PSNI's Operation Exposure and the publication of images of children and young people in Ardoyne.

This study also identified further examples of the longer-term consequences of social reaction. The content analysis illustrated the prominence of calls for 'harsher sentences' for young people. Journalists typically made reference to sentencing policies and called for sentences that were in line with sentences issued in England and Wales. In particular, the riots in July 2010 continued to be employed in media discourse as an example of why there should be 'harsher sentences'. For example, Mr Terry Spence, Chairman of the Police Federation Northern Ireland, stated that more punitive sentencing would give 'rioters ... the wake up call ... that their behaviour will not be tolerated' (*News Letter*, 27 October 2011). In calling for judges to respond, Mr Spence specified the 'context' of Northern Ireland:

> Because the rioting here has been usually politically and criminally inspired, rioters were judged in the soft context of the social and political difficulties of Northern Ireland, inching its sporadically violent way to stability. (*News Letter*, 27 October 2011)

He framed the responses that followed from July 2010 as soft in order to justify a call for swift, harsher measures to be implemented, in particular a review of the sentencing guidelines that are currently in operation in Northern Ireland. Therefore, within media and political discourses were calls and support for the transference of UK policies. Such calls did not include or acknowledge the context or special circumstances of Northern Ireland. As evident in the above quotation, the Conflict was employed as a reason why policies have been deemed soft. Subsequently, demands for 'harsher' punishments have been reinforced in order to secure stability and security, as part of Northern Ireland's transition from conflict.

The findings indicate that in light of the existing concerns about stability in the ongoing period of transition, anxieties were heightened. In particular, the case study of July 2010 highlights the impact of social reaction on political debate and the consequences for children and young people. Throughout the media coverage prominence was given to calls for the transferral of UK policies, such as parenting orders and longer sentences. These recommendations were proposed without consideration of the wider context of the legacy of the Conflict. Thus, it is evident that post-devolution of policing and justice, the UK legacy in terms of criminal justice policies and practices continue to be inherited.

Engagement, Participation and Challenging the Media

Theoretically, the literature review outlined the structured relationship between the media and institutional definers (see Allan 1999). Previous research has discussed the existence of a hierarchy of access to the media (see Becker 1963), which ensures that authority figures and moral entrepreneurs are provided with 'organized media access' (van Dijk 1991). In contrast, 'other' marginalised voices or 'alternative' viewpoints are excluded or hidden. Thus, the media and moral entrepreneurs are able to set the agenda and establish the boundaries within which discussion and debate on 'problem youth' takes place.

Against this theoretical backdrop, this study considered the prominence given to certain voices and the exclusion or marginalisation of other voices in newspaper content. In prioritising an exploration of the broad themes of inclusion, access, engagement and participation, the focus groups with children and young people, as well as the interviews with advocates, considered their experiences of direct engagement with editors and journalists. The findings identify difficulties routinely experienced by children, young people and their advocates when challenging negative media representations. The study also explored the views of editors, journalists and politicians with regard to current and future engagement with children, young people and advocates. A new theme emerged in relation to children and young people's own forms of media (for example, their own newspapers, publications and online media). This theme highlights adults' reliance on mainstream media representations and their significance in generating social reaction.

The literature review established that most communications are shaped and take place 'within settings of inequality' (Corner and Hawthorn 1993). As the content analysis and case study confirms, marginalised social groups in Northern Ireland experience inequality in relation to access to, and participation with the media. Children, young people and their advocates' voices were typically excluded, missing, hidden or marginalised in media discourse. The findings demonstrate how the codified journalistic conventions operated in the media to naturalise and reaffirm the existing social divisions and inequalities (Allan 1999). This was reflected in responses from editors who acknowledged their preference for interviewing those in power, such as 'businessmen', 'entrepreneurs' or 'politicians'. Thus, the interview responses provide further evidence of the inequality perpetuated by editors and journalists in their construction and promotion of meanings, and in the 'privileged' access given to certain social groups.

Significantly, the review of previous studies indicated that there is limited contemporary research that has considered the direct impact of exclusion and marginalisation in media discourse on children, young people and advocates. Prioritising the inclusion of their voices addressed this gap and contributed to an understanding of the impact of inequality in relation to access, participation and inclusion. Children, young people and their advocates collectively observed that editors and journalists typically engaged with, and gave prominence to the voices of 'adults in power', who were most likely to 'condemn' the perceived behaviour of this social group. This finding reflected Hall's (1986: 9–12, original emphasis) observation that 'the hierarchy of *power* in … society is reproduced, in the media, as a structure of *access*', which is 'systematically skewed in relation to certain social groups'.

Children, young people and their advocates routinely described the frustration they felt when seeking access to mainstream newspapers. In particular they described the limited opportunities to be included in news items, as well as the 'tokenistic' and 'condescending' nature of the current practice of 'youth sections' in some newspapers. Significantly, a few editors and journalists agreed when they referred to youth sections as 'tokenistic'. However, they did not make suggestions for how meaningful participation could be achieved. This limited access and means to participate also extended to politics, with several responses from politicians clearly indicating their reluctance to engage with children and young people. These findings demonstrate the hierarchy of access to the media in Northern Ireland, the marginalisation of youth in political discourse, as well as the existence of dismissive attitudes towards children and young people.

The empirical findings also reveal the impact that dismissive attitudes have on advocates, on community perceptions of their work and on service provision. Advocates described the negative impact that labels such as 'quangos' and personal attacks had on *'staff morale'*. Further, advocates discussed the difficulties they experienced when attempting to have mainstream news items address issues that they had raised. Their descriptions of the work and effort involved and the time taken to write articles, find appropriate photographs and submit items to newspapers, most of which are *'not picked up and printed'*, emphasised their frustration. When included, alternative voices typically were framed within the angle taken by the journalists. These findings reflected Gross's (1992: 131) assertion that when outsiders do attain visibility, their views are included only within a framework set out by editors and journalists.

An additional theme of children and young people's own forms of media emerged from the print media content analysis and focus groups. While this theme has not been identified in previous content analysis studies, Crane's (1997) analysis did make reference to student-operated newspapers. Crane (1997: 94) proposes that they pay 'relatively little attention to sensational issues such as crime' and avoid 'age-based labelling'. Significantly, this new theme emerged during focus groups with children and young people. In particular, two focus groups discussed the creation and use of their own forms of media to challenge stereotypes and negative media representations. The difficulties in relation to the limited access and meaningful participation children and young people have with the mainstream media, were clearly a consequence of the ideological process. Children and young people's experiences emphasised how certain individuals and social groups were positioned on the margins, with little or no means of challenging their position or how they were represented.

The empirical research addressed the call by McRobbie and Thornton (1995) to explore whether 'folk devils' play a role in the 'moral panic' process. In considering this, the study explored children and young people's experiences of employing their own forms of media to challenge negative representations. Collectively, this social group and their advocates were clearly frustrated and identified the difficulties they experienced. Children and young people considered that the newspaper editors and journalists *'did not take seriously'* or acknowledge the media output they produced (Focus Group 1, aged 15–19). These findings challenge McRobbie and Thornton's (1995) argument and concluded that it did not fully consider power relations, the impact of the mainstream media on social reactions and policy responses, as well as the maintenance of negative adult perceptions of youth.

Further, the literature review illustrated that previous research had not explored the negative consequences of social groups producing their own forms of media, particularly as a means of challenging mainstream representations. Significantly, children and young people spoke of physical injuries and punishment beatings following the creation of their own forms of media that challenged the mainstream representations (Focus Group 6, aged 14–16). While existing research has documented the 'policing' of young people and the impact of punishment beatings (see Whitman 1992; Hamill 2002, 2011), this finding in relation to retribution for creating a form of media to challenge stereotypes, had not been identified in previous academic studies. It provides a unique insight into the impact of social reactions towards youth in transitioning societies. Further, it demonstrates how significant the unaddressed context of the legacy of the Conflict was for the lives and experiences of children and young people in the 'new' Northern Ireland.

As the analysis illustrates, children and young people in Northern Ireland are not afforded social, political or economic power. The empirical findings in relation to the broad themes of access, participation and inclusion, reinforce the proposition that this social group is denied its right to be heard and freedom of expression (Articles 12 and 13 of the UNCRC). The findings also establish that the recommendations contained within the CRC Concluding Observations (2008) have not been addressed or placed on the political agenda (see Chap. 1). Further, the lack of opportunities for meaningful participation with the mainstream media is further evidence of a backlash against children's rights and this impacts negatively on those who advocate for greater opportunities for children and young people's participation in the media. Their experiences confirm the need for greater opportunities for children and young people to form their own views and freely express their ideas. This remains a challenge and will only be possible if the media and politicians work to provide opportunities whereby children and young people are afforded meaningful and equal access to participate and be represented in media coverage.

Challenges

Planning and conducting a critical study combining several research methods, brought many challenges. The demands of collecting, managing and analysing large amounts of print media content were overcome through designing and implementing a tabular system. This provided the point of reference for drawing out the prominent themes and analysing the news items. Many of the prominent themes to emerge from the content analysis were highly sensitive and personal, and were also raised and discussed at interviews and focus groups. These include the media's representations of youth suicide, media intrusion, examples of the role of the media in naming and shaming children and young people and discussions of experiences of being the targeted victims of punishment beatings, shootings and exiling from the community.

From the outset, the primary research set out to reflect the dynamics of age-related power and power relations, institutionally and inter-personally, in Northern Ireland. The review of literature demonstrated that as a social group, children and young people are not afforded the same social, political or economic power as adults. Thus, theoretically and methodologically differential access to power emerged as a prominent theme and consideration. In terms of methodology, research methods texts, such as Jupp (1989), advise that when designing, conducting and analysing empirical material, critical researchers should be aware of the balance of power between the researcher and the participants involved. As discussed elsewhere, power imbalances were identified and measures put in place, particularly in relation to children and young people.

Further challenges in relation to power imbalances emerged during the interviewing process, particularly when interviewing those within a media industry not previously the subject of contemporary critical social research. Initially I had not anticipated that as a researcher I would personally experience the effects of an imposed 'power imbalance'. At the time of conducting the empirical research, I was a young female research student, the social determinants of my age, gender and assumed social status were evident dynamics in several interviews, in particular those conducted with newspaper editors. The analysis in Chap. 6 made reference to several of the personalised comments directed at me during interviews, such as: *'drunken students ... causing mayhem ... including [researcher's name]'* (ED1). As previously outlined, these responses were closely related to defensiveness on the part of several editors and journalists.

Significantly, interviewing trained and experienced interviewers brought a significant dynamic to the primary research, with defensiveness a common response throughout several interviews with editors and journalists. These interviews were the most challenging. A number of the interviewees strongly expressed statements, posed questions and directed criticisms towards the validity of the empirical research. For instance, one editor asserted that focus groups with children and young people and interviews with their advocates would *'produce'* no more than a collection of *'anecdotal stories'* (ED5). My experiences as a researcher reflected Becker's (1967) observations. Specifically, that by presenting the view from below, research may 'draw the criticism, from those in authority', in particular views 'that the researcher has become biased, an advocate of those they seek to present' (David and Sutton 2011: 38).

The approach taken, in particular the open questioning and semi-structured nature of the interviews ensured that I did not present any personal opinions or responses. However, it appeared that many of those working in the media presumed that due to the research topic, I was in essence 'questioning' the integrity of journalism in Northern Ireland. While such experiences were initially challenging, on reflection the approach on the part of several interviewees represented the existing denial of inequalities in relation to the hierarchy of access to the media. Their comments also represented the reinforcement of a dominant discourse that many of those working in the media maintain in the news items they personally produce. Thus, the way in which several editors and journalists responded to me as a researcher was very similar to the experiences outlined by those advocating on behalf of children and young people.

In contrast, my age appeared to be an advantage when creating an appropriate environment in which children and young people felt comfortable to discuss personal experiences and sensitive subjects.[4] During several of the focus groups, the conversations flowed to the extent that the participants became inclusive of me as a researcher. This environment aided direct engagement. Significantly I was questioned and challenged about the research. Having been involved in previous research focus groups, one young woman questioned what impact this research would have, as *'we never heard back from [organisation's name] who did one of these focus group things and what difference does this all make anyway?'* (Focus Group 3, aged 15–21). In response both the youth worker and I stated that advocates and researchers should *'always try to challenge such representations'*, *'challenge politicians and lobby government, to try and bring about some sort of change'* and we highlighted the need for young people's voices to be heard.

The young woman's question outlined above was poignant, not least because it reflects a key objective of critical research, that of ensuring 'the view from below' is included, while challenging those in power. It emphasises the importance of critical social research in providing an opportunity for hidden or marginalised individuals and social groups to have their voices heard and their difficulties and experiences acknowledged. In striving to make a difference, critical social research can be an important tool for advocates to use in lobbying government to bring about change.

Future Considerations

The reflection on the empirical findings has identified several significant future considerations for scholars, policy makers, advocates and society. This monograph provides a foundation for scholars to critically analyse the impact of media representations on other social groups in the 'new' Northern Ireland. While the research analyses the representation of children and young people in newspaper coverage over an extensive period of six months, it does not address broadcast media. The empirical interviews demonstrate the perceived *'high readership'* figures and the *'close'* relationship between the media and their readership. These findings reinforce the importance of this analysis of newspaper content. In adding an interesting dynamic to the research, the interviews involved participants working in different media (for example, newspapers, radio and televised news). This enabled the inclusion of a range of opinions on the role, significance and impact of the media.

Future research could extend to include content analysis of radio and televised news bulletins, in order to compare and contrast the representations and impact of broadcast and online media. In addition, an important future focus for research must be the exploration of the audience/readership's perceptions and interpretations of newspaper representations of children and young people. As part of a larger study on older victims of crime, the author is addressing this 'gap' in the research-based literature by exploring how older victims perceive and interpret print media portrayals of young people 'in conflict with the law'.

Several future considerations for the media, moral entrepreneurs and children and youth sector organisations emerge from the empirical findings. It was acknowledged that media training at College and University level does not include training in children's rights or how to appropriately engage with children and young people. As Chap. 7 demonstrated, there appears to be a clear reluctance on the part of the media to engage with children and young people. Several interviewees described engagement as posing *'difficulties'* and *'hassle'* (JOURN1), due to perceived *'cotton wool'* (JOURN3) surrounding this social group. In order to move beyond the attitude of *'don't work with animals or little children'* (JOURN1), education on children's rights and training on engaging with children, young people and their advocates could have the potential to address the current *'issues'* (YW4) interviewees discussed.

Beyond training, there should be a genuine willingness on the part of the media to include and value the voices of children, young people and their advocates. As noted above, in the course of the interviews, several advocates considered that current engagement was typically *'tokenistic'* and that it typically resulted in this social group being used by the media in order to serve their own agenda or purposes. The personal experiences of advocates made them *'sceptical'* and *'wary'* of engaging with the media. These experiences of negative engagement with the media, alongside the issue of the 'hierarchy of access' to the media need to be addressed, if the content of media reporting is to be fully representative. Thus, the findings in this study identify a need for contact and engagement to be inclusive and promote equality and participation, which values the voices, opinions and experiences of children and young people. These findings are in line with children and young people's best interests, and their right to participate and be consulted (UNCRC Articles 3 and 12).

Critical research advocates for academics to expose and monitor media content in order to 'widen accountability' (Hall 1986: 13). As this study demonstrates, accountability goes hand-in-hand with media regulatory arrangements. Significantly, the Leveson report[5] based on Lord Leveson's Inquiry on the culture, practices and ethics of the press in the UK outlined recommendations, which were to provide impetus for reform in the area of media regulation. While several recommendations have been enacted, the protection and accessibility to routes or mechanisms for vulnerable individuals and social groups to seek redress, still need to be fully addressed.

Against this contemporary backdrop, this research establishes that while those working in the media asserted that the Press Complaints Commission (PCC) are *'effective'* (ED4) and *'have teeth'* (ED5), in contrast advocates strongly disagreed by arguing that, *'self-regulation is not working'* (YS2). It is poignant that each advocate called for immediate reform in the area of media regulation. Significantly, children and young people were not aware of the then PCC, Office of Communications (OFCOM) and avenues open to them to complain about negative media coverage. Therefore, a central future consideration for policy makers is to ensure that all members of the public are provided with information, education and details on accessing the regulatory bodies in order to make a complaint. Further, in order to hold the media accountable, children, young people and their advocates must have the opportunity to utilise all avenues in an accessible form to challenge the media and seek redress.

The vulnerability of children and young people was revealed in the media's reporting and treatment of highly sensitive issues, and the experiences of intrusion. When discussing the effectiveness of current regulatory bodies with regard to vulnerable social groups, such as children and young people, typical responses from the media were that it was *'a question for them [regulatory bodies] whether they help vulnerable members of society or not'* (ED7). This placed emphasis and responsibility on regulatory bodies, rather than on individual newspapers, editors and journalists. Examples of intruding on the privacy of those who are the subject of news items were outlined during interviews with advocates and focus groups with children and young people. In light of these findings, in the future greater emphasis should be placed on the ethics that operate within a newsroom where stories are produced.

Suggestions for the development of *'guidelines and booklets'* and *'intensive training'* (CS1) for the media that prioritise the rights of children and young people is an important future consideration for advocates, policy makers, academics and those working in the media. This suggestion is similar to guidelines and a handbook published by MediaWise in partnership with United Nations Children's Fund (UNICEF) (Jempson 2010). The development of Northern Ireland specific guidelines to address the findings of the empirical study on which this monograph is based, would have the potential to promote inclusiveness and the fair and accurate portrayal of children and young people. The guidelines could also aid and establish ongoing communication between children and young people's advocates, editors and journalists. Ensuring that the media participate and implement the guidelines would be key to such an initiative's success.

In addition, there are further considerations and challenges identified by the research as being specific to Northern Ireland. The amplification, construction and representation of children and young people's perceived involvement in anti-social behaviour, crime and violence, clearly reinforces anxiety and fear surrounding the stability of a society in transition from conflict. At times of profound change, uncertainty and transition, youth becomes an easy target. In addressing the impact of the negative media, social and ideological constructions and representations of children and young people, there are specific challenges for advocates, practitioners, politicians, policy makers and scholars. Several of these challenges relate to the larger questions, in particular the unaddressed legacy of the Conflict and the current structure of society.

However, Cohen (2002: 172) is pessimistic in relation to 'the chances of changing social policy', predicting:

> More moral panics will be generated and other, as yet nameless, folk devils will be created ... because our society as presently structured will continue to generate problems for some of its members – like working-class adolescents – and then condemn whatever solution the groups find.

Therefore, change must be generated at the local community and political levels. As a theoretical perspective 'moral panics' continues to 'expose' the process of the criminalisation and demonisation of youth, however unless such change occurs 'we face the prospect of living in a society where the marginalisation of youth continues to produce the devils we fear' (Simpson 1997: 15).

In moving beyond the resources of theory into praxis, critical analysis seeks to expose inequalities and speak out about injustices, in order to ultimately bring about social, economic and political change (Scraton 2007: 240). This takes political responsibility on the part of the researcher, who not only gives a voice to those who are silenced, marginalised and vulnerable, but sets out to act on existing social and political injustices (Scraton 2007: 240). This is what makes critical social research so important. These core elements of critical social research will remain central in terms of building on the contribution this monograph makes to contemporary academic debates and policy development. While the vibrant and committed children and youth sectors in Northern Ireland have long highlighted, campaigned and challenged the media on the negative portrayal of young people, academic research-based literature has not focused on this issue in great depth.

Many editors and journalists asserted that they were *'yet to be convinced'* that children and young people are negatively represented in media coverage, however as one editor stated, *'I'm open to being shown the evidence ... interested in seeing your findings'* (ED7). In their debates and discussions on how to bring about change, on how to challenge the media and those in power, particularly politicians, children and young people's advocates have highlighted the need for evidence. As one advocate asserted, in order 'to achieve this [change], we need to have clear irrefutable evidence, patience, passion and commitment because we are right' (Yiasouma 2010). The empirical research evidence-base contained within this monograph, provides that evidence and, most importantly, it has given the previously marginalised, hidden or excluded voices of children and young people, a position at the centre of debate on this significant issue. Future debates, discussions, policies and practices in this area must ensure that children and young people's voices and experiences are valued and considered central to their development.

Notes

1. See: http://news.bbc.co.uk/1/hi/northern_ireland/8584603.stm (accessed on 24 March 2010).

2. Throughout this chapter direct quotations are presented in italics. Consistent with previous chapters, individual comments are attributed to the interviewee using the reference system outlined in the appendices. However, where a word or phrase has not been attributed, this denotes use by more than one interviewee.

3. The media's position concerned the potential danger to staff and 'risk' to their safety. The National Union Journalists (NUJ) and Broadcasting, Entertainment, Cinematograph and Theatre Union (BECTU) issued statements of concern. As a letter from the broadcast union BECTU stated, editors and journalists do not want to be perceived as 'evidence gatherers for the State', particularly given the dissident threat. See: http://www.u.tv/News/Broadcasters-warn-PSNI-over-demands-for-footage/80562d4c-57bd-4e42-8f6f-1e7c627358c9 (accessed on 18 August 2011); http://www.belfasttelegraph.co.uk/news/local-national/northern-ireland/psni-demand-for-riot-footage-could-put-journalists-at-risk-16037940.html#ixzz21Ntq8Wt2 (accessed on 18 August 2011); http://www.4rfv.co.uk/industrynews.asp?id=130785 (accessed on 19 August 2011).

4. One youth worker who observed a focus group stated that: *The young people seemed to enjoy the opportunity to have their voices heard on the issues. They are not always as forthcoming with researchers* (e-mail correspondence, dated 11 January 2011).

5. See: http://www.levesoninquiry.org.uk/ (accessed on 30 March 2012).

Appendix 1: Sample Newspapers and Media Coverage

Sample Newspapers

The following newspapers are referred to throughout the monograph as the 'sample newspapers' that were collected over the six months data collection period (1 March 2010 to 31 August 2010).

Andersonstown News
Belfast Telegraph
Irish News
News Letter
North Belfast News
South Belfast News
Sunday Life
Sunday World, Northern Edition

In selecting the newspapers, the ideological differences existing within Northern Ireland's media have been considered and the selection is representative (i.e. *The Irish News* aligns with the Nationalist viewpoint, whereas the *Newsletter* aligns with the Unionist viewpoint and the *Belfast Telegraph* appears not to favour or align with one specific cultural tradition or particular political ethos).

© The Author(s) 2018
F. Gordon, *Children, Young People and the Press in a Transitioning Society*,
Palgrave Socio-Legal Studies, https://doi.org/10.1057/978-1-137-60682-2

Table A1.1 Sample newspapers circulation figures, December 2010

Newspaper	Type	Circulation figure	Ownership
Belfast Telegraph	Daily	58,491	Belfast Telegraph Newspapers
Irish News	Daily	44,222	Irish News Ltd
News Letter	Daily	23,669	Johnston Publishing (NI)
Andersonstown News	Twice-weekly	12,090 6,761 (Monday)	Belfast Media Group
North Belfast News	Weekly	4,438	Belfast Media Group
South Belfast News	Weekly	Not available	Belfast Media Group
Sunday Life	Weekly	54,435	Belfast Telegraph Newspapers
Sunday World, Northern Edition	Weekly	Not available	Not available

Table A1.2 Other local newspapers cited
The following newspapers were collected during July and August 2010 and further news items were accessed from the online archives. Both newspapers provided a local insight into the PSNI's Operation Exposure in Derry/Londonderry.

Newspaper	Type	Circulation figure	Ownership
Derry Journal	Twice-weekly	15,848 (Tuesday) 18,182 (Friday)	Johnston Publishing (NI)
Londonderry Sentinel	Weekly	4,451	Johnston Publishing (NI)

Figures above published and supplied in 2011 by the Audit Bureau of Circulation (ABC). For further information, see: http://www.abc.org.uk/Certificates-Reports/Our-Reports/ (accessed on 1 June 2011).

Table A1.3 National and international print media
The following newspapers were accessed in hard copy and online during July and August 2010. The media content collected for analysis related to what was framed in media and political discourse as 'sectarian rioting' in Northern Ireland. The collection of national and international print media provided an interesting dynamic and insight into the reporting and representations of Northern Ireland's children, young people and the transition period.

Newspaper	Form
Daily Mail	Hard copy
Daily Mirror	Hard copy
Financial Times	Online version
Global Post	Online version
San Diego Union – Tribune	Online version
The Economist	Hard copy
The Guardian	Hard copy
The Hindu	Online version
The Irish Times	Hard copy
The Irish Times Weekend Review	Hard copy
The New York Times	Online version
The Observer	Hard copy
The Sun	Hard copy
The Sunday Telegraph	Hard copy
The Sunday Times	Hard copy

Appendix 2: Interview and Focus Group Schedule

Reference System

Table A2.1 Focus groups schedule and reference system

Date	Focus group reference	Age group	Location
2 October 2010	Focus Group 1	15–19 years	Derry/Londonderry
27 October 2010	Focus Group 2	17–21 years	Belfast
10 January 2011	Focus Group 3	15–21 years	Belfast
1 February 2011	Focus Group 4	16–20 years	North Down
2 February 2011	Focus Group 5	17–23 years	Belfast
7 February 2011	Focus Group 6	14–16 years	Belfast

Table A2.2 Interview schedule and reference system

Date	Interviewee	Location	Reference
2 October 2010	Youth Worker and former local journalist	Derry/ Londonderry	YW1
13 October 2010	Northern Ireland Human Rights Commission	Belfast	NIHRC1
20 October 2010	Ulster Unionist Party MLA (UUP)	Lisburn	POL1
20 October 2010	Youth Worker	Belfast	YW2
27 October 2010	The Northern Ireland Children's Commissioner	Belfast	NICCY1
28 October 2010	Senior Broadcast Journalist [Television]	Belfast	JOURN1
29 October 2010	Broadcast Journalist [Radio]	Belfast	JOURN2
1 November 2010	Senior Broadcast Journalist [Television and Radio]	Belfast	JOURN3
2 November 2010	Inspector, PSNI Strand Road (Derry/Londonderry)	Belfast	PSNI1
3 November 2010	Independent MLA	Belfast	POL2

(*continued*)

© The Author(s) 2018
F. Gordon, *Children, Young People and the Press in a Transitioning Society*,
Palgrave Socio-Legal Studies, https://doi.org/10.1057/978-1-137-60682-2

Table A2.2 (continued)

Date	Interviewee	Location	Reference
5 November 2010	Democratic Unionist Party MLA (DUP)	Belfast	POL3
9 November 2010	Director of Children's Rights Organisation/NGO	Belfast	CS1
11 November 2010	Senior Research and Policy Officer, Children's Sector Organisation/NGO	Belfast	CS2
12 November 2010	Community and Youth Worker	Belfast	YW3
16 November 2010	Senior Programme Manager in the Youth Sector	Belfast	YS1
16 November 2010	Director of a Youth Sector NGO	Belfast	YS2
19 November 2010	Youth Worker	Belfast	YW4
26 November 2010	Social Democratic and Labour Party MLA (SDLP)	Belfast	POL4
6 December 2010	Director of Children's sector Organisation/NGO	Belfast	CS3
13 January 2011	Equality Commission for Northern Ireland	Belfast	EQ1
13 January 2011	Editor	Belfast	ED1
18 January 2011	Sinn Féin Councillor (SF) for West Belfast	Lisburn	POL5
19 January 2011	Editor [Sample Weekly Newspaper]	Belfast	ED2
21 January 2011	Editor [Sample Twice Weekly Newspaper]	Belfast	ED3
25 January 2011	Editor [Sample Daily Newspaper]	Belfast	ED4
28 January 2011	Group Editor and Reader's Editor [Two Sample Newspapers, Daily and Weekly]	Belfast	ED5
2 February 2011	Tabloid Editor	Belfast	ED6
9 February 2011	Editor, Head of News [Sample Daily Newspaper]	Belfast	ED7

Bibliography

Aggleton, P. (1987) *Deviance*, London: Tavistock Publications.

Albertazzi, D. and Cobley, P. (2010) *The Media: An Introduction* (Third Edition), Essex: Pearson Education Limited.

Aldridge, J. and Cross, S. (2008) 'Young People Today: Media, Policy and Youth Justice', *Journal of Children and Media*, Volume 2, Number 3, pages 203–218.

Aldridge, J., Medina-Ariza, J. and Ralphs, R. (2007) *Youth Gangs in an English City: Social Exclusion, Drugs and Violence*, Manchester: University of Manchester.

Allan, S. (1999) *News Culture*, Buckingham: Open University Press.

Allen, J. and Cooper, S. (1995) 'Howard's Way - A Farewell to Freedom?', *The Modern Law Review*, Volume 58, Issue 3, pages 364–389.

Andersson, G. and Lundstrom, T. (2007) 'Teenagers as Victims in the Press', *Children and Society*, Volume 21, Number 3, pages 175–188.

Ang, I. (1990a) 'Culture and Communication', *European Journal of Communication*, Volume 5, Number 2, pages 239–260.

Anthony, T. and Cunneen, C. eds. (2008) *The Critical Criminology Companion*, New South Wales, Australia: Hawkins Press.

Appleby, L., Kapur, N., Shaw, J., Hunt, I. M., Flynn, S., While, D., Windfuhr, K., Williams, A. and Rahman, M. S. (2011) *The National Confidential Inquiry into Suicide and Homicide by People with Mental Illness: Suicide and Homicide in Northern Ireland*, DHSSPNI, PHA and University of Manchester, Manchester: University of Manchester Press.

Archers, J. and Jones, J. (2003) 'Headlines from History: Violence in the Press, 1850–1914', in E. A. Stanko (ed.) *The Meanings of Violence*, London: Routledge, pages 17–32.

Arthur, P. (2000) *Special Relationships: Britain, Ireland, and the Northern Ireland Problem*, Belfast: Blackstaff Publishing.

© The Author(s) 2018

F. Gordon, *Children, Young People and the Press in a Transitioning Society*, Palgrave Socio-Legal Studies, https://doi.org/10.1057/978-1-137-60682-2

Arthur, R. (2010) *Young Offenders and the Law: How the Law Responds to Youth Offending*, London: Routledge.

Audit Commission (1996) *Misspent Youth: The Challenge for Youth Justice*, London: The Audit Commission.

Aughey, A. (2005) *The Politics of Northern Ireland: Beyond the Belfast Agreement*, London: Routledge.

Austin, J. and Willard, M. N. (1998) 'Introduction: Angels of History, Demons of Culture', in J. Austin and M. N. Willard (eds.) *Generations of Youth: Youth Cultures and History in Twenty-Century America*, London: New York University Press, pages 1–20.

Bachman, R. and Schutt, R. K. (2003) *The Practice of Research in Criminology and Criminal Justice* (Third Edition), California, USA: SAGE Publications Limited.

Bagdikian, B. H. (2004) *The New Media Monopoly*, Boston, USA: Beacon Press.

Bairner, A. and Shirlow, P. (2003) 'When Leisure Turns to Fear: Fear, Mobility, and Ethno-Sectarianism in Belfast', *Leisure Studies*, Volume 22, Number 3, pages 203–221.

Balen, R., Blyth, E., Calabretto, H., Fraser, C., Horrocks, C. and Manby, M. (2006) 'Involving Children in Health and Social Research: "Human Becomings" or "Active Beings"?', *Childhood*, Volume 13, Number 1, pages 29–48.

Ball, C. (2004) 'Youth Justice? Half a Century of Responses to Youth Offending', *Criminal Law Review*, 50th Anniversary Edition, pages 28–41.

Bandalli, S. (2000) 'Children, Responsibility and the New Youth Justice', pages 81–96, in B. Goldson (ed.) *The New Youth Justice*, Lyme Regis: Russell House.

Barber, B. K. (2009) *Adolescents and War: How Youth Deal with Political Violence*, Oxford: Oxford University Press.

Barker, C. (1999) *Television, Globalization and Cultural Identities*, Buckingham: Open University Press.

Barker, C. (2000) *Cultural Studies: Theory and Practice*, London: SAGE Publications Limited.

Barker, J. and Weller, S. (2003) '"Is It Fun?" Developing Children Centred Research Methods', *International Journal of Sociology and Social Policy*, Volume 23, Number 1, pages 33–58.

Blood, M. (2008) 'What We Can Do for Young People', in *Northern Ireland Big Times*, Belfast: Big Lottery Fund, pages 6–7.

Barrat, D. (1994) *Media Sociology* (Fourth Edition), London: Routledge.

Barry, M. ed. (2005) *Youth Policy and Social Inclusion: Critical Debates with Young People*, Oxfordshire: Routledge.

Barthes, R. (1977) '"The Photograph Message", Translated by Stephen Heath, 1977, An Excerpt', in V. Goldberg (ed.) *Photography in Print: Writings from 1816 to Present*, Albuquerque, New Mexico: University of New Mexico Press, pages 15–31.

Batchelor, S. A. (2001) 'The Myth of Girl Gangs', *Criminal Justice Matters*, Volume 43, Number 1, pages 26–27.

Batchelor, S. (2009) 'Girls, Gangs and Violence: Assessing the Evidence', *Probation Journal*, Volume 56, Number 4, pages 399–414.

Bean, K. (2007) *The New Politics of Sinn Féin*, Liverpool: Liverpool University Press.

Bean, K. (2011) 'Civil Society, the State and Conflict Transformation in the Nationalist Country: A Violence from the Past?', in M. Power (ed.) *Building Peace in Northern Ireland*, Liverpool: Liverpool University Press, pages 154–171.

Beck, U. (1992) *Risk Society: Towards a New Modernity*, Translation by Mark Ritter, London: SAGE Publications Limited.

Becker, H. S. (1953) 'Becoming a Marihuana User', *The American Journal of Sociology*, Volume 59, Number 3, November, pages 235–242.

Becker, H. (1963) *Outsider: Studies in the Sociology of Deviance,* New York and London: Free Press.

Becker, H. (1967) 'Whose Side Are We On?', *Social Problems*, Volume 14, Number 3, pages 234–247.

Bell, J. (2007) *Parades and Protests: An Annotated Bibliography*, Belfast: Institute for Conflict Research.

Bentley, T., Oakley, K., Gibson, S., Kilgour, K. (1999) *What Young People Really Think About Government, Politics and Social Exclusion*, London: Demos.

Berger, A. A. (1998) *Media Analysis Techniques* (Second Edition), London: SAGE Publications Limited.

Berrington, E. and Honkatukia, P. (2002) 'An Evil Monster and a Poor Thing: Female Violence in the Media', *Journal of Scandinavian Studies in Criminology and Crime Prevention*, Volume 3, pages 50–72.

Bessant, J. (1997) 'What the Papers Say: The Media, the "Underclass" and Sociology', in J. Bessant and R. Hil (eds.) *Youth Crime and the Media: Media Representations of and Reactions to Young People in Relation to Law and Order*, Hobart, Australia: Australian Clearinghouse for Youth Studies, pages 23–34.

Bessant, J. (2003) 'Precursors to a Media Frenzy: Supervised Chroming Young People in Care and Victorian Drug Policy', *Youth Studies Australia*, Volume 22, Number 3, pages 11–17.

Bessant, J. and Hil, R. eds. (1997) *Youth Crime and the Media: Media Representations of and Reactions to Young People in Relation to Law and Order*, Hobart, Australia: Australian Clearinghouse for Youth Studies.

Bessant, J. and Watts, R. (1998) 'History, Myth Making and Young People in a Time of Change', *Family Matters*, Australian Institute of Family Studies, Number 49, pages 4–10.

Bignell, J. (1997) *Media Semiotics: An Introduction*, Manchester: Manchester University Press.

Bird, S. E. (2003) *The Audience in Everyday Life: Living in a Media World*. New York: Routledge.

Birrell, D. and Murie, A. (1980) *Policy and Government in Northern Ireland: Lessons of Devolution*, Dublin: Gill and Macmillan.

Black, J. and Roberts, C. (2011) *Doing Ethics in Media: Theories and Practical Applications*, Oxon: Routledge.

Blair, T. (1998) *The Third Way: New Politics for the New Century*, Fabian Pamphlet, 588, September, London: The Fabian Society.

Blumler, J. and Gurevitch, M. (1995) *The Crisis of Public Communication*, London: Routledge.

Bowes, J. (1977) 'Stereotyping and Communication Accuracy', *Journalism Quarterly*, Volume 54, Spring, pages 70–76.

Box, S. (1983) *Power, Crime, and Mystification*, New York, USA: Tavistock.

Boyce, S. (2010) 'PSNI Release of Images of Children and Young People to the Media: A Case Study', Presented at *Media Representations of Children and Young People Seminar*, Childhood, Transition and Social Justice Initiative, Queen's University Belfast, 14 September 2010.

Braham, P. (1982) 'How the Media Report Race', in M. Gurevitch, T. Bennett, J. Curran and J. Woollacott (eds.) *Culture, Society and the Media*, London: Methuen, pages 274–275.

Branston, G. and Stafford, R. (2003) *The Media Student's Book* (Third Edition), London: Routledge.

Brewer, J., Lockhart, B. and Rodgers, P. (1997) *Crime in Ireland: 'Here Be Dragons'*, Oxford: Clarendon.

Briggs, A. and Cobley, P. eds. (1998) *The Media: An Introduction*, Essex: Addison Wesley Longman.

Briggs, A. and Cobley, P. eds. (2002) *The Media: An Introduction* (Second Edition), Essex: Addison Wesley Longman.

British Society of Criminology (2008) *Code of Ethics*, London: British Society of Criminology. Accessed from: http://www.britsoccrim.org/codeofethics.htm (accessed on 20 February 2009).

Brocklehurst, H. (1999) *Children as Political Bodies: Concepts, Cases and Theories*, University of Wales, unpublished thesis.

Brocklehurst, H. (2006) *Who's Afraid of Children? Children, Conflict and International Relations*, Hampshire: Ashgate Publishing Limited.

Brocklehurst, H., Stott, N., Hamber, B. and Robinson, G. (2001) 'Lesson Drawing: Northern Ireland and South Africa', *Indicator*, South Africa, Volume 18, Number 1, pages 89–95.

Brown, S. (1998) *Understanding Youth and Crime: Listening to Youth?*, Buckingham: Open University Press.

Brown, S, (2005) *Understanding Youth and Crime: Listening to Youth?* (Second Edition), Berkshire: Oxford University Press.

Brownlee, I. (1998) 'New Labour – New Penology? Punitive Rhetoric and the Limits of Managerialism in Criminal Justice Policy', *Journal of Law and Society*, Volume 25, Number 3, pages 313–335.

Brownlie, J. (2005) 'An Unsolvable Justice Problem? Punishing Young People's Sexual Violence', *Journal of Law and Society*, Volume 30, Number 4, pages 506–531.

Brunt, R. (1990) 'Engaging with the Popular: Audiences for Mass Culture and What to Say About Them', in C. N. L. Grossberg and P. Treichler (ed.) *Cultural Studies*, London: Routledge, pages 69–80.

Bryant, J. and Zillmann, D. (2002) *Media Effects: Advances in Theory and Research*, London: Routledge.

Bryman, A. (2004) *Social Research Methods*, Oxford: Oxford University Press.

Bucholtz, M. (2002) 'Youth and Cultural Practice', *Annual Review of Anthropology*, Volume 31, Number 1, pages 525–552.

Buckland, G. and Stevens, A. (2001) *Review of Effective Practice with Young Offenders in Mainland Europe*, Canterbury: European Institute of Social Sciences.

Byrne, J., Conway, M. and Ostermeyer, M. (2005) *Young People's Attitudes and Experiences of Policing, Violence and Community Safety in North Belfast*, Belfast: Northern Ireland Policing Board.

Byrne, J., Hansson, U. and Bell, J. (2006) *Shared Living: Mixed Residential Communities in Northern Ireland*, Belfast: Institute for Conflict Research.

Cadwallader, A. (2004) *Holy Cross: The Untold Story*, Belfast: Brehon Press Limited.

Cairns, E. (1987) *Caught in Crossfire: Children and the Northern Ireland Conflict*, Belfast: The Appletree Press Limited.

Cairns, E. and Darby, J. (1998) 'The Conflict in Northern Ireland: Causes, Consequences and Controls', *American Psychologist*, Volume 53, pages 754–760.

Caliendo, S. M. (2011) 'Race, Media and Popular Culture', in S. M. Caliendo and C. D. Mcllwain (eds.) *The Routledge Companion to Race and Ethnicity*, Oxon: Routledge, pages 73–81.

Callanan, V. J. (2005) *Feeding the Fear of Crime: Crime-related Media and Support for Three Strikes*, New York, USA: LFB Scholarly.

Camargo Heck, M. (1980) 'The Ideological Dimension of Media Messages', in S. Hall, D. Hobson, A. Lowe and P. Willis (eds.) *Culture, Media, Language*, Oxon: Routledge, pages 122–127.

Chadwick, K. and Scraton, P. (2006) 'Criminalization', in E. McLaughlin and J. Muncie (eds.) *The SAGE Dictionary of Criminology* (Second Edition), London: SAGE Publications Limited, pages 95–97.

Chibnall, S. (1973) 'The Production of Knowledge by Crime Reporters', in S. Cohen and J. Young (eds.) *The Manufacture of News: Deviance, Social Problems and the Mass Media* (First Edition), London: Constable, pages 75–98.

Chibnall, S. (1975) 'The Crime Reporter: A Study in the Production of Commercial Knowledge', *Sociology*, Volume 9, Number 1, pages 49–66.

Chibnall, S. (1977) *Law and Order News: An Analysis of Crime Reporting in the British Press*, London: Tavistock Publications.

Chibnall, S. (2003) *Law and Order News*, London: Routledge.

Children in Northern Ireland (2010) *NIO Consultation Paper: A Bill of Rights for Northern Ireland, Next Steps*, Belfast: Children in Northern Ireland.

Cicourel, A. (1968) *The Social Organization of Juvenile Justice*, New York: The Free Press.

Cochrane, F. (1997) *Unionist Politics and the Politics of Unionism Since the Anglo Irish Agreement*, Cork: Cork University Press.

Codd, H. (2008) *In the Shadow of Prison: Families, Imprisonment and Criminal Justice*, Cullompton: Willan Publishing.

Cohen, A. (1955) *Delinquent Boys: The Culture of the Gang*, London: Collier-Macmillan.

Cohen, L., Manion, L. and Morrison, K. (2007) *Research Methods in Education*, Oxon: Routledge.

Cohen, S. (1972) *Folk Devils and Moral Panics: The Creation of the Mods and Rockers* (First Edition), Oxford: Martin Robertson.

Cohen, S. (1980) *Folk Devils and Moral Panics: The Creation of the Mods and Rockers* (Second Edition), Oxford: Martin Robertson.

Cohen, S. (2002) *Folk Devils and Moral Panics: The Creation of the Mods and Rockers* (Third Edition), London: Routledge.

Cohen, S. and Young, J. eds. (1981) *The Manufacture of News: Social Problems, Deviance and the Mass Media* (Second Revised Edition), London: Constable.

Cole, P. (2005) 'The Structure of the Print Industry', in R. Keeble (ed.) *Print Journalism: A Critical Introduction*, Oxon: Routledge, pages 21–38.

Coleman, R. and McCahill, M. (2011) *Surveillance and Crime*, London: SAGE Publications Limited.

Collins, J., Noble, G., Poynting, S. and Tabar, P. (2000) *Kebabs, Kids, Cops and Crime: Youth, Ethnicity and Crime*, Sydney, Australia: Pluto Press.

Collins, S. and Cattermole, R. (2006) *Anti-social Behaviour and Disorder: Powers and Remedies*, London: Sweet and Maxwell.

Conboy, M. (2006) *Tabloid Britain: Constructing a Community Through Language*, London: Routledge.

Convery, U. and Moore, L. (2006) *Still in Our Care. Protecting Children's Rights in Custody in Northern Ireland*, Belfast: Northern Ireland Human Rights Commission.

Convery, U., Haydon, D., Moore, L. and Scraton, P. (2008) 'Children, Rights and Justice in Northern Ireland: Community and Custody', *Youth Justice*, Volume 8, Number 3, pages 245–263.

Conway, M. and Byrne, J. (2005) *Interface Issues: An Annotated Bibliography*, Belfast: Belfast Institute for Conflict Research.

Coogan, T. P. (2002) *The Troubles: Ireland's Ordeal and the Search for Peace*, New York, USA: Palgrave Publishers Limited.

Cormack, M. (2000) 'The Reassessment of Ideology', in D. Fleming (ed.) *21st Century Media Studies Textbook*, Manchester: Manchester University Press, pages 93–95.

Corner, J. and Hawthorn, J. eds. (1993) *Communication Studies: An Introductory Reader* (Fourth Edition), London: Arnold Publishers.

Corner, J., Schlesinger, P. and Silverstone, R. eds. (1998) *International Media Research: A Critical Survey*, London: Routledge.

Cornwell, B. and Linders, A. (2002) 'The Myth of "Moral Panic": An Alternative Account of LSD Prohibition', *Deviant Behavior*, Volume 23, Number 4, July–August, pages 307–330.

Cote, S. (2002) *Criminological Theories: Bridging the Past to the Future,* London: SAGE Publications Limited.

Cotter, C. (2010) *News Talk: Investigating the Language of Journalism*, Cambridge: Cambridge University Press.

Cottle, T. J. (2001) *At Peril: Stories of Injustice*, Amherst, USA: University of Massachusetts Press.

Cox, M., Guelke, A. and Stephen, F. eds. (2006) *A Farewell to Arms? Beyond the Good Friday Agreement*, Manchester: Manchester University Press.

Craig, G. (2004) *The Media, Politics and Public Life,* New South Wales, Australia: Allen and Unwin.

Crane, P. (1997) 'Whose Views? Whose Interests? The Absence of Young People's Voices in Mainstream Media Reports on Crime', in J. Bessant and R. Hil (eds.) *Youth Crime and the Media: Media Representations of and Reactions to Young People in Relation to Law and Order*, Hobart, Australia: Australian Clearinghouse for Youth Studies, pages 93–104.

Crawford, A. and Burden, T. (2005) *Integrating Victims in Restorative Youth Justice*, Bristol: The Policy Press.

Crawford, A., and Newburn, T. (2002) Recent Development in Restorative Justice for Young People in England and Wales, *British Journal of Criminology*, Volume 42, Number 3, pages 476–495.

Criminal Justice Inspectorate (2008) *Anti-Social Behaviour Orders: An Inspection of the Operation and Effectiveness of ASBOs,* October, Belfast: Criminal Justice Inspection Northern Ireland.

Critcher, C. (2003) *Moral Panics and the Media*, Milton Keynes: Open University Press.

Croft, S. ed. (1991) *British Security Policy: The Thatcher Years and the End of the Cold War*, London: Harper Collins Academic.

Croteau, D. and Hoynes, W. (2003) *Media Society: Industries, Imagery, and Audiences*, London: SAGE Publications Limited.

Centre for Social Justice (2010) *Breakthrough Northern Ireland*, London: Centre for Social Justice.

Curran, J. (1998) 'Newspapers: Beyond Policy Economy', in A. Briggs and P. Cobley (eds.) *The Media: An Introduction*, Essex: Longman, pages 81–96.

Curran, J. (2002) *Media and Power,* London: Routledge.

Curran, J. and Seaton, J. (1992) *Power Without Responsibility: The Press and Broadcasting in Britain* (Fourth Edition), London: Routledge.

Curran, J., Douglas, A. and Whannel, G. (1980) 'The Political Economy of the Human-Interest Story', in A. Smith (ed.) *Newspapers and Democracy*, Cambridge: MIT Press, pages 288–347.

Curran, J., Ecclestone, J., Oakley, G. and Richardson, A. eds. (1986) *Bending Reality: The State of the Media*, London: Pluto Press Limited.

Curran, J., Gurevitch, M. and Woollacott, J. (1988) 'The Study of the Media: Theoretical Approaches', in M. Gurevitch, T. Bennett, J. Curran and J. Woollacott (eds.) *Culture, Society and the Media*, London: Routledge, pages 11–29.

Dantzker, R. D. and Hunter, M. L. (2005) *Crime and Criminality: Causes and Consequences*, Colorado, USA: Lynne Rienner Publishers.

Darby, J. (1986) *Intimidation and the Control of Conflict in Northern Ireland*, New York, USA: Syracuse University Press.

David, C. D. and Sutton, M. (2011) *Social Research: An Introduction* (Second Edition), London: SAGE Publications Limited.

David, T. (1992) 'Do We Have to Do This?', *Children and Society*, Volume 6, Number 3, pages 204–211.

Davies, S. (1997) 'A Sight to Behold: Media and the Visualisation of Youth, Evil and Innocence', in J. Bessant and R. Hil (eds.) *Youth Crime and the Media: Media Representations of and Reactions to Young People in Relation to Law and Order*, Hobart, Australia: Australian Clearinghouse for Youth Studies, pages 55–66.

Davis, H. and Bourhill, M. (1997) '"Crisis": The Demonization of Children and Young People', in P. Scraton (ed.) *Childhood in 'Crisis'?*, London: UCL Press/ Routledge, pages 28–57.

Davis, J. M. (1998) 'Understanding the Meaning of Children: A Reflexive Process', *Children and Society*, Volume 12, Number 5, pages 325–335.

DeLisi, M. (2003) 'Self-control Pathology: The Elephant in the Living Room', *Advances in Criminological Theory*, Volume 12, Number 1, pages 21–38.

Department of Justice (2011) *'Building Safer, Shared and Confident Communities': A Consultation on a New Community Safety Strategy for Northern Ireland*, January, Belfast: Department of Justice Northern Ireland.

Department of Justice (2012a) *Perceptions of Crime: Findings from the 2010/2011 Northern Ireland Crime Survey, Research and Statistical Bulletin*, February, Belfast: Department of Justice Northern Ireland.

Department of Justice Northern Ireland (2012) *Building Safer, Shared and Confident Communities: A Community Safety Strategy for Northern Ireland 2012–2017*, July, Belfast: Department of Justice Northern Ireland.

Derry District Policing Partnership (2010) *District Policing Partnerships 9-Month Report, Foyle District Command Unit, Figures Extracted 6 January 2010*, Derry/ Londonderry: Derry District Policing Partnership.

Devereux, E. (2003) *Understanding the Media*, London: SAGE Publications Limited.

Devereux, E. (2007) *Understanding the Media* (Second Edition), London: SAGE Publications Limited.

Dickson, B. (1989) *The Legal System of Northern Ireland* (Second Edition), Belfast: SLS Legal Publications.

Dickson, B. (2001) *The Legal System of Northern Ireland* (Fourth Edition), Belfast: SLS Legal Publications.

Dickson, B. (2010) *The European Convention on Human Rights and the Conflict in Northern Ireland*, Oxford: Oxford University Press.

Dignan, J. (1999) 'The Crime and Disorder Act and the Prospects for Restorative Justice', *Criminal Law Review,* January, pages 48–60.

Ditton, J. and Duffy, J. (1983) 'Bias in the Newspaper Reporting of Crime News', *British Journal of Criminology*, Volume 23, Number 2, pages 159–165.

Donoghue, J. (2010) *Anti-social Behaviour Order. A Culture of Control?*, Basingstoke: Palgrave Macmillan.

Dorfman, L. and Schiraldi, V. (2001) *Off Balance: Youth, Race and Crime in the News*, New Hampshire, USA: The Police Policy Studies Council.

Downes, D. and Rock, P. (2007) *Understanding Deviance*, Oxford: Oxford University Press.

Downing, J. (1980) *The Media Machine*, London: Pluto Press Limited.

Durham, A. M., Elrod, H. P. and Kinkade, P. T. (1995) 'Images of Crime and Justice: Murder and the "True Crime" Genre', *Journal of Criminal Justice*, Volume 23, Number 2, pages 143–152.

DSHSSPS, (2006) *The Bamford Review of Mental Health and Learning Disability (Northern Ireland)*, Northern Ireland: DSHSSPS.

Dyer, R. (1993) *The Matters of Images: Essays on Representations,* London: Routledge.

Eldridge, J., Kitzinger, J. and Williams, K. (1997) *The Mass Media Power in Modern Britain*, London: Oxford University Press.

Elliott, S. and Flackes, W. D. (1999) *Northern Ireland: A Political Directory, 1968–1999*, Belfast: Blackstaff Press.

Ellison, G. (2001) *Young People, Crime, Policing and Victimisation in Northern Ireland*, Research Series 2001–2002, Belfast: Queen's University Belfast.

Ellison, G. and Smyth, J. (2000) *The Crowned Harp: Policing Northern Ireland*, London: Pluto Press.

Elrod, P. and Scott Ryder, R. (2005) *Juvenile Justice: A Social, Historical and Legal Perspective*, Burlington, USA: Jones and Bartlett Publishers.

Entman, R. M. (1993) 'Framing: Toward Clarification of a Fractured Paradigm', *Journal of Communication*, Volume 43, Number 4, pages 51–58.

Ericson, R. V., Baranek, P.M. and Chan, J. B. L. (1987) *Visualizing Deviance: A Study of News Organization*, Milton Keynes: Open University Press.

Ericson, R. V., Baranek, P. M. and Chan, J. B. L. (1999) 'Negotiating Control: A Study of News Sources', in H. Tumber (ed.) *News: A Reader*, Oxford: Oxford University Press, pages 297–307.

Erikson, K. T. (1962) 'Notes on the Sociology of Deviance', *Social Problems*, Volume 9, Number 4, pages 307–314.

Erikson, K. T. (1966) *Wayward Puritans: A Study in the Sociology of Deviance*, New York, USA: John Wiley and Sons.

Erjavec, K. (2001) 'Media Representation of the Discrimination Against the Roma in Eastern Europe: The Case of Slovenia', *Discourse and Society*, Volume 12, Number 6, pages 699–727.

Eschholz, S. (2003) 'The Color of Prime-Time Justice: Racial Characteristics of Television Offenders and Victims', in M. D. Free (ed.) *Racial Issues in Criminal*

Justice: The Case of African Americans, California, USA: Greenwood Publishing Groups Limited, pages 59–76.

Evans, E. J. (2004) *Thatcher and Thatcherism*, London: Routledge.

Evelegh, R. (1978) *Peace-Keeping in a Democratic Society: The Lessons of Northern Ireland*, London: C. Hurst and Co. Publishers Limited.

Fahey, T., Hayes, B. C. and Sinnott, R. (2005) *Conflict and Consensus: A Study of Values and Attitudes in the Republic of Ireland and Northern Ireland*, Dublin: Institute of Public Administration.

Farnen, R. F. (1990) 'Decoding the Mass Media and Terrorism Connection: Militant Extremism As Systematic and Symbiotic Processes', in C. R. Sander (ed.) *Marginal Conventions, Popular Culture, Mass Media and Social Deviance*, Ohio, USA: Bowling Green State University Popular Press, pages 98–116.

Farr, K. A. (2001) 'Women on Death Row: Media Representations of Female Evil', in D. E. Eber and A. G. Neal (eds.) *Memory and Representation: Constructed Truths and Competing Realities*, Ohio, USA: Bowling Green State University Popular Press, pages 73–87.

Farrell, S. (2000) *Rituals and Riots: Sectarian Violence and Political Culture in Ulster 1784–1886*, Kentucky, USA: The University Press of Kentucky.

Fields, R. M. (1977) *Northern Ireland: Society Under Siege*, Philadelphia, USA: Temple University Press.

Fionda, J. (1999) 'New Labour, Old Hat: Youth Justice and the Crime and Disorder Act 1998', *Criminal Law Review*, January, pages 36–47.

Fionda, J. (2005) *Devils and Angels: Youth Policy and Crime*, Oxford: Hart Publishing.

Fishman, M. (1980) *Manufacturing the News*, Texas, USA: University of Texas Press.

Fiske, J. (1991) *Television Culture*, London: Routledge.

Fiske, J. and Hartley, J. (1989) *Reading Television*, London: Routledge.

Fitch, K. (2009) *Teenagers at Risk: The Safeguarding Needs of Young People in Gangs and Violence Peer Groups*, London: NSPCC.

Foreman, G. (2011) *The Ethical Journalist: Making Responsible Decisions in the Pursuit of News*, West Sussex: Wiley-Blackwell.

Foster, P. (2006) 'Observational Research', in R. Sapsford and V. Jupp (eds.) *Data Collection and Analysis* (Second Edition), London: SAGE Publishers Limited, pages 57–92.

Fourie, P. J. (2001) *Media Studies, Volume One: Institutions, Theories and Issues*, Landsdowne, South Africa: Juta Education.

Fowler, R. (1994) *Language in the News: Discourse and Ideology in the Press*, London: Routledge.

France, A. (2007) *Understanding Youth in Late Modernity*, Berkshire: Open University Press.

Franklin, B. (1996) 'The Case for Children's Rights: A Progress Report', in B. Franklin (ed.) *The Handbook of Children's Rights: Comparative Policy and Practice*, London: Routledge, pages 3–24.

Franklin, B. (1999) *Social Policy, the Media and Misrepresentation*, London: Routledge.

Franklin, B. (2002) *The New Handbook of Children's Rights: Comparative Policy and Practice*, London: Routledge.

Franklin, B. and Murphy, D. eds. (1997) *Making the Local News: Local Journalism in Context*, London: Routledge.

Franklin, B. and Petley, J. (1996) 'Killing the Age of Innocence: Newspaper Reporting of the Death of James Bulger', in J. Pilcher and S. Wagg (eds.) (1996) *Thatcher's Children*, London: Frances Pinter, pages 134–155.

Franzese, R. J. (2009) *The Sociology of Deviance: Differences, Tradition, and Stigma*, Illinois, USA: Charles C. Thomas Publisher.

Fraser, T. G. (2000) *Ireland in Conflict 1922–1998*, London: Routledge.

Frost, C. (2000) *Media Ethics and Self-Regulation*, Essex: Longman.

Frost, C. (2010) *Reporting for Journalists* (Second Edition), Oxon: Routledge.

Gabriel, J. (1998) *Whitewash: Racialized Politics and the Media*, London: Routledge.

Gado, M. (2008) *Death Row Women: Murder, Justice, and the New York Press*, California, USA: Greenwood Publishing Group.

Gaffikin, F. and Morrissey, M. (2011) *Planning in Divided Cities*, Chichester, USA: Wiley-Blackwell.

Gallagher, M. (1982) 'Negotiation of Control in Media Organizations', in M. Gurevitch, T. Bennett, J. Curran and J. Woollacott (eds.) *Culture, Society and the Media*, London: Routledge, pages 148–171.

Galtung, J. and Ruge, M. H. (1965) 'The Structure of Foreign News: The Presentation of the Congo, Cuba and Cyprus Crises in Four Norwegian Newspapers', *Journal of Peace Research*, Volume 2, Number 1, pages 64–91.

Galtung, J. and Ruge, M. H. (1982) 'Structuring and Selecting News', in S. Cohen and J. Young (eds.) *The Manufacture of News: Deviance, Social Problems and the Mass Media* (First Edition), London: Constable, pages 52–64.

Gans, H. J. (1980) *Deciding What's News. A Study of CBS Evening News, NBC Nightly News, Newsweek and Time*, New York, USA: Vintage.

Garratt, D., Roche, J. and Tucker, S. (1997) *Changing Experiences of Youth*, London: SAGE Publications Limited.

Gieber, W. (1999) 'News Is What Newspapermen Make It', in H. Tumber (ed.) *News: A Reader*, Oxford: Oxford University Press, pages 218–223.

Gil-Robles, A. (2005) 'Commissioner for Human Rights on His Visit to UK, 4–12 November 2004', Comm DHL 2005/6, Council of Europe: Office of Commissioner for Human Rights.

Gillespie, G. (2009) *The A to Z of the Northern Ireland Conflict*, New Jersey, USA: Scarecrow Press.

Glover, D. (1984) *The Sociology of the Mass Media*, Cornwall: Causeway Press Limited.

Golding, P. and Elliott, P. (1999) 'Making the News' (Excerpt), in H. Tumber (ed.) *News: A Reader*, Oxford: Oxford University Press, pages 102–111.

Golding, P. and Murdock, G. (1991) 'Culture, Communications, and Political Economy', in J. Curran and M. Gurevitch (eds.) *Mass Media and Society*, London: Edward Arnold, pages 15–32.

Goldson, B. (2002) *Vulnerable Inside: Children in Secure and Penal Settings,* London: Children's Society.

Goldson, B. (2005) 'Taking Liberties: Policy and the Punitive Turn', in H. Hendrick (ed.) *Child Welfare and Social Policy: An Essential Reader*, Bristol: The Policy Press, pages 255–268.

Goldson, B. (2006) 'Penal Custody: Intolerance, Irrationality and Indifference', in B. Goldson and J. Muncie (eds.) (2006) *Youth Crime and Justice*, London: SAGE Publications Limited, pages 139–156.

Goode, E. and Ben-Yehuda, N. (1994) *Moral Panics: The Social Construction of Deviance*, Oxford: Blackwell.

Goode, E. and Ben-Yehuda, N. (2009) *Moral Panics: The Social Construction of Deviance* (Second Edition), West Sussex: Wiley-Blackwell.

Goodwin, A. (1990) 'TV News: Striking the Right Balance?', in A. Goodwin and G. Whannel (eds.) *Understanding Television*, London: Routledge, pages 42–59.

Gordon, F. (2007) *Children's Rights in a Media Culture,* Queen's University Belfast, Unpublished Dissertation.

Gordon, F. (2010) 'Construction, Portrayal and Treatment of Contemporary 'Folk Devils': Media, Political and Public Reactions to Children and Young People in Northern Ireland', Paper Presented at the *Moral Panics in the Contemporary World*, International Conference, Brunel University London, 10–12 December.

Gordon, F., Haydon, D., Marshall, C., McAlister, S. and Scraton, P. (2009) *'The Childhood, Transition and Social Justice Initiative' Response to the NIO Consultation Document -'Together. Safer. Stronger'*, Belfast: CTSJI, Queen's University Belfast.

Gordon, F. (2016) 'Publication of Children's Images, Privacy and Article 8: Judgment in the Matter of an Application by JR38 for Judicial Review (Northern Ireland) [2015] UKSC 42' *Northern Ireland Legal Quarterly*, Volume 67, Number 2, pages 257–261.

Gorton, K. (2009) *Media Audiences: Television, Meaning and Emotion.* Edinburgh: Edinburgh University Press.

Graham, B. (2011) 'Sharing Space? Geography and Politics in Post-conflict Northern Ireland', in P. Meusburger, M. Heffernan and E. Wunder (eds.) *Cultural Memories: The Geographical Point of View*, London: Springer, pages 87–100.

Graham, J. and Bowling, B. (1995) *Young People and Crime*, Home Office Research Study 145, London: Home Office.

Grattan, A. (2008) 'The Alienation and Radicalisation of Youth: A "New Moral Panic?"' *The International Journal of Diversity in Organisations, Communities and Nations*, Volume 8, Number 3, pages 255–263.

Green, D. A. (2008a) 'Suitable Vehicles: Framing Blame and Justice When Children Kill a Child', *Crime Media Culture*, Volume 4, Number 2, August, pages 197–220.

Green, D. A. (2008b) *When Children Kill Children: Penal Populism and Political Culture*, Oxford: Clarendon Press.

Greenslade, R. (2003) *Press Gang: How Newspapers Make Profits from Propaganda*, London: Macmillan.

Greer, C. (2003) *Sex Crime and the Media: Sex Offending and the Press in a Divided Society*, Devon: Willan Publishing.

Greer, C. (2005) 'Crime and Media', in C. Hale, K. Hayward, A. Wahidin and E. Wincup (eds.) *Criminology*, Oxford: Oxford University Press, pages 152–182.

Greer, C. (2007) 'News Media, Victims and Crime', in P. Davies, P. Francis and C. Greer (eds.) *Victims, Crime and Society*, London: SAGE Publications Limited, pages 20–50.

Griffin, C. (2009) 'Representations of the Young', in J. Roche, S. Tucker, R. Thomson and R. Flynn (eds.) *Youth in Society* (Second Edition), London: SAGE Publications Limited, pages 10–18.

Gross, L. (1992) 'Out of the Mainstream: Sexual Minorities and the Mass Media', in E. Seiter, H. Borchers, G. Kreutzner and E. M. Warth (eds.) *Remote Control: Television, Audiences and Cultural Power*, London: Routledge, pages 130–149.

Grover, S. (2004) 'Why Won't They Listen to Us? On Giving Power and Voice to Children Participating in Social Research', *Childhood*, Volume 11, Number 1, pages 81–93.

Gurevitch, M., Bennett, T., Curran, J. and Woollacott, J. (eds.) (1982) *Culture, Society and the Media*, London: Routledge.

Hall, S., Critcher, C., Jefferson, T., Clarke, J., and Roberts, B. (1978) *Policing the Crisis: Mugging, the State and Law and Order,* London: Macmillan.

Hall, S. (1986) 'Media Power and Class Power', in J. Curran, J. Ecclestone, G. Oakley and A. Richardson (eds.) *Bending Reality: The State of the Media*, London: Pluto Press Limited, pages 5–14.

Hall, S. (1997) 'Discourse, Power and the Subject', in S. Hall (ed.) *Representation: Cultural Representations and Signifying Practices*, London: SAGE Publications Limited, pages 41–74.

Hall, S. (1998) 'The Great Moving Nowhere Show', *Marxism Today*, November – December, pages 9–14.

Hall, S. and Jefferson, T. eds. (2006) *Resistance Through Rituals: Youth Subcultures in Post-war Britain*, Oxon: Routledge

Hall, S. and Scraton, P. (1981) 'Law, Class and Control', in M. Fitzgerald, G. McLennan and J. Pawson (eds.) *Crime and Society*, London: RKP, pages 460–498.

Hamill, H. (2002) 'Victims of Paramilitary Punishment Attacks in Belfast', in C. Hoyle and R. Young (eds.) *New Visions of Crime Victims*, Oxford: Hart Publishing, pages 49–69.

Hamill, H. (2011) *The Hoods: Crime and Punishment in Belfast*, Oxfordshire: Princeton University Press.

Hamilton, J., Radford, K. and Jarman, N. (2003) *Policing, Accountability and Young People,* Belfast: Institute for Conflict Research.

Hancock, L., Mooney, G. and Neal, S. (2010) 'The "Broken Society" and Anti-Welfarism: A Moral Panic About 'Problem' Behaviours?' Paper Presented at *Moral Panics in the Contemporary World*, International Conference, Brunel University London, 10–12 December.

Harland, K. (2010) 'Violent Youth Culture in Northern Ireland: Young Men, Violence and the Challenges of Peacebuilding', *Youth and Society*, Volume XX, Number 1, pages 1–19.

Harnett, A. (2010) 'Aestheticized Geographies of Conflict: The Politicization of Culture and the Culture of Politics in Belfast's Mural Tradition', in H. Silverman (ed.) *Contested Cultural Heritage: Religion, Nationalism, Erasure, and Exclusion in a Global World*, London: Springer, pages 69–108.

Harrison, M. (1985) *TV News: Whose Bias?* London: Policy Journals.

Hart, A. (1991) *Understanding the Media: A Practical Guide*, London: Routledge.

Harvey, D. (1996) 'Possible Urban Worlds', The Fourth Megacities Lecture, November 2000. Accessed from: http://www.megacities.nl/lecture_4/invitation.html (accessed on 13 February 2009).

Harvey, D. (2007) 'Cities or urbanization?', City, Volume 1, Number 1, pp. 38–61.

Haudrup Christensen, P. (2004) 'Children's Participation in Ethnographic Research: Issues of Power and Representation', *Children and Society*, Volume 18, Number 2, pages 165–176.

Haydon, D. and Scraton, P. (2000) "Condemn a Little More, Understand a Little Less': The Political Context and Rights Implications of the Domestic and European Rulings in the Venables - Thompson Case', *Journal of Law and Society*, Volume 27, Number 3, pages 416–448.

Haydon, D. and Scraton, P. (2008) 'Conflict, Regulation and Marginalisation in the North of Ireland: The Experiences of Children and Young People', in P. Scraton (ed.) *Current Issues in Criminal Justice*, Volume 20, Number 1, pages 59–78.

Haydon, D. (2008) *Northern Ireland NGO Alternative Report to the UN Committee on the Rights of the Child*, Belfast: Save the Children and the Children's Law Centre Northern Ireland.

Hayward, K. and Yar, M. (2006) 'The "Chav" Phenomenon: Consumption, Media and the Construction of a New Underclass', *Crime Media Culture*, Volume 2, Number 1, pages 9–28.

Heenan, D. and Birrell, D. (2011) *Social Work in Northern Ireland: Conflict and Change*, London: The Policy Press.

Heintz-Knowles, K. E. (2000) *Images of Youth: A Content Analysis of Adolescents in Prime-time Entertainment Programming*, Washington, USA: Frameworks Institute.

Hendrick, H. (2005) *Child Welfare and Social Policy: An Essential Reader*, London: The Policy Press.

Hendrick, H. (2006) 'Histories of Youth Crime and Justice', in B. Goldson and J. Muncie (eds.) *Youth, Crime and Justice: Critical Issues,* London: SAGE Publications Limited, pages 3–16.

Henn, M., Weinstein M. and Foard, N. (2009) *A Critical Introduction to Social Research* (Second Edition), London: SAGE Publications Limited.

Hennessey, T. (2000) *The Northern Ireland Peace Process. Ending the Troubles?*, Dublin: Gill and Macmillan.

Herman, E. (1990) 'Media in the U.S. Political Economy', in J. Downing, A. Sreberny-Mohammadi and A. Mohammadi (eds.) *Questioning the Media*, London: SAGE Publications Limited, pages 75–87.

Herman, E. S. and Chomsky, N. (1988) *The Political Economy of the Mass Media*, New York, USA: Pantheon.

Herman, E. S. and Chomsky, N. (1994) *Manufacturing Consent* (Second Edition), London: Vintage.

Heskin, K. (1980) *Northern Ireland: A Psychological Analysis*, Dublin: Gill and Macmillan.

Hillyard, P. (1987) 'The Normalisation of Special Powers: From Northern Ireland to Britain', in P. Scraton (ed.) *Law, Order and the Authoritarian State*, Milton Keynes: Open University Press, pages 279–309.

Hillyard, P. (1988) 'Political and Social Divisions of Emergency Law in Northern Ireland', in A. Jennings (ed.) *Justice Under Fire. The Abuse of Civil Liberties in Northern Ireland*, London: Pluto Press, pages 191–212.

Hillyard, P. (1993) 'Paramilitary Policing and Popular Justice in Northern Ireland', in M. Findlay, and U. Zvekic (eds.) *Alternative Policing Styles: Cross Cultural Perspectives*, Boston, USA: Kluwer Law and Taxation Publishers, pages 139–156.

Hillyard, P., Rolston, B., Tomlinson, M. (2005) *Poverty and Conflict in Ireland: An International Perspective*, Issue 36 of Research Report Series, Belfast: Combat Poverty Agency.

Holland, P. (1992) *What Is a Child? Popular Images of Childhood*, London: Virago.

Holland, P. (1997) *The Television Handbook*, London: Routledge.

Holland, P. (2004) *Picturing Childhood: The Myth of the Child in Popular Imagery*, London: I.B. Tauris.

Holsti, O. R. (1969) *Content Analysis for the Social Sciences and Humanities*, Reading, USA: Addison - Welsey Publications Company.

Home Office (1980) *Young Offenders* (White Paper) Cmnd. 8045, London: Home Office.

Home Office (1996) *Misspent Youth*. Audit Commission Report, London: Home Office.

Home Office (1997a) *No More Excuses – A New Approach to Tackling Youth Crime in England and Wales*, London: Home Office.

Home Office (1997b) *Tackling Youth Crime: A Consultation Paper*, London: Home Office.

Home Office (2005) *Publicising Anti-Social Behaviour Orders: Home Office Guidance*, March, London: Home Office.

Hopkins Burke, R. (2008) *Young People, Crime and Justice*, Devon: Willan Publishing.

Horgan, G. (2005) *The Particular Circumstances of Children in Northern Ireland*, November, Belfast: The Children's Law Centre Northern Ireland. Available from: http://www.childrenslawcentre.org/ParticularCircumstancesofChildreninNorther nIreland-GorettiHorgan.htm (accessed on 10 March 2011).

Hornig Priest, S. (2010) *Doing Media Research: An Introduction* (Second Edition), London: SAGE Publications Limited.

Horrie, C. (2003) *Tabloid Nation: From the Birth of the Daily Mirror to the Death of the Tabloid*, London: Carlton Publishing Group.

House of Commons (2003) *Culture, Media and Sport Committee: Privacy and Media Intrusion, Fifth Report of Session 2002–2003*, Volume 1, London: House of Commons.

Human Rights Watch members (unnamed) (1991) *Human Rights in Northern Ireland*, Helsinki Watch Report, Volume 1245, USA: Human Rights Watch.

Hunt, G., Moloney, M. and Evans, K. (2010) *Youth, Drugs, and Nightlife*, Oxon: Routledge.

Hyman, H. H., with Cobb, W. J., Feldman, J. J., Hart, W. C. and Stember, C. H. (2004) 'Interviewing in Social Research', in C. Seale (ed.) *Social Research Methods: A Reader*, London: Routledge, pages 88–95.

Include Youth (2004) *Response to Measures to Tackle Anti-Social Behaviour in Northern Ireland Consultation Document*, Belfast: Include Youth.

Include Youth (2009) *Response to the Department of Health, Social Services and Public Safety's Consultation of A Legislative Framework for Mental Capacity and Mental Health Legislation in Northern Ireland*, March, Belfast: Include Youth.

Irvine, M. (1991) *Northern Ireland: Faith and Faction*, London: Routledge.

Jamieson, J. and Yates, J. (2009) 'Young People, Youth Justice and the State', in R. Coleman, J. Sim, S. Tombs and D. Whyte (eds.) *State, Power, Crime*, London: SAGE Publications Limited, pages 76–89.

Jarman, N. (1997) *Material Conflicts: Parades and Visual Displays in Northern Ireland*, Oxford: Berg.

Jarman, N. (2002) *Managing Disorder: Responding to Interface Violence in North Belfast*, Belfast: OFMDFM.

Jarman, N. (2004) 'From War to Peace? Changing Patterns of Violence in Northern Ireland 1990–2003', *Terrorism and Political Violence*, Volume 16, Number 3, Autumn, pages 420–438.

Jarman, N. (2005) 'Teenage Kicks: Young Women and Their Involvement in Violence and Disorderly Behaviour', *Child Care in Practice*, Volume 11, Number 3, July, pages 341–356.

Jarman, N. (2006) 'Peacebuilding and Policing: The Role of Community-based Initiatives', *Shared Space*, Number 3, November, pages 31–44.

Jarman, N. (2008) 'Security and Segregation: Interface Barriers in Belfast', *Shared Space*, Number 6, June, pages 21–33.

Jarman, N. and O'Halloran, C. (2001) 'Recreational Rioting: Young People, Interface Areas and Violence', *Child Care in Practice*, Volume 7, Number 1, pages 2–16.

Jarman, N., Quinn, G., Murphy, J. and Nichol, S. (2002) 'Escaping to the Happy Planet? Drug Use, Education and Professional Support in North Belfast', *Child Care in Practice*, Volume 8, Number 3, pages 159–175.

Jempson, M. (2010) *The Media and Children's Rights: A Resource for Journalists by Journalists* (Third Edition), London: MediaWise and UNICEF.

Jewkes, Y. (2004) *Media and Crime*, London: SAGE Publications Limited.

Jewkes, Y. (Ed) (2009) *Crime and Media*, Volume One of Three-Volume Set, SAGE Library of Criminology, London: SAGE Publications Limited.

Jewkes, Y. (2011) 'The Media and Criminological Research', in P. Davis, P. Francis and V. Jupp (eds.) *Doing Criminological Research*, London: SAGE Publications Limited, pages 245–261.

Jones, T. and Newburn, T. (2002) 'Policy Convergence and Crime Control in the USA and the UK: Streams of Influence and Levels of Impact', *Criminology and Criminal Justice*, Volume 2, Number 2, pages 173–203.

Jupp, V. (1989) *Methods of Criminological Research*, New York, USA: Routledge.

Jupp, V. (2006a) *The SAGE Dictionary of Social Research Methods*, London: SAGE Publications Limited.

Jupp, V. (2006b) 'Documents and Critical Research', in R. Sapsford and V. Jupp (eds.) *Data Collection and Analysis* (Second Edition), London: SAGE Publications Limited, pages 272–290.

Kaufmann, E. P. (2007) *The Orange Order: A Contemporary Northern Irish History*, Oxford: Oxford University Press.

Kay, S. (2011) *Celtic Revival? The Rise, Fall, and Renewal of Global Ireland*, Plymouth: Rowan and Littlefield.

Keeble, R. (2009) *Ethics for Journalists* (Second Edition), Oxon: Routledge.

Keeble, R. L. and Mair, J. eds. (2012) *The Phone Hacking Scandal: Journalism on Trial*, Suffolk: Arima Publishing.

Kelly, L. (2011) 'Belfast, August 1969: The Limited and Localised Pattern(s) of Violence', in W. Sheehan and M. Cronin (ed.) *Riotous Assemblies: Rebels, Riots and Revolts in Ireland*, Cork: Mercier Press, pages 228–242.

Kelso, W. (1994) *Poverty and the Underclass: Changing Perceptions of the Poor in America*, New York: New York University Press.

Kennedy, L. (2001) *They Shoot Children, Don't They? An Analysis of the Age and Gender of Victims of Paramilitary 'Punishments' in Northern Ireland*, A Report Prepared for the Northern Ireland Committee Against Terror and the Northern Ireland Affairs Committee of the House of Commons, Belfast: Queen's University Belfast.

Kenway, P., MacInnes, T., Kelly, A. and Palmer, G. (2006) *Monitoring Poverty and Social Exclusion in Northern Ireland 2006*, York: Joseph Rowntree Foundation.

Khabaz, D. V. (2006) *Manufactured Schema: Thatcher, the Miners and the Culture Industry*, Leicester: Matador.

Kidd-Hewitt, D. (1995) 'Crime and the Media: A Criminological Perspective', pages 9–24, in D. Kidd-Hewitt and R. Osborne (eds.) *Crime and the Media: The Post-Modern Spectacle*, London: Pluto Press.

Kieran, M. (1998) *Media Ethics*, London: Routledge.

Kilkelly, U., Moore, L. and Convery, U. (2002) *In Our Care: Promoting the Rights of Children in Custody*, Belfast: Northern Ireland Human Rights Commission.

Kilkelly, U., Kilpatrick, R., Lundy, L., Moore, L., Scraton P., Davey, C., Dwyer, C. and McAlister, S. (2004) *Children's Rights in Northern Ireland*, Belfast: Northern Ireland Commissioner for Children and Young People.

Kitsuse, J. I. (1962) 'Social Reaction to Deviant Behavior: Problems of Theory and Method', *Social Problems*, Volume 9, Number 1, pages 247–256.

Koffman, L. (2006) 'The Use of Anti-Social Behaviour Orders: An Empirical Study of a New Deal for Communities Area', *Criminal Law Review*, July, pages 593–613.

Knight, V. (2016) *Remote Control Television in Prison*, Hampshire: Palgrave Macmillan.

Krinsky, C. ed. (2008) *Moral Panics over Contemporary Children and Youth*, Surrey: Ashgate Publishing Limited.

Lacey, N. (1998) *Image and Representation: Key Concepts in Media Studies*, Hampshire and London: Macmillan Press Limited.

Laidler, T. (1997) 'Media Portrayals of Young People', in J. Bessant and R. Hil (eds.) *Youth Crime and the Media: Media Representations of and Reactions to Young People in relation to Law and Order*, Hobart, Australia: Australian Clearinghouse for Youth Studies, pages 105–108.

Lansdown, G. (1994) 'Children's Rights', in B. Mayall (ed.) *Children's Childhoods Observed and Experienced*, London: The Falmer Press, pages 33–44.

Lashmar, P. (2010) 'The Journalist, Folk Devil', Paper Presented at the *Moral Panics in the Contemporary World*, International conference, Brunel University London, 10–12 December.

Lemert, E. M. (1951) *Social Pathology: A Systematic Approach to the Theory of Sociopathic Behavior*, New York: McGraw-Hill.

Lemert, E. M. (1967) *Human Deviance, Social Problems, and Social Control*, Englewood Cliffs, USA: Prentice Hall.

Lemert, E. M. (1972) *Human Deviance, Social Problems, and Social Control* (Second Edition), Englewood Cliffs, USA: Prentice Hall.

Leonard, M. (2006) 'Teens and Territory in Contested Spaces: Negotiating Sectarian Interfaces in Northern Ireland', *Children's Geographies*, Volume 4, Number 2, pages 225–238.

Leonard, M. (2009) 'Children's Agency in Politically Divided Societies: The Case of Northern Ireland', in J. Quortrup (ed.) *Structural, Historical, and Comparative Perspectives*, Sociological Studies of Children and Youth, Volume 12, Bingley, USA: Emerald Group Publishing Limited, pages 115–138.

Leonard, M. (2010a) 'What's Recreational about Recreational Rioting', *Children and Society*, Volume 24, Number 1, pages 38–50.

Leonard, M. (2010b) 'Parochial Geographies: Growing up in Divided Belfast', *Childhood*, Volume 17, Number 3, pages 329–342.

Leonard, M. (2011) 'A Tale of Two Cities: Political Tourism in Belfast', *Irish Journal of Sociology*, Volume 19, Number 2, pages 110–125.

Leonard, M. and McKnight, M. (2010) 'Teenagers' Perceptions of Belfast as a Divided/Shared City', *Shared Space*, Volume 10, pages 23–39.

Leonard, M and McKnight, M. (2011) 'Bringing Down the Walls: Young People's Perspectives on Peace Walls in Belfast', *International Journal of Sociology and Social Policy*, Volume 31, Number 9/10, pages 569–583.

Lilly, J., Cullen, F. T. and Ball, R. A. (2011) *Criminological Theory: Context and Consequences*, (Fifth Edition), London: SAGE Publications Limited.

Lister, R. and Bennett, F. (2010) 'The New "Champion of Progressive Ideals?" Cameron's Conservative Party: Poverty, Family Policy and Welfare Reform', *Renewal*, Volume 18, Numbers 1–2, pages 84–109.

Little, A. (2008) *Democratic Piety: Complexity, Conflict and Violence,* Edinburgh: Edinburgh University Press Limited.

Loughlin, J. (1998) *The Ulster Question Since 1945*, London: Macmillan.

Lumsden, K. (2009) '"Do We Look Like Boy Racers?" The Role of the Folk Devil in Contemporary Moral Panics', *Sociological Research Online*, Volume 14, Number 2, electronic format.

Lysaght, K. (2008) 'Speaking of Contested Sites: Narrative and Praxis of Spatial Competition in Belfast, Northern Ireland', in T. Levin (ed) *Violence: 'Mercurial Gestalt'*, Netherlands: Rodopi, pages 151–172.

Machin, D. and Niblock, S. (2006) *News Production: Theory and Practice*, London: Routledge.

Marsh, I. and Melville, G. (2009) *Crime, Justice and the Media*, Oxon: Routledge.

Masterman, L. (1990) *Teaching the Media*, London: Routledge.

Maruna, S. and King, A. (2008) 'Giving Up on the Young', in P. Scraton (ed.) *Current Issues in Criminal Justice*, Volume 20, Number 1, pages 129–134.

Mauthner, M. (1997) 'Methodological Aspects of Collecting Data from Children: Lessons from Three Research Projects', *Children and Society*, Volume 11, Number 1, pages 16–28.

Mawby, R. C. (2010) 'Chibnall Revisited: Crime Reporters, the Police and "Law-and-Order News"', *British Journal of Criminology*, Volume 50, Number 6, pages 1060–1076.

Mawby, R. C. (2011) 'Using the Media to Understand Crime and Criminal Justice', in P. Davis, P. Francis and V. Jupp (eds.) *Doing Criminological Research*, London: SAGE Publications Limited, pages 223–244.

McAlinden, A. (2011) '"Transforming Justice": Challenges for Restorative Justice in an Era of Punishment-based Corrections', *Contemporary Justice Review: Issues in Criminal, Social, and Restorative Justice*, Volume 14, Number 4, pages 383–406.

McAlister, S., Scraton, P. and Haydon D. (2009) *Childhood in Transition: Experiencing Marginalisation and Conflict in Northern Ireland*, Belfast: Queen's University Belfast, Save the Children and Prince's Trust Northern Ireland.

McAlister, S., Scraton, P. and Haydon, D. (2010) '"Insiders" and "Outsiders": Young People, Place and Identity in Northern Ireland', *Shared Space*, Number 9, pages 69–83.

McAlister, S., Scraton, P. and Haydon, D. (2011) 'Place, Territory and Young People's Identity in the "New" Northern Ireland', in B. Goldson (ed.) *Youth in Crisis? Gangs, Territoriality and Violence*, London: Routledge, pages 89–109.

McAra, L. (2012) 'Models of Youth Justice', in D. J. Smith (ed.) *A New Response to Youth Crime*, Oxon: Routledge, pages 287–318.

McCrudden, C. (2007) 'Northern Ireland and the British Constitution since the Belfast Agreement', in J. Jowell and D. Oliver (2007) *The Changing Constitution* (Sixth Edition), Oxford: Oxford University Press, pages 227–270.

McEldowney, O., Anderson, J. and Stuttleworth, I. (2011) 'Sectarian Demography: Dubious Discourses of the Ethno-nationalist Conflict', in K. Hayward and C. O'Donnell (eds.) *Political Discourse and Conflict Resolution: Debating Peace in Northern Ireland*, London: Routledge, pages 160–176.

McEvoy, K. and Ellison, T. eds. (2003) *Criminology, Conflict Resolution and Restorative Justice,* Hampshire: Palgrave Macmillan.

McEvoy, J. (2008) *The Politics of Northern Ireland*, Edinburgh: Edinburgh University Press Limited.

McGarry, J. (2001) 'Introduction: The Comparable Northern Ireland', in J. McGarry (ed.) *Northern Ireland and the Divided: The Northern Ireland Conflict and the Good Friday Agreement in Comparative Perspective*, Oxford: Oxford University Press, pages 1–35.

McGarry, J. and O'Leary, B. (1999) *Policing Northern Ireland: Proposals for a New Start*, Belfast: Blackstaff Press.

McGarry, J. and O'Leary, B. (2004) *The Northern Ireland Conflict: Consociational Engagements*, Oxford: Oxford University Press.

McGarry, J. and O'Leary, B. (2009) 'Power Shared After the Deaths of Thousands', in R. Taylor (ed.) *Consociational Theory: McGarry & O'Leary and the Northern Ireland Conflict*, Oxon: Routledge, pages 15–84.

McGrellis, S. (2004) 'Pushing the Boundaries in Northern Ireland: Young People, Violence and Sectarianism', Families and Social Capital ESRC Research Group Working Paper Number 8, London: London South Bank University.

McKnight, D. (2012) *Rupert Murdoch: An Investigation of Political Power*, UK: Allen and Unwin.

McLaughlin, G. (2006) 'Profits, Politics and Paramilitaries: The Local News Media in Northern Ireland', in B. Franklin (ed.) *Local Journalism and Local Media: Making the Local News,* London: Routledge, pages 60–70.

McMahon, A. (1997) 'Rough Justice: Juveniles and the Reporting of Crime in Townsville', in J. Bessant and R. Hil (eds) *Youth Crime and the Media: Media Representations of and Reactions to Young People in Relation to Law and Order*, Hobart, Australia: Australian Clearinghouse for Youth Studies, pages 75–80.

McNair, B. (1994) *News and Journalism in the UK*, London: Routledge.

McNair, B. (2009) *News and Journalism in the UK* (Fifth Edition), London: Routledge.

McQuail, D. (1972) *Sociology of Mass Communications*, Harmondsworth: Penguin Publishers.

McQuail, D. (1991) 'Mass Media in the Public Interest: Towards a Framework of Norms for Media Performance', in J. Curran and M. Gurevitch (eds.) *Mass Media and Society*, London: Edward Arnold, pages 68–81.

McQuail, D. (2000) *McQuail's Mass Communication Theory* (Fourth Edition), London: SAGE Publications Limited.

McRobbie, A. (1994) *Postmodernism and Popular Culture*, London: Routledge.

McRobbie, A. and Thornton, S. (1995) 'Rethinking "Moral Panic" for Multi-mediated Social Worlds', *British Journal of Sociology*, Volume 46, pages 559–574.

McRobbie, A. and Thornton, S. (2002) 'Rethinking "Moral Panic" for Multi-mediated Social Worlds', in J. Muncie, G. Hughes and E. McLaughlin (eds.) *Youth Justice: Critical Readings*, London: SAGE Publications Limited, pages 68–79.

Meadows, S. (2010) *The Child as Social Person*, East Sussex: Routledge.

Mentor, K. (1997). 'Why Don't We Just Ask? Qualitative Interviews in Criminology Research'. Accessed from: http://kenmentor.com/papers/qual_int.htm (accessed on 22 March 2009).

Mercer, C. (1992) 'Regular Imaginings: The Newspaper and the Nation', in T. Bennett, P. Buckridge, D. Carter and C. Mercer (eds.) *Celebrating the Nation: A Critical Study of Australia's Bicentenary*, Sydney, Australia: Allen and Unwin, pages 26–46.

Merton, R. K. (1968) *Social Theory and Social Structure*, New York, USA: The Free Press.

Meyer, P. (2009) *The Vanishing Newspaper*, Missouri, USA: University of Missouri.

Miller, D. (1993) *Don't Mention the War: Northern Ireland, Propaganda and the Media*, London: Pluto Press.

Mishna, F., Antle, B. J. and Regehr, C. (2004) 'Tapping the Perspectives of Children: Emerging Ethical Issues in Qualitative Research', *Qualitative Social Work*, Volume 3, Number 4, pages 449–468.

Monteith, M., Lloyd, K. and McKee, P. (2008) *Persistent Child Poverty in Northern Ireland: Key Findings*, Belfast: Save the Children.

Mooney, G. (2009) 'The "Broken Society" Election: Class Hatred and the Politics of Poverty and Place in Glasgow East', *Social Policy and Society*, Volume 3, Number 4, pages 1–14.

Moore, J. (1997) 'Paramilitary Prisoners and the Peace Process in Northern Ireland', in A. O'Day (ed.) *Political Violence in Northern Ireland: Conflict and Conflict Resolution,* Westport, USA: Praeger Publishers, pages 81–95.

Moore, L. and Convery, U. (2008) 'Barred from Change: The Incarceration of Children and Young People in Northern Ireland', in P. Scraton (ed.) *Current Issues in Criminal Justice*, Volume 20, Number 1, pages 79–94.

Moores, S. (1993) *Interpreting Audiences: The Ethnography of Media Consumption*, London: SAGE.

Morgan, R. (2009) 'Children in Custody', in M. Blyth, R. Newman and C. Wright (eds.) *Children and Young People in Custody*, Bristol: The Policy Press, pages 9–22.

Morley, D. (1997) *Television, Audiences and Cultural Studies,* London: Routledge.

Morris, A. and Gelsthorpe, L. (2000) 'Something Old, Something Borrowed, Something Blue, but Something New? A Comment on the Prospects for Restorative Justice Under the Crime and Disorder Act 1998', *Criminal Law Review*, January, pages 18–27.

Morris, A. and Giller, H. (1987) *Understanding Juvenile Justice,* London. Croom Helm.

Mulcahy, A. (2002) 'The Impact of the Northern "Troubles" on Criminal Justice in the Irish Republic', in P. O'Mahony (ed.) *Criminal Justice in Ireland*, Dublin: Institute of Public Administration, pages 275–296.

Mulcahy, A. (2006) *Policing Northern Ireland: Conflict, Legitimacy and Reform*, Devon: Willan Publishing.

Mulholland, M. (2002) *Northern Ireland: A Very Short History*, Oxford: Oxford University Press.

Muncie, J. (2004) *Youth and Crime* (Second Edition), London: SAGE Publications Limited.

Muncie, J. (2006) 'Labelling', in E. McLaughlin and J. Muncie (eds.) *The SAGE Dictionary of Criminology* (Second Edition), London: SAGE Publications Limited, pages 229–231.

Muncie, J. (2009) *Youth and Crime* (Third Edition), London: SAGE Publications Limited.

Muncie, J. and Fitzgerald, M. (1981) 'Humanising the Deviant: Affinity and Affiliation Theories', in M. Fitzgerald, G. McLennan and J. Pawson (eds.) *Crime and Society: Readings in History and Theory*, London: Routledge and Kegan Paul/The Open University Press, pages 403–429.

Muraskin, R. and Domash, S. F. (2007). *Crime and the Media: Headlines vs. Reality*, New Jersey, USA: Pearson Education.

Murdock, P. and Golding, P. (1977) 'Capitalism, Communication and Class Relations', in J. Curran, M. Gurevitch and J. Woolacott (eds.) *Mass Communication and Society*, London: Edward Arnold, pages 12–43.

Nairn, T. (1981) *The Break-Up of Britain*, London: Verso.

Naylor, B. (2001). 'Reporting Violence in the British Print Media: Gendered Stories', *The Howard Journal*, Volume 40, Number 2, pages 180–194.

Negrine, R. M. (1989) *Politics and the Mass Media in Britain*, London: Routledge.

Neocleous, M. (2008) *Critique of Security*, Edinburgh: Edinburgh University Press.

New Labour (1997) *New Labour Because Britain Deserves Better*, London: The Labour Party.

Newburn, T. (1995) *Crime and Criminal Justice Policy*, London: Longman.

Newburn, T. (1997) 'Youth Crime and Justice', in M. Maguire, R. Morgan and R. Reiner (eds.) *The Oxford Handbook of Criminology*, Oxford: Oxford University Press, pages 613–660.

Newburn, T. (2002) 'Atlantic Crossings: "Policy Transfer" and Crime Control in the USA and Britain', *Punishment and Society*, Volume 4, Number 2, pages 165–194.

Newburn, T. (2007) *Criminology*, Devon: Willan Publishing.

NIACRO (2009) *NIACRO's Response to 'Together. Stronger. Safer' Community Safety in Northern Ireland Consultation*, January, Belfast: NIACRO.

NICCY (2004) *Northern Ireland Commissioner for Children and Young People Applies for Judicial Review Over Anti-Social Behaviour Order Consultation*, Belfast: NICCY.

NICCY (2005) *The Northern Ireland Commissioner for Children and Young People, Nigel Williams, Today Welcomed the Equality Commission's Recommendation That the*

Northern Ireland Office Must Carry Out an Equality Impact Assessment on Anti-social Behaviour Orders (ASBOs), Belfast: NICCY.

Nicholas, J. and Price, J. eds. (1998) *Advanced Studies in Media*, Cheltenham: Nelson Thornes.

Nichols, B. (2010) *Introduction to Documentary* (Second Edition), Indiana, USA: Indiana University Press.

Northern Ireland Human Rights Commission (2010) *Letter Addressed to Ald. Joe Miller, MBE Regarding Operation Exposure*, 2 September, Belfast: NIHRC.

Northern Ireland Office (1998) *The Agreement* (The Belfast/Good Friday Agreement), Belfast: Northern Ireland Office.

Northern Ireland Office (1999) *A New Beginning: Policing in Northern Ireland: The Report of the Independent Commission on Policing for Northern Ireland*, Belfast: Northern Ireland Office.

Northern Ireland Office (2000) *Review of the Criminal Justice System in Northern Ireland, the Report of the Criminal Justice System Review,* 30 March , Belfast: Northern Ireland Office.

Northern Ireland Office (2002) *Explanatory Notes on 2002 Justice Act Northern Ireland*, Belfast: NIO. Accessed from: http://www.legislation.gov.uk/ukpga/2002/26/notes/contents (accessed on 1 June 2011).

Northern Ireland Office (2004) *Measures to Tackle Anti-Social Behaviour in Northern Ireland: A Consultation Document*, Belfast: Criminal Justice Policy Branch, Northern Ireland Office.

Northern Ireland Office (2006) *The St Andrews Agreement*, Belfast: Northern Ireland Office.

Northern Ireland Office (2008) *Together. Safer. Stronger Consultation Document*, Belfast: Community Safety Unit, Northern Ireland Office.

Northern Ireland Office (2010) *Agreement at Hillsborough Castle,* 5 February, Belfast: Northern Ireland Office. Accessed from: http://www.nio.gov.uk/agreement_at_hillsborough_castle_5_february_2010.pdf (accessed on 12 February 2010).

Noaks, L. and Wincup, E. (2004) *Criminological Research – Understanding Qualitative Methods*, London: SAGE Publications Limited.

North, L. (2009) *The Gendered Newsroom: How Journalists Experience the Changing World of Media*, Cresskill, USA: Hampton Press, Inc.

Northern Ireland Policing Board (2010a) AEPs, September. http://www.nipolicing-board.org.uk/index/our-work/content-humanrights/content-lesslethal/content-aeps.htm (accessed on 30 July 2011).

Northern Ireland Policing Board (2010b) September. http://www.nipolicingboard.org.uk/index (accessed on 30 July 2011).

O'Connor, A. (1989) 'The Problem of American Cultural Studies', *Critical Studies in Mass Communication*, December, pages 405–413.

O Dochartaigh, N. (1997) *From Civil Rights to Armalites: Derry and the Birth of the Irish Troubles*, Cork: Cork University Press.

O'Rawe, A. (2003) *An Overview of NI Child and Adolescent Mental Health Services*, Belfast: Children's Law Centre Northern Ireland.

O'Rawe, M. (2011) 'Security System Reform and Identity in Divided Societies: Lessons from Northern Ireland', in P. Arthur (ed.) *Identities in Transition: Challenges for Transitional Justice in Divided Societies*, Cambridge: Cambridge University Press, pages 87–117.

O'Sullivan, T., Dutton, B. and Rayner, P. (2003) *Studying the Media* (Third Edition), London: Arnold Publishers.

Osgerby, B. (2004) *Youth Media*, Oxon: Routledge.

Pearson, G. (1983) *Hooligan: A History of Respectable Fears*, Basingstoke: Macmillan.

Pearson, G. (2011) 'Perpetual Novelty: Youth, Modernity and Historical Amnesia', in B. Goldson (ed.) *Youth in Crisis? Gangs, Territoriality and Violence*, London: Routledge, pages 20–37.

Perakyla, A. (2004) 'Reliability and Validity in Research Based on Tapes and Transcripts', in C. Seale (ed.) *Social Research Methods: A Reader*, London: Routledge, pages 325–330.

Perry, D. K. (2002) *Theory and Research in Mass Communication Contexts and Consequences* (Second Edition), New Jersey, USA: Laurence Erlbaum Associates Inc. Publisher.

Pinkerton, J. (1994) *In Care at Home: Parenting, the State, and Civil Society*, Aldershot: Avebury.

Pitts, J. (1988) *The Politics of Juvenile Crime*, London: SAGE Publications Limited.

Pitts, J. (2001) *The New Politics of Youth Crime: Discipline or Solidarity*, London: Routledge.

Potter, W. J. (2010) *Media Literacy*, London: SAGE Publications Limited.

Poynting, S., Noble, G., Tabar, P. and Collins, J. (2004) *Bin Laden in the Suburbs: Criminalising the Arab Other*, Sydney Institute of Criminology Series, Number 18, Sydney: The Sydney Institute of Criminology.

Pratt, M. (1980) *Mugging as a Social Problem*, London: Routledge and Kegan Paul.

Pratt, J. (2000) 'The Return of the Wheelbarrow Men, or the Arrival of Postmodern Penality?', *British Journal of Criminology*, Volume 40, Number 1, page 127–145.

Presdee, M. (2009) 'Young People, Culture and the Construction of Crime: Doing Wrong Versus Doing Crime', in B. Goldson and J. Muncie (eds.) *Youth Crime and Juvenile Justice*, Volume 1, SAGE Library of Criminology, London: SAGE Publications Limited, pages 283–290.

Prout, A. (2000) 'Control and Self-realisation in Late Modern Childhoods', *Children and Society*, Volume 14, Number 4, pages 304–315.

Prus, R. and Grills, S. (2003) *The Deviant Mystique: Involvements, Realities and Regulation*, Westport, USA: Praeger Publishers.

PSNI (2010) *Operation Exposure*, July 2010, Derry/Londonderry: PSNI.

PSNI (undated document) *Operation Exposure: Guidance on the Release of Unidentified Images and Facial Composites of Suspects to the Local Media in G District*, Derry/Londonderry: PSNI.

Puech, K., and Evans, R. (2001) 'Reprimands and Warnings: Populist Punitiveness or Restorative Justice', *Criminal Law Review*, October, pages 794–805.

Punch, S. (2002) 'Research with Children: The Same or Different from Research with Adults?', *Childhood*, Volume 9, Number 3, pages 321–341.

Queen's University Belfast (undated) *School of Law Ethical Guidelines*, Belfast: Queen's University. Accessed from: http://www.qub.ac.uk/schools/SchoolofLaw/Research/EthicsApproval/ (accessed on 23 November 2009).

Quinn, K. and Jackson, J. (2003) 'The Detention and Questioning of Young Persons by the Police in Northern Ireland', NIO Research and Statistical Series, Report Number 9, Belfast: NIO.

Radway, J. (1984) *Reading the Romance*, Chapel Hill: University of North Carolina Press.

Ramsay, P. (2004) 'What Is Anti Social Behaviour?', *Criminal Law Review*, November, pages 908–925.

Regoli, R., Hewitt, J. and DeLisi, M. (2011) *Delinquency in Society: The Essentials*, London: Jones and Bartlett.

Reilly, P. (2010) *Anti-social Networking in Northern Ireland: An Exploratory Study of Strategies for Policing Interfaces in Cyberspace*, Oxford: Oxford Internet Institute.

Reilly, P. (2011) '"Anti-social" Networking in Northern Ireland: Policy Responses to Young People's Use of Social Media for Organizing Anti-social Behavior', *Policy and Internet*, Volume 3, Issue 1, Article 7, pages 1–23.

Reiner, R. (2000) *The Politics of the Police* (Third Edition), Oxford: Oxford University Press.

Reiner, R. (2002) 'Media-made Criminality: The Representation of Crime in the Mass Media', in M. Maguire, R. Morgan and R. Reiner (eds.) *The Oxford Handbook of Criminology*, Oxford: Oxford University Press, pages 302–340.

Reiner, R. (2007) 'Media-made Criminality: The Representation of Crime in the Mass Media', in M. Maguire, R. Morgan and R. Reiner (eds.) *The Oxford Handbook of Criminology* (Fourth Edition), Oxford: Oxford University Press, pages 302–340.

Ripley, T. and Chappell, M. (1993) *Security Forces in Northern Ireland 1969–92*, Oxford: Osprey Publishing.

Roberts, R. (1971) *The Classic Slum: Salford Life in the First Quarter of the Century*, Manchester: Manchester University Press.

Robinson, J. (2009) 'The Social Construction of Deviant Identities: The Devil Wears a Hoodie', in D. Kassem, L. Murphy and E. Taylor (eds.) *Key Issues in Childhood and Youth Studies*, Oxon: Routledge, pages 123–135.

Robson, G. (2004) *"No One Likes Us, We Don't Care": The Myth and Reality of Millwall Fandom*, Oxford: Berg.

Rolston, B. ed. (1991) *The Media and Northern Ireland: Covering the Troubles*, London: Macmillan.

Rolston, B. and Miller, D. eds. (1996) *War and Words: The Northern Ireland Media Reader*, Belfast: Beyond the Pale Publications.

Ross, M. H. (2007) *Cultural Contestation in Ethnic Conflict*, Cambridge: Cambridge University Press.

Ruane, J. and Todd, J. (1996) *The Dynamics of Conflict in Northern Ireland: Power, Conflict and Emancipation*, Cambridge: Cambridge University Press.

Rutherford, A. (2000) 'An Elephant on the Doorstep: Criminal Policy Without Crime in New Labour's Britain', in P. Green and A. Rutherford (eds.) *Criminal Policy in Transition*, Oxford: Hart Publishing, pages 33–62.

Ryder, C. (1990) *The RUC: A Force Under Fire*, London: Mandarin.

Samaritans (2011) *Culture, Practice and Ethics of the Press, Submission to the Leveson Inquiry by Samaritans*, November, London: Samaritans.

Save the Children and ARK (2008) *Persistent Child Poverty in Northern Ireland*, Belfast: Save the Children and ARK.

Save the Children (2011) *Severe Child Poverty in Northern Ireland: Briefing*, February, Belfast: Save the Children.

Schirato, T. and Yell, S. (2000) *Communication and Culture: An Introduction*, London: SAGE Publications Limited.

Schissel, B. (1997) *Blaming Children: Youth Crime, Moral Panics and the Politics of Hate*, Nova Scotia, Canada: Fernwood Publishing.

Schissel, B. (2006) *Still Blaming Children: Youth Conduct and the Politics of Child Hating*, Nova Scotia, Canada: Fernwood Publishing.

Schissel, B. (2008) 'Justice Undone: Public Panic and the Condemnation of Children and Youth', in C. Krinsky (ed.) *Moral Panics Over Contemporary Children and Youth*, Surrey: Ashgate Publishing Limited, pages 15–30.

Schlesinger, P. (1987) *Putting 'Reality' Together: BBC News*, London: Methuen and Company.

Schlesinger, P. and Tumber, H. (1994) *Reporting Crime: The Media Politics of Criminal Justice*, Oxford: Clarendon Press.

Schlesinger, P. Murdock, G. and Elliott, P. (1983) *Televising Terrorism*, London: Comedia.

Schlesinger, P. and Murdock, G. (1991) 'The Media Politics of Crime and Criminal Justice', *British Journal of Sociology*, Volume 42, Number 3, pages 397–420.

Schudson, M. (1978) *Discovering the News: A Social History of American Newspapers*, New York, USA: Basic Books.

Schudson, M. (1996) 'The Sociology of News Production Revisited', in J. Curran and M. Gurevitch (eds.) *Mass Media and Society* (Second Edition), London: Arnold Publishers, pages 141–159.

Schulman, M. (1990) 'Control Mechanisms Inside the Media', in J. Downing, A. Sreberny-Mohammadi and A. Mohammadi (eds.) *Questioning the Media*, London: SAGE Publications Limited, pages 125–138.

Scott, S. and Haydon, D. (2005) *Barnardo's Statement of Ethical Research Practice*, Belfast: Barnardo's.

Scott, J. (2006) 'Content Analysis', in E. McLaughlin and J. Muncie (eds.) *The Sage Dictionary of Criminology* (Second Edition), London: SAGE Publications Limited, pages 40–41.

Scraton, P. (Ed) (1997) *'Childhood' in 'Crisis'?*, London: UCL Press/Routledge.

Scraton, P. (2004) 'Streets of Terror: Marginalisation, Criminalisation and Moral Renewal', *Social Justice*, Volume 3, Numbers 1–2, pages 130–158.

Scraton, P. (2005) 'The Denial of Children's Rights and Liberties in the U.K. and the North of Ireland', in ECLN Essays, Number 14. Accessed from: http://www.ecln.org (accessed on 12 September 2009).

Scraton, P. (2007) *Power, Conflict and Criminalisation*, London: Routledge.

Scraton, P. (2008) 'The Criminalisation and Punishment of Children and Young People: Introduction', in P. Scraton (ed.) *Current Issues in Criminal Justice*, Volume 20, Number 1, pages 1–13.

Scraton, P. and Moore, L. (2005) (Revised edition). *The Hurt Inside: The Imprisonment of Women and Girls in Northern Ireland*, Belfast: Northern Ireland Human Rights Commission.

Scraton, P. and Moore, L. (2007) *The Prison Within: The Imprisonment of Women in Hydebank Wood 2004–2006*, Belfast: Northern Ireland Human Rights Commission.

Scraton, P., Sim, J. and Skidmore, P. (1991) *Prisons Under Protest*, Milton Keynes: Open University Press.

Shawcross, W. (1992) *Rupert Murdoch: Ringmaster of the Information Circus*, London: Random House.

Sheptycki, J. (2003) 'Against Transnational Organized Crime', in M. E. Beare (ed.) *Critical Reflections on Transnational Organized Crime, Money Laundering and Corruption*, Canada: University of Toronto Press, pages 120–144.

Shipman, M. (2002) *'The Penalty Is Death': US Newspaper Coverage of Women's Executions*, Missouri, USA: University of Missouri Press.

Shirlow, P. and Murtagh, B. (2006) *Belfast: Segregation, Violence and the City*, London: Pluto Press.

Shirlow, P. (2008) 'Belfast: A Segregation City', in C. Coulter and M. Murray (eds.) *Northern Ireland After the Troubles: A Society in Transition*, Manchester: Manchester University Press, pages 73–87.

Siegel, L. J. (2008) *Criminology* (Fifth Edition), New York, USA: West Publishing Company.

Silverblatt, A. (2004) 'Media as Social Institution', *American Behavioral Scientist*, Volume 48, Number 1, pages 35–41.

Silverman, H. (2010) 'Contested Cultural Heritage: A Selective Historiography', in H. Silverman (ed.) *Contested Cultural Heritage: Religion, Nationalism, Erasure, and Exclusion in a Global World*, London: Springer, pages 1–50.

Silverstone, R. (1999a) *Why Study the Media?* London: SAGE Publications Limited.

Silverstone, R. (1999b) *Television and Everyday Life*. London: Routledge.

Sim, J., Scraton, P. and Gordon, P. (1987) 'Introduction: Crime, the State and Critical Analysis', in P. Scraton (ed) *Law, Order and the Authoritarian State*, Milton Keynes: Open University Press, pages 1–70.

Simpson, B. (1997) 'Youth Crime, the Media and Moral Panic', in J. Bessant and R. Hil (eds.) *Youth Crime and the Media: Media Representations of and Reactions to Young People in Relation to Law and Order*, Hobart, Australia: Australian Clearinghouse for Youth Studies, pages 9–16.

Slattery, M. (2003) *Key Ideas in Sociology*, Cheltenham: Nelson Thornes Limited.

Smith, R. (2003) *Youth Justice: Ideas, Policy and Practice*, Devon: Willan Publishing.

Smith, D. J. and Bradshaw, P. (2005) 'Gang Membership and Teenage Offending', *Edinburgh Study of Youth Transitions and Crime Research Digest*, Number 8, Edinburgh: University of Edinburgh, pages 1–25.

Smithey, L. A. (2011) *Unionists, Loyalists and Conflict Transformation in Northern Ireland*, Oxford: Oxford University Press.

Smyth, M. (1998) *Half the Battle: Understanding the Effects of the Troubles on Children and Young People in Northern Ireland*, Derry/Londonderry: INCORE.

Smyth, M., Fay, M. T., Brough, E. and Hamilton, J. (2004) *The Impact of Political Conflict on Children in Northern Ireland*, Belfast: Institute for Conflict Research.

Socio-Legal Studies Association (2009) *SLSA Statement of Principles of Ethical Research Practice*, January, UK: Socio-Legal Studies Association. Accessed from: http://www.slsa.ac.uk/ethics-statement (accessed on 1 February 2009).

Springhall, J. (2008) '"The Monsters Next Door: What Made Them Do It?" Moral Panics Over the Causes of High School Multiple Shootings (Notably Columbine)', in Krinsky, C. (ed.) *Moral Panics Over Contemporary Children and Youth*, Surrey: Ashgate Publishing Limited, pages 47–70.

Squires, P. ed. (2008) *ASBO Nation: The Criminalisation of Nuisance*, Bristol: The Policy Press.

Sreberny-Mohammadi, A. (1990) 'Small Media for Big Revolution: Iran', *International Journal of Politics, Culture, and Society*, Volume 3, Number 3, pages 341–371.

Stephen, D. (2006) 'Community Safety and Young People: 21st-Century *Homo Sacer* and the Politics of Injustice', in P. Squires (ed) *Community Safety: Critical Perspectives on Policy and Practice*, Bristol: The Policy Press, pages 219–237.

Stubbs, M. (2008) 'Three Concepts of Keywords', Revised Version of Paper Presented at Keyness in Text, Certosa di Pontignano, University of Siena, 2007. Accessed from: http://www.uni-trier.de/fileadmin/fb2/ANG/Linguistik/Stubbs/stubbs-2008-keywords.pdf. (accessed on 10 February 2011).

Such, E., Walker, O. and Walker, R. (2005) 'Anti-war Children: Representation of Youth Protests Against the Second Iraq War in the British National Press', *Childhood*, Volume 12, Number 3, pages 301–326.

Surette, R. (1998) *Media, Crime and Criminal Justice: Images and Realities* (Second Edition), California, USA: Wadsworth.

Labour Party (1996) *Tackling the Causes of Crime*, London: The Labour Party.

Tait, G., Kendall, G. and Carpenter, B. (1997) 'Violence in the Media: Youth, Government and Censorship', in J. Bessant and R. Hil (eds.) *Youth Crime and the Media: Media Representations of and Reactions to Young People in Relation to Law and Order*, Hobart, Australia: Australian Clearinghouse for Youth Studies, pages 17–22.

Tait, R. (2012) 'Never Waste a Good Crisis: The British Phone Hacking Scandal and Its Implications for Politics and the Press', in H. A. Semetko and M. Scammell (eds.) *The SAGE Handbook of Political Communication*, London: SAGE Publications Limited, pages 518–527.

Tannenbaum, F. (1938) *Crime and the Community*, New York: Columbia University Press.

Taylor, R. (2001) 'Northern Ireland: Consociation or Social Transformation?', in J. McGarry (ed) *Northern Ireland and the Divided: The Northern Ireland Conflict and the Good Friday Agreement in Comparative Perspective*, Oxford: Oxford University Press, pages 36–52.

Taylor, I., Walton, P. and Young, J. (1973) *The New Criminology: For a Social Theory of Deviance*, London: Routledge and Kegan Paul plc.

Teo, P. (2000) 'Racism in the News: A Critical Discourse Analysis of News Reporting in Two Australian Newspapers', *Discourse and Society*, Volume 11, Number 1, pages 7–49.

Thompson, J. (1990) *Ideology and Modern Culture*, Cambridge: Polity Press.

Thompson, K. ed. (1997) *Media and Cultural Regulation*, London: SAGE Publications Limited.

Thompson, K. (1998) *Moral Panics: Key Ideas*, London: Routledge.

Thompson, J. E. (2001) *American Policy and Northern Ireland: A Saga of Peacebuilding*, California, USA: Greenwood Publishing Group.

Tierney, J. (2010) *Criminology: Theory and Context* (Third Edition), Harlow: Longman.

Tolson, A. (1996) *Mediations: Text and Discourse in Media Studies*, London: Arnold Publishers.

Tomlinson, M. (2007a) *The Trouble with Suicide. Mental Health, Suicide and the Northern Ireland Conflict: A Review of the Evidence*, Belfast: Department of Health, Social Services and Public Safety Northern Ireland.

Tomlinson, M. (2007b) 'Suicide and Young People: The Case of Northern Ireland', *Child Care in Practice*, Volume 13, Number 4, pages 435–443.

Tonge, J. (2002) *Northern Ireland: Conflict and Change* (Second Edition), Essex: Pearson Education Limited.

Tonge, J. (2006) *Northern Ireland*, Cambridge: Polity Press.

Tuchman, G. (1972) 'Objectivity as Strategic Ritual: An Examination of Newsmen's Notions of Objectivity', *American Journal of Sociology*, Number 77, pages 660–679.

Tuchman, G. (1974) *Making News: The Social Construction of Reality*, New York: Free Press.

Unger, S. (2001) 'Moral Panic Versus the Risk Society: The Implications of the Changing Sites of Social Anxiety', *British Journal of Society*, Volume 52, June, pages 271–291.

United Nations Committee on the Rights of the Child (2008) *UK Concluding Observations,* October, United Nations: UN Committee on the Rights of the Child.

van Dijk, T. A. (1991) *Racism and the Press: Critical Studies in Racism and Migration*, London: Routledge.

van Zoonen, L. (1996) *Feminist Media Studies*, London: SAGE Publications Limited.

Waddington, P. A. J. (1986) 'Mugging as a Moral Panic: A Question of Proportion', *British Journal of Sociology*, Volume 37, June, pages 245–259.

Waiton, S. (2008) *The Politics of Antisocial Behaviour: Amoral Panics*, London: Routledge.

Walker, C. (2011) *Terrorism and the Law*, Oxford: Oxford University Press.

Walklate, S. (1998) *Understanding Criminology: Current Theoretical Debates*, Buckingham, UK: Open University Press.

Walliman, N. (2001) *Your Research Project*, London: SAGE Publications Limited.

Walters, R. and Woodward, R. (2007) 'Punishing "Poor Parents": "Respect", "Responsibility" and Parenting Orders in Scotland', *Youth Justice: An International Journal*, Volume 7, Number 1, pages 5–20.

Wardrip-Fruin, N. and Montfort, N. (2003) *The New Media Reader*, Cambridge, USA: MIT Press.

Watson, T. and Hickman, M. (2012) *Dial M for Murdoch: News Corporation and the Corruption of Britain*, London, UK: Penguin.

Wearing, M. (1997) 'The Crime-youth Unemployment Link: Textual Representations', in J. Bessant and R. Hil (eds.) *Youth Crime and the Media: Media Representations of and Reactions to Young People in Relation to Law and Order*, Hobart, Australia: Australian Clearinghouse for Youth Studies, pages 35–42.

West, D. J. (1976) *The Young Offender*, Middlesex: Penguin Books Limited.

Whale, J. (1980) *The Politics of the Media* (Revised Edition), Glasgow: William Collins Sons and Co. Limited.

Wharton, C. (2006) 'Document Analysis', in V. Jupp (ed.) *The SAGE Dictionary of Social Research Methods*, London: SAGE Publications Limited, pages 79–81.

White, R. W. (1993) 'On Measuring Political Violence: Northern Ireland, 1969 to 1980', *American Sociological Review*, Volume 58, pages 575–585.

White, R. (2002) *Understanding Youth Gangs*, Canberra, Australia: Australian Institute of Criminology.

Whitman, L. (1992) *Children in Northern Ireland Abused By Security Forces and Paramilitaries*, USA: Human Rights Watch.

Whyte, B. (2007) 'Change, Evidence, Challenges: Youth Justice Developments in Scotland', in M. Hill, A. Lockyer and F. Stone (eds.) *Youth Justice and Child Protection*, London: Jessica Kingsley Publishers, pages 158–174.

Whyte, J. (1981) 'Why Is the Northern Ireland Problem so Intractable?', *Parliamentary Affairs*, Volume XXXIV, Number 4, pages 422–435.

Wilkins, L. T. (1960) *Delinquent Generations*, London: HMSO.

Wilkins, L. T. (1964) *Social Deviance: Social Policy, Action, and Research*, London: Tavistock.

Williams, R. (1977) *Marxism and Literature*, Oxford: Oxford University Press.

Williams, P. and Dickinson, J. (1993) 'Fear of Crime: Read All About It? The Relationship Between Newspaper Crime Reporting and Fear of Crime', *British Journal of Criminology*, Volume 33, Number 1, pages 33–56.

Winston, B. (1986) *Misunderstanding Media*, Cambridge: Harvard University Press.

Wolfsfeld, G. (2004) *Media and the Path to Peace*, Cambridge: Cambridge University Press.

Wood, I. S. (2006) *Crimes of Loyalty: A History of the UDA*, Edinburgh: Edinburgh University Press.

Wood, R. (2010) 'UK: The Reality Behind the "Knife Crime"', *Race Class*, Volume 52, Number 2, October, pages 97–103.

Worrall, M. (2006) 'Discourse Analysis', in E. McLaughlin and J. Muncie (eds.) *The Sage Dictionary of Criminology* (Second Edition), London: SAGE Publications Limited, pages 132–134.

Wright Mills, C. (1976) *The Sociological Imagination*, New York: Oxford University Press.

Wykes, M. (2001) *News, Crime, and Culture*, London: Pluto.

Yates, J. (2008) 'Naming and Shaming', in B. Goldson (ed.) *Dictionary of Youth Justice*, Devon: Willan Publishing, pages 239–240.

Yiasouma, K. (2010) 'Fluffy Bunny Philosophy: The Media and Policy Advocacy', Presented at *Media Representations of Children and Young People Seminar*, Childhood, Transition and Social Justice Initiative, Queen's University Belfast, 14 September.

Young, J. (1971) *The Drugtakers: The Social Meaning of Drug Use*, London: McGibbon and Kee.

Young, J. (2008) 'Moral Panics', in L. Kontos and D. C. Brotherton (eds.) *Encyclopedia of Gangs*, California, USA: Greenwood Publishing Group, pages 174–176.

Young, J. (2007) *The Vertigo of Late Modernity*, London: SAGE Publications Limited.

Young, T., Fitzgerald, M., Hallsworth, S. and Joseph, I. (2007) *Groups, Gangs and Weapons*, London: Youth Justice Board.

Freedom of Information Requests

Police Service Northern Ireland (2010a), Freedom of Information Request, Reference: F – 2010 – 02165, *Subject: Recruitment of Op Exposure PSNI Officer in Strand Road*, Northern Ireland: PSNI.

Police Service Northern Ireland (2010b), Freedom of Information Request, Reference: F – 2010 – 02516, *Subject: Cost of Ardoyne Riots on 12 July 2010*, Northern Ireland: PSNI.

Police Service Northern Ireland (2010c), Freedom of Information Request, Reference: F – 2010 – 02745, *Subject: Operation Exposure*, Northern Ireland: PSNI.

Police Service Northern Ireland (2010d), Freedom of Information Request, Reference: F – 2010 – 02764, *Subject: Cost of a Leaflet Drop in Londonderry*, Northern Ireland: PSNI.

Police Service Northern Ireland (2011), Freedom of Information Request, Reference: F – 2011 – 00341, *Subject: Paramilitary Style Incidents*, Northern Ireland: PSNI.

Internet Sources

4NI.CO.UK, *Anti-social Behaviour Legislation Sought for NI: The Outgoing Chairman of the Northern Ireland Housing Executive Has Called on the Government to Introduce Anti-social Behaviour Legislation in Northern Ireland*, 3 September 2003. Accessed from: http://www.4ni.co.uk/northern_ireland_news.asp?id=19675 (accessed on 1 August 2011)

4RFV.CO.UK, *Union Backs NI Media Over Riot Tapes: The Broadcast Union, BECTU Is Throwing Its Weight Behind an Appeal to the PSNI to Adopt a More 'Responsible Approach' to Applications for Access to Media Footage*, 19 August 2011. Accessed from: http://www.4rfv.co.uk/industrynews.asp?id=130785 (accessed on 19 August 2011).

Association of Chief Police Officers (ACPO). Accessed from: http://www.acpo.police.uk/ (accessed on 1 August 2011).

Banning Mephedrone. Accessed from: http://www.direct.gov.uk/en/N11/Newsroom/DG_186993 (accessed on 27 April 2010).

BBC News NI, *Boy Wins Right to Challenge PSNI Operation Exposure*, 29 September 2010a. Accessed from: http://www.bbc.co.uk/news/uk-northern-ireland-11435661 (accessed on 4 July 2011).

BBC News NI, *Police's Operation Exposure Photo 'Invaded Privacy'*, 28 September 2010b. Accessed from: http://www.bbc.co.uk/news/uk-northern-ireland-11429160 (accessed on 4 July 2011).

BBC News, *PM hails 'Historic' Northern Ireland Justice Vote*, 9 March 2010a. Accessed from: http://news.bbc.co.uk/1/hi/northern_ireland/8558466.stm (accessed on 27 April 2010).

BBC News, *Police Transfer Over Final Hurdle*, 24 March 2010b. Accessed from: http://news.bbc.co.uk/1/hi/northern_ireland/8584603.stm (accessed on 24 March 2010).

BBC News, *PSNI Release Pictures of Ardoyne Riot Suspects*, 9 September 2010c. Accessed from: http://www.bbc.co.uk/news/uk-northern-ireland-11249047 (accessed on 4 July 2011).

BBC Newsline NI, *Derry Police Publish Wanted Photos on Website*, 22 November 2011. Accessed from: http://www.bbc.co.uk/news/uk-northern-ireland-foyle-west-15833297 (accessed on 22 November 2011).

BBC Newsline NI, *Timeline: Devolution of Policing and Justice*, 5 February 2010a. Accessed from: http://news.bbc.co.uk/1/hi/northern_ireland/8457650.stm (accessed on 10 February 2010).

BBC Newsline NI, *What Will Happen When Policing and Justice Is Devolved?* 12 April 2010b. Accessed from: http://news.bbc.co.uk/1/hi/8459824.stm (accessed on 27 April 2010).

BBC Newsline, *Robinson and McGuinness Meet Matt Baggott Over Rioting*, 14 July 2010. Accessed from: http://www.bbc.co.uk/news/uk-northern+ireland-politics-10636126 (accessed on 14 July 2010).

BBC Newsline, *Silly ASBOs*, 11 April 2006. Accessed from: http://news.bbc.co.uk/1/hi/wales/south_east/4902092.stm (accessed on 1 August 2011).

Belfast Telegraph, *Psni Demand for Riot Footage 'Could Put Journalists at Risk'*, 18 August 2011. Accessed from: http://www.belfasttelegraph.co.uk/news/local-national/northern-ireland/psni-demand-for-riot-footage-could-put-journalists-at-risk16037940.html#ixzz21Ntq8Wt2 (accessed on 18 August 2011).

Belfast Telegraph, *Family Seeking Tough Sentences Over Harry Holland Murder*, 25 June 2009. Accessed from: http://www.belfasttelegraph.co.uk/news/local-national/family-seeking-tough-sentences-over-harry-holland-murder-14359177.html (accessed on 12 August 2009).

Crime Watch UK, *Belfast Riots*. Accessed from: http://www.bbc.co.uk/crimewatch/appeals/2010/09/belfast_riots.shtml (accessed on 4 July 2011).

Criminal Justice Inspectorate Report and Documentation. Accessed from: http://www.cjini.org/CJNI/files/74/743c0eb6-5bcl-4a27-b08f-e0d17ad490e3.pdf (accessed on 1 August 2011).

Department of Justice, *Perceptions of Crime: Findings from the 2010/11 Northern Ireland Crime Survey*, 29 February 2012b. Accessed from: http://www.northernireland.gov.uk/index/media-centre/news-doj-29022012 perceptions-of-crime.htm (accessed on 30 August 2012).

Derry News, Commissioner's Concern Over PSNI Leaflets, 20 August 2010. Accessed from: http://www.derrynews.net/2010/08/20/commissioner's-concern-over-psni-leaflets/ (accessed on 21 August 2010).

Justice Girvan's Judgment in Relation to NICCY's Judicial Review Application (ASBOs). Accessed from: http://www.courtsni.gov.uk/NR/rdonlyres/705ED37E-0CC3-46CA-8D89-3B0B3CB9E372/0/j_i_GIRF4194.htm (accessed on 1 August 2011).

New Labour's 1997 Election Manifesto, 'New Labour Because Britain Deserves Better'. Accessed from: http://www.labour-party.org.uk/manifestos/1997/1997-labour-manifesto.shtml (accessed on 1 August 2011).

NIO, Explanatory Notes on NI Act 2002. Accessed from: http://www.nio.gov.uk/justice_ni_act_2002_explanatory_notes.pdf (accessed on 1 August 2011).

OFMDFM, 'UNCRC Northern Ireland's Priorities and Plans'. Accessed from: http://www.ofmdfmni.gov.uk/uncrc_statement_northern_ireland_annex_to_executive_5.11.2009-2.pdf (accessed on 2 June 2010).

Parades Commission in Northern Ireland. Accessed from: http://www.paradescommission.org/ (accessed on 30 July 2011).

Patten Commission Report (1999) *A New Beginning: Policing in Northern Ireland: The Report of the Independent Commission on Policing for Northern Ireland*. Belfast: Northern Ireland Office. Accessed from: http://www.nio.gov.uk/a_new_beginning_in_policing_in_northern_ireland.pdf (accessed on 23 March 2011).

PSNI, Operation Relentless. Accessed from: http://www.psni.police.uk/operation_relentless (accessed on 25 November 2011).

PSNI, Operation Snapper. Accessed from: http://www.psni.police.uk/operation-snapperfoylejuly (accessed on 1 July 2012).

Queen's University Belfast, Research Governance, 'Policy on the Ethical Approval of Research and Guidelines for Schools'. Accessed from: http://www.qub.ac.uk/directorates/ResearchEnterprise/ResearchPolicyOffice/ResearchGovernance/PolicyontheEthicalApprovalofResearchGuidelinesforSchools/ (accessed on 13 February 2010).

Queen's University Belfast, School of Law, 'Ethical Guidelines for Research'. Accessed from: http://www.law.qub.ac.uk/schools/SchoolofLaw/Research/EthicsApproval/ (accessed on 2 September 2009).

Safeguarding Vulnerable Groups (NI) Order2007. Accessed from: http://www.legislation.gov.uk/nisr/2012/320/article/6/made (accessed on 14 February 2010).

The 1998 referendums (Belfast/Good Friday Agreement). Accessed from: http://www.ark.ac.uk/elections/fref98.htm (accessed on 22 March 2011).

The Centre for Social Justice. Accessed from: http://www.centreforsocialjustice.org.uk/ (accessed on 3 April 2011).

The Guardian Online, *Stormont Votes to Take Over Northern Ireland Policing Powers*, 9 March 2010. Accessed from: http://www.guardian.co.uk/politics/2010/mar/09/stormont-northern-ireland-policing-vote (accessed on 10 March 2010).

The Leveson Inquiry. Accessed from: http://www.levesoninquiry.org.uk/ (accessed on 30 March 2012).

The North Report. Accessed from: http://cain.ulst.ac.uk/issues/parade/north.htm (accessed on 20 August 2011).

The Northern Ireland Association for the Care and Resettlement of Offenders (NIACRO). Accessed from: http://www.niacro.co.uk/about-niacro/ (accessed on 1 August 2011).

The Police Ombudsman's Office. Accessed from: http://www.policeombudsman.org/Publicationsuploads/PONI_BATON_REPORT_2005.pdf (accessed on 1 August 2011).

The Youth Justice Review (2011). Accessed from: http://www.dojni.gov.uk/index/publications/publication-categories/pubs-criminal-justice/review-of-youth-justice---large-print-version-of-report.pdf (accessed on 1 October 2011).

UTV, *Broadcasters Warn PSNI Over Riot Footage*, 18 August 2011a. Accessed from: http://www.u.tv/News/Broadcasters-warn-PSNI-over-demands-for-footage/80562d4c-57bd-4e42-8f6f-1e7c627358c9 (accessed on 18 August 2011).

UTV, *Police Pictures Risk Children's Rights*, 26 January 2011b. Accessed from: http://www.u.tv/news/Police-pictures-risk-childrens-rights/d2e7b577-d003-4da3-9e87-2a744216c202 (accessed on 4 July 2011).

UTV, *PSNI Put Warrant Wanted Pictures Online*, 22 November 2011c. Accessed from: http://www.u.tv/News/PSNI-put-warrant-wanted-pictures-online/aab87fbd-f6ca-4743-ba73-19e2aa90b819 (accessed on 22 November 2011).

Legislation

Anti-Social Behaviour Act 2003
Beijing Rules 1985
Children and Young Persons Act (Northern Ireland) 1968
Children Order (Northern Ireland) 1995
Civil Authorities (Special Powers) Act (Northern Ireland) 1922
Crime and Disorder Act 1998
Criminal Justice Act 1982
Criminal Law Act (Northern Ireland) 1967
Data Protection Act 1998
Emergency Provisions Act 1973 (updated in 1978)
European Convention of Human Rights
Havana Rules 1990
Human Rights Act 1998
Justice (Northern Ireland) Acts 2002 and 2004
Northern Ireland Act 1998
Northern Ireland Emergency Provisions Act 1973
PACE Codes of Practice 2007
Police and Criminal Evidence (Amendment) Order 2007, No. 288 (N.I.2)
Police and Criminal Evidence (Northern Ireland) Order 1989
Prevention of Terrorism Act 1974 (updated in 1976)
Protection of Children and Vulnerable Adults (Northern Ireland) Order 2003
Public Order (Northern Ireland) Order 1987
Riyadh Guidelines 1990
Safeguarding Vulnerable Groups (Northern Ireland) Order 2007
Serious Organised Crime and Police Act 2005
United Nations Convention on the Rights of the Child
Youth Justice and Criminal Evidence Act 1999

Media Content

The following list of media content relates to news items cited throughout the monograph that were printed outside of the data collection period (see Appendix 2).

Daily Mail Reporter (2009) Thousands of England's Worst Families to Be Placed In 'Sin Bins' to Improve Behaviour, *Daily Mail,* 22 July 2009.

Daily Mail Reporter (2010) 'Scourge of Society': Gang of Teen Bullies Who Terrorised City and Even Beat Up Disabled Man Are Named and Shamed, *Daily Mail*, 5 November 2010.

Little, A. (2009) Sin Bins for Worth Families, *Daily Express,* 23 July 2009.

MacIntyre, D. (1993) Major on Crime: "Condemn More, Understand Less", *Mail on Sunday,* 21 February 1993.

McDonald, H. and Watt, N. (2010) Stormont Votes to Take Over Northern Ireland Policing Powers, *Guardian*, 9 March 2010.

News Letter Reporter (2011) Terry Spence: Judges Should Have More Options on Sentencing, *News Letter*, 27 October 2011.

Other Correspondence

E-mail correspondence from a youth worker, dated 11 January 2011.

Index[1]

---

[1] Notes: Page numbers followed by 'n' refer to notes.

© The Author(s) 2018
F. Gordon, *Children, Young People and the Press in a Transitioning Society*,
Palgrave Socio-Legal Studies, https://doi.org/10.1057/978-1-137-60682-2

CPI Antony Rowe
Chippenham, UK
2018-05-02 21:36